Toward a New Image of Paramārtha

Bloomsbury Studies in World Philosophies

Series Editor:
Monika Kirloskar-Steinbach

Comparative, cross-cultural, and intercultural philosophy are burgeoning fields of research. Bloomsbury Studies in World Philosophies complements and strengthens the latest work being carried out at a research level with a series that provides a home for thinking through ways in which professional philosophy can be diversified. Ideal for philosophy postgraduates and faculty who seek creative and innovative material on non-Euroamerican sources for reference and research, this series responds to the challenges of our postcolonial world, laying the groundwork for a new philosophy canon that departs from the current Eurocentric sources.

Titles in the Series:
Andean Aesthetics and Anticolonial Resistance, by Omar Rivera
Chinese Philosophy of History, by Dawid Rogacz
Chinese and Indian Ways of Thinking in Early Modern European Philosophy, by Selusi Ambrogio
Indian and Intercultural Philosophy, by Douglas Berger
Toward a New Image of Paramārtha, by Ching Keng

Toward a New Image of Paramārtha

Yogācāra and Tathāgatagarbha Buddhism Revisited

Ching Keng

BLOOMSBURY ACADEMIC
LONDON • NEW YORK • OXFORD • NEW DELHI • SYDNEY

BLOOMSBURY ACADEMIC
Bloomsbury Publishing Plc
50 Bedford Square, London, WC1B 3DP, UK
1385 Broadway, New York, NY 10018, USA
29 Earlsfort Terrace, Dublin 2, Ireland

BLOOMSBURY, BLOOMSBURY ACADEMIC and the Diana logo are trademarks of Bloomsbury Publishing Plc

First published in Great Britain 2023
This paperback edition published 2024

Series design by Louise Dugdale
Cover image © Olga Kurbatova/Getty Images

A catalogue record for this book is available from the British Library.

A catalog record for this book is available from the Library of Congress.

ISBN: HB: 978-1-3503-0390-4
PB: 978-1-3503-0394-2
ePDF: 978-1-3503-0391-1
eBook: 978-1-3503-0392-8

Series: Bloomsbury Studies in World Philosophies

Typeset by Deanta Global Publishing Services, Chennai, India

To my grandmother and my parents

Contents

List of Illustrations viii
Acknowledgements x
List of Abbreviations and Convention xii

Introduction 1
1 Two Competing Readings of the Notion of *Jiexing* 解性 21
2 Doubts about the Connection between the *Awakening of Faith* and Paramārtha 37
3 A Philological Investigation of Dunhuang Fragment T2805 51
4 Doctrinal Coherence between T2805 and the Works of Paramārtha 107
5 Two Shelun Lineages and How the *Awakening of Faith* Came to Be Attributed to Paramārtha 123
6 What Exactly Is *Jiexing*? 151
7 Paramārtha as a Successor to Vasubandhu 177
8 Conclusion 211

Notes 219
Bibliography 257
Index 268

Illustrations

Figures

4.1	Before and after the transformation of the basis according to MSgBh	118
5.1	Mapping between the two theories in Jizang onto T2805 and its opponent	126
5.2	Doctrinal differences between the two Shelun lineages	134
7.1	Dharma-body as Thusness disclosed	185
7.2	Doctrinal differences between the two Shelun lineages	204

Tables

0.1	Numbers of Works Attributed to Paramārtha by Chinese Buddhist Catalogs	8
0.2	Idiosyncratic Translation of the Sanskrit Term *anāsrava* by Paramārtha	9
1.1	Permanence vs. Impermanence Reading	34
2.1	Dates of the Translation of the *Awakening of Faith* Given by Chinese Buddhist Catalogs	39
3.1	Estimate of the Total Fascicles of T2805	53
3.2	Different Terminology Used by Paramārtha and Xuanzang	54
3.3	The Division of *Pin* and *Zhang* in *Shelun*	55
3.4	Terminology in T2805, Paramārtha's Works Compared to Others	61
3.5	New Translation Terms Coined by Paramārtha's Group	69
3.6	Special Transliterations by Paramārtha's Group	69
3.7	Various Transliterations of the Five Stages of the Fetus	69
3.8	Newly Introduced School Names	70
3.9	Special Technical Terms from Sanskrit	70
3.10	Special Concept Not Directly from Sanskrit	70
3.11	Terminology in T2805, *Suixiang lun* Compared to Others	72
3.12	The Phrase *Jiwufu* in T2805, *Suixiang lun* and Other Works	73
3.13	The Phrases *Jiwufu* and *Qifuyou* in T2805, *Suixiang lun* and Jizang	73
3.14	Translations of Four Kinds of Wholesomeness in T2805 and *Suixiang lun*	74
3.15	Terminology in T2805 Never Used by Paramārtha	76
3.16	T2805's Connection with the Southern Tradition	77
3.17	More Examples for T2805's Connection with the Southern Tradition	81
3.18	Exegetical Tools from the Southern Tradition	84
3.19	Terminology in T2805 Never Used by Authors from the North	91
3.20	Causal Systems in **Tattvasiddhi* and **Saṃyuktābhidharma-hṛdaya-śāstra*	92
3.21	Names of the Stage Immediately Preceding the First Bodhisattva Stage	93
3.22	Three Systems of *Gotras* in the South, North, and Zhiyi	95

3.23 Terminology in T2805 Never Appeared before 600 97
3.24 Terminology in T2805 Never Appeared in the South but in the North 98
3.25 Three Kinds of Pure Lands According to T2805 and Huiyuan 102
4.1 *Shelun* in Parallel with Other Translations of MSg and MSgBh X.35 117
5.1 Permanence vs. Impermanence Reading 125
5.2 Two Interpretations of Permeation of Hearing Attributed to Shelun Masters 128
5.3 Two Interpretations of *Buddha-gotra* Attributed to Shelun Masters 132
5.4 Summary of the Two Interpretations Attributed to Shelun Masters 133
6.1 Summary of All the Information about *Jiexing* from *Shelun* and T2805 158
7.1 Translations of the Five Similes by Takasaki and Ruegg 198
7.2 Mapping among the Five Similes, Two *Buddha-gotras* and Three Buddha-bodies 199
7.3 Two-*gotra* Theory in Some Indian Buddhist Texts 207

Acknowledgements

In 2001, my wife and I, newlyweds at the time, came to Harvard University to start our academic adventure. Twenty years later, with the generous support of the Harvard-Yenching Institute, we came back again, but this time with our beloved son. I have a feeling that fate has led me along the path to the final publication of this book.

This book is a revision of my PhD dissertation, which was submitted to Harvard in 2009. I decided to work on Paramārtha for two reasons. First, I was very much intrigued by the issue of the Sinicization of Buddhism, as reflected in the debates between Paramārtha and Xuanzang. This interest was inspired mainly by my advisor, Professor Robert M. Gimello. Second, through Professor Gimello and my classmate Michael Radich, I learned that Professor Tōru Funayama at Kyōto University was about to conduct a five-year research seminar on Paramārtha. I then decided to work on Paramārtha, because I was hoping to take advantage of Professor Funayama's seminar and learn from him and his colleagues. I am most grateful to these three people for leading me to this journey of discovery.

My ideas about how to do research changed completely after I came to study at Harvard. In addition to Professor Gimello, I benefited greatly from the instruction of professors Parimal G. Patil, Leonard W. J. van der Kuijp, and David D. Hall. I was extremely lucky to sit in Sanskrit classes with professors Patrick Olivelle and Joel Brereton at UT Austin. I also want to thank my cohort at Harvard, Michael Radich and Eyal Aviv in particular, for their friendship and intellectual exchange.

My challenge to the traditional image of Paramārtha would never have been effectively laid out without the work of CBETA (the Chinese Buddhist Electronic Texts Association), which ushered in a new era in working with Chinese Buddhist texts. I here express my gratitude to Professor Ven. Huimin and the late Professor Aming Tu. I have also taken advantage of the Thesaurus Literaturae Buddhicae hosted by Professor Jens Braarvig. I am also grateful to Dr Susan Whitfield, director of the International Dunhuang Project back in 2007, for kindly agreeing to make freely available the scanned image of Taishō 2805, a major focus of this book.

After I received my PhD degree, I was extremely fortunate to teach at the National Chengchi University, Taiwan, and had Professor Chen-kuo Lin as my mentor. He kindly shared his long-term vision and taught me a great deal about how to promote Buddhist Philosophy in Taiwan by means of international collaboration. Teaching excellent students is a real privilege, and it helped a lot with my own research. I am also indebted to the following respected teachers and colleagues in Taiwan: the late Ah-yueh Yeh, Chih-fu Lee, Pochi Huang, and Chien-hsing Ho. I benefited greatly from participating in projects led by Professor John Makeham. I also received invaluable help and instruction from professors Shōryū Katsura, Michael Zimmermann, and Zhihua Yao.

I am deeply indebted to the people of Taiwan for generously supporting me and my wife to study in the United States. Without their generous help, my dream of becoming a scholar would never have been realized. I shall dedicate my remaining academic life to them in return.

Thanks also to Michael Radich, Robert Kritzer, Jeffrey Kotyk, and Ernest Brewster for their generous help editing my manuscript at various stages. I also thank Colleen Coalter and Venkat Perla Ramesh at Bloomsbury Academic for their kind and professional help.

This work was supported by the Academy of Korean Studies (KSPS) Grant funded by the Korean Government (MOE) (AKS-2012-AAZ-2102). My special thanks are due to Professor Jeson Woo for involving me in that very prestigious project.

Finally, I express my deepest gratitude to my family. I came from a mediocre background. In retrospect, I probably should not have followed my own scholarly interests and pursued an academic career. It is simply by the grace of God that I was born into a family full of love and managed to build my own beautiful family. Words cannot express how much I cherish every single day with my dear wife and son. It is a great pity I cannot share this book with my late grandmother and father. This book is dedicated to my grandmother and my parents for their love, education and understanding.

Abbreviations and Convention

AKBh	*Abhidharmakośabhāṣya* by Vasubandhu. "Paramārtha's AKBh" refers to Paramārtha's Chinese translation of the AKBh (T1559).
Awakening of Faith	*Awakening of Faith in Mahāyāna* 大乘起信論 (T1666).
CWSL	*Cheng weishi lun* 成唯識論 compiled by Xuanzang (T1585).
DT	sDe-dge bsTan 'gyur (Tōhoku 東北 Edition).
FDJL	*Fodi jing lun* 佛地經論 translated by Xuanzang[1] (T1530).
FXL	*Foxing lun* 佛性論 translated by Paramārtha (T1610).
MAV	*Madhyāntavibhāga* (verses only).
MAVBh	*Madhyāntavibhāgabhāṣya*.
MSA	*Mahāyānasūtrālaṃkāra* (verses only).
MSABh	*Mahāyānasūtrālaṃkārabhāṣya*.
MSg	*Mahāyānasaṃgraha* by Asaṅga. I follow the section numbers designated by Lamotte (1973), Nagao (1982-1987), or Griffiths et al. (1989).
MSgBh	*Mahāyānasaṃgrahabhāṣya* by Vasubandhu.
RGV	*Ratnagotravibhāga* (verses only).
RGVV	*Ratnagotravibhāgavyākhyā*.[2]
Shelun	Paramārtha's Chinese translation of the *Mahāyānasaṃgrahabhāṣya* (T1595).
T2805	The Dunhuang fragment No. 2805 in the *Taishō shinshū Daizōkyō*.
T	TAKAKUSU Junjirō 高楠順次郎 and WATANABE Kaigyoku 渡辺海旭, 1940. *Taishō shinshū Daizōkyō* 大正新修大蔵経. Tōkyō: Daizō Shuppan.
Tanyan shu 曇延疏	*Dasheng qixin lun yishu* 大乘起信論義疏 (X755).
X	KAWAMURA Kōshō 河村孝照, ed., 1975-1989. *Shinsan Dai Nihon zoku Zōkyō* 新纂大日本續藏經. Tōkyō: Kokusho Kankōkai.
XGSZ	*Xu gaoseng zhuan* 續高僧傳 (T2060).
Ch.	terms in Chinese

Skt.	terms in Sanskrit
Tib.	terms in Tibetan

[] Brackets in English translation: insertion by the author.
() Parenthesis in English translation: paraphrase, explanations, and so on.
In citing the *Taishō* (T) and the *Zoku Zōkyō* (X) Chinese canons, I give the number of the text, followed by the volume, page, register, and line numbers, for example: T1595:31.156c9-22. Unless otherwise noted, all translations are the author's.

Introduction

0.1 Yogācāra and Tathāgatagarbha as Two Competing Traditions

In this book, I argue that our current understanding of Paramārtha (Zhendi 真諦 499–569), an important Indian scholar-monk and translator in China, is fundamentally distorted. I assert that the traditional image of Paramārtha, to which many modern scholars still subscribe, is a product of later Chinese reinterpretations of his work through the lens of the *Awakening of Faith in Mahāyāna* (*Dasheng qixin lun* 大乘起信論, T1666; henceforth abbreviated as *Awakening of Faith*).[1] More importantly, by establishing that a long-lost fragment preserved only in Dunhuang 敦煌 (numbered 2805 in the *Taishō shinshū Daizōkyō* 大正新修大藏經 [henceforth abbreviated as T]; henceforth abbreviated as T2805[2]) is closely related to Paramārtha, I try to recover the authentic teachings of Paramārtha, which were lost within a few decades following his death. Finally, I elucidate how my refutation of the traditional image of Paramārtha helps us to better understand the development of Buddhist thought in both India and China.

This chapter is a general introduction to the whole book. It consists of four parts: (1) background information about the Buddhist intellectual context in India and China at the time of Paramārtha; (2) a brief description of the traditional image of Paramārtha, which is my main target of criticism; (3) a review of previous scholarship on Paramārtha, in which I identify three dubious assumptions that have misled previous scholars; and (4) an outline of the remaining chapters of the book.

0.1.1 Yogācāra Tradition[3] (Acquired Undiscriminating *Jñāna*) vs. Tathāgatagarbha Tradition (Innate Undiscriminating *Jñāna*)[4]

Among the world's religious traditions, Buddhism occupies a special position as it emphasizes neither faith in God nor the merits of good actions, but rather stresses that once sentient beings realize the true nature of the world, then they will naturally be freed from suffering and other forms of bondage, as these are all merely derivatives of their initial ignorance. Such a cognitive state is called undiscriminating *jñāna* (Ch. *wufenbie zhi* 無分別智; Skt. *nirvikalpa-jñāna*). It is undiscriminating because it is not conceptualized. It is *jñāna* because it is cognitive. Note that, throughout this book, I do not translate *jñāna* (Ch. *zhi* 智) in the case of undiscriminating *jñāna* in order to keep it vague enough to accommodate the sense of "unconditioned undiscriminating *jñāna*" that I will discuss in Chapters 4 and 6. It would sound weird in English to say "unconditioned undiscriminating cognition" because the English word "cognition" always implies a causal process.

In terms of soteriology, the Yogācāra tradition argues that sentient beings do not have innate *jñāna* and that only a very few people, such as the Buddha, can acquire it. This is because human consciousness, according to Yogācāra, is fundamentally flawed and thus is not capable of liberating itself. Undiscriminating *jñāna* must come from outside—in particular, from hearing the teachings of the Buddha. The more one hears the Buddhist teachings, the weaker the power of the flawed consciousness becomes. Before undiscriminating *jñāna* is acquired, however, consciousness remains defiled and projects mental representations that are mistakenly regarded as externally real, which then become the objects of cognitive and emotional attachments. This is why Yogācāra endorses idealism in terms of ontology.[5] Since *jñāna* is not innate to sentient beings, there is no guarantee that one can acquire it. One Yogācāra interpretation even suggests that some people innately lack certain factors and, as a result, can never become Buddhas.[6]

In contrast, the Tathāgatagarbha tradition insists that *jñāna* is innate to all sentient beings. The term *tathāgatagarbha,* literally "containing a Tathāgata,"[7] implies that buddhahood is innate to all sentient beings. But what prevents us from exercising this innate *jñāna*? The Tathāgatagarbha tradition answers that the problem is our ignorance. The innate *jñāna* will be revealed as soon as ignorance is eliminated through proper Buddhist practice.

Interestingly, since as early as the late sixth century, it has been accepted in China that the great Indian translator Paramārtha had successfully created a syncretism between the two conflicting positions of Yogācāra and Tathāgatagarbha. This idea that Paramārtha reconciled the Yogācāra and Tathāgatagarbha traditions became the standard image of Paramārtha by the early seventh century and has largely shaped our current understanding of him. In what follows, I shall refer to "the traditional image of Paramārtha."

It is the goal of this book to challenge this traditional image of Paramārtha. But before further elucidating the details of this image, I first briefly review Paramārtha's life and works.

0.1.2 Paramārtha's Life and Work in China[8]

Paramārtha came to southern China from Ujjayanī (present Ujjain) in western India. When he arrived in China at the age of forty-eight in 546, China had already been divided into 2 regions for almost 200 years. Native Han Chinese regimes held sway in the South, whereas the North was governed by a succession of "barbarian" peoples. The unremitting tensions between North and South, as well as constant political strife within both regions, imposed conditions of severe political and social hardship. These conditions made life difficult for Paramārtha, and his translation work suffered many interruptions. In fact, Paramārtha might have been the only major translator of Buddhist texts in China who did not receive imperial subsidy during his missionary career.

We do not really know how well Paramārtha spoke, read, or wrote Chinese. According to the preface to his Chinese translation of the *Abhidharmakośa-bhāṣya* (*Api damo jushe shilun* 阿毘達磨俱舍釋論, T1559; henceforth abbreviated as Paramārtha's AKBh) and the epilogue to his translation of the *Jingang bore boluomi jing* 金剛般若波羅蜜經 (*Vajracchedikā-prajñāpāramitā-sūtra*), Paramārtha, at least in his later career, was well versed in Buddhist Chinese, so he could translate directly into Chinese without an intermediate interpreter (*duyu* 度語 or *chuanyu* 傳語).[9] He was so distressed by the obstacles to his translation that he was nearly driven to suicide.[10] A few months after his favorite disciple died prematurely, Paramārtha died in China at the age of seventy-one.

During his stay in China, Paramārtha translated several Indian Buddhist texts, mostly from the Yogācāra tradition. Among the texts he translated, Paramārtha reportedly most valued *A Summary of the Great Vehicle* (Skt. *Mahāyānasaṃgraha*; Ch. *Shedasheng lun* 攝大乘論; henceforth abbreviated as MSg) by Asaṅga (fourth to fifth centuries) together with *A Commentary on the Summary of the Great Vehicle* (Skt. *Mahāyānasaṃgraha-bhāṣya*; Ch. *Shedasheng lun shi* 攝大乘論釋; henceforth abbreviated as MSgBh when referring to Vasubandhu's text and as *Shelun* when referring to Paramārtha's Chinese translation [T1595]) by Vasubandhu (fourth to fifth centuries).[11]

In addition to his translations of the Yogācāra texts, Paramārtha is also regarded in the later Chinese Buddhist tradition as the translator of the *Awakening of Faith*, a seminal Tathāgatagarbha text that has been highly influential in East Asian Buddhist traditions. Beginning from the twentieth century, serious doubt has been cast on the traditional attribution of the *Awakening of Faith* to Paramārtha.[12] This attribution is an essential part of the traditional image of Paramārtha.

0.2 Problems with the Traditional Image of Paramārtha and His Translation

0.2.1 The Traditional Image of Paramārtha

As mentioned earlier, the tradition holds that Paramārtha was the person who successfully created a syncretism between the conflicting Yogācāra and Tathāgatagarbha traditions. This image is based on two essential assumptions: (1) Paramārtha is the translator of the *Awakening of Faith*; (2) Paramārtha often interpolates into his translations Tathāgatagarbha notions or passages in order to reinterpret Yogācāra texts. Both points are taken as proof of Paramārtha's affiliation with the Tathāgatagarbha tradition.

The *Awakening of Faith* is a seminal Tathāgatagarbha text that incorporates major Yogācāra doctrines. It accepts the Yogācāra theory regarding the defiled function of consciousness but maintains the Tathāgatagarbha tenet of universal buddhahood. While agreeing with Yogācāra that external objects are illusory because they are merely projections of consciousness, the *Awakening of Faith* does not agree that consciousness is completely defiled. It maintains that consciousness is defiled only when it is agitated by ignorance. When consciousness is not agitated, it is restored to its own original tranquility, which is none other than the innate undiscriminating *jñāna*. Consciousness hence is both defiled and undefiled: it is defiled regarding its agitated function; it is undefiled regarding its tranquil basis, namely, undiscriminating *jñāna*. The *Awakening of Faith* crafts a unique notion of "original awakening" (*benjue* 本覺) to refer to this undiscriminating *jñāna*. All sentient beings equally possess original awakening as the undefiled basis for consciousness and are therefore capable of becoming Buddhas.

With respect to the concepts or passages interpolated by Paramārtha, a remark on the way Paramārtha produced his "translations" is necessary. A feature of his translations is that he often interpolates various ideas or inserts passages into the original text. Scholars generally agree that such interpolated portions, which have no parallels in other versions of the same text, are "lecture notes" from Paramārtha's oral explanations of the text that were recorded by his Chinese colleagues and immediate disciples.[13] This practice was not uncommon among early translators,[14] but it has created a lot of confusion and controversy among later scholars due to uncertainty about the precise meaning of these passages.

The notion of *jiexing* 解性—the focal point of this book—is one such an interpolation,[15] inserted by Paramārtha into his *Shelun*. This allows a reinterpretation of *jiexing* from the perspective of the *Awakening of Faith*. This traditional interpretation of *jiexing* and the attribution of the *Awakening of Faith* to Paramārtha constitute the two pillars supporting the traditional image of Paramārtha as a figure who created a syncretism between Yogācāra and Tathāgatagarbha. Herein, I illustrate how these two pillars work together to produce a certain picture of Paramārtha.

0.2.2 The Traditional Interpretation of *Jiexing*: *Jiexing* = Original Awakening

According to the traditional image, *jiexing* is a hallmark of Paramārtha's Tathāgatagarbha thought because it is taken to mean "the permanent nature (*xing* 性) of *jñāna* (*jie* 解)" in all sentient beings. In this traditional interpretation, *jiexing* refers to the unchanging and undefiled element within defiled consciousness. The existence of *jiexing* therefore explains why all sentient beings are capable of becoming Buddhas.

According to this traditional interpretation of *jiexing*, *jiexing* in Paramārtha's *Shelun* is just another version of the notion of original awakening found in the *Awakening of Faith*: both notions refer to the unchanging and undefiled basis of consciousness that underlies universal buddhahood. In fact, as we shall see in Chapter 1, almost all the early authors gloss *jiexing* in terms of original awakening.

The traditional image hence offers a fairly consistent picture of Paramārtha: he was an Indian Yogācāra scholar sympathetic to Tathāgatagarbha thought (such as that in the *Awakening of Faith*), who incorporated the Tathāgatagarbha claim of universal buddhahood into his translations of Yogācāra texts. This explains why Paramārtha translated the *Awakening of Faith* and also why Paramārtha interpolated notions such as *jiexing*—which is synonymous with original awakening—into his *Shelun*.

Due to the influence of this traditional image, Paramārtha has long been regarded as the Indian authority behind the Chinese Tathāgatagarbha tradition (the so-called *Faxing zong* 法性宗 ["The Tradition of the Nature of Dharmas"]), which is heavily influenced by the *Awakening of Faith*.[16] For the same reason, he was also harshly criticized for having transmitted heterodox Yogācāra teachings to China by the Chinese Yogācāra tradition (the so-called *Faxiang zong* 法相宗 ["The Tradition of the Characteristics of Dharmas"]), which can be traced to the great pilgrim and translator Xuanzang 玄奘 (602–64) and his disciple Master Ji 基法師.[17] According to the Chinese Yogācāra tradition, Tathāgatagarbha doctrine is incompatible with orthodox Yogācāra teachings. The conflict between these two camps subsided soon after the rapid decline of the Chinese Yogācāra tradition. After around the ninth century, Tathāgatagarbha doctrine as expressed in the *Awakening of Faith* was accepted by almost all the major East Asian Buddhist traditions.

The traditional image of Paramārtha held sway right down to the early twentieth century when modern Buddhist scholars began to question the Indian provenance of the *Awakening of Faith*. The old debates between the Chinese Yogācāra and the Chinese Tathāgatagarbha traditions revived and continue even today. But the jury is still out concerning the central issues involved in these debates, such as the exact meaning of the notion of *jiexing* and whether the *Awakening of Faith* was a work by Paramārtha at all (either as a translation or an original composition). This book hopes to contribute to the final resolution of these issues.

0.2.3 Problematizing the Traditional Image of Paramārtha

The traditional image of Paramārtha has remained unquestioned for more than a millennium until the early twentieth century. In Chapter 2, I challenge the traditional image of Paramārtha by focusing on two major problems. Here, I briefly summarize these problems: (1) the questionable authorship of the *Awakening of Faith*; (2) the idea in the *Awakening of Faith* that Thusness as an unconditioned dharma can ever be permeated.

(1) The doubts cast on the authorship of the *Awakening of Faith* raise many questions about the traditional image of Paramārtha. MOCHIZUKI Shinkō 望月信亨 (1869–1948), an early-twentieth-century Japanese scholar of Chinese Buddhism, was the first modern scholar to suggest that the *Awakening of Faith* is a Chinese composition rather than a translation by Paramārtha.[18] Nowadays, almost all scholars agree that the *Awakening of Faith* could not have been a direct translation from an Indic text.[19] In recent decades an increasing number of scholars agree with the suggestion made by TAKEMURA Makio 竹村牧男 (1993) that there is a close relationship, both philological and philosophical, between the *Awakening of Faith* and the so-called Dilun tradition 地論宗. Following Takemura, ŌTAKE Susumu 大竹晉 (2017) convincingly demonstrates that the *Awakening of Faith* was actually a patchwork from previous Chinese texts.

The Dilun tradition was the most influential philosophical tradition in sixth-century northern China. It was named after a text entitled *A Commentary on the Ten*

Stages [of the Bodhisattva Path] (Skt. *Daśabhūmika-sūtra-śāstra*; Ch. *Shidi jinglun* 十地經論, or simply *Dilun* 地論), traditionally attributed to Vasubandhu. For a long time, scholars knew little about the Dilun tradition. Recently, groundbreaking work has been produced by AOKI Takashi 青木隆, ISHII Kōsei 石井公成, and the research team organized by the Geumgang University of South Korea based on the information about the Dilun tradition found in Dunhuang materials.[20]

A Commentary on the Ten Stages is a commentary on the Chapter of the Ten Stages (*Shidi pin* 十地品) in the *Buddhāvataṃsaka-sūtra* (*Huayan jing* 華嚴經). The famous claim made by this chapter is that "All the three realms (*dhātu*) are unreal, merely made by the mind."[21] To this extent, it betrays a strong bent for idealism. For this reason, Vasubandhu's *Twenty Verses* also cites this claim in the very beginning as a scriptural authority.[22] Following this claim, the central claim made by the Dilun tradition was that the arising of phenomena from the mind must rely upon the mixture of the truth (i.e., the pure mind) and the untruth (i.e., ignorance) (*zhenwang hehe* 真妄和合) or the interdependence between the truth and the untruth (*zhenwang xiangyi* 真妄相依).[23]

What underlies this Dilun claim is that all phenomena must have the pure mind as the undefiled ultimate basis.[24] To this extent, it seems that the Dilun tradition opposes the Indian Yogācāra tradition, which insists that the basis of all phenomena is the storehouse consciousness that is fundamentally defiled.[25]

The key issue with understanding the Dilun thought lies in how to understand the mixture of truth and untruth, namely, what exactly it means by the mixture of the pure mind and ignorance, and why phenomena thereby arise. Most scholars have assumed that what is meant by the mixture of truth and untruth is precisely the same conceptual scheme underlying the mixture between "neither-arising-nor-ceasing" (*busheng bumie* 不生不滅) and "arising-and-ceasing" (*shengmie* 生滅) in the *Awakening of Faith*, and hence take the *Awakening of Faith* as coherent with Dilun thought. But in Keng (2014b), I have argued that the doctrine of the *Awakening of Faith* is not derived directly from the Dilun tradition. I shall come back to this issue in 7.5.

(2) Another problem with the *Awakening of Faith* is that it claims that Thusness, being unconditioned (Ch. *wuwei* 無為; Skt. *asaṃskṛta*), is subject to permeation (Ch. *xunxi* 熏習; Skt. *vāsanā*), either by ignorance or by the deluded mind.[26] This goes against the basic presumption in Indian Buddhism that Thusness is unconditioned and hence cannot change. Because Thusness never changes, it cannot be permeated, given that the idea of "being permeated" implies "change." In 2.4, I shall pinpoint this distinction between unconditioned vs. conditioned as the major point where the *Awakening of Faith* deviates from Indian Yogācāra. That is, Indian Yogācāra insists on the strict distinction between the two, but the *Awakening of Faith* blurs or even obliterates this distinction.

This distinction cannot be overemphasized in terms of understanding *jiexing* because, as shown in 1.3, the difference between the two readings of *jiexing* lies precisely in this distinction: the permanence reading (closely connected with the *Awakening of Faith*) identifies *jiexing* as the original awakening of the *Awakening of Faith*, and hence construes it as being both unconditioned and conditioned; the impermanence reading (preserved in T2805[27]) in contrast construes *jiexing* as being conditioned.

More broadly, such a distinction also looms large in the distinction between dharma-body (unconditioned) and enjoyment-body (conditioned) (see 4.5 & 7.2), between unconditioned undiscriminating *jñāna* and conditioned undiscriminating *jñāna* (see 4.3 and 6.8), a strong vs. weak reading of *tathāgatagarbha* (see 7.5). In fact, I shall argue that this distinction is the most important key for understanding Tathāgatagarbha thought in India as a whole. This is why this distinction becomes a recurring theme throughout this book.

These two problems in the *Awakening of Faith* depicted earlier are, I believe, sufficient reasons to remain suspicious about the traditional attribution of the *Awakening of Faith* to Paramārtha and hence about the usual understanding of Paramārtha. This also motivates us to move toward a new image of Paramārtha.

0.3 Toward a New Image of Paramārtha: Methodological Considerations

My approach is historical, philological, and philosophical. I show how the current image of Paramārtha is a construct of his Chinese successors and hence does not properly reflect Paramārtha's actual thinking. I analyze the terminology adopted in Paramārtha's works to demonstrate that T2805 is closely affiliated with Paramārtha's group and hence might well preserve Paramārtha's authentic teachings (Chapter 3). I reconstruct the philosophical claims made in this fragment regarding *jiexing* and the understanding of dharma-body to recover Paramārtha's original teaching on *jiexing* and the much-neglected teachings of Vasubandhu on the notion of dharma-body (Chapters 6 and 7).

More broadly, this book provides a case study about how, in the development of a religious tradition, a later text, which includes a new interpretation, is attributed to an earlier master and hence turns the tradition toward a new direction. In the Buddhist tradition, the most famous examples might be the attribution of the Mahāyāna texts to the historical Buddha[28] and the production of the *Platform Scripture*.[29]

In this book, I argue that a similar situation occurred regarding the attribution of the *Awakening of Faith* to Paramārtha. A group of people who were not Paramārtha's direct disciples introduced the *Awakening of Faith* in their reinterpretation of Paramārtha and hence shifted what were considered to be Paramārtha's teachings in a new direction. Later Chinese Buddhist tradition failed to differentiate these new teachings based on the *Awakening of Faith* from Paramārtha's original teachings and hence mistakenly accepted the attribution of the *Awakening of Faith* to Paramārtha. Here lies the root of our confusion about Paramārtha. It is the goal of my book to distinguish the teachings that were introduced later from Paramārtha's original teachings and to uncover the lost history behind this false attribution.

After the *Awakening of Faith* was attributed to Paramārtha, the traditional image of him was formed, and a new philosophical tradition (the Huayan tradition 華嚴宗) was then founded on that image. With the demise of the Chinese Yogācāra tradition and the flourishing of the Huayan tradition in China, such a traditional image became deeply rooted in the Chinese Buddhist tradition after the Tang dynasty. This makes it extremely difficult to reconstruct the original teachings of Paramārtha.

0.3.1 Difficulties in Reconstructing the Original Teachings of Paramārtha

In the previous section, I have pointed out some reasons for doubting the traditional image of Paramārtha. The next question is how to correct this traditional image and to recover the original teachings of Paramārtha.

It is almost impossible to reconstruct the development of Yogācāra thought in general and Paramārtha's original teachings in particular based on the available Indian sources, for the simple reasons that there are very few extant texts and we know too little about the dates of the available texts and the relationships among them. Moreover, most extant Sanskrit manuscripts are of a very late date. We cannot judge whether the Sanskrit texts we have now are exactly the same as they were more than a thousand years ago.

One useful approach is to seek help from later Chinese reports and testimonies, but these reports and testimonies may turn out to be more misleading than useful for the following reasons:

(A) We are not certain about which are Paramārtha's authentic works. The attribution of the *Awakening of Faith* to Paramārtha is the most conspicuous example, but it is also noteworthy that, Paramārtha's corpus fluctuates and increases over time according to various Chinese Buddhist catalogs, as can be seen clearly in Table 0.1.[30]

From this brief summary, we clearly see that the number of works attributed to Paramārtha fluctuates significantly. Most dramatically, the *Datang neidian lu* (ed. 664) attributes sixty-eight works to Paramārtha, more than twice the number attributed by the *Zhongjing mulu* (ed. 594).

(B) The biography of Paramārtha in the *Xu gaoseng zhuan* 續高僧傳 (*The Continued Biographies of Eminent Monks*, T2060; henceforth XGSZ) may turn out to be a hagiography conflating what might be historically true about Paramārtha and what happened only after Paramārtha's death but was superimposed back onto him. I discuss this in 5.3.

Given the aforementioned two problems, it is inevitable that later reports or testimonies are also fraught with conflicting information about what constituted Paramārtha's original teachings. For example, regarding the notion of "three ways of subduing forbearance" (*san furen* 三伏忍), Wŏnch'ŭk seems to cite at least two

Table 0.1 Numbers of Works Attributed to Paramārtha by Chinese Buddhist Catalogs

	Year of Editing	Total Number of Works Attributed to Paramārtha
Zhongjing mulu 眾經目錄	594	25
Lidai sanbao ji 歷代三寶紀	597	64
Zhongjing mulu 眾經目錄	602	34
Datang neidian lu 大唐內典錄	664	68
Gujin yijing tuji 古今譯經圖記	666	50

different views that are affiliated with Paramārtha: one is based on "original notes" (*benji* 本記) allegedly written by Paramārtha; the other is based on Paramārtha's *Shelun*.[31] As a result, scholars have had difficulty deciding which view, if either, was the original teaching of Paramārtha.

The conflicting information provided by later Buddhist catalogs as well as later reports strongly suggests that some people composed texts *in the name of* Paramārtha. Later catalogs and eventually the whole Chinese Buddhist tradition failed to distinguish between authentic and inauthentic works of Paramārtha and simply attributed all of them to Paramārtha. A foremost example of this is, of course, the attribution of the *Awakening of Faith* to Paramārtha. This conflation of authentic and inauthentic teachings is the most important factor underlying all the confusion we now have about Paramārtha.

0.3.2 A New Approach to the Study of Paramārtha

I believe that the first step toward removing obstacles to an accurate understanding of Paramārtha's thought is to find a way to determine which works are authentic. I briefly introduce my philological approach here.

Scholars have failed to notice that Paramārtha used a special terminology in his later career,[32] a terminology mostly unique to him. This distinctive terminology provides us with an excellent criterion for judging whether Paramārtha translated a given text during his later career. The most telling example is the term *wuliu* 無流 (Skt. *anāsrava*): almost all other authors in the Chinese Buddhist canon use the term *wulou* 無漏 to translate *anāsrava*. The usage of *wuliu* is summarized in Table 0.2.

Using this terminological analysis extensively, I show in Chapter 3 that the author of T2805 must have been closely connected with Paramārtha's group. This conclusion then allows us to make use of the information preserved in the fragment to reconstruct Paramārtha's original teachings. However, not all problems concerning Paramārtha can be resolved simply by means of terminological analysis. In his early career, Paramārtha still followed the prevalent convention of translating *anāsrava* as *wulou*. A philological approach needs to be supplemented by other methods, such as doctrinal and historical analyses, as I have done in Chapters 4 and 5.

The philological approach helps build a solid foundation for distinguishing the original works of Paramārtha from later Chinese works composed in his name.

Table 0.2 Idiosyncratic Translation of the Sanskrit Term *anāsrava* by Paramārtha

Term/Total Occurrences[a]	Paramārtha's Corpus	Before Paramārtha	After Paramārtha
wuliu dao 無流道/22	17	0	2
wuliu ding 無流定/12	11	0	0
wuliu jie 無流界/22	19	0	1
wuliu shan 無流善/15	8	0	3
youliu shan 有流善/36	12	5 (in different senses)	8

[a]"Total occurrences" here refers to the total occurrences of a term in CBReader released in February 2007 (v 3.6). See 3.3.4 for more details.

Based on this foundation, I hope to refute the traditional image of Paramārtha and to portray him in a completely new way. In addition, we also must eliminate a few dubious assumptions that have arisen due to the traditional image of Paramārtha. In what follows, I review previous modern scholarship on Paramārtha in order to point out three dubious assumptions still held by most scholars.

0.4 Review of Previous Scholarship: Three Dubious Assumptions

In this section, I review previous modern scholarship and identify three major dubious assumptions that scholars currently accept about Paramārtha. Among these three, the first and most basic is the attribution of the *Awakening of Faith* to Paramārtha. It is mainly due to this attribution (from around 590, less than thirty years after Paramārtha's death) that the later Chinese tradition as well as modern scholarship accepts the remaining two assumptions: that Paramārtha and Xuanzang upheld opposing doctrinal views and that Yogācāra and Tathāgatagarbha are antagonistic to each other. To a large extent, all three of these assumptions still hold sway today. Before I challenge them, I first show how they have misled previous scholarships.

0.4.1 Assumption 1: The *Awakening of Faith* Was Somehow Related to Paramārtha

The modern interest in Paramārtha began mainly with the Japanese Buddhologist UI Hakuju 宇井伯寿 (1882–1963). Long before Ui, the Chinese Buddhist tradition had established the Chinese Yogācāra Tradition as the orthodox Yogācāra teaching. Countering this traditional interpretation, Ui argued that Paramārtha *alone* preserved the deeper Yogācāra teachings of Asaṅga and Vasubandhu because Paramārtha presented a syncretism between Yogācāra and Tathāgatagarbha. The reason was that Paramārtha's thought advanced to the level of the ultimate truth (Ch. *zhen shengyi* 真勝義; Skt. *paramārtha-satya*) of Yogācāra—which, according to Ui, *is* Tathāgatagarbha thought—whereas the Chinese Yogācāra Tradition stayed merely at the level of the conventional truth (Ch. *li shisu* 理世俗; Skt. *saṃvṛti-satya*). According to Ui, therefore, Yogācāra and Tathāgatagarbha are not incompatible. Taken together—Yogācāra as the conventional truth and Tathāgatagarbha as the ultimate truth—they form a unified system that is faithful to the deeper Yogācāra teachings of Asaṅga and Vasubandhu.[33]

Ui's conception of Tathāgatagarbha thought as the ultimate truth of Yogācāra thought is no doubt based on his acceptance of the traditional attribution of the *Awakening of Faith* to Paramārtha. Ui thinks it is proper to read Asaṅga's and Vasubandhu's works from the perspective of "dependent origination on the basis of *tathāgatagarbha*" (*rulaizang yuanqi* 如來藏緣起). And this is particularly true, according to Ui, if we read Paramārtha's *Shelun*.[34] What Ui means here by "dependent origination on the basis of *tathāgatagarbha*" is precisely the scheme of the *Awakening of Faith*: the dependent origination of objects as illusory projections out of consciousness, which, if not agitated by ignorance, is fundamentally undefiled. This fundamentally undefiled consciousness is called *tathāgatagarbha*.

Although most scholars currently do not accept Ui's premise that the *Awakening of Faith* was translated by Paramārtha, they almost all still view Paramārtha under the influence of Ui's idea that Paramārtha's works represent a syncretism between Yogācāra and Tathāgatagarbha.[35] For example, neither IWATA Taijō 岩田諦静 (2004) nor Shengkai 聖凱 (2006) subscribes to the view that the *Awakening of Faith* was translated by Paramārtha, but they both still depict Paramārtha as creating a kind of syncretism between Yogācāra and Tathāgatagarbha thought.[36]

In Chapter 2, I review the debates regarding the attribution of the *Awakening of Faith* to Paramārtha. I argue that, despite all the counter-evidence, the only remaining argument supporting this traditional attribution of the *Awakening of Faith* to Paramārtha is made by KASHIWAGI Hiroo 柏木弘雄 (1981). Drawing on the fact that there is a close connection between the masters who taught Paramārtha's *Shelun* and those who taught the *Awakening of Faith*, Kashiwagi argues that we should trust the traditional attribution.[37] Countering Kashiwagi's claim, I point out in Chapter 5 that Kashiwagi fails to notice that there existed two lineages of Shelun masters 攝論師, and that the dissemination of the *Awakening of Faith* was closely related *only* to the indirect lineage of Shelun masters, who based their understanding of Paramārtha on the *Awakening of Faith*. This observation, I hope, will help settle the controversy regarding the relation between the *Awakening of Faith* and Paramārtha.

0.4.2 Assumption 2: Paramārtha Opposed Xuanzang

Ui's claim implies that there is a sharp tension between Paramārtha's and Xuanzang's doctrines: Paramārtha expresses the ultimate truth, while Xuanzang conveys merely the conventional truth. Ui's claim, as indicated earlier, is based on the traditional image of Paramārtha, according to which the *Awakening of Faith* is connected to Paramārtha.

But even scholars who do not agree with Ui in attributing the *Awakening of Faith* to Paramārtha still assume that there is a conflict between Paramārtha and Xuanzang: one represents the authentic Yogācāra and the other does not.

The most famous example is UEDA Yoshifumi 上田義文 (1904–93), a student of Ui. In contrast to Ui, Ueda was quite aware of the differences between Paramārtha and the *Awakening of Faith*. According to him, Paramārtha's *Shelun,* together with Asaṅga's MSg and Vasubandhu's MSgBh, must be regarded as upholding the idea of "dependent origination on the basis of the storehouse consciousness (*ālayavijñāna*)" (*alaiye shi yuanqi* 阿賴耶識緣起) instead of "dependent origination on the basis of *tathāgatagarbha,*" which is suggested in the *Awakening of Faith.*[38]

The main question posed by Ueda is this: "If the theories of Paramārtha and Hsuang-tsang [Xuanzang] are fundamentally different, the problem arises as to which transmission is faithful to the theories of Maitreya, Asaṅga, and Vasubandhu?"[39] Based on his differentiation between Xuanzang's and Paramārtha's teachings regarding the theory of three natures (*trisvabhāva-nirdeśa*) and the notion of the transformation of consciousness (*vijñāna-pariṇāma*), Ueda contends that Paramārtha's transmission was more faithful to Vasubandhu than that of Xuanzang.[40]

My major objection to Ueda is that he is particularly invested in the presumption that either Paramārtha or Xuanzang must be wrong. According to Ueda, it is impossible for both authors to be faithful to Vasubandhu's original teaching while disagreeing with each other. As I point out in Chapter 6, arguing that one of them must be unfaithful is not the best way to understand the differences between Paramārtha and Xuanzang. Rather, given that there is a 100-year gap between the two, each represents a different period in the development of Yogācāra thought. In fact, they frequently agree with each other. For instance, they both think that the storehouse consciousness becomes the enjoyment-body (*saṃbhoga-kāya*) of the Buddhas (see 4.5). Ideas expressed by Paramārtha in an undeveloped form are sometimes further elaborated by Xuanzang. For instance, I argue in Chapter 6 (6.3–6.6) that Paramārtha's idea of *jiexing* is further developed in *A Treatise for the Establishment of Consciousness-and-representation-only* (*Cheng weishi lun* 成唯識論, T 1585; henceforth abbreviated as CWSL) and in the *Commentary on the Scripture of the Buddhaland* (*Fodijing lun* 佛地經論, T1530; henceforth abbreviated as FDJL). On the other hand, some ideas are more prominent in Paramārtha than in Xuanzang. For instance, the idea of *tathāgatagarbha* is almost completely missing in Xuanzang's works (see Chapter 7). These discrepancies, I argue, should be explained by the fact that Paramārtha and Xuanzang were active during different periods in the development of Yogācāra.[41]

0.4.3 Assumption 3: Yogācāra and Tathāgatagarbha Are Two Distinct and Antagonistic Traditions

The implication of the first two assumptions is that the *Awakening of Faith* and Xuanzang, representing the Tathāgatagarbha tradition and the Yogācāra tradition, respectively, are considered to be diametrically opposed. And almost all scholars place Paramārtha somewhere between the two.

In this way of thinking, Paramārtha is usually considered to be halfway between Tathāgatagarbha and Yogācāra. For example, Shengkai (2006), in his comprehensive study of the Shelun tradition 攝論宗, argues that Yogācāra is one extreme, in which the mind is regarded as fundamentally untrue (i.e., deluded; *wangxin* 妄心); Tathāgatagarbha is the other extreme, in which mind is regarded as fundamentally true (i.e., undeluded; *zhenxin* 真心).[42] Throughout his two-volume work, Shengkai forcefully argues his thesis that Paramārtha should be situated halfway between Yogācāra and Tathāgatagarbha.

Shengkai's fundamental limitation is that he still accepts the premise that Yogācāra and Tathāgatagarbha are opposed to each other. His basic strategy is to divide the Buddhist Path of Cultivation into two parts: before and after the attainment of buddhahood. According to Shengkai's interpretation of Paramārtha, Thusness—as something transcendent—is distinct from the storehouse consciousness before one becomes a Buddha; it is only after the attainment of buddhahood that Thusness and undiscriminating *jñāna* become one.[43] To put it simply, the untrue consciousness and the true mind are separate before one becomes a Buddha. These two become united, or better, the original unity between these two is disclosed, only after one becomes a Buddha. Thus, Shengkai argues that Paramārtha's understanding of the stage before the attainment of buddhahood is closer to Yogācāra, while his understanding of the stage after the attainment of buddhahood is closer to Tathāgatagarbha. Shengkai concludes that Paramārtha represents a middle ground between Yogācāra and Tathāgatagarbha: starting from Yogācāra and moving toward Tathāgatagarbha. To this extent, we can discern that Shengkai is still heavily influenced by Ui's distinction between Yogācāra as the conventional truth and Tathāgatagarbha as the ultimate truth.

From Shengkai's discussion, it is not difficult to tell that, by Tathāgatagarbha, what he has in mind is the *Awakening of Faith*. Hence his real thesis is that Paramārtha is halfway between Indian Yogācāra transmitted by Xuanzang and the *Awakening of Faith*. My question for Shengkai then would be this: since he does not accept the traditional attribution of the *Awakening of Faith* to Paramārtha,[44] why does he not just completely remove the *Awakening of Faith* from any consideration about Paramārtha? As I show in Chapters 6 and 7, if we completely dissociate the *Awakening of Faith* from Paramārtha, then we will realize that there is not that much antagonism between Paramārtha and Xuanzang, on the one hand, and between Indian Yogācāra and Indian Tathāgatagarbha on the other.

0.4.4 The Internal Diversity of Yogācāra

More broadly, the relationship between Yogācāra and Tathāgatagarbha must be reexamined. Regarding Yogācāra, contemporary Japanese scholars have called attention to the diversity and heterogeneity of Yogācāra texts. Suguro (1989) has drawn our attention to the differences between the "Maitreya texts" and the "Asaṅga texts." Kitano (1999) examines the development of the theory of three natures and argues that there is a syncretism between the "Maitreya texts" and the "Asaṅga texts" in Vasubandhu's works.

I (Keng 2014a, 2015) have shown that there are two models for the theory of three natures, the single-layer model, which is earlier, and the double-layer model, which is later. For example, in Chapter 1 of the *Treatise on the Distinction between the Middle and the Ends* (Skt. *Madhyāntavibhāga*; Ch. *Zhongbian fenbie lun song* 中邊分別論頌; henceforth abbreviated as MAV), we find the single-layer model but in Chapter 3 we find the double-layer model. Similarly, in Chapter 6 of the *Ornament of the Mahāyāna Scriptures* (Skt. *Mahāyānasūtrālaṃkāra*; Ch. *Dasheng zhuangyan jing lun* 大乘莊嚴經論; henceforth abbreviated as MSA) we find the single-layer model but in Chapter 11 we find the double-layer model.[45] Given this diversity within the Yogācāra tradition itself, we should not expect the relationship between Tathāgatagarbha and the various strands of Yogācāra to be uniform.[46]

0.4.5 More Than One Kind of Tathāgatagarbha Thought

Regarding the Tathāgatagarbha tradition, a serious issue is that we fail to distinguish between the different senses of *tathāgatagarbha* when we use the term. The problem is that there is a fundamental difference between what I call in 7.5 the strong understanding of *tathāgatagarbha* in the *Awakening of Faith* vs. the weak understanding of *tathāgatagarbha* in, for example, *the Treatise on the Jewel-like Gotra* (Skt. *Ratnagotravibhāga*; Ch. *Jiujing yisheng baoxing lun* 究竟一乘寶性論; henceforth abbreviated as RGV). To put it simply, under the weak understanding of *tathāgatagarbha*, a Tathāgata (i.e., the dharma-body of the Buddhas) is identified with unconditioned (*asaṃskṛta*) and unchangeable (*avikāra*) Thusness (*tathatā*). All sentient beings are regarded as "containing a Tathāgata" (*tathāgata-garbha*) because they are pervaded by Thusness. In contrast, under the strong understanding of *tathāgatagarbha*, as suggested in the *Awakening of Faith*, a Tathāgata (i.e., the dharma-body of the Buddhas), while being identical with Thusness and being unconditioned, when agitated by ignorance, is transformed into the storehouse consciousness, from which illusory phenomena are projected. Again, this shows that the *Awakening of Faith* blurs or even obliterates the distinction between unconditioned and conditioned.

Moreover, I point out in Chapter 7 that Vasubandhu, arguably the most important Yogācāra thinker, in his MSgBh already incorporated into his Yogācāra system the weak understanding of *tathāgatagarbha*. Vasubandhu endorses the Tathāgatagarbha claim that "all sentient beings are *tathāgatagarbhas*" for the same reason as the RGV, namely, on the ground that Thusness pervades all sentient beings. Given that Vasubandhu already subscribes to the idea of *tathāgatagarbha*, it seems that the notion that there is some antagonism between Yogācāra and Tathāgatagarbha may be the result of interpreting earlier Indian Buddhism in light of later events in China (namely, the debates between the Chinese Yogācāra tradition and the Chinese Tathāgatagarbha tradition).

0.4.6 The Unawareness of the Heterogeneity of the Shelun Masters

The three dubious assumptions about Paramārtha mentioned earlier are closely related. Namely, the antagonism between Yogācāra and Tathāgatagarbha is partly due to the debates in China between the followers of Xuanzang and the followers of Paramārtha. The disputes between Xuanzang and Paramārtha are also partly due to the attribution of the *Awakening of Faith* to Paramārtha. Now I ask: Why was the *Awakening of Faith* attributed to Paramārtha?

Studies of the Shelun tradition by YOSHIMURA Makoto 吉村誠 are very inspiring in this connection.[47] Yoshimura suggests that our confusion about Paramārtha originates from the historical junction where Paramārtha's works were re-interpreted by the Shelun masters, who had been trained under the Dilun tradition before they were exposed to Paramārtha's teachings. For example, Yoshimura (2007, 2013: 163ff.) claims that, despite the absence of the notion of "the ninth consciousness" in Paramārtha's works, the Shelun masters took advantage of Paramārtha's notion of "spotless consciousness" (Ch. *amoluo shi* 阿摩羅識; Skt. **amalavijñāna*), reinterpreting it as the ninth consciousness in order to justify presuppositions based on their connection with the Dilun tradition and their study of the *Awakening of Faith*.

What is inspiring in Yoshimura's work is that he rightly sees that the traditional image of Paramārtha is basically a reinterpretation of Paramārtha based on the *Awakening of Faith*. But there is a major shortcoming in Yoshimura's approach: Yoshimura (2013: 9, 183) takes "Shelun masters" to be a monolithic body of people, all of whom came from the southern branch of the Dilun tradition. For this reason, Yoshimura denies all doctrines proclaimed by the Shelun masters as being authentic teachings of Paramārtha. But, as I show in 5.3 later, it is very likely that the so-called Shelun masters consist of two groups of people. One indirect lineage was headed by Tanqian 曇遷 (542–607), who never studied with Paramārtha nor any of his direct disciples, but the other direct lineage was headed by Paramārtha's immediate disciple Daoni 道尼 (d.u., died after 590) and hence should have reflected Paramārtha's original teaching. By discarding all doctrines proclaimed by the Shelun masters as being unfaithful to Paramārtha, Yoshimura actually misses the opportunity of discerning Paramārtha's authentic teachings.

Based on the existence of two groups of Shelun masters around 590, I give in Chapter 5 an explanation of why the *Awakening of Faith* came to be attributed to Paramārtha. Namely, the *Awakening of Faith* is closely related *only* to Tanqian, but because the later Chinese tradition treats Tanqian as a true heir of Paramārtha, the *Awakening of Faith* came to be attributed to Paramārtha.[48]

0.4.7 Other Related Studies of Paramārtha and Sixth-Century Chinese Buddhism

There is even less Western than Japanese scholarship on Paramārtha's works. Paul (1984) was the first monographic study of Paramārtha, mainly focusing on the text entitled *A Treatise on the Transformation of Consciousness*[49] (*Zhuanshi lun* 轉識論; T1587) traditionally attributed to Paramārtha. One of Paul's merits is that she has nicely summarized in English the Japanese scholarship from her time. In addition, she tries to make Yogācāra theory as well as Paramārtha's terminology more accessible by referring to contemporary Analytic Philosophy. The major limitation of her book for my purpose is that she does not cover Paramārtha's *A Treatise on the Buddha-gotra* (*Foxing lun* 佛性論, T1610; henceforth abbreviated as FXL), a major focus of Chapter 7. Nonetheless, Paul's book is a qualified introduction to Paramārtha in English.

In contrast, King (1991) is a study of Paramārtha's FXL, an important text about the notion of *buddha-gotra* (Buddha-lineage) that is closely related to the notions of *tathāgatagarbha* and dharma-body. I will discuss this notion of *buddha-gotra* in the FXL in detail in 7.6 later. A shortcoming of King's book is that she did not realize that the term *foxing* in the title means "*buddha-gotra*" instead of "Buddha nature" (as the title of her book suggests). More importantly, King does not show any awareness of the doctrinal differences between Paramārtha and the *Awakening of Faith*. In fact, King (1991: 18–19) seems to take the *Awakening of Faith*, Paramārtha's FXL and the *Laṅkāvatāra-sūtra* as belonging to the same group of texts that seek to incorporate Tathāgatagarbha ideas into Yogācāra. For this reason, King's book does not pose any challenge to the traditional image of Paramārtha.

Among current Japanese scholars, FUNAYAMA Tōru 船山徹 (2002, 2006) has produced the most noteworthy studies on Paramārtha. Funayama draws our attention to the peculiarities in Paramārtha's method of translating, namely, that he inserts lecture notes into his translations. This practice, according to Funayama, is not limited to Paramārtha but is common to many early translators before the Sui dynasty. More broadly, Funayama (2005a, 2007) addresses the issue of "Sinicization" by focusing on the transformations a text undergoes when it is translated, edited, and compiled. These transformations can include omission, deletion, interpolation, and adoption of a previous Chinese version of the same text, modified or not. Funayama draws our attention to how "Sinicization" takes place not only at the doctrinal or linguistic level but also at the level of the "materiality" of texts, namely, the process in which a text comes into existence.[50]

Funayama (2012) is the most important contribution to the study of Paramārtha in decades, the product of a six-year-long (2005–11) seminar on Paramārtha at Kyoto University led by Funayama. This volume is a collection of essays entitled *Shindai sanzō kenkyū ronshū* 真諦三藏研究論集 (*Studies of the Works and Influence of Paramārtha*) with contributions from young as well as established scholars. Funayama in the beginning gives a general introduction to Paramārtha's activities and the features of his works. What is particularly relevant to this book are the contributions from ISHII Kōsei 石井公成, ŌTAKE Susumu 大竹晋, and Michael Radich. Ishii (2012) employs the computerized terminological analysis called NGSM (N-Gram-based System for Multiple document comparison and analysis), and he makes observations about the relations among Paramārtha's works. What is relevant to this book are two: (a) The *Suixiang lun* 隨相論 (T1641) and the *Shiba kong lun* 十八空論 (T1616) resemble each other very closely and should be regarded as the products of the same hand; (b) The FXL is close to Paramārtha's works, but it also employs terminology and syntax resembling that of the *Awakening of Faith*. In Chapter 3, I shall criticize Ishii's method and suggest that the evidence provided by Ishii is not conclusive. In Chapter 5, I shall refute the relation between the *Awakening of Faith* and Paramārtha.

Ōtake (2012) suggests that a mysterious work entitled *Jiushi zhang* 九識章 (*Chapter on the Nine Consciousnesses*) should be attributed to Paramārtha. I disagree with Ōtake mainly because the XGSZ attributes the *Jiushi zhang* to Tanqian rather than to Paramārtha.[51] I reserve a more detailed criticism of Ōtake in 5.3.4.

Finally, Radich (2012) in the aforementioned volume examines the traditional attributions of works to Paramārtha in the Chinese Buddhist catalogs. The major finding, which I cannot agree more with, is the observation that we should not rely only on the catalogs when trying to decide whether a work was created by Paramārtha. In 0.3.1, I have shown how various numbers of texts were attributed to Paramārtha by different Buddhist catalogs. Moreover, the Buddhist catalogs themselves are not consistent with each other. Radich indicated that two threads in *Zhongjing mulu* 眾經目錄 edited in 594 and in *Lidai sanbao ji* 歷代三寶紀 edited in 597 merged into the *Kaiyuan shijiao lu* 開元釋教錄 edited in 730. The inconsistency is particularly noteworthy when the 594 *Zhongjing mulu* 眾經目錄 treats the *Awakening of Faith* as being of a dubious origin,[52] but all the later catalogs accept that it was translated by Paramārtha.

More broadly, LI Zijie 李子捷 (2020) has a monograph devoted to the impacts of the RGV on East Asian Buddhism, focusing on the three notions of *tathāgatagarbha*,

Thusness and *buddha-gotra*. These are also the key notions throughout this book, Chapters 6 and 7 in particular. Li and I both agree that the distinction between unconditioned vs. conditioned is crucial for understanding the RGV. We differ, however, in that Li (2020: 281ff.) thinks that, for the RGV, Thusness, while being unconditioned, can still function in the manner of conditioned dharmas. Li seems to think that, before the *Awakening of Faith*, the RGV has already begun to obliterate the distinction between unconditioned vs. conditioned, and claims this to be the feature of Ratnamati (Lenamoti 勒那摩提, d.u., active around the beginning of the sixth century), the Indian Buddhist scholar who translated the RGV into Chinese. I disagree with Li's interpretation of the RGV, which is probably based on a back-reading of the *Awakening of Faith* into the RGV.

In contrast, I think the story is much more complicated than Li suggests. In Keng (2013a) I argued that the RGV is acutely aware of the difficulty brought about by identifying the dharma-body with Thusness because the dharma-body would then become incapable of teaching sentient beings.[53] Hence the RGV employs several strategies to suggest that, despite being unconditioned, the dharma-body can still function to a minimum degree. I then carefully examined all those strategies to show that neither of the strategies adopted is successful. I conclude by pointing to the fundamental soteriological impasse faced by the RGV: on the one hand, if the dharma-body is not identified with Thusness, which is unconditioned and hence is pervasive, then the claim made by the Tathāgatagarbha tradition that "all sentient beings are *tathāgatagarbhas*" cannot be established; but on the other hand, if the dharma-body is considered to be unconditioned, then it would be unable to function at all. So what happens with the RGV is not that it just obliterates the distinction between unconditioned vs. conditioned as Li seems to have suggested. Rather, the RGV presupposes this distinction and is aware of the fundamental impasse depicted above. It tries hard to overcome it but, in my opinion, to no avail.

Finally, the best work in English incorporating a broader perspective on Buddhist thought in the sixth century is still Gimello (1976). Of special concern for Gimello is the issue of the Sinicization of Buddhism. As Gimello has noted, scholars of Chinese Buddhism have long sensed that Buddhism in China is generally more "this-worldly" than Buddhism in India. This trend is most clearly expressed in the rise of indigenous Chinese Buddhist traditions in the sixth century, a phenomenon that the Japanese scholar YŪKI Reimon 結城令聞 calls New Buddhism. Yūki suggests that the motivation for the rise of new Buddhist traditions in China was "the need to affirm the spiritual potential of the humanly [*sic*] and worldly life."[54] Yūki also proposes that the Sinicization of Buddhism should be understood in this light. The limitation of Yūki's approach is that he investigates the transformation of Buddhism in China almost exclusively from a sociopolitical point of view and seems to suggest that the harsh governmental persecution of Buddhists adequately explains the rise of the New Buddhism.

I do not reject Yūki's thesis as a whole. However, it seems important also to trace the development of ideas in order to explain more completely why New Buddhism arose. In Chapter 5, I show how the *Awakening of Faith* differs from the original teachings of Paramārtha. I regard this contrast between the *Awakening of Faith* and Paramārtha as a crucial point in the Sinicization of Buddhist thought.[55] I also think that the *Awakening of Faith* paved the way for the philosophical system of New Buddhism.[56] In other words, I would like to supplement Yūki's ideas by arguing that the Sinicized form of Buddhism should be understood in philosophical as well as sociopolitical terms.

By arguing that the *Awakening of Faith* was not connected with Paramārtha, however, I do not want to essentialize the contrast between what is Chinese and what is Indian. I do not claim that the *Awakening of Faith* is an original masterpiece characteristic *only* of the "Chinese mind." I am fully aware of the fact that although the *Awakening of Faith* is not directly connected with Paramārtha, this does not mean that the issues and problems addressed by the *Awakening of Faith* are completely foreign to those addressed in Paramārtha's works. By "Sinicization," I mean that the ideas in Paramārtha are somewhat transformed in the *Awakening of Faith* and that this transformation to some extent marks the beginning of a new era in Buddhist thought. I do not mean that there is something typically Chinese that requires ideas originating outside of China to be filtered or reshaped according to this pre-existing scheme.[57]

0.5 Outline of Chapters

I begin the long journey of this book with two passages from the Dunhuang fragment T2805. These two passages are special because they offer an interpretation of the notion of *jiexing*, what I call in Chapter 1 the "Impermanence reading," that is different from the traditional account, what I call the "Permanence reading." These two passages contribute to my doubts about the reliability of the traditional account. However, almost all early Chinese sources agree on the meaning of *jiexing*. Most modern scholars have simply followed this traditional interpretation and voiced no objections.[58] While a few scholars have realized potential problems with this interpretation, the alternatives they have proposed are unsatisfactory.[59]

This Introduction is followed by seven chapters. In Chapter 1, I trace the history of the interpretation of *jiexing* and show that the dominant modern interpretation actually does not differ from the traditional Chinese interpretation. The traditional interpretation is closely related to the *Awakening of Faith* and can be traced as far back as 590, only two decades after Paramārtha's death. In Chapter 2, I suggest two major reasons for doubting the traditional attribution of the *Awakening of Faith* to Paramārtha. Thus, the first two chapters suggest that there are good reasons to question the traditional interpretation of *jiexing* and that T2805 deserves careful study.

An investigation of the relationship between T2805 and Paramārtha is particularly difficult. Its author and date are unknown, and only a single brief Japanese article has touched on it.[60] A breakthrough occurred when I realized that T2805 uses several technical terms that rarely appear in the Chinese Buddhist canon *except* in Paramārtha's corpus.[61] Thus, in Chapter 3, I employ a philological investigation to demonstrate that T2805 should have been composed by a direct disciple of Paramārtha. In Chapter 4, I examine the doctrinal similarities between T2805 and Paramārtha's corpus in order to further support the close connection between these two. In Chapter 5, I reexamine all available historical information about the spread of Paramārtha's teachings in order to give a coherent account of how the *Awakening of Faith* came to be attributed to Paramārtha. Chapters 3 through 5 suggest that the interpretation of *jiexing* in T2805 is closer to Paramārtha's original interpretation than is the traditional interpretation.

In Chapter 6, I draw on Paramārtha's corpus, T2805, and later sources translated by Xuanzang to propose that the closest approximation to Paramārtha's interpretation of *jiexing* is the idea of an "innate seed (Skt. *bīja*; Ch. *zhongzi* 種子) of *jñāna*," which can also be described as "originally existent uncontaminated seeds" or "innate *gotra*."

Finally, in Chapter 7, I point out that Vasubandhu subscribed to Tathāgatagarbha thought well before Paramārtha. I also point out how in Paramārtha's works we find a further development of Vasubandhu's legacy. In light of this, I suggest that the generally accepted idea that Yogācāra and Tathāgatagarbha were two separate and hostile traditions in India is highly questionable. A major hindrance to our knowledge of the relation between these two traditions is the distorted image of Paramārtha. The first step toward a better understanding of the relation between Yogācāra and Tathāgatagarbha is to reach a more accurate understanding of Paramārtha. This is the mission of my book.

1

Two Competing Readings of the Notion of *Jiexing* 解性

In this chapter, I establish that there are two interpretations of the notion of *jiexing*: the traditional interpretation, which is still largely accepted by modern scholars, and the interpretation preserved in the Dunhuang fragment T2805, which has long escaped attention and is not the subject of any extensive study by a modern scholar. I first outline the development of the traditional interpretation in order to show that it can be traced to around the year 590, only two decades after Paramārtha's death. Then I review the interpretation of *jiexing* in T2805 and highlight the key differences between the two interpretations. I conclude this chapter with translations of a few early passages that support the interpretation of *jiexing* preserved in T2805.

1.1 The Initial Passages on *Jiexing*

Strictly speaking, the term "*jiexing*" makes its appearance only once in Paramārtha's *Shelun*, in Fascicle 3, but it is quite likely that the concept is found in a slightly different phrasing in Fascicle 1. Let me begin with these two passages.

1.1.1 *Shelun Jiexing* Passage (1)

> [MSg:] It is first explained that the basis for the knowable (**jñeyāśraya*) is named the "*aliye shi*" 阿黎耶識 ("storehouse consciousness"; Skt. *ālayavijñāna*). [Ask:] Where has the World-honored One spoken of this consciousness? Where did he call it "*aliye*"? [Answer:] In the **Mahāyāna-abhidharma-sūtra* (*Scripture of the Mahāyāna Abhidharma*), he said:
> From beginningless time this element (*dhātu*),
> Is the basis for all dharmas (*sarvadharmasamāśraya*),
> Only if it exists do all the destinies exist,
> And there is an access to nirvana. (A modification of the translation by Keenan [2003: 13])
>
> [*Shelun*:] Commentary: Now [the author of the MSg] wants to prove the substance (*ti* 體) and the name of the storehouse consciousness by referring to the Āgama (i.e.

the teachings of the Buddha). Āgama here refers to the **Mahāyāna-abhidharma-sūtra*, in which the World-honored One says the verses. The term "this" [in the MSg] refers to the element (*dhātu*), i.e., the storehouse consciousness (*aliye shi jie* 阿黎耶識界), *which has jie as its xing* (*yi jie wei xing* 以解為性).[1] This element has five senses: (1) the sense of "substance-genus" (*tilei* 體類): all sentient beings do not go beyond this substance-genus and all sentient beings are not different due to this substance-genus; (2) the sense of "cause" (*yin* 因): all [wholesome] dharmas for sentient beings to become noble people (Ch. *shengren* 聖人; Skt. *ārya*), i.e., the four bases of mindfulness (*smṛtyupasthāna*), etc., arise because of [the existence of] this element (*yuan cijie sheng* 緣此界生); (3) the sense of "birth" (*sheng* 生):[2] the dharma-body (Ch. *fashen* 法身; Skt. *dharmakāya*) attained by all noble people are accomplished by the Dharma-gates (*famen* 法門) of having the aspiration from confidence (Ch. *xinle* 信樂; Skt. *adhimukti*) in this element; (4) the sense of "being real": it is not destroyed in this mundane world, nor is it exhausted in the supramundane world; (5) the sense of "being contained" (Ch. *cang* 藏; Skt. *garbha*): if any [dharma] is associated with (Ch. *ying* 應; Skt. **saṃyukta*) this dharma (i.e., the element)—which is wholesome by its nature—then it would lie inside [of this element]; if any [dharma] lies outside of this dharma (i.e., the element), then even if it is associated with [this element], it would become the shell (i.e., outside of this element). (My emphasis)[3]

1.1.2 *Shelun Jiexing* Passage (2)

The supramundane transformation of the basis (Ch. *chushi zhuanyi* 出世轉依; Skt. **lokōttarāśraya-parāvṛtti*)[4] is also like this. As the power of the base consciousness (Ch. *benshi* 本識; Skt. *mūla-vijñāna*) gradually diminishes and the permeation of hearing (Ch. *wenxunxi* 聞熏習; Skt. *śrutavāsanā*), etc., increase step by step, the basis for ordinary people (Ch. *fanfu yi* 凡夫依; Skt. **pṛthagjanāśraya*) is discarded and the basis for noble people (Ch. *shengren yi* 聖人依; Skt. **āryāśraya*) is made. What is called "the basis for noble people" comes from *the mixture of the permeation of hearing and jiexing* (*wenxunxi yu jiexing hehe* 聞熏習與解性和合). With this being the basis, all noble paths are born." (My emphasis)[5]

1.1.3 The Relation between the Two "*Shelun Jiexing* Passages"

The foremost question raised by the *Shelun Jiexing* Passage (1) is how to read the Chinese phrase, *yi jie wei xing* 以解為性. Before I examine this phrase, I want to refute the explanation of Iwata.[6]

Iwata suggests that the word "*jie*" here means "to clearly understand" (Skt. *abhi-sam-√i*). He refers to Paramārtha's use of the same term *jie* in his translation of the four senses of "higher teaching" (Skt. *abhidharma*). Here, Iwata takes *jie* to mean "to explain," and takes *xing* in *jiexing* as *gotra* in Sanskrit, meaning "family" or "lineage." Hence Iwata proposes that the phrase *yi jie wei xing* 以解為性 means "it is to be explained as the *gotra*" (解釈を以って性とする).[7] Iwata's explanation of *xing* is worth further exploration.[8] However, there is a serious problem with Iwata's explanation of the compound: Paramārtha never uses the formula "*yi* 以 x *wei* 為 y" in the way Iwata suggests. In Paramārtha's *Shelun*, all phrases that have the form of "*yi* x *wei* y" invariably mean that something has x as its y.[9] This construction may well be used to translate Sanskrit *Bahuvrīhi* compounds.

In light of the *Shelun jiexing* passage (2), I suggest that the phrase *yi jie wei xing* in the first passage alludes to *jiexing* as a single technical term. This passage then states that the element (the storehouse consciousness) has *jie* as its *xing*, or alternatively, the element is endowed with *jiexing*. This way of treating *jiexing* as a single technical term accords well with the readings of most modern Japanese scholars, including Ui,[10] ETŌ Sokuō 衛藤即応 (1888–1958),[11] and NAGAO Gajin 長尾雅人 (1907–2005).[12] Moreover, as will become clear, almost the entire later Chinese Buddhist tradition also takes *jiexing* as a single technical term.

I begin by examining how the idea of *jiexing* was understood by Ui, whose reading has become the standard, although not entirely undisputed, interpretation.[13]

1.1.4 Ui's Interpretation of *Jiexing*

In the *Shelun Jiexing* Passage (1), Paramārtha says that the storehouse consciousness is endowed with *jiexing* and can be understood in five ways. According to Ui, this shows that Paramārtha follows the doctrine of "dependent origination on the basis of *tathāgatagarbha*." This is because those five senses are also mentioned in the RGV and the *Śrīmālādevīsiṃhanāda-sūtra* (*The Lion's Roar of Queen Śrīmālā*), as well as in the FXL and the *Xianshi lun* 顯識論 (*A Treatise on Consciousness as Appearance*, T1618) compiled by Paramārtha, as characterizations of *tathāgatagarbha*.[14] Based on the resemblances among these texts, Ui argues that Paramārtha promotes the idea of "dependent origination based on *tathāgatagarbha*" by suggesting that there is something pure (i.e., *tathāgatagarbha*) within the impure storehouse consciousness. Thus, Ui argues that, by *yi jie wei xing*, Paramārtha means that the storehouse consciousness has *jie* 解 (undiscriminating *jñāna*) as its *xing* 性 ("nature") (界は解を以て性と為す). In other words, the storehouse consciousness is taken as a mixture of both pure and impure aspects (*ranjing hehe* 染淨和合) or a mixture between true and untrue aspects (*zhenwang hehe* 真妄和合). It has something pure—*jiexing*, *tathāgatagarbha*, Thusness (*tathatā*)—as its underlying substance (*ti* 體).[15]

Ui further supports his reading of *jiexing* as the true (i.e., pure) aspect within the storehouse consciousness by referring to the theory of the three natures (*tri-svabhāva-nirdeśa*) commonly adopted in the Yogācāra texts.[16] The theory of the three natures was first mentioned in the *Saṃdhinirmocana-sūtra* (*The Scripture on the Explication of the Profound Meaning*) independent from the theory of the storehouse consciousness. It was in Asaṅga's MSg, where the idea of the dependent nature (*paratantra-svabhāva*) is evoked to explain how consciousness (*vijñāna*) or consciousness-and-representation (*vijñapti*) function, that these two theories are combined.[17] Ui argues that, according to the theory of the three natures in the MSg, the dependent nature is a mixture of the imagined nature (*parikalpita-svabhāva*) and the perfected nature (*parinişpanna-*

svabhāva), so the storehouse consciousness must also be a mixture of both the true (i.e., pure) and false (i.e., impure) aspects. And *jiexing* refers precisely to the true aspect (i.e., the perfected nature) within the storehouse consciousness.[18]

Ui's interpretation of *jiexing* also seems to accord well with the *Shelun Jiexing* Passage (2). According to Ui, *jiexing* refers to the pure substance (*ti* 體) that lies hidden inside the storehouse consciousness. Under the influence of the permeation of hearing (Ch. *wenxunxi* 聞熏習; Skt. *śrutavāsanā*), which acts as a trigger from outside, *jiexing* becomes activated and leads one toward liberation.

Ui's interpretation depicted earlier clearly was heavily influenced by the *Shōdaijōronshaku ryakusho* 攝大乘論釋略疏 (*A Brief Commentary on the Shelun*) by an eighteenth-century Japanese Hossō 法相 monk Fujaku 普寂 (1707–81). A distinct feature of Fujaku's reading of *jiexing* was his identification of *jiexing* with the notion of "original awakening" in the *Awakening of Faith*. In his commentary, Fujaku says:

> (Quotation 1.1)
> First, [the *Shelun*] uses "nature" (*xing* 性) to explain the "element" (*dhātu*). [The phrase] "having *jie* as its nature' (*yi jie wei xing* 以解為性) refers to the sense of the awakening and illuminating (*juezhao* 覺照) of the *tathāgatagarbha*. This is in general terms similar to the notion of "original awakening" in the *Awakening of Faith*.[19]

Fujaku's understanding of *jiexing* in terms of original awakening of the *Awakening of Faith* was later followed by Ui. According to the *Awakening of Faith*, because original awakening is named as neither-arising-nor-ceasing (Ch. *busheng bumie* 不生不滅) and is identified with the dharma-body of the Buddhas, it signifies what is pure and permanent within the storehouse consciousness.[20] For this reason, both Fujaku and Ui regard *jiexing* as a synonym for *tathāgatagarbha*.

Until now, Ui's reading of *jiexing* has been the only persuasive interpretation and hence has dominated our current understanding of *jiexing*.[21] It is my purpose to refute this reading and to offer another, more convincing, reading. In the next chapter, I point out the major problems with Ui's reading. But before doing that, I trace the background of Ui's reading and show that both Ui and Fujaku inherited their specific reading of *jiexing* from a long interpretive tradition in medieval China.

1.2 The Background of Our Current Understanding of *Jiexing*

Fujaku's reading of *jiexing* can be further traced back to as early as around 590 when the *Awakening of Faith* made its first appearance. Herein, I cite a number of texts to show that, since its earliest reception, the notion of *jiexing* has been interpreted in close connection with the *Awakening of Faith*. In all cases, *jiexing* was understood in terms of original awakening in the *Awakening of Faith*, whether this identification was made directly or indirectly.

1.2.1 *Dasheng qixin lun yishu* 大乘起信論義疏 Attributed to Tanyan 曇延 (516–88)

Scholars debate whether this *Dasheng qixin lun yishu* (*A Commentary on the Awakening of Faith*, X755; henceforth abbreviated as *Tanyan shu*) was really composed by Tanyan (516–88), a high official monk in the early Sui dynasty. Kashiwagi (1981) suggests that this is the earliest extant commentary on the *Awakening of Faith*.[22] Ikeda (2012) instead proposes that Hane 333V, a fragmentary commentary on the *Awakening of Faith* preserved in the collection of Dunhuang manuscripts by HANEDA Tōru 羽田亨 (1882–1955), was the earliest commentary. It is noteworthy that Hane 333V has a close relation to the *Tanyan shu* because both share some identical sentences. I tentatively agree with Jorgensen et al. (2019: 42) that Ikeda's proposal is not conclusive.

The *Tanyan shu* introduces the notion of *jiexing* in the context of commenting on key phrases from the *Awakening of Faith*. I first quote the original passage from the *Awakening of Faith*:

> (Quotation 1.2) (from the *Awakening of Faith*)
> The sense of awakening means that the substance (*ti* 體) of the mind is devoid of all thoughts (*xin ti li nian* 心體離念). The characteristic of "being devoid of all thoughts" is identical to the realm of empty space (*xukong jie* 虛空界) and is all-pervasive. The unitary characteristic (*yixiang* 一相) of the Dharma-element (Ch. *fajie* 法界; Skt. *dharmadhātu*) is none other than the uniform (*pingdeng* 平等) dharma-body of the Tathāgatas. It is on the basis of this dharma-body that one speaks of original awakening.[23]

The *Tanyan shu* comments as follows:

> (Quotation 1.3)
> The phrase "identical to the realm of empty space" aims to show that it (i.e., awakening) has the same characteristic (*xiang* 相) with empty space. Empty space has two meanings: (1) the sense of "all-pervasive" (*zhoubian* 周遍); (2) the sense of "without distinction" (*wuchabie* 無差別). Original awakening also [has these two meanings]. Because these two meanings are shared by both these two (i.e., empty space and original awakening), it (the empty space) is compared [to original awakening]. . . . The phrase "the unitary characteristic of the Dharma-element" refers to the second meaning [of the empty space mentioned above], because all dharmas share the same nature (*tongyi xing* 同一性). The word "element" (*jie* 界) means "nature" (*xing* 性). In the phrase "is none other than the uniform dharma-body of the Tathāgatas," the [original] term [of Dharma-element] is replaced [by the term of dharma-body] in order to show that just this substance of the mind (*xinti* 心體), i.e., *jiexing*, is equal to Thusness. For this reason, it [i.e., the substance of the mind, i.e., *jiexing*,] is named the dharma-body.[24]

Here, keeping in mind that this passage is a gloss on the original passage about original awakening in the *Awakening of Faith*, we see that, according to the *Tanyan shu*, *jiexing* is identified with the substance of mind, Thusness, the dharma-body of the Buddhas, and also with original awakening.

Moreover, the *Tanyan shu* also uses the term "*jiexing*" in a way that accords with the *Shelun Jiexing* Passage (2). Thus, it is obvious that the author of *Tanyan shu* was familiar with Paramārtha's *Shelun*.

> (Quotation 1.4)
> The phrase "destroy the characteristic of the mixed consciousness" (*po hehe shi xiang* 破和合識相) means that, from the beginningless time, the storehouse consciousness (*zangshi* 藏識) has been mixed with defiled dharmas and, in dependence upon them, it arises together [with them]. Not until one attains the highest path is this (i.e., mixture of the storehouse consciousness with defiled dharmas) destroyed. This [path] is divided into four levels: (1) the stage of aspiration from confidence (Ch. *yuanle wei* 願樂位;[25] Skt. *adhimukti*): Based on [hearing] the teaching of the "consciousness-and-representation-only" (*vijñapti-mātratā*), the permeation by three kinds of understanding (*prajñā*)[26] arises. This permeation advances the force of *jiexing* and harms the power of the seeds. This is what is called "the transformative stage of advancing the force and harming the power" (Ch. *yili sunneng zhuan* 益力損能轉; Skt. **durbalīkaraṇopabṛṃhaṇa-parāvṛtti*).[27] This can only harm the power [of the seeds] bit by bit but cannot break them right on, because one [at this level] still has not realized the original nature of the mind.[28]

From this passage, we can tell that, for the author of the *Tanyan shu*, *jiexing* functions like an inherent pure nature that is empowered by the permeation of hearing the Buddhist teachings. Clearly, this understanding of *jiexing* follows the same pattern as the notion of original awakening in the *Awakening of Faith*.

The *Tanyan shu* is the earliest extant text that maintains the identity of *jiexing* with original awakening. Herein, we can see how this idea was adopted by later authors.

1.2.2 Jingying Huiyuan 淨影慧遠 (523–92)

Huiyuan 慧遠 of the Jingying temple 淨影寺 was one of the most knowledgeable scholar-monks in the early Sui dynasty.[29] He was trained in the Dilun tradition, which, according to most modern scholars, is closely connected to the origin of the *Awakening of Faith*.[30] In *Dasheng yizhang* 大乘義章 (T1851), Huiyuan writes:

> (Quotation 1.5)
> The wholesome practices that are cultivated in the six consciousnesses will permeate the base consciousness (*benshi* 本識, i.e., the storehouse consciousness). The Buddha nature (*foxing* 佛性),[31] the true mind (*zhenxin* 真心) within the base consciousness is called "*jiexing*." As the *jiexing* is permeated by those pure dharmas, pure seeds are established. After these pure seeds are established, they permeate ignorance and reduce it. As ignorance is reduced, in the six consciousnesses, which

> are transformed from [the pure seeds], wholesome [dharmas] arise and become superior, and in this manner one [wholesome dharmas] occurs after another until the ultimate goal (i.e., buddhahood). Therefore, the six consciousnesses and the base consciousness serve as the cause and effect for each other. Here this is taught by the Treatise (i.e., the *Shelun*).[32]

After Paramārtha, this is the earliest passage on *jiexing* among sources for which dates are known.[33] Although Huiyuan knew about the *Awakening of Faith* and the notion of original awakening, he did not explicitly establish the connection between *jiexing* and original awakening. *Jiexing* was simply identified with Buddha nature, which is the true mind, that is, the pure aspect within the storehouse consciousness.

Nonetheless, it is clear from this passage that Huiyuan was following the conceptual scheme of the *Awakening of Faith*. For example, the idea that the true mind is permeated by hearing the teaching, after which it can permeate the ignorance within the storehouse consciousness, clearly came from the *Awakening of Faith*.[34] Although Huiyuan did not explicitly identify *jiexing* with original awakening, we can infer this identification if we recall that original awakening is none other than "true mind within the storehouse consciousness."

1.2.3 *Dasheng zhiguan famen* 大乘止觀法門

Dasheng zhiguan famen 大乘止觀法門 (*The Dharma-gates of the Mahāyāna Calm and Insight Meditation*) is a text that bases its method of meditation on the idea of "dependent origination on the basis of the *tathāgatagarbha*," which has its origin in the *Awakening of Faith*. Based on this, *Dasheng zhiguan famen* can also be regarded as a commentary on the *Awakening of Faith*.

This text is traditionally attributed to Huisi 慧思 (515–77), the teacher of Zhiyi 智顗 (538–97), the founder of the Tiantai 天台 tradition in China. However, there is some dispute about Huisi's authorship.[35] Yoshizu (2000) argues that it is more likely that the author was Tanqian. Kashiwagi (1981) also holds a similar view and argues that the *Dasheng zhiguan famen* was composed by people surrounding Tanqian in the latter half of the sixth century.[36] Here I cite only one passage from this text which glosses *jiexing*:[37]

> (Quotation 1.6)
> Question: When the base consciousness is permeated, is the true mind also permeated?
>
> Answer: When one touches the currents of water, one also touches water. Hence what I said before, i.e., the "enhancement of the power of *jiexing*" is also the enhancement of the power of the undeluded mind that is innately pure. For this reason, the Treatise (i.e., the *Awakening of Faith*) states: There are two aspects of the *aliye shi* 阿梨耶識 (i.e., the storehouse consciousness), one is awakening; the other is non-awakening. Awakening means the pure mind (*jingxin* 淨心). Non-awakening means ignorance. The mixture of these two is named the base

consciousness. Therefore, when one talks about the pure mind, there is no separate *aliye shi* [from the pure mind]; when one talks about the *aliye shi*, there is no separate pure mind [from the *aliye shi*]. It is just in view of the difference of meaning between the substance (*ti* 體) (i.e., the mind) and the characteristic (*xiang* 相) (i.e., the *aliye shi*) that there are these two different names.[38]

The close connection between *jiexing* and the *Awakening of Faith* is clear in the passage earlier. Quotation 1.6 identifies *jiexing* as the pure aspect within the mind, and the *Awakening of Faith* is cited immediately after *jiexing* is discussed. If we consider that original awakening refers to the pure aspect within the storehouse consciousness, it is clear that the underlying identification between original awakening and *jiexing* is intended.

1.2.4 *Shedasheng lun chao* 攝大乘論抄 (T2806)

In addition, a fragmentary commentary on Paramārtha's *Shelun* entitled *Shedasheng lun chao* is preserved in Dunhuang. According to Oda Akihiro 織田顯祐,[39] this commentary was probably the work of a Chinese monk named Fachang 法常 (567–645). Ikeda (2009) and Ikeda (2010) are extensive studies of this fragment. Ikeda traces the origin of this fragment to the collection made by Moriya Kōzō 守屋孝藏 (1876–1954). Ikeda also suggests that this fragment and Stein collection S.2554 should belong to the same document. Finally, Ikeda suggests that the author should be a Shelun master in northern China during the Sui dynasty because the doctrines expressed in this fragment were criticized by Lingrun 靈潤 (590?–682?). No matter whether the aforementioned attributions are correct or not, my opinion is that this commentary does not show any awareness of Xuanzang's translation of the MSgBh and hence was likely composed at a time before Xuanzang became influential. Again, here I just pick one passage from this fragment:[40]

(Quotation 1.7)
Regarding the substance (*ti* 體) and the name of the five meanings of "containing" (Ch. *zang* 藏; Skt. *garbha*). . . . Secondly, with respect to their substance, they all employ [the notions of] original awakening, the mind of understanding (*jiexin* 解心), *tathāgatagarbha*, and have them (i.e., original awakening, etc.) as the nature [of the storehouse consciousness].[41]

Quotation 1.7 identifies the mind of understanding (*jiexin* 解心) with original awakening and *tathāgatagarbha*. It further claims that the nature of the storehouse consciousness is original awakening, the mind of understanding, and *tathāgatagarbha*. Thus, T2806 interprets the phrase *yi jie wei xing* 以解為性 of the *Shelun* as meaning that the storehouse consciousness has the mind of understanding as its nature.

1.2.5 Jizang 吉藏 (549–623)

Jizang, the most important scholar-monk of the Sanlun tradition 三論宗 (Tradition based on Three Treatises), which claims itself to be the true heir of Nāgārjuna, also links *jiexing* with the idea of "neither-arising-nor-ceasing" (*wu shengmie* 無生滅) in the *Awakening of Faith*. This can be seen in a passage from Jizang's *Zhongguanlun shu* 中觀論疏 (*A Commentary on the Mūlamadhyamakakārikā*), composed in 608:

> (Quotation 1.8) (cf. quotation 5.6)
> Further, the old Dilun masters claim that the seventh consciousness is false (*xuwang* 虛妄) but the eighth consciousness is true (*zhenshi* 真實). The Shelun masters (*Shedasheng shi* 攝大乘師) regard the eighth consciousness as false but the ninth consciousness as true. They also say (*youyun* 又云) that the eighth consciousness has two different senses: first, false; second, true. It is true in the sense that it has *jiexing*; it is false [in the sense] that it has the consciousness of retribution (Ch. *guobao shi* 果報識; Skt. *vipāka-vijñāna*). The mixture of arising-and-ceasing (*shengmie* 生滅) and neither-arising-nor-ceasing (*busheng bumie* 不生不滅) [as discussed] in the *Awakening of Faith* is taken to be the substance (*ti* 體) of the *aliye shi* (i.e., the storehouse consciousness).[42]

Apparently, Jizang was already aware that the Shelun masters saw a close association between *jiexing* and the notion of "neither-arising-nor-ceasing" in the *Awakening of Faith*. Although Jizang does not explicitly use the term "original awakening" in this passage, we can easily see the connection between *jiexing* and original awakening because the concept of original awakening is identical with "neither-arising-nor-ceasing," that is, the pure aspect within the storehouse consciousness, which, according to the *Awakening of Faith*, is a mixture of the pure aspect (i.e., neither-arising-nor-ceasing) and the impure (i.e., arising-and-ceasing) aspect.

1.2.6 Huayan Tradition:[43] Fazang 法藏 (643–712)

In the same way as the aforementioned texts, the Huayan master Fazang identifies *jiexing* with original awakening:[44]

> (Quotation 1.9)
> Question: Whenever we talk about the [*buddha-*]*gotra* (*zhongxing* 種性), it must be conditioned. How then could this doctrine take Thusness as the [*buddha-*]*gotra*?
> Answer: By adjusting to conditions (*suiyuan* 隨緣), Thusness is mixed with defilement (*ran* 染) and becomes the base consciousness. [Despite this], in that Reality [i.e., Thusness] there is the uncontaminated (Ch. *wulou* 無漏; Skt. *anāsrava*) original awakening that permeates sentient beings from within and serves as the cause of reversing transmigration (Ch. *fanliu yin* 返流因; Skt. **nivṛtti-hetu*). For this reason, [sentient beings] are regarded as having the [*buddha-*]*gotra*. The *Shelun* translated in the Liang dynasty claims this (i.e., original awakening) to be *jiexing* within the storehouse consciousness. This is also the original awakening as explained in the *Awakening of Faith* under the two senses of the storehouse consciousness."[45]

After Fazang, the notion of *jiexing* did not seem to receive much attention. It appears only in a few commentaries on the *Dasheng zhiguan famen* 大乘止觀法門 and the works of Fazang. In those works, *jiexing* is invariably understood in terms of original awakening. There is nothing new in any of these later interpretations. It is also this specific reading of *jiexing* as identical to original awakening that Fujaku and Ui accept uncritically. This interpretation of *jiexing* is still prevalent today.

1.3 Permanence Reading (*Awakening of Faith*) vs. Impermanence Reading (T2805)

Having reviewed interpretations of *jiexing* from the late sixth century through modern times, I conclude that the current scholarly consensus regarding *jiexing*—that it refers to the pure aspect within the storehouse consciousness which is identical with original awakening as it is explained in the *Awakening of Faith*—has not changed much since the late sixth century. This traditional interpretation has implications related to original awakening in the *Awakening of Faith*. Next I point out that according to the traditional account, *jiexing* is permanent (*nitya*), just like original awakening. At the end of this section, I introduce the contrary interpretation in T2805, in which *jiexing* is understood as being impermanent (*anitya*).

1.3.1 The Implications of Understanding *Jiexing* as Original Awakening

I have shown that *jiexing* has been closely associated with original awakening in the *Awakening of Faith* in several early sources about *jiexing*, beginning with *Tanyan shu* around the end of the sixth century in China and continuing through Ui Hakuju in the modern period. The traditional attribution of the *Awakening of Faith* to Paramārtha also seems to justify the affinity between *jiexing* and original awakening.[46]

Regarding the doctrinal significance of the identification between *jiexing* and original awakening, I must return to the *Awakening of Faith* and investigate how original awakening is depicted there.

At the beginning of the *Awakening of Faith*, the famous scheme of One Mind in Two Aspects (*yixin ermen*一心二門) is introduced. The basic idea is that the mind of sentient beings is responsible for both aspects: "neither-arising-nor-ceasing" (*busheng bumie* 不生不滅) and "arising-and-ceasing" (*shengmie* 生滅), that is, for both purity and impurity. The first aspect is called the aspect of Thusness of the mind (*xin zhenru men* 心真如門), and the second aspect is called the aspect of arising-and-ceasing of the mind (*xin shengmie men* 心生滅門). Under these two aspects, the *Awakening of Faith* suggests that all dharmas (i.e., phenomena) are merely delusive mental representations projected by the One Mind (*yixin*一心), which is innate and pure. The reason why this Mind projects delusive representations is that it is agitated by ignorance and functions like the storehouse consciousness.[47] This is called the Aspect of arising-and-ceasing. But when the Mind is no longer agitated by ignorance, it is restored to its original calmness and purity. This is called the aspect of Thusness. In both cases, there is only one substance, namely the One Mind.

In this system, the storehouse consciousness is understood as the agitated state of the pure Mind. It is a mixture of the pure aspect of "neither-arising-nor-ceasing" and the impure aspect of "arising and ceasing" because it is still pure in its underlying uncontaminated substance. This pure substance, the Mind in its calm state, is also called original awakening, which is also identified with the dharma-body according to quotation 1.2 earlier. I discuss the notion of dharma-body in more detail in Chapter 7. It is important to note here that the dharma-body is also identified with such notions as Thusness and *tathāgatagarbha* according to the *Awakening of Faith*:

> (Quotation 1.10)
> Furthermore, the characteristic of Thusness itself (*zhenru zitixiang* 真如自體相) is as follows: [It] does not increase nor decrease for any ordinary sentient beings, the Hearers (*śrāvaka*), the Solitary Realizers (*pratyekabuddha*), the bodhisattvas, or the Buddhas. It is neither that [Thusness] arose in the former time, nor that it will cease at some future time. It is permanent throughout time. From the beginningless time Thusness by its nature is replete with all excellent qualities . . . it is called "containing a tathāgata" (Ch. *rulaizang* 如來藏; Skt. *tathāgatagarbha*) and also the dharma-body of the Tathāgatas.[48]

Hence, the Mind, original awakening, dharma-body, and *tathāgatagarbha* are all synonymous. All are permanent and unconditioned because none of them ever changes.

1.3.2 The Permanence Reading of *Jiexing*

The crucial point in these interpretations of *jiexing*, which are closely associated with the *Awakening of Faith*, is that *jiexing* is permanent and unconditioned: it is identified with original awakening, Thusness, dharma-body, *tathagatagarbha*, and the Dharma-element (*dharmadhātu*). This will have great significance in our later discussion.

I call this interpretation the Permanence Reading of *jiexing*. In the next chapter, I challenge this Permanence Reading, which is closely connected to the *Awakening of Faith*. First, however, I introduce a different understanding of *jiexing* found in T2805.

1.4 An Alternative Reading of *Jiexing* Suggested by T2805

A different reading of *jiexing*—the only other that I have found so far—survives in T2805. I reserve a more elaborate discussion and philological analysis of T2805 for Chapter 3. Here, I examine some comments in T2805 on the *Shelun Jiexing* Passage (2).

1.4.1 T2805 *Jiexing* Passage (1)

> [Quotation from *Shelun*:] "What is called the 'basis for noble people' (Ch. *shengren yi* 聖人依; Skt. **āryāśraya*) comes from the mixture between the permeation of

hearing (Ch. *wenxunxi* 聞熏習; *śrutavāsanā*) and *jiexing*. With this being the basis, all noble paths are born."

[Commentary by T2805:] This is the tenth point, which means to clarify that when the understanding arising from hearing (Ch. *wen [hui]* 聞[慧]; *śrutamayī[-prajñā]*) and the understanding arising from pondering (Ch. *si [hui]* 思[慧]; *cintāmayī[-prajñā]*) permeate the impermanent (Ch. *wuchang* 無常; Skt. *anitya*) *jiexing* of the base consciousness (Ch. *benshi* 本識; Skt. *mūla-vijñāna*), [the practitioners] are still ordinary people (*pṛthagjana*). [The practitioners] become noble people (Ch. *shengren* 聖人; Skt. *ārya*) only after the permeation increases, further resides in the sixth mental consciousness (*manovijñāna*) and establishes the uncontaminated path (Ch. *wuliu dao* 無流道; Skt. *anāsrava-mārga*), i.e., the understanding arising from cultivating (Ch. *xiuhui* 修慧; Skt. **bhāvanāmayī-prajñā*). Hence it is said that all noble paths are based upon it (i.e., the permeation of hearing).

Question: Regarding the *jiexing* that is permeated by the seeds of [the understanding arising from] hearing and [the understanding arising from] pondering, an explanation says that *jiexing* refers to the true and pure dharma-body (*zhenjing fashen* 真淨法身). How can you (my master) claim that it is an impermanent dharma?

Answer: [This explanation] is arbitrary words (*manyu* 漫語) that, based on one's own [incorrect] thinking (*zigui shi xin* 自歸識心), arise from a dark discriminating mind (*fenbie anxin* 分別闇心). This is not the correct interpretation. A permanent dharma cannot be permeated, unlike an impermanent [dharma], which can be permeated in six contexts (*liuyi* 六義).[49] The understanding arising from hearing and the understanding arising from pondering permeate [the storehouse consciousness], and only when they further reside in the sixth, i.e., the mental consciousness and establish the understanding arising from cultivating, is the uncontaminated path established. These seeds [arising from] hearing and pondering give birth to [the understanding of] consciousness-and-representation-only (*vijñaptimātratā*) with no external objects and the *jñāna* arising from contemplation (*guanzhi* 觀智) [on the reality of dharmas]. At this moment, [these seeds] serve as the causes for the dharmas [that lead to liberation] and belong to the dependent nature (*paratantra-svabhāva*). When afflictions are cut off completely, one experiences the transformation of the basis (Ch. *zhuanyi* 轉依; Skt. *āśrayaparāvṛtti* or *āśrayaparivṛtti*) and attains liberation as the effect. [Only at that time] does the body [of liberation (*jietuo shen* 解脫身)?][50] transform its basis and have [as its new basis] the true and pure mind (*zhenjing xin* 真淨心), which is the dharma-body and [contains] the merits from the effect (*guode* 果德) [of liberation].

How[51] can one [at that time] again have [the dharma-body] mixed with the seeds [arising from] hearing and pondering to become the cause to the noble path? When one is associated with (*xiangying* 相應) the dharma-body (i.e., when one attains the dharma-body), only the merits from the effect [of liberation] are based on the dharma-body. [The dharma-body] does not have the further (*wufu* 無復) sense of being a seed or a cause."[52]

1.4.2 T2805 *Jiexing* Passage (2)

> The undiscriminating *jñāna* has the Dharma-element as its faculty (Ch. *gen* 根; Skt. *indriya*). Its substance (*ti* 體) is the faculty of having learned (Ch. *zhigen* 知根; Skt. *ājñātendriya*), because it is born from the faculty of resolving to know something unknown (Ch. *zhiweizhi gen* 知未知根 or *weizhi yuzhi gen* 未知欲知根; Skt. *ājñāsyāmīndriya*). It is also called "having a faculty" (*yougen* 有根) because it has the faculty of resolving to know something unknown, which is born from the *jñāna* of things as they really are (Ch. *rushi zhi* 如實智; Skt. *yathābhūta-parijñāna*). Moreover, from the perspective of the contributory cause (*yuanyin* 緣因) [for the undiscriminating *jñāna*], the arising of *jiexing* is also called "having a faculty." [Moreover, the undiscriminating *jñāna*] is also called "having a faculty" because it can bring about the subsequently acquired *jñāna* (Ch. *houzhi* 後智; i.e., 後得智; Skt. *pṛṣṭhalabdha-jñāna*) and advance to the applied *jñāna* (*jiaxing zhi* 加行智) at later stages (*bhūmi*). "Having a faculty" means having something that serves as the substance (*you dangti* 有當體). Why? Because once this [undiscriminating] *jñāna* is attained, the other kinds of *jñāna* will cease. Based on this [undiscriminating] *jñāna*, the merits and wisdom at higher stages will be born. For this reason, it [the undiscriminating *jñāna*] is a faculty.[53]

These two passages from T2805 are difficult to understand not only because of the missing characters but also because of their opaqueness. Unfortunately, the only study of this fragmentary commentary is Kimura (1985), which is not helpful.[54] In 6.2, I explore these two passages at greater length.

1.4.3 Preliminary Observations on *Jiexing* in T2805

Notwithstanding its obscurities, T2805 clearly gives a picture of *jiexing* that is almost the complete opposite of the traditional interpretation, which is closely associated with the *Awakening of Faith*. The first assertion we can make about *jiexing* according to T2805 is that *jiexing* is not a permanent dharma and hence cannot be identical with the dharma-body.

T2805 also makes a clear-cut distinction between unconditioned and conditioned dharmas: it says that the dharma-body, as an unconditioned dharma, cannot be permeated. In contrast, since *jiexing* can be permeated by the understanding arising from hearing and pondering (*wensi hui* 聞思慧), it must be conditioned.

Following this point, T2805 makes it clear that the role played by the dharma-body—again, as an unconditioned dharma—in the path toward liberation is not as a cause. The dharma-body only functions as the final goal, to which the merits from the effect (*guode* 果德) belong. In other words, the fact that the dharma-body is permanent implies that it does not serve as the cause for attaining liberation.

In Chapter 6, I offer a tentative resolution of these two difficult passages. These preliminary observations, however, are sufficient in hinting at an interpretation of *jiexing* diametrically opposed to the traditional account.

1.4.4 Impermanence Reading of *Jiexing*

T2805 interprets *jiexing* as impermanent, conditioned, and different from the dharma-body. All this information is contrary to the traditional account of *jiexing*. I call the reading suggested by T2805 the Impermanence Reading. According to this understanding, *jiexing* has yet to be permeated by the understanding arising from hearing and pondering and must be conditioned and impermanent. For the same reason, *jiexing* must not be identified with the dharma-body.

Now the contrast between two different readings of *jiexing*—the Permanence Reading in the *Awakening of Faith*, and the Impermanence Reading in T2805—can be summarized in Table 1.1.

1.4.5 Testimonies for the Impermanence Reading of *Jiexing*

As mentioned earlier, T2805 contains a reading of *jiexing* that is contrary to that of the interpretative tradition connected with the *Awakening of Faith*. Now the question is whether we can find any other textual evidence that supports this Impermanence Reading.

In contrast to the wealth of passages supporting the traditional account of *jiexing* (as surveyed earlier), I found only two passages that seem to echo what is said about *jiexing* in T2805. The first one is by Jizang:

> (Quotation 1.11) (= quotation 5.2)
> Seventhly, the Shelun masters (*Shedasheng shi* 攝大乘師) explain [as follows]: All sentient beings of the six destinies originate from the base consciousness. Because there are seeds for the six destinies in the base consciousness, the six destinies arise. Issuing from the pure Dharma-element, the twelve sections of scriptures arouse the permeation of hearing in just one thought (*yinian* 一念), which then becomes attached to the base consciousness. This is the beginning of returning (Ch. *fanqu* 返去; Skt. *nivṛtti*) [to nirvana]. As the permeation of hearing increases, the base consciousness also decreases. Once the realization (*jie* 解) is perfectly established, the base consciousness ceases entirely. The enjoyment[-body of a] Buddha (Ch. *baofo* 報佛; Skt. *buddha-saṃbhoga-*[*kāya*]) is established by adopting the *jiexing* within the base consciousness. This *jiexing* will not cease [when the

Table 1.1 (= Table 5.1) Permanence vs. Impermanence Reading

Permanence Reading (*Awakening of Faith*)	Impermanence Reading (T2805)
Jiexing is permanent/unconditioned.	*Jiexing* is impermanent/conditioned.
Jiexing is the dharma-body.	*Jiexing* is not the dharma-body.
Jiexing (i.e., original awakening, Thusness, dharma-body) permeates ignorance.	*Jiexing* has yet to be permeated by the understanding arising from hearing and pondering.
Jiexing (i.e., original awakening, Thusness, dharma-body) functions as the cause/seed for liberation.	The dharma-body does not function as the cause/seed for liberation but is the final goal for the Buddhist path.

> enjoyment-body is established]. The innate pure mind (Ch. *zixing qingjing xin* 自性清淨心; Skt. *prakṛtiprabhāsvara-citta*) is the dharma-body of a Buddha. When *jiexing* always agrees with (*changhe* 常合)[55] the innate pure mind and reaches the ultimate stage, *jiexing* and the innate pure mind are associated with each other and become [united in] one substance (*yiti* 一體). And hence not only is the dharma-body permanent but also is the enjoyment-body permanent.[56]

It is apparent from Jizang's understanding of the Shelun masters that they say that ultimate liberation lies in *jiexing*'s becoming the enjoyment-body of a Buddha when the base consciousness (i.e., the storehouse consciousness) ceases, namely, when one attains buddhahood. This suggests that *jiexing* is different from the dharma-body, which is also called the innate pure mind. Only when one attains buddhahood does *jiexing* or the enjoyment-body agree with the dharma-body or the innate pure mind. This clearly suggests that *jiexing* is different from the dharma-body, at least before one attains buddhahood. The idea that *jiexing* is related to the enjoyment-body and wisdom will be further explored in Chapters 4 and 6.[57]

1.4.6 Zhiyi 智顗 (538–97)

Zhiyi of the Tiantai tradition similarly describes an interpretation agreeing with the Impermanence Reading:

> (Quotation 1.12)
> If there are seeds for birth and death (*shengsi zhongzi* 生死種子) in the storehouse consciousness, then when they are permeated, they increase and become the discriminating consciousness. If there are seeds for wisdom (*zhihui zhongzi* 智慧種子) in the storehouse consciousness, then when they are permeated, they increase and, after the transformation of the basis, become Thusness after the Path (*daohou zhenru* 道後真如) and are named the pure consciousness (*jingshi* 淨識). If [the storehouse consciousness is discussed via the aspect other than the former two types of consciousness (i.e., the discriminating consciousness and the pure consciousness)], then it is [simply] the storehouse consciousness. This is what I mean by discussing via three [aspects] in one dharma and to discuss one [dharma] along three aspects.[58]

It is striking here that when Zhiyi says that there are "seeds for wisdom" (*zhihui zhongzi* 智慧種子) in the storehouse consciousness, he may be alluding to a reading according to which *jiexing* is regarded as seeds. It is evident that seeds, being conditioned, cannot be identified with the dharma-body, which is unconditioned. Thus, Zhiyi's passage can also be taken as supporting the Impermanence Reading of *jiexing* as preserved in T2805.

It is not easy to judge whether Zhiyi makes this comment based on his own understanding of the *Shelun* or on what he has heard about Paramārtha's teachings. Nor is it easy to judge whether the idea that there are seeds for wisdom within the storehouse consciousness was based on the *Shelun* teachings in the South or in the North.

Apparently, Zhiyi knew about the disputes between the Dilun and Shelun masters in the North.[59]

1.5 Conclusion

In this chapter, I have briefly traced the history of the reception of the notion of *jiexing*, which appears only twice in Paramārtha's *Shelun*. I have shown that our current understanding of this notion, which owes much to the modern Japanese scholar Ui Hakuju, is heavily influenced by the traditional interpretation of *jiexing* that is closely connected with the *Awakening of Faith*. Almost all early authors followed this reading of *jiexing*. The most distinctive feature of this interpretation, which I call the Permanence Reading, is that *jiexing* is identified with original awakening, the dharma-body of the Buddhas and Thusness and hence is regarded as permanent and unconditioned.

In contrast, a different reading of *jiexing* is preserved in T2805, a fragment of a commentary on Paramārtha's *Shelun*. T2805 refutes outright the idea that *jiexing* should be identified with the dharma-body. Instead, *jiexing* is something waiting to be permeated and hence must be conditioned and impermanent. For this reason, I call the interpretation offered by T2805 the Impermanence Reading.

In the light of two contradictory readings of *jiexing*, how can we decide which better represents Paramārtha's original teaching? In Chapter 2, I cast doubt on the traditional Permanence Reading of *jiexing* by referring to the convincing evidence adduced by previous scholars for doubting the traditional attribution of the *Awakening of Faith* to Paramārtha. Thus, I suggest that we should remain skeptical about the traditional Impermanence Reading, according to which *jiexing* is identified with original awakening in the *Awakening of Faith*.

2

Doubts about the Connection between the *Awakening of Faith* and Paramārtha

There have long been debates among scholars, especially Japanese scholars, about the provenance of the *Awakening of Faith*. In the first part of this chapter, I briefly review these debates. My goal is to show that most scholars currently agree that the *Awakening of Faith* could not have been translated by Paramārtha. Nevertheless, there is a convincing argument for a connection between the *Awakening of Faith* and Paramārtha, namely, the strong tie between the dissemination of the *Awakening of Faith* and the dissemination of Paramārtha's *Shelun*. For this reason, any refutation of the traditional attribution of the *Awakening of Faith* must provide a satisfactory explanation for this connection. In the second part of the chapter, I argue that there is a crucial doctrinal difference that separates the *Awakening of Faith* from all known Indian Yogācāra sources, namely, the idea that Thusness, an unconditioned dharma, can be permeated. This deviation found in the *Awakening of Faith* casts further doubt on its possible Indian provenance.

2.1 The Early Reception of the *Awakening of Faith*

The first mention of the *Awakening of Faith* appeared around 590 in the *Tanyan shu* 曇延疏. As already mentioned in Chapter 1, Kashiwagi (1981) suggests that this was the first commentary written on the *Awakening of Faith*.[1]

Slightly later, the *Awakening of Faith* appeared in the works of Jingying Huiyuan, including *Da boniepan jing yiji* 大般涅槃經義記 (*A Record of the Doctrines of the Mahāparinirvāṇa-mahāsūtra*), *Dasheng yizhang*, and *Weimo yiji* 維摩義記 (*A Record of the Doctrines of the Vimalakīrtinirdeśa-sūtra*). We do not know the exact dates of the composition of these works.

It is noteworthy that another commentary on the *Awakening of Faith* entitled *Dasheng qixin lun yishu* 大乘起信論義疏 (*A Commentary on the Doctrines of the Awakening of Faith*) was also attributed to Huiyuan, but there are good reasons for doubting this attribution.[2] After Huiyuan, the *Awakening of Faith* became influential and appeared in the works of many authors. Among the earlier authors are Jizang of the Sanlun tradition and Zhiyan 智儼 (602–68) of the early Huayan tradition.

It should be noted that although the *Awakening of Faith* was already attributed to Paramārtha around 594 in the capital, Chang'an 長安,[3] none of the aforementioned prominent authors explicitly identified Paramārtha as the translator. They referred to the *Awakening of Faith* either as the *Qixin lun* 起信論 (*The Treatise that [Aims at] Arousing one's Faith [in the Mahāyāna]*) or as the *Maming lun* 馬鳴論 (*The Treatise by Aśvaghoṣa*). Fazang 法藏 (643–712), in his *Dasheng qixin lun yiji* 大乘起信論義記 (*A Record of the Doctrines of the Awakening of Faith*), was the first known prominent Chinese monk to mention that Paramārtha was the translator of the *Awakening of Faith*.[4] In other words, the attribution of the translation of the *Awakening of Faith* to Paramārtha may not have been generally accepted at the earliest stage of its circulation.

To support the attribution of the *Awakening of Faith* to Paramārtha, Hirakawa (1990) argues that, although these authors did not mention Paramārtha by name, they actually had Paramārtha in mind, even though they referred to the text as *Maming lun*. It is true, as Hirakawa claims, that their convention was to designate a text by the name of its Indian author without mentioning the translator's name. However, this does not prove that the authors before Fazang actually thought Paramārtha was the translator. It is equally possible that these authors never directly associated the *Awakening of Faith* with Paramārtha because they entertained doubts about this attribution.

2.2 Inconsistencies in Chinese Buddhist Catalogs

The situation is no clearer with respect to the catalogs of the Buddhist canon in China, either.[5] The first catalog that mentions the *Awakening of Faith*, namely, the *Zhongjing mulu* 眾經目錄 (*A Catalog of All Scriptures*), edited by Fajing 法經 (d.u.) in 594, included the *Awakening of Faith* in the category of "Dubious Works" (*yihuo* 疑惑) and commented as follows:

> (Quotation 2.1)
> The *Awakening of Faith*; One fascicle. (Some people say that this was translated by Paramārtha. *I have consulted the catalog of Paramārtha's works but [the Awakening of Faith] is not listed there*, and hence I put this into the category of "Dubious Works"). (My emphasis)[6]

The first catalog that includes the *Awakening of Faith* is the *Lidai sanbao ji* 歷代三寶紀 (*A History of Buddhism throughout the Dynasties*), edited by Fei Changfang 費長房 (d.u.) in 597. Fei Changfang claims that the *Awakening of Faith* was translated by Paramārtha in 550, that is, the fourth year of Taiqing 太清 during the reign of Emperor Wu 武帝 (reigned during 502–49) of the Liang 梁 dynasty (502–57). The *Lidai sanbao ji* generally gives the year and/or the place of translation for many of Paramārtha's works. However, the *Lidai sanbao ji* is widely distrusted by modern scholars,[7] and serious doubts must be cast on the information it provides regarding Paramārtha's works. To just give one example, Emperor Wu died in the third year of Taiqing, and hence the fourth year of Taiqing never existed.

With the notable exception of the *Zhongjing mulu* 眾經目錄 by Fajing 法經 mentioned earlier, all the later catalogs of the Buddhist canon follow the *Lidai san*

Table 2.1 Dates of the Translation of the *Awakening of Faith* Given by Chinese Buddhist Catalogs

	Year of Editing	Date of the *Awakening of Faith*
Zhongjing mulu (Fajing)	594	Does not accept attribution to Paramārtha
Lidai sanbao ji	597	550
Zhongjing mulu (Yancong)	602	During Chen dynasty (557–69)
Datang Dongjing Dajing'ai si yiqiejinglun mu[lu]	664	During Chen dynasty (557–69)
Datang neidian lu	664	Listed during both Liang dynasty (546–57) and Chen dynasty (557–69)
Gujin yijing tuji	666	554 (Chengsheng 承聖 3 of the reign of Emperor Wu of the Liang dynasty)
Dazhou kanding zhongjing mulu	695	During the Liang dynasty (546–57)
Kaiyuan shijiao lu	730	553 (Chengsheng 2 of the reign of Emperor Wu of the Liang dynasty)
Zhenyuan xinding shijiao mulu	800	553

bao ji in attributing the *Awakening of Faith* to Paramārtha, including the *Zhongjing mulu* 眾經目錄 (602) by Yancong 彥琮 (557–610), the *Datang Dongjing Dajing'ai si yiqiejinglun mu[lu]* 大唐東京大敬愛寺一切經論目[錄] (664), the *Datang neidian lu* 大唐內典錄 (664), the *Gujin yijing tuji* 古今譯經圖記 (666), the *Dazhou kanding zhongjing mulu* 大周刊定眾經目錄 (695), the *Kaiyuan shijiao lu* 開元釋教錄 (730), the *Zhenyuan xinding shijiao mulu* 貞元新定釋教目錄 (800), and a few later catalogs edited by Japanese and Korean Buddhist scholars. Despite their agreement about Paramārtha being the translator, they disagree about the exact date of translation. The dates of the translation of the *Awakening of Faith* given by various Chinese Buddhist catalogs are shown in Table 2.1.

Hence, the Chinese tradition is not unanimous regarding the date of the *Awakening of Faith*. Since the earliest catalog, Fajing's *Zhongjing mulu*, edited in 594, questions the attribution of the *Awakening of Faith* to Paramārtha, we can assume that this attribution must have been current even before 594.

2.3 Three Claims Regarding the Provenance of the *Awakening of Faith*

2.3.1 Hirakawa: Paramārtha Translated the *Awakening of Faith*

Few scholars still believe that Paramārtha himself was the translator of the *Awakening of Faith*. The most recent exposition of this view appears in a long article by HIRAKAWA Akira 平川彰. Hirakawa (1990) tries to refute the claim that the *Awakening of Faith* is a Chinese, rather than an Indian, work. However, I do not find his arguments convincing in most cases, nor do most scholars today. Here I discuss some of his points and his strategies that are relevant to my discussion later.

2.3.1.1 *Regarding the Doubt Cast by Fajing's Zhongjing mulu*

Concerning the suspicions expressed by the earliest catalog, that is, Fajing's *Zhongjing mulu*, Hirakawa's strategy is to discredit the catalog itself. He points out that, according to its postscript, this catalog was finished in only two months (May–July, 594), and Hirakawa suggests that it must therefore have contained many mistakes. A clue to the untrustworthiness of this catalog, according to Hirakawa, is that Yancong, one of its editors, compiled another catalog eight years later (602), in which the *Awakening of Faith* was attributed to Paramārtha.[8] Moreover, Hirakawa seems to suggest that the earliest catalog must be mistaken, since it is the only one that differs from all later catalogs.[9]

There are at least two problems with Hirakawa's arguments. First, the fact that there are several mistakes in Fajing's *Zhongjing mulu* does not prove that it was wrong to doubt the attribution of the *Awakening of Faith* to Paramārtha. Second, the fact that later catalogs all agree that Paramārtha was the translator does not prove that it is true.

2.3.1.2 *Regarding the Terminological Differences between the* **Awakening of Faith** *and Other Works by Paramārtha*

A major challenge to the traditional attribution of the *Awakening of Faith* to Paramārtha is that there are significant terminological differences between it and other works of Paramārtha. Hirakawa iterates Ui's defense and argues that the reason for such substantial differences is that Paramārtha had been in China for only four years when he translated the *Awakening of Faith*. According to these two scholars, the terminological inconsistency was due to Paramārtha's inadequate Chinese proficiency as well as his Chinese colleagues' unfamiliarity with the terminology of Indian Buddhism.[10]

This argument looks persuasive at first glance. However, the terminology of the *Awakening of Faith* coincides with the terminology prevalent in northern China but not the terminology in southern China, where Paramārtha was active and where his Chinese colleagues presumably originated. Ui's argument would make sense only if he could convincingly explain why Paramārtha's Chinese colleagues were more familiar with the northern Chinese terminology than with the southern.[11]

2.3.1.3 *The* **Awakening of Faith** *Was Based on Indian Scriptures*

Hirakawa also tries to refute the idea that the *Awakening of Faith* was composed in China by reminding us that the issues it addresses originated in scriptures composed in India. That is to say, the major doctrines of the *Awakening of Faith* belong completely to Indian Mahāyāna Buddhist philosophy and do not contain any "Chinese element."[12]

Hirakawa is arguing against opponents, notably Mochizuki, who suggest that the *Awakening of Faith* must have been composed by Chinese monks in order to resolve debates that occurred only in China, namely, between the Dilun and the Shelun traditions (see 5.5). Now we turn to Mochizuki and examine the strong evidence he provides against the traditional attribution of the *Awakening of Faith* to Paramārtha.

2.3.2 Mochizuki, Takemura and Ōtake: Paramārtha Had Nothing to Do with the *Awakening of Faith*

The traditional attribution of the *Awakening of Faith* to Paramārtha is almost completely rejected, especially in the West. Very few scholars still believe that Paramārtha was the translator of the *Awakening of Faith*. In Japan, scholars did not begin to doubt the traditional attribution until early in the twentieth century. In the West, Paul Demiéville (1929) wrote a long article arguing in favor of the traditional attribution. But thanks to Walter Liebenthal (1958), most Western scholars now reject this attribution.[13]

2.3.2.1 Mochizuki

The Japanese scholars Mochizuki (1869–1948), Takemura (born in 1948), and Ōtake (born in 1974) are noteworthy among those who have challenged the traditional attribution. Kashiwagi (1981) extensively surveys the modern Japanese scholarly debate about the author/translator of the *Awakening of Faith*. He summarizes Mochizuki's main points supporting the Chinese provenance of the *Awakening of Faith*.[14] Here I slightly modify Kashiwagi's summary for clarity:

1. The description in the *Lidai sanbao ji* was fabricated; in contrast, the treatment of the *Awakening of Faith* in the *Fajing lu* should be correct.
2. The Preface to Paramārtha's translation is not genuine. Its description of the process of the translation process is fabricated.
3. Some terminology used in the *Awakening of Faith* goes against the usual translations in Paramārtha's other works.
4. The *Awakening of Faith* was composed based on the *Zhancha shan'e yebao jing* 占察善惡業報經 (*The Scripture on the Divination of the Effects of Good and Evil Actions*).
5. The *Awakening of Faith* quotes the *Renwang bore jing* 仁王般若經 (*The Perfection of Wisdom Scripture for Humane Kings*) and the *Pusa yingluo benye jing* 菩薩瓔珞本業經 (*The Scripture on the Bracelet-like Previous Deeds of Bodhisattvas*). In addition, in the section entitled *Duizhi xiezhi* 對治邪執 (Antidotes to Erroneous Views), the *Awakening of Faith* criticizes five views of selfhood; among them are those held by prominent monks in China, such as Kumārajīva 鳩摩羅什 (344–413), Daosheng 道生 (355–434), and Sengzhao 僧肇 (374–414?).
6. Sentences in the *Awakening of Faith* seem to have been extracted from scriptures that were all translated before the Liang dynasty.
7. The terms for the three bodies of the Buddha in the *Awakening of Faith*, namely, the *fashen* 法身, *baoshen* 報身 (i.e., enjoyment-body), and *yingshen* 應身 (response-body; Skt. *nirmāṇakāya*), are adopted from the scriptures translated in northern China. According to Mochizuki, this implies that the *Awakening of*

Faith represents a reconciliation made by the northern Dilun tradition when it encountered and tried to incorporate the teachings of the Shelun tradition which had been earlier transmitted from southern China. From this, Mochizuki infers that the *Awakening of Faith* was composed after Paramārtha translated the *Shelun* and the *Jinguangming jing* 金光明經 (Skt. *Suvarṇaprabhāsottama-sūtra*, *The Scripture of Golden Light*).[15]

8. Regarding what it says about the theory of three bodies, the doctrine of the "three greats" (*sanda* 三大, i.e., substance [*ti* 體], characteristics [*xiang* 相], and function [*yong* 用]) of the *Awakening of Faith* represents a compromise with the three-bodies theory prevalent in northern China, that is, the idea of "breaking up the true (body) [into two parts] and fusing [one part] with the response(-body)" (*kaizhen heying* 開真合應).[16]
9. The *Awakening of Faith,* based on the doctrine of "Thusness as basis" (*zhenru yichi* 真如依持) of the southern branch of the Dilun tradition, states that Thusness is "the substance (*ti* 體) of Dharma-gates (*famen ti* 法門體)," that is, that Thusness is the ontological basis for all dharmas.
10. The *Awakening of Faith* defines the storehouse consciousness as both true and false by saying that it is "a mixture of neither-arising-nor-ceasing and arising-and-ceasing, with these two neither different from nor identical to each other."[17] This is the result of compromises among various teachings about the storehouse consciousness in the two branches of the Dilun tradition and in the Shelun tradition.
11. The order of the seven types of consciousnesses, that is, the storehouse consciousness, the five sense consciousnesses, and mental consciousness (*aliye shi* 阿梨耶識, *wuyi* 五意, *yishi* 意識) is based on the *Laṅkāvatāra-sūtra* (*The Sutra on [the Buddha's] Entering [the Country of] Lanka*) in four fascicles translated by Guṇabhadra 求那跋陀羅 (394–468). As for the terms "*yeshi* 業識," "*zhuanshi* 轉識," "*xianshi* 現識," "*zhishi* 智識," "*xiangxu shi* 相續識," and "*fenbieshi shi* 分別事識," they are a blend of the doctrine of consciousnesses in the Chinese translations of the *Laṅkāvatāra-sūtra* by Guṇabhadra and by Bodhiruci (菩提流支, date unknown; arrived in China in 508).
12. Regarding the authorship of the *Awakening of Faith*, Mochizuki speculates that the text was probably written down by Tanqian, based on the oral teaching of Tanzun 曇遵 (d. 588), and hence originated from the southern branch of the Dilun tradition. Mochizuki's suggestion is based on the relation between the *Awakening of Faith* and the *Dasheng zhiguan famen*, which Mochizuki regarded as the work of Tanqian.
13. The so-called new translation by Śikṣānanda 實叉難陀 (652–710) was composed in order to counter the criticism by the Chinese Yogācāra tradition regarding the authenticity of the *Awakening of Faith.*

Finally, the following testimony should be added to the aforementioned list.[18]

14. The Japanese monk Chinkai 珍海 (?–1152) reported that Huijun 慧均 (var. Junzheng 均正; dates unknown, active *c.* 600), in his text entitled *Silun xuanyi* 四論玄義 (*On the Profound Meanings of the Four Treatises*), pointed out that the *Awakening of Faith* was composed by a Dilun master in northern China and hence was not composed by Aśvaghoṣa.[19]

2.3.2.2 The Terminological Differences between the Awakening of Faith *and Paramārtha*

I cannot examine each of the aforementioned points in detail. Here I offer a discussion only of the terminology adopted in the *Awakening of Faith* itself. I deal with some of the historical and doctrinal issues in later chapters.

With respect to the terminology of the *Awakening of Faith*, it is most startling that it includes several terms that are never used by Paramārtha but are closely connected to works belonging to the Dilun tradition. This strongly supports Mochizuki's points 10 and 12, that the *Awakening of Faith* was composed by a Chinese monk from the Dilun tradition.

Three prominent examples follow of the inconsistency of terminology between the *Awakening of Faith* and other works of Paramārtha, first pointed out by Mochizuki.[20]

1. Terms for the three Buddha-bodies. The terms "*fashen* 法身," "*yingshen* 應身," and "*huashen* 化身" are used by Paramārtha in his translations of the *Shelun*, the FXL, and the *Sanshen fenbie pin* 三身分別品 (*A Chapter on the Distinction among the Three Bodies*) of the *Jinguangming jing*. In contrast, the terms used in the *Awakening of Faith* are *fashen* 法身, *baoshen* 報身, and *yingshen* 應身, respectively. The set of terms in the *Awakening of Faith* is identical to the terms used by Bodhiruci, for example, in northern China.[21]
2. Way of quoting from scriptures. When Paramārtha quotes from a scripture, he usually begins with either the exact title of the scripture or the phrase *jing shuo* 經說 ("Thus says the Scripture"), in which the word for "Scripture" is translated. In contrast, the *Awakening of Faith* consistently uses the phrase *xiuduoluo (zhong) shuo* 修多羅（中）說 ("The Scripture says"), in which the word for "Scripture" is represented phonetically, eleven times in all. Again, *xiuduoluo (zhong) shuo* appears in texts such as the *A Commentary on the Ten Stages [of the Bodhisattva Path]* and the RGV, both from the north.[22]
3. The pair *fannao'ai* 煩惱礙 (obstruction related to afflictions) and *zhi'ai* 智礙 (obstruction related to cognitive objects). This pair, which occurs only in the *Awakening of Faith*, differs from the pair *fannaozhang* 煩惱障 and *zhizhang* 智障, which occurs both in Paramārtha and in translations from the north.

Unfortunately, Mochizuki's examples are not a conclusive argument against the attribution of the *Awakening of Faith* to Paramārtha. This is mainly because the terms employed by the *Awakening of Faith,* although never used by Paramārtha, are found in Chinese Buddhist texts contemporary with Paramārtha. It is possible that some of Paramārtha's Chinese colleagues simply used terms with which they were already familiar.

2.3.2.3 Strengthening Mochizuki's Arguments: Takemura's Observations

Given the inconclusiveness of Mochizuki's argument, it is useful here to look at the reasons provided by Takemura (1990) for doubting an association between Paramārtha and the *Awakening of Faith*.[23]

1. The compound *xinyiyishi* 心意意識 (*citta-mano-manovijñāna*). The *Awakening of Faith* uses the compound *xinyiyishi* in the following passage:

   (Quotation 2.2)
   Furthermore, the "cause and condition for the arising-and-ceasing [of sentient beings]" is: all sentient beings evolve (*zhuan* 轉) based on the mind, the mentation, and the mental consciousness (Ch. *xinyiyishi* 心意意識; Skt. *citta-mano-manovijñāna*).[24]

   The point here is that this specific rendering of the compound *citta-mano-manovijñāna* is found only in translations by Guṇabhadra, Bodhiruci, and Ratnamati. According to Takemura, this phrase is especially associated with the *Laṅkāvatāra-sūtra,* which typically belongs to the Dilun tradition. More importantly, Takemura does not mention the fact that Paramārtha never uses this Chinese compound to translate the Sanskrit term *citta-mano-manovijñāna*. Instead, he consistently translates *citta-mano-manovijñāna* as *xinyishi* 心意識 in the *Juedingzang lun* 決定藏論 (*A Collection of the Settled Views*) as well as in Paramārtha's AKBh and *Shelun*, two of his last works.[25]
2. The terms "*shemota guan* 奢摩他觀" and "*piboshena guan* 毘鉢舍那觀." The *Awakening of Faith* says:

   (Quotation 2.3)
   How to cultivate the gate of "Cessation and Observation" (*zhiguan men* 止觀門)? "Calming" (*zhi* 止) means the cessation of all the appearances of objects (*jingjie xiang* 境界相) as one follows the sense of the observation of *shemota* (Ch. 奢摩他; Skt. *śamatha*). "Observing" (*guan* 觀) means the analysis of the appearances of the arising and ceasing of causes and conditions (*yinyuan shengmie xiang* 因緣生滅相), as one follows the sense of observation of *piboshena* (Ch. 毘鉢舍那; Skt. *vipaśyanā*).[26]

   According to Takemura, the issue here is the phrase *piboshena guan* 毘鉢舍那觀, since the Chinese *piboshena* is already a transliteration of the Sanskrit *vipaśyanā*, meaning either "observation" or the *jñāna* gained from observation. Taken literally, the *piboshena guan* in the *Awakening of Faith* would mean something like "the observation of observing."

   In fact, as Takemura pointed out, *piboshena guan* was copied by the *Awakening of Faith* from Bodhiruci's translation of the *Saṃdhinirmocana-sūtra*.[27] But in the *Saṃdhinirmocana-sūtra*, the Chinese term *guan* 觀 is a translation either of the Sanskrit term *ālambana* or *bimba* and never means *vipaśyanā* (observation) in its original context. The author of the *Awakening of Faith* mistakenly copied this Chinese phrase and used it in the wrong context.
3. The term *nian* 念 ("thought") as a key term in the *Awakening of Faith*. The term *nian* 念, as Takemura points out, is always used pejoratively in the *Awakening of Faith*. This term is already employed in the *Laṅkāvatāra-sūtra* and the *Daśabhūmika-sūtra-śāstra,* both translated by Bodhiruci, and the RGV, translated by Ratnamati. In particular, in the RGV, the Chinese term *nian* is a translation of the Sanskrit term *manasikāra*, for example, in translation of *ayoniśo-manasikāra* as *xienian* 邪念.

Again, Paramārtha never uses the term *nian* in the same way as the *Awakening of Faith*. He translated *ayoniśo-manasikāra* as *buzheng siwei* 不正思惟 ("incorrect thought").

4. The term *rushi xiuxing* 如實修行 (*abhisamaya-dharma*; *yoga-parāyaṇa*; *yoga-vāhin*).[28] Moreover, Takemura refers to the argument of SAKURABE Hajime 櫻部建, that the term *rushi xiuxing* 如實修行 belongs exclusively to the Dilun tradition.[29]

   More recently, Ōtake (2017) also argues that the *Awakening of Faith* is a patchwork of quotations from previous Chinese Buddhist texts. Based on this observation, Ōtake joins Takemura in claiming that the author must have come from the Dilun tradition.

2.3.3 C. Kashiwagi, Yoshizu: The *Awakening of Faith* is connected with Paramārtha, although he may not have translated it

Notwithstanding Takemura's compelling evidence for refuting the attribution of the *Awakening of Faith* to Paramārtha, some scholars, especially Japanese, are still not entirely convinced. Chief among them is Kashiwagi (1981).

Kashiwagi agrees that it is quite unlikely that Paramārtha himself translated the *Awakening of Faith*.[30] But he nonetheless argues that the *Awakening of Faith* was not composed by Chinese people, as suggested by Mochizuki and Takemura. Instead, Kashiwagi insists that the *Awakening of Faith* was closely embedded in the Indian Buddhist context. According to Kashiwagi:

> (Quotation 2.4)
> The *Awakening of Faith* was translated during the fifth to the sixth century, either in India or in China (also including such places as *Funan* 扶南 [i.e. Cambodia today]), *with its theory being constructed based on the direct extended line of Indian Buddhist thought*, by Paramārtha or someone belonging to the translation group surrounding Paramārtha. As to the situation of its translation, in addition to being based upon the recitation by a translator, the extant text is composed also based on the hands of the translation group that included Chinese Buddhists.[31] (My emphasis)

Although Kashiwagi agrees that it is unlikely that Paramārtha was the translator of the *Awakening of Faith*, he still insists on the association between the *Awakening of Faith* and Paramārtha. His main reason is his belief that the issues of concern (*mondai ishiki* 問題意識) in the *Awakening of Faith* are more Indian than Chinese. Paying close attention to the earliest reception of the *Awakening of Faith*, he points out that, at first, the *Awakening of Faith* was more closely connected to Paramārtha than to other indigenous Chinese Buddhist traditions, such as the Dilun tradition.[32]

For example, Kashiwagi examines three works that belong to this early phase: the *Tanyan shu*, *Zhancha shan'e yebao jing*, and the *Dasheng zhiguan famen*. Particularly relevant here are the first and the third texts. Briefly, regarding the *Tanyan shu*, Kashiwagi points out that it is a commentary on the *Awakening of*

Faith that repeatedly quotes from Paramārtha's *Shelun* and the RGV.[33] As for the *Dasheng zhiguan famen*, Kashiwagi suggests that it must have been composed by "Tanqian, or people surrounding him."[34] Tanqian was the foremost teacher who spread Paramārtha's Shelun from the south to the north. I will say more about him in Chapter 5.

Most importantly, Kashiwagi points out that several disciples of Tanyan (the probable author of the *Tanyan shu*) were also teachers on the *Shelun*.[35] In fact, Kashiwagi shows that all the teachers of the *Awakening of Faith* recorded in the XGSZ studied and lectured on the *Shelun*.[36] He also mentions that, according to Ui, the general tendency among the Shelun masters, that is, the disciples of Paramārtha, was to understand the *Shelun* from the perspective of the *Awakening of Faith*.[37] Based on the same reason offered by Kashiwagi, Yoshizu (2003: 282ff.) goes further to claim that the *Awakening of Faith* was indeed translated by Paramārtha.

To conclude, it has almost become a consensus among scholars that Paramārtha himself could not have been the translator of the *Awakening of Faith*. Nevertheless, some scholars still claim that the *Awakening of Faith* was closely connected with Paramārtha due to the strong tie between the dissemination of the *Awakening of Faith* and Paramārtha's *Shelun*. It seems to me that this tie is the strongest, perhaps the only, basis for arguing for an Indian provenance of the *Awakening of Faith* despite the strong counter-evidence. In Chapter 5, I refute this so-far unchallenged assumption.

However, there is a crucial place in the *Awakening of Faith* where it seems to diverge from the Indian sources.

2.4 The Divergence of the *Awakening of Faith* from Indian Yogācāra

With its notion of original awakening, the *Awakening of Faith* in fact initiates a completely new approach toward liberation that distinctively marks itself off from all major Yogācāra texts in India. The major difference here is the drastically altered idea of Thusness (*tathatā*) in the *Awakening of Faith*.

As I mentioned earlier, Thusness, like the dharma-body, the Dharma-element, nirvana, and space, is unconditioned.[38] And the essential character of the unconditioned dharmas is that they do not change over time. For this reason, these unconditioned dharmas lie outside the chain of cause and effect. Because of this, the unconditioned dharmas can serve as causes only in some special cases.[39] Since the unconditioned dharmas can never be altered, they cannot be permeated.

2.4.1 *Awakening of Faith*: Thusness Is Permeated

But the *Awakening of Faith* deviates from the principle that Thusness, as an unconditioned dharma, cannot be permeated. For example, the *Awakening of Faith* states,

(Quotation 2.5)
How is it that the permeation [of ignorance] gives rise to the defiled dharmas without interruption? This means that based on the dharma of Thusness (*zhenru fa* 真如法), ignorance arises. Because ignorance exists as the cause of defiled dharmas, it (i.e., ignorance) then permeates Thusness. Due to this permeation, the false mind (*wangxin* 妄心) comes to exist. Because the false mind exists, it (i.e., false mind) then permeates ignorance. [As a result, the false mind] does not understand the dharma of Thusness. The thought of non-awakening arises and so does the false cognitive objects (*wang jingjie* 妄境界).[40]

(Quotation 2.6)
How is it that the permeation [of Thusness] gives rise to the pure dharmas without interruption? This means that due to [the existence of] the dharma of Thusness, it (i.e., Thusness) permeates ignorance. Because of the power of the causes and conditions of permeation, [this power] leads the false mind to loathe sufferings and to aspire for nirvana. Because this false mind has the causes and conditions, i.e., loathing [of sufferings] and aspiring [for nirvana], [this false mind] then permeates Thusness. [As a result, the mind] has self-confidence that there is [Buddha] nature in oneself. [One] knows that the mind is agitated due to falsity and that the cognitive objects before it do not really exist, and hence cultivates the dharmas (i.e., practices) [that lead one] away from [these false cognitive objects].[41]

In both passages, the *Awakening of Faith* states that Thusness can be permeated by ignorance (quotation 2.5) and the false mind (quotation 2.6). As I mentioned earlier, this idea that Thusness can be permeated goes against the fundamental doctrine that Thusness is unconditioned.

2.4.2 MSg, MSgBh, CWSL: Unconditioned Dharmas Cannot Be Permeated

As opposed to the *Awakening of Faith*, Asaṅga's MSg (I.23) lists four characteristic marks of something that can be permeated. Among these four, the third one is "permeability" (Ch. *kexun* 可熏; Skt. *bhāvya*).[42] Here I quote Vasubandhu's explanation of permeability from Paramārtha's *Shelun*:

(Quotation 2.7)
Third, by "permeability" (*kexun* 可熏) I mean something that can be permeated. Hence [things like] gold, silver, stone, etc., are not permeable because they cannot be permeated. Because things such as clothes, oil, etc., can be permeated, they are named "permeable."[43]

It is true that in this paragraph Vasubandhu does not say explicitly that an unconditioned dharma cannot be permeated. But we can assume this must be the case. If even conditioned things such as gold, whose nature is that they are difficult to change, cannot be permeated, then how could unconditioned dharmas, whose nature is that they are impossible to change, be permeated? In contrast to the MSg and the MSgBh, the CWSL make this point explicitly:

> (Quotation 2.8)
> Third, "permeability": with regard to a dharma that is independent (*svatantra*), if its nature is not firm (Ch. *jianmi* 堅密; Skt. *dhruva* or *dṛḍha*[44]) so as to receive permeation, then such a dharma is what is permeable (*suoxun* 所熏). This excludes dharmas such as mental factors (Ch. *xinsuo* 心所; Skt. *caitta*) and unconditioned dharmas. [The former is] dependent upon others and [the latter has a nature that is] firm, and hence these two cannot be permeated.[45]

Moreover, the CWSL also mentions four characteristic marks of a thing that can permeate something else and states that an unconditioned dharma cannot permeate something else:

> (Quotation 2.9)
> First, "[a thing that] has arising-and-ceasing" (*you shengmie* 有生滅): if a dharma is not permanent (Ch. 非常 *feichang*; Skt. *anitya*) and can function to produce and increase permeation (Ch. *xiqi* 習氣; Skt. *vāsanā*), then it is what permeates (*nengxun* 能熏). This excludes unconditioned dharmas, which do not change during a previous moment and a successive one and have no function of producing and increasing [something else]. Hence it is not what permeates.[46]

This claim made in the MSg, the MSgBh, and the CWSL resonates with the point made in T2805, namely, that the dharma-body cannot be permeated since it is unconditioned dharma. For this reason, *jiexing*, which resides in the storehouse consciousness and is permeated by the "permeation of hearing," cannot be identified with the dharma-body.

2.4.3 Thusness as the Object of Undiscriminating *Jñāna* in Paramārtha

If Thusness, as an unconditioned dharma, cannot permeate nor be permeated, then what role does it play in Buddhist soteriology? In this section, I point out that the exclusive role Paramārtha assigns to Thusness is to serve as the cognitive object of undiscriminating *jñāna* (*nirvikalpa-jñāna*). When Paramārtha uses term "*jñāna* about Thusness" (*ruruzhi* 如如智) several times, it is clear from the context that he is referring to the *jñāna* that has Thusness as its cognitive object.[47] Here I provide several examples:[48]

1. From Paramārtha's *Jin guangming jing* 金光明經:

> (Quotation 2.10)
> O sons of good families! There is no superior *jñāna* beyond the undiscriminating *jñāna*. There is no superior object beyond the Thusness of dharmas (*fa ruru* 法如如). The Thusness of dharmas and the *jñāna* about Thusness are two kinds of Thusness. These two [kinds of Thusness] are neither identical nor different.[49]

2. From Paramārtha's MAV:

 (Quotation 2.11)
 What is the Ultimate Reality (*paramārtha*)? [The Ultimate Reality is threefold]: (1) [the Reality of] object (*artha-paramārtha*); (2) [the Reality of] proper cultivation (*prapatti*); (3) [the Reality of] (ultimate) attainment (*prāpti*). [Among these three] "The Reality of object" means the Thusness of dharmas, [which is the object] of the ultimate *jñāna* (*paramasya jñānasya*).[50]

3. From Paramārtha's FXL:

 (Quotation 2.12)
 The perfected nature (Ch. *zhenshi xing* 真實性; Skt. *parinişpanna-svabhāva*) refers to the Thusness of all dharmas, which is the object (Ch. *jing* 境; Skt. *vişaya*) of the undiscriminating *jñāna* of the noble people.[51]

4. From Paramārtha's *San wuxing lun* 三無性論 (*Treatise on the Three Kinds of the Absence of Self-nature*):

 (Quotation 2.13)
 What is meant by "Thusness" is the object (*vişaya*) of the noble *jñāna* (*shengzhi* 聖智) that is characterized by (*suoxian* 所顯)[52] the emptiness of dharmas. What is meant by "undiscriminating *jñāna*" is [the *jñāna*] by which all noble people penetrate into (Ch. *tongda* 通達; Skt. *prativedha*) Thusness.[53]

5. From Paramārtha's *Shelun*:

 (Quotation 2.14)
 Explanation: When a bodhisattva enters into the true observation (*zhenguan* 真觀), the *jñāna* of the bodhisattva is based upon ten kinds of equality, as is said in the *Daśabhūmika-sūtra*. In addition, [the *jñāna* of the bodhisattva] is based on two kinds of equality, namely the equality between the cognizer (Ch. *nengyuan* 能緣; Skt. *ālambaka*[54]) and the cognized (Ch. *suoyuan* 所緣; Skt. *ālambya/ālambana*). The cognizer [here] is the undiscriminating *jñāna*. This *jñāna* is called equality because it is devoid of discrimination. The cognized is Thusness as a cognitive object (*zhenru jing* 真如境). Since the object is also devoid of discrimination, [these two] are called equal [to each other].[55]

6. From Paramārtha's *Juedingzang lun*:

 (Quotation 2.15)
 [Objection:] . . . Furthermore, the [negative] permeation (Ch. *xiqi* 習氣; Skt. *vāsanā*) is the dharmas of negative faults that pervade everywhere (*bianyiqiechu zhu ezuifa* 遍一切處諸惡罪法). Now if the seeds of all dharmas [come to exist] based on this [negative] permeation, then on what basis can various supramundane dharmas arise?

 [Answer:] the seeds of negative dharmas (*efa zhong* 惡法種) are not the causes of [supramundane dharmas]. These supramundane dharmas arise by having

> Thusness as the condition of object-support (Ch. *zhenru jingjie zuoyuan* 真如境界作緣; Skt. *tathatālambanapratyaya*).[56]

To sum up, in all the previous examples, Paramārtha consistently maintains that Thusness is the object of undiscriminating *jñāna*. Nowhere does he mention (as the *Awakening of Faith* does) that Thusness is capable of permeating ignorance,[57] although he does claim that all sentient beings are endowed with Thusness.[58] This idea that Thusness can serve only as a condition of object-support (Skt. *ālambana-pratyaya*; Ch. *suoyuan yuan* 所緣緣 [Xuanzang]; *yuanyuan* 緣緣 or *suoyuan* 所緣 [Paramārtha]) but not as a causally efficacious seed can also be corroborated by the *Yogācārabhūmi*.[59]

2.5 Conclusion

In this chapter, I first showed that serious doubts have been cast on the traditional attribution of the *Awakening of Faith* to Paramārtha. After reviewing the arguments for and against the traditional attribution, I pointed out that the only remaining convincing argument for the traditional attribution is provided by Kashiwagi, who draws on the fact that there was a close tie between the spread of the *Awakening of Faith* and the spread of Paramārtha's *Shelun*. The traditional attribution cannot definitively be rejected without refuting Kashiwagi's argument, a task I undertake in Chapter 5.

In the second part of this chapter, I pinpointed a fundamental difference between the *Awakening of Faith* and all known Indian Yogācāra sources, including those translated by Paramārtha: Thusness as an unconditioned dharma cannot be permeated according to these Indian sources, whereas the *Awakening of Faith* declares outright that Thusness can be permeated. This striking difference casts further doubts on the Indian provenance of the *Awakening of Faith*.

In Chapter 1, I reviewed two readings of *jiexing*: the Permanence Reading, which is closely connected with the *Awakening of Faith* and has become the traditional interpretation of *jiexing*, and the Impermanence Reading, which is preserved only in T2805, a Dunhuang fragment that was hidden and unknown for more than a thousand years. If the traditional attribution of the *Awakening of Faith* is discredited, the Impermanence Reading in T2805 might be closer to Paramārtha's original teaching than the Permanence Reading. In the following chapters, I establish the close connection between T2805 and Paramārtha by showing the striking similarity between them from philological (Chapter 3) and doctrinal (Chapter 4) perspectives, and I argue that the Impermanence Reading of *jiexing* found in T2805 is more likely to have preserved the original teaching of Paramārtha.

3

A Philological Investigation of Dunhuang Fragment T2805

In Chapter 1, I showed that the Impermanence Reading of *jiexing*, which is different from the traditional Permanence Reading connected with the *Awakening of Faith*, is preserved in T2805. In Chapter 2, I pointed out several doubts cast on the traditional attribution of the *Awakening of Faith* to Paramārtha. The goal of this chapter is to show that, from the philological perspective, T2805 bears a striking similarity to other works of Paramārtha. For this reason, I propose in later chapters that the author of T2805 must be closely related to Paramārtha and his group; hence, it is the Impermanence Reading of *jiexing* in T2805, rather than the Permanence Reading associated with the *Awakening of Faith*, that most likely represents Paramārtha's original teaching regarding *jiexing*.

3.1 An Introduction to T2805

T2805, which is the focus of this and the next two chapters, is the fragmentary text numbered 2805 in the T, which includes T2805 in the section of texts whose date and authorship are unknown (*koitsu* 古逸). T2805 was discovered in the early twentieth century by Sir Aurel Stein (1862–1943) in the Mogao 莫高 cave, number Ch.80. VII.27. It is cataloged in the Stein collection as Stein 2747 (Or.8210/S.2747) and in Giles's *Descriptive Catalogue of the Chinese Manuscripts from Tunhuang in the British Museum* as Giles 5766.[1] It has been photographically reproduced in the collection entitled *Dunhuang baozang* 敦煌寶藏.[2]

Thanks to the International Dunhuang Project (IDP), the scanned image of T2805 is available.[3] It is written in ink in Chinese characters. Giles describes it as "in good bold MS. (i.e., handwriting), sometimes becoming careless, of late 6th century, (?). Thin buff paper. 30 ft."[4] In fact, as pointed out by Giles, the original manuscript consists of two fragments on both sides of the same scroll. On one side, it is entitled *Shedasheng shu juan di wu* 攝大乘疏卷第五 (fascicle 5 of *A Commentary on the Shelun*); on the other side, it is entitled *Shedasheng lun yiji di qi* 攝大乘論義記第七 (fascicle 7 of *A Record of the Doctrines of the Shelun*). Notwithstanding the different titles, these two fragments must belong to the same original text because the calligraphy and the style in which they comment on the *Shelun* are the same. Both fragments comment on Asaṅga's MSg as well as on Vasubandhu's MSgBh. Furthermore, as Shengkai 聖凱 (2006) points out, when commenting on Asaṅga's MSg, both fragments consistently use the phrase *lunben yun* 論本云 ("the root text [Paramārtha's translation of the MSg] says"); when commenting on Vasubandhu's MSgBh, they both say *shilun yue* 釋論曰 ("the commentary says"). Moreover, both fascicles comment selectively on difficult sentences or notions in Paramārtha's *Shelun*.[5]

In addition to T2805, four other fragmentary commentaries on Paramārtha's *Shelun* are included in the T, namely, T2806, T2807, T2808, T2809. Among these, I discussed T2806 in Chapter 1 (1.2.4). T2807 and T2808 were both found in Dunhuang. T2807 was included in the Stein collection as S. 2435 (Giles 5767), while T2808 was included as S. 2048 (Giles 5765). Shengkai made the important discovery that T2807 and S.6715 are fragments of the same text.[6] The note attached to the end of T2808 indicates that it was copied in 601, which means that it must have been composed before 601.[7] T2809 is included in the fragment preserved by the Japanese scholar ŌYA Tokujō大屋德城. Katsumata suggests that T2809 was probably composed by Daoji 道基 (?–637).[8]

Giles dates T2805 to the late sixth century with a question mark. In fact, we know nothing about by whom, when, or where it was written. In this and the next two chapters, I try to establish the probable date, author, and place of production of T2805.

3.2 Some Preliminary Observations about T2805

T2805 as we have it constitutes only parts of the original texts, namely, part of fascicle 5 and part of fascicle 7. If we compare the number of fascicles in T2805 and in Paramārtha's *Shelun*, we have the following estimate in Table 3.1.

Given that fascicle 5 of T2805 corresponds to fascicles 3–4 of Paramārtha's *Shelun* and that fascicle 7 covers fascicles 7–8 of the *Shelun*, we can assume that fascicle 6 covered fascicles 5–6 of the *Shelun*. If this pattern continues, fascicle 8 covers *Shelun* fascicles 9–10; fascicle 9 covers *Shelun* fascicles 11–12; fascicles 10 and probably 11 cover *Shelun* fascicles 13–15. Thus, the original length of T2805 was probably 10–11 fascicles.

3.2.1 Preliminary Dating of T2805

T2805 clearly must have been composed either contemporaneously with, or subsequent to, Paramārtha's translation of the *Shelun*, since it is a selective commentary on the *Shelun*. The *Shelun*, according to its preface, was translated by Paramārtha and disciple Huikai 慧愷 (var. Zhikai 智愷, 518–68) shortly before Paramārtha died in 569. Thus, T2805 was definitely composed after 568.

3.2.2 T2805 Could Not Have Been Written by Paramārtha

There are a few reasons why T2805 could not have been a sub-commentary on the *Shelun* by Paramārtha. First, as I discuss in 6.1, there is an inconsistency in the

Table 3.1 Estimate of the Total Fascicles of T2805

T2805	**[Fascicles 1–4]**		**Fascicle 5 = *Shelun* 3–4 (end of *Shelun* 3- end of *Shelun* 4) 175a–181b**		**[Fascicle 6]**		**Fascicle 7 = *Shelun* 7–8 (beginning of *Shelun* 7-end of *Shelun* 8) 199b–212c**		**[Fascicle 8]**		**[Fascicle 9]**		**[Fascicles 10–11]**		
Shelun	1	2	3	4	5	6	7	8	9	10	11	12	13	14	15
15 fascicles (total pages)	(9)	(8)	(8)	(7)	(9)	(8)	(8)	(7)	(9)	(8)	(9)	(9)	(8)	(9)	(8)
Page numbers in T (119 in total)	152a–160b	160b–167c	167c–175a	175b–181b	181b–190c	191a–198c	198c–205c	206a–212c	212c–220c	221a–229a	229b–238b	238c–247a	247a–254b	254c–262c	263a–270b

Shelun regarding the stage at which practitioners become noble people. But T2805 unequivocally maintains that it is at the first bodhisattva stage that one becomes noble. This difference between T2805 and the *Shelun* means that there must have been a gap in time between the translation of the *Shelun* and T2805.

Second, as I argue toward the end of this chapter, T2805 shows obvious signs of contact with Jingying Huiyuan and Buddhism in Chang'an 長安 around 590. This also implies that it is impossible that Paramārtha was the author of T2805.

3.2.3 T2805 Predates Xuanzang.

Further, it is noteworthy that T2805 shows no awareness of Xuanzang or his works. Xuanzang returned to China and began translating Buddhist texts in 645; thus, T2805 should predate 645. In addition, Xuanzang's characteristic terminology is not used in T2805, as shown by the following Table 3.2.[9]

3.2.3.1 The Style of T2805

The style of T2805 also has a distinct feature that sets it apart from the other four fragmentary commentaries on Paramārtha's *Shelun*. As I mentioned earlier, T2805 comments on the *Shelun* selectively. It focuses only on particular sentences or specific ideas. When commenting, it first quotes the sentence from the root text (either Paramārtha's MSg or *Shelun*) and then provides a detailed explanation.

The sentence-by-sentence style of T2805 seems to be the common style of writing commentaries in sixth-century southern China. The standard method of exegesis is displayed in the *Da boniepan jing jijie* 大般涅槃經集解 (*A Collection of Commentaries on the Mahāparinirvāṇa-mahāsūtra*) edited by Baoliang 寶亮 (444–509) in 509.[10] In this collection, different comments by different authors are arranged under each

Table 3.2 Different Terminology Used by Paramārtha and Xuanzang

Sanskrit Term/ Meaning	T2805	Paramārtha	Xuanzang	Before Paramārtha
catvāraḥ pratyayāḥ (four conditions)	因緣, 緣緣, 次第緣, 增上緣	因緣, 緣緣, 次第緣, 增上緣	因緣, 所緣緣, 等無間緣, 增上緣	因緣, 緣緣, 次第緣, 增上緣
anāsvara (uncontaminated)	無流	無流/無漏	無漏	無漏
bhājana-loka (the world of inanimate things)	器世界	器世界	器世間	器世間
yogin (yoga-practitioner)	觀行人	觀行人/修觀行人/觀人	瑜伽師/瑜伽者/觀者/修法觀者	行者 (Guṇabhadra); 行者/修行者 (Bodhiruci);
pañca-skandha (five aggregates)	五陰	五陰	五蘊	五陰
indriya-viṣaya-vijñāna (organ-cognitive object-consciousness)	根塵識	根塵識	根境識	根塵識

sentence that is commented upon. As a whole, it looks as though each sentence is commented upon, but it is not the case that each commentator comments on every sentence, so it is selective in nature.

3.2.4 The Division in Terms of *pin* 品 and *zhang* 章

It is also noteworthy that one section of Paramārtha's *Shelun* itself is divided into *pin* and *zhang*. Only the first chapter of the *Shelun* is divided into four *pin*, each of which is further divided into several *zhang*, as shown in Table 3.3.

It is not clear why the last five chapters are not divided into *zhang*. As these divisions are missing from all the other translations of the *Shelun*, it is likely that they were added in China. Moreover, it is significant that the division of *zhang* in the *Shelun* agrees with what we find in T2805. If, as I attempt to prove in this chapter and in Chapters 4 and 5, the author of T2805 belonged to Paramārtha's group, this division into *zhang* must have originated in Paramārtha's group.[11]

It is even possible that this division was made during Paramārtha's own lectures because, according to the XGSZ, Paramārtha gave his lectures only through Chapter 5 (until the middle of fascicle 11). The remaining chapters (from the middle of fascicle 11 until the end of fascicle 15) of the current edition of the *Shelun* were completed by Paramārtha's disciple Sengzong 僧宗 (d.u.).[12] Since Chapter 6 is particularly short, Paramārtha might not have felt the need to divide it into *zhang*, and for some reason Sengzong also failed to divide the remaining chapters. Paramārtha's *Shelun* includes a brief introduction to each *pin* and *zhang*, as does T2805.

3.2.5 No Reference to the *Awakening of Faith* in T2805

What is even more striking about T2805 is that it neither quotes from nor refers to the *Awakening of Faith*. This is an especially important feature if we bear in mind that, as emphasized by Kashiwagi, all the earliest teachers of Paramārtha's *Shelun* were teaching the *Awakening of Faith* at the same time according to the XGSZ.[13] This observation made by the XGSZ is supported by the fact that the *Awakening of Faith* looms large in all the other four fragmentary commentaries on Paramārtha's *Shelun*. As early as 601,[14] T2808 already shows the confluence of Paramārtha's *Shelun* and the *Awakening of Faith*. T2805, however, is an exception, showing no connection to the *Awakening of Faith*.

Moreover, it is distinctive of T2805 that it refers to neither of the two most popular treatises in sixth-century China: the **Tattvasiddhi* 成實論 and the **Saṃyuktābhidharma-hṛdaya-śāstra* (*Za apitan xin lun* 雜阿毘曇心論). These texts

Table 3.3 The Division of *Pin* and *Zhang* in *Shelun*

Shelun	Ch. 1				Ch. 2	Ch. 3	Ch. 4	Ch. 5	Ch. 6	Ch. 7	Ch. 8	Ch. 9	Ch. 10
pin	1	2	3	4	-	-	-	-	-	-	-	-	-
zhang	3	7	6	7	4	10	11	5	-	-	-	-	-

are either cited or mentioned repeatedly in T2807, T2808, and T2809,[15] as well as by authors in both the south and north, for example, Huiyuan and Jizang and, less frequently, Zhiyi and Zhiyan.

In fact, the only text cited in T2805 is the *Juedingzang lun* translated by Paramārtha. In an explanation of three kinds of *buddha-gotra* (*sanzhong foxing* 三種佛性), T2805 refers to an unspecified *yizhang* 義章.[16] It also refers to a *yizhang* in a text it calls *Niepan ji* 涅槃記 (*Notes about Nirvāṇa*).[17] Furthermore, it explains ten kinds of equality in an unacknowledged reference to the *Daśabhūmika*.[18]

All these observations about T2805 point to one thing: it is a distinctive commentary on Paramārtha's *Shelun*, quite different from the other Dunhuang fragments of commentaries on Paramārtha's *Shelun* in terms of its style and the texts it cites. In the remainder of this chapter, I compare the terminology in T2805 with that of other contemporaneous Chinese works.

3.3 Methodology of the Terminological Analysis

Next, I demonstrate that T2805 is closely related to Paramārtha by carefully comparing its terminology with the terminology in Paramārtha's other works. Chinese terms and phrases that are used in the same sense in T2805 and in Paramārtha's works but rarely elsewhere are adduced as evidence for their affinity.

The underlying presupposition of my terminological analysis is that the spread of terms, especially new translations of technical terms, can provide information about the relationships among the people using these terms. My approach is surprisingly effective in determining the connection between Paramārtha and T2805 because the translations of many technical terms adopted by Paramārtha and his group were not used by later Chinese translators.

3.3.1 Ishii's NGSM Method

Although this kind of terminological analysis is not uncommon in philological studies of, for example, Shakespeare's works, it has not been widely employed in the study of Buddhist texts. In the fields of Paramārtha and the *Awakening of Faith*, the only studies that take an approach similar to mine are the computational analysis of the phrases of the *Awakening of Faith* by ISHII Kōsei 石井公成 (2003).[19] Ishii's work tries to make suggestions about the provenance of the *Awakening of Faith*. He adopts the NGSM (N-gram Based System for Multiple Document Comparison and Analysis) computational analysis to investigate how the phrases in the *Awakening of Faith* resemble the phrases in works by Bodhiruci and Ratnamati.

The major criticism I have of Ishii's work is that, in his computerized analysis, he fails to take into account the syntactical features of the Chinese language. For example, in analyzing how the word *yi* 依 is used, Ishii lists a few sentences such as *yi rulaizang gu* 依如來藏故 and *yi zhenru yi shuo* 依真如義說. The problem here is that the terms *rulaizang* and *zhenru* can be substituted by any other terms without changing the pattern of the original sentence. Hence, I suggest that the more meaningful patterns are *yi* X *gu* and *yi* X *yi shuo*, or simply *yi* X *shuo* and *yi* X *yi*. It is these patterns, rather than whole sentences, that should be analyzed by computer. Nonetheless, I firmly believe that Ishii's work is useful, and all available approaches should supplement each other to produce the most fruitful possible hypotheses about the textual history of Chinese Buddhist texts of uncertain origin.

3.3.2 Features of Paramārtha's Terminology

The major reason why there is an overlap between those who shared Paramārtha's terminology and those who belonged to the lineage of his disciples is that his work consists of translations of highly technical, philosophical texts written in Sanskrit. Therefore, it is unlikely that someone outside Paramārtha's group would have come up with exactly the same new translation for a technical term. Further, most of the texts translated by Paramārtha and many of the technical terms they contained were rendered into Chinese for the first time, and Chinese Buddhists had no other access to those texts.[20] Moreover, given the highly technical style of the philosophical treatises translated by Paramārtha, it must have been extremely difficult, if not impossible, to properly understand the terminology without help from a teacher or a commentary affiliated with Paramārtha.[21]

On the other hand, we cannot ignore the fact that Paramārtha and his group did not translate the texts from scratch. Before Paramārtha, many texts had been translated, and the translations of many Buddhist terms had been standardized by some of his foremost predecessors, such as Kumārajīva and Dharmakṣema 曇無讖 (385–433). We must always keep in mind the Chinese Buddhist context in which Paramārtha and his group worked when we examine why he adopted some, but not all, of the standardized translation terms.

3.3.3 Features of the Chinese Language

The particular characteristics of the Chinese language must always be taken into consideration in this kind of terminological analysis. For example, sometimes it is not a single term, but a group of terms sharing the same structure and expressing closely related ideas that should be considered as a meaningful pattern. An example of this is phrases such as *ci yi bu cheng* 此義不成 ("This thesis cannot be established"), *ci yi ruo cheng* 此義若成 ("If this thesis is established"), *and ci yi ying cheng* 此義應成 ("This thesis should be established"). These three phrases express identical or opposite ideas but still display some variation in the exact wording. In this case, I think we should treat these three phrases as a single meaningful pattern.

A feature related to the spoken language, namely, abridgment, must also be taken into account. For example, a phrase such as *chengshou xiuxi* 成熟修習 may be shortened to *shuxiu* 熟修, and hence these two terms should be treated as a single pattern.

Another complication arises from different ways of writing the same phrase, for example, *keluoluo* 柯羅邏 and *keluoluo* 柯羅囉. This is further complicated by the fact that the Chinese canon has been continuously re-edited; hence, the original form of a character has sometimes been replaced by a form that has become popular later.[22]

Another problem is that Paramārtha was not always consistent in his choice of terminology. We can find a mixture of old and new terminology in the same work. For example, both *wulou* 無漏 and *wuliu* 無流 are used in the FXL and the *Shiba kong lun* 十八空論 (*A Treatise on Eighteen Kinds of Emptiness*) to translate the Sanskrit term *anāsrava*. There are two possible reasons. These two texts may have been translated during a transitional period in Paramārtha's career. In his earlier works, Paramārtha tended to use *wulou*, the standard translation in his time, whereas in his later works, he used *wuliu*, which was his new translation. Alternatively, the mixture of terminology may be the result of later additions to the original text. The current edition of FXL apparently includes both the original text and later interpolations, which are marked by phrases like *jiyue* 記曰 ("Notes") and *shiyue* 釋曰 ("Commentary"). Unfortunately, there is no consistency regarding which alternative appears in the original text and which appears in the later interpolations.

Finally, I do not argue that this kind of terminological analysis is completely reliable. In order for it to be so, the texts we are working with would have to be exactly the same as Paramārtha's original versions, and we would need to have a complete collection of his authentic works. Unfortunately, there is no way to be sure that these conditions have been met.

3.3.4 Methodological Considerations about Working with the CBReader 2007

Before presenting my analysis of terminology, I must mention a few specific methodological concerns about searching through the Chinese Buddhist Electronic Text Association (CBETA) collection of texts. The search engine I used is the version of the CBReader, developed by the CBETA, that was released in February 2007 (v 3.6). This version includes Vol. 1–55, 85 of the T and Vol. 1–88 of the X. This version is particularly useful for my purpose, because starting from 2009 (v 3.8), other versions of the Chinese Buddhist canon (including those edited in modern times) were added to the database, which makes it difficult to ascertain Paramārtha's authentic terminology. My concerns are as follows:

1. The most difficult part of the terminological analysis is that some terms have more than one sense, and it is sometimes quite difficult to establish the meaning appropriate to the context. The problem here is that merely counting the occurrences of a term without regard to the context can be very misleading. Much more terminological analysis must be done to resolve this problem. At this stage, I have done my best to avoid relying upon ambiguous terms, to read the terms in their original context as much as possible, and to bear in mind the date and location of the text in which a term appears. Similar usages are usually shared only among authors who are close in time and space.

2. Some of the works of some authors, such as Jingying Huiyuan and Zhiyi, may have been rewritten by their later disciples. For example, the XGSZ states that Huiyuan's *Da boniepan jing yiji* (T1764) was added to and rewritten by Huiyuan's disciple Shanzhou 善胄 (550–620), who was reported to have been dissatisfied with Huiyuan's original works.[23] Zhiyi's case is even more complicated. What we have of his works are his disciples' lecture notes, some of which were re-edited by his later disciples.

   In the cases of Huiyuan and Zhiyi, it is difficult to tell whether any term in their work was really their own. There is no way to solve this problem without distinguishing different layers of their works and paying attention to the inconsistencies in terminology.[24] This will require comprehensive philological study of their works.
3. The case of Jizang is also complicated by the fact that he moved from the south to the capital, Chang'an, at the age of 51 (599) and stayed there until the end of his life (623). While he was in Chang'an, Jizang wrote most of his major works. For this reason, it becomes difficult to trace whether a specific term occurring in Jizang's works originated in southern or northern China. The situation of Huijun, a fellow student of Falang 法朗 (507–81), is similar.

   It is possible that both Jizang and Huijun finished their basic training in the south. For this reason, more of their vocabulary, especially non-technical and stylistic terms and phrases, may have come from the south than from the north. At the same time, however, it is also true that they absorbed some vocabulary from the north after they arrived in Chang'an.

   Much more study is required in this respect, but, in any case, I suggest that Jizang and Huijun's terminology should not be exclusively relied on and must be supplemented by other evidence.
4. A problem with searching with CBReader v3.6 is that sometimes the same text in T has been re-edited later and is repeated in X. For example, Zhiyi's *Renwang huguo bore jing shu* 仁王護國般若經疏 (*A Commentary on the Perfection of Wisdom Scripture for Humane Kings*) included in T as T1705 is repeated in a later edition, *Renwang jing heshu* 仁王經合疏 (*A Collective Commentary on the Perfection of Wisdom Scripture for Humane Kings*), which is included in X as X513. Similarly, Zhiyi's *Weimo jing lüeshu* 維摩經略疏 (*A Rough Commentary on the Vimalakīrtinirdeśa-sūtra*) included in T as T1778 is repeated and included in X as X338 under the title of *Weimo jing wenshu* 維摩經文疏 (*A Commentary on Passages of the Vimalakīrtinirdeśa-sūtra*).

   This situation makes it difficult to calculate the total number of occurrences of a specific term in Zhiyi's works. Due to the repetition of texts, the frequency of a term's occurrence may be doubled or even tripled. At this stage, I have no good way to avoid this inaccuracy. But, for my purpose, whether Zhiyi uses a term is more important than how often he uses it. Therefore, my failure to exclude repeated texts of Zhiyi is not likely to significantly distort the general picture of the results of my terminological analysis.
5. The exact dates and locations of the other fragmentary Dunhuang commentaries on Paramārtha's *Shelun* are not known. But given the fact that T2806, T2807,

T2808, and T2809 all comment on Paramārtha's *Shelun*, we can safely assume that all four are dated between 569 and 645.[25]

6. Finally, with respect to the scope of Paramārtha's works, I have excluded the *Dazongdi xuanwen benlun* 大宗地玄文本論 (T1669), which is considered to be an apocryphal work.[26] Moreover, for the reasons given in Chapter 2, I have also excluded the *Awakening of Faith*.

3.4 Terminological Affinity between T2805 and the Works of Paramārtha

Table 3.4 juxtaposes the terminology used in T2805, in Paramārtha's works, and in Chinese Buddhist texts before Paramārtha, between Paramārtha and Xuanzang, and after Xuanzang. I aim to show that T2805 consistently adopts the terminology of Paramārtha, which rarely appears in any of the other Chinese texts. Some explanations are necessary.

1. The number following a Chinese term in the first column is the total number of occurrences of this term retrieved with the CBReader.
2. When I give a term, followed by "near," followed by a number in parentheses, followed by a second term, the number in parentheses indicates the range of characters between the two terms. For example, "*benshi* 本識 near (20) *bianyi* 變異" means that these two terms occur within a range of twenty Chinese characters.
3. In the column, "Before P," I list the total number of occurrences of a term in works that predate Paramārtha, namely, before 569. "Between P and X" indicates the period between Paramārtha's death and Xuanzang's return to China, namely, between 569 and 645. In these two columns, I usually give the title of the text in which a term is found. But if an author/translator uses a term in more than one work, or in the case of certain important figures, I give the author's name rather than listing all their works. This calls attention to the practices of specific author/translators.

A problem here, however, is that some authors, such as Huiyuan (523–92), Zhiyi (538–97), Jizang (549–623), and Zhiyan (602–68), were active in two periods. As shown in Table 3.4 below, all these authors seem to have pick up Paramārtha's terminology to some degree, Huiyuan's *Bashi yi* in particular. For this reason, I put these authors under the group of "Between P and X."

Based on Table 3.4, I summarize the most distinctive examples in groups, as shown in tables 3.5–3.10.

Table 3.4 Terminology in T2805, Paramārtha's works Compared to Others (the symbol "~" means "roughly")

Term/Total	T2805	Paramārtha	Before P	Between P and X	X and After
bidu 比度/348	1	16	2 (Zhu Fonian); 1 (different sense)	2 (different sense) 7 (Huiyuan); 1 (T2806)	318
benshi 本識 near (20) *bianyi* 變異/35	6	15	0	4 (Huiyuan's *Bashi yi*)	10
bianyi shi 變異事/15	1	2	1 (Kumārajīva's **Tattvasiddhi*)	0	7
bianyi zuo 變異作/14	5	2	0	0	7
buliaobie 不了別/73	1	14	1 (*Fangbianxin lun*)	1 (*Foshuo wenshushili xing jing*)	~56
chihena 持訶那 or *chiena*持阿那 (*dhyāna*)/ 29	1	19	0	2 (Zhiyan); 1 (Wŏnhyo); 1 (XGSZ)	5
chi zhongzi 持種子/220	3	4	1?	7 (Dharmgupta); 1 (Jizang); 1 (Zhiyan)	~203
da gongyong 大功用/45	2	12	4 (*Apitan piposha lun*)	1 (Jizang)	
Dazhong bu 大眾部/805	2	13	0	29 (Jizang); 2 (Prabhākaramitra); 1 (Zhiyan);	~758
ganwei 噉味/33	1	17	2	1 (Zhiyan); 2 (Prabhākaramitra)	10
dengliuguo 等流果/1188	3	41	0	1 (Zhiyan)	~1143
dujue 獨覺 near (20) *shengwen* 聲聞/6180[a]	3	38	0	~146 (mainly Sui dynasty)	~5993
duo wenxunxi 多聞熏習/129	1	11	0	3 (Dharmagupta); 1 (Prabhākaramitra)	~113
fashi 發識/718	1	1	0	7 (Zhiyi); 2 (Jizang); 1 (*Tanyan shu*); 1 (Zhiyan)	~705

(*Continued*)

Table 3.4 (Continued)

Term/Total	T2805	Paramārtha	Before P	Between P and X	X and After
fawo zhi 法我執/71	1	4	0	1 (Jizang); 1 (Zhiyan); 2 (T2807)	62
fawosuo zhi 法我所執/8	1	1	0	0	6
fei anlidi 非安立諦/276	6	13	0	1 (Zhiyi); 5 (Jizang); 1 (Zhiyan);	250
fei zemie 非擇滅/2041	2	25	0	1 (Zhiyan)	2013
guanxing ren 觀行人/217	5	83	0	4 (Zhiyi); 2 (Jizang); 3 (T2809)	120
guoju 過聚/29	1	8	3 (different sense)	3 (Prabhākaramitra)	14
guoshi fa 過失法/28	1	2	0	1 (Prabhākaramitra); 1 (in different sense)	23
hanyang 含養/29	2	1	0	0	26
heng xiangying 恒相應/140	2	9	3	1 (Jizang)	125
jitong jing 極通境/12	5	5	0	1 (Zhiyan)	1
qiehena 伽訶那 (*ghana*)/18	2	4	0	0	12
jiaxing dao 加行道/873	2	5	0	1 (T2806); 1 (T2807); 1 (T2809)	863
*jingzhi wuchabie*境智無差別/6	1	5	0	0	0
keluoluo 柯羅邏/43 or *keluoluo* 柯羅囉 (kalala)/2	1	37	2 (Saṅghavarman)	0	5
keyan ti 可言體/21	2	11	0	2 (Zhiyan)	6
liutong hui 六通慧/20	1	6	2 (Zhu Fonian)	1 (Zhiyan)	10

miexin ding 滅心定/126	18	63	1 (*Apitan piposha lun*)	1 (Dharmagupta); 3 (T2806); 1 (Zhiyan)	39
polike 頗梨柯 (*sphaṭika*) /23	3	18	0	0	2
pusa zhenwei 菩薩真位/2	1	1	0	0	0
puti ziliang 菩提資糧/364	1	7	0	2 (Upaśūnya[b]); 30 (Dharmagupta)	324
qi shijie 器世界 (*bhājana-loka*)/403	1	43	1? (Bodhiruci[c]); 1 (*Apitan piposha lun*); 6 (*Za apitan xin lun*)	5 (Dharmagupta); 4 (Jizang); 1 (T2807); 1 (*Shi mohoyan lun*); 2 (*Dasheng zhiguan famen*); 4 (Zhiyan)	334
qing'an 輕安 (*praśrabdhi*)/2911	2	23	1 (Buddhabhadra); 1 (Saṅghavarman);	1 (Huiyuan); 3 (Dharmagupta); 1 (Prabhākaramitra); 1 (Zhiyan)	2878
ranzhuo zhongzi 染濁種子/6	3	3	0	0	0
ruzhenguan 入真觀/55	3	10	0	2 (Jizang)	40
ruzhuchu 入住出/226	2	10	1 (Kumārajīva); 1 (Sengzhao)	9 (Zhiyi), 1 (Jizang); 1 (Zhiyan)	201
ruozuo 若作before (5) yi 義/123	1	2	0	19 (Zhiyi); 13 (Jizang); 1 (Huiying)	~87
*sanwuxing zhenru*三無性真如/9	2	3	0	2 (T2807)	2
shangxin huo 上心惑/53	1	31	0	2 (T2807); 1 (T2809); 1 (Zhiyan)	27

(*Continued*)

Table 3.4 (Continued)

Term/Total	T2805	Paramārtha	Before P	Between P and X	X and After
shi bianyi 識變異 (*vijñāna-pariṇāma*)/58	2	22	0	1 (Huiyuan's *Bashi yi*); 1 (Dharmagupta); 1 (Jizang)	31
shuxi 數習/675	11	76	8 (scattered); excluding occurrences of 數數習	13 (Dharmagupta); 4 (Prabhākaramitra); 2 (Huiyuan); 1 (*Tanyan shu*); 5 (Zhiyi); 1 (Jizang); 1 (T2808);	553
siwei 四微/495	8	5	1? (*Hongming ji*)	1 (Dharmagupta); 4 (Huiyuan); 51 (Zhiyi); 67 (Jizang); 4 (Huiying); 3 (Zhiyan)	351
sizhong shengsi 四種生死/63	3	10	0	12 (Jizang); 1 (Zhiyan)	37
suiyu 隨與 near (20) *xiangying* 相應/38	1	3	0	1 (Zhiyi)	33
tongdafen shan (*gen*) 通達分善(根)/18	3	10 (*Juedingzang lun*: 1)	0	1 (Dharmagupta); 1 (Prabhākaramitra)	3
dafen shangen 達分善根/68	0	2 (*Juedingzang lun*)	51 (*Apitan piposha lun*); 3 (**Tattvasiddhi*); 2 (*Apitan xin lun jing*)	1 (Huiyuan)	9
tonglei yin 同類因/1580	2	78	0	3 (Huiyuan); 2 (Zhiyan)	1495

tuiqu 退屈/1125	8	11	0	10 (Dharmagupta); 1 (Zhiyi); 4 (Jizang); 13 (Prabhākaramitra)	1078
weishi guan 唯識觀/375	26	45	0	6 (Dharmagupta); 1 (Jizang); 1 (T2806); 5 (T2807); 6 (Zhiyan)	285
weishi wuchen 唯識無塵/30	1	7	0	1 (T2806)	21
weishi zhi 唯識智/58	3	14	0	1 (T2807); 2 (T2808); 1 (Zhiyan)	37
wenxunxi 聞熏習/515	4	70	0	1 (Huiyuan's *Bashi yi*); 26 (Dharmagupta); 1 (Zhiyi); 3 (Prabhākaramitra); 3 (*Tanyan shu*); 11 (Jizang); 1 (T2806); 6 (T2807); 6 (T2809); 1 (Zhiyan)	382
wufenbie hou zhi 無分別後智/55	1	42	0	0	12
wufu wuji 無覆無記/2432	3	46	0	2 (Jizang); 2 (T2807); 1 (T2806); 1 (Prabhākaramitra); 1(Zhiyan)	2376

(*Continued*)

Table 3.4 (Continued)

Term/Total	T2805	Paramārtha	Before P	Between P and X	X and After
wujian dao 無間道/2556	3	47	1 (*Avataṃsaka-sūtra* [Buddhabhadra trans.]); 3 (*Shelifo apitan lun*); 1 (Saṅghavarman)	1 (T2809); 1 (Prabhākaramitra)	2499
wuliu dao 無流道/22	3	17	0	0	2
wuliu ding 無流定/12	1	11	0	0	0
wuliu jie 無流界/22	1	19	0	1 (T2806)	1
wuliu shan 無流善/15	4	8	0	0	3
wuxiang xing 無相性/175	5	18	2 (Kumārajīva); 1 (Dharmakṣema); 1 (Naredrayaśas)	2 (Huiyuan's *Bashi yi*); 1? (Zhiyi); 1 (*Tanyan Shu*); 1 (T2808); 1 (Jizang); 3 (*Dasheng zhiguan famen*); 3 (Zhiyan)	136
xiqing 細輕 near(20) *cuzhong* 麤重/88	2	7	0	0	79
ximei 細昧/6	1	2	0	0	3
xiadi huo 下地惑/65	1	3	1 (Baoliang)	0	60
xiaosheng yi 小乘義/170	3	2	0	1 (Zhiyi); 39 (Jizang); 4 (Huijun)	121
xinle wei 信樂位/13	3	3	0	1 (Zhiyan)	6
xiuguan ren 修觀人/21	1	8	0	0	12
xunsi 尋思/2951	18	97	1 (*Bieyi za ahan jing*); 2 (*Zhong benqi jing*); 1 (*Mohesengqi lü*); 1 (*Youposai wujie weiyi jing*); 1 (*Fenbie gongde lun*); 1 (*Hongming ji*)	1 (*Dafaju tuoluoni jing*); 3 (Dharmagupta); 7 (Zhiyi); 1 (T2806); 1 (*Tanyan shu*); 54 (Zhiyan)	2762

yiqi bao 一期報/67	1	4	0	3 (Zhiyi)	59
yiwei 移位/11	1	2	0	0	8
yiyan fenbie 意言分別/238	13	55	0	2 (Huiyuan's *Bashi yi*); 3 (*Jin'gang sanmei jing*); 2 (Dharmagupta)	163
yi budecheng 義不得成/21	1	5	1? (*yi bude chengjiu* 義不得成就: *Zhengfa nianchu jing*)	1 (Dharmagupta); 1 (Jizang)	12
ye xunxi 業熏習or *ye xunxi* 業薰習/86	1	20	0	1? (Huiyuan); 1 (*Fo benxing ji jing*); 2 (T2806); 3 (T2807); 1 (*Dasheng zhiguan famen*); 1 (Prabhākaramitra); 2 (Zhiyan)	54
yinsheng 引生/2361	16	31	0	2 (Huiyuan's *Bashi yi*); 16 (Dharmagupta); 6 (Zhiyi); 1 (T2807); 1 (Dushun); 3 (Zhiyan)	2285
yingruchu 應入處/3	2	1	0	0	0
youliu shan 有流善/36	5	12	5 (different sense, i.e., 有流, 善)	4 (Dharmagupta); 2 (T2809)	8
zemie 擇滅/4907	2	97	0	4 (Zhiyi); 6 (Zhiyan)	4798
zengyi zhi 增益執/44	1	4	0	1 (Zhiyan)	37
Zhengliang bu 正量(部)/778	1	6	0	25 (Jizang); 2 (T2806); 1 (T2807); 5 (Prabhākaramitra)	738

(*Continued*)

Table 3.4 (Continued)

Term/Total	T2805	Paramārtha	Before P	Between P and X	X and After
zhuanyi 轉依/2908	50	168	3 (diff senses); 2 (Bodhiruci); 1 (*Za apitan xin lun*)	3 (Huiyuan's *Bashi yi* [1]; *Shidi jing lun yiji* [2]); 41 (Dharmagupta); 2 (Zhiyi); 1 (*Sanlun youyi yi*); 9 (T2807); 5 (T2809); 2 (T2806); 1(T2808); 40 (Prabhākaramitra); 13 (Zhiyan)	2567
zhuanyi ti 轉依體/15	6	1	0	0	8
ziliang dao 資糧道/122	1	1	2 (different senses)	3 (Dharmagupta)	115
zita chabie 自他差別/111	2	8	0	3 (Dharmagupta); 3 (T2806); 1 (T2807); 1 (Prabhākaramitra); 2 (Zhiyan)	91
ruci zhi 如此執/42	3	19	0	1 (Huiyuan); 3 (Zhiyi) 1 (Jizang); 1 (*Dasheng zhiguan famen*); 2 (Prabhākaramitra)	12
zuo ruci zhi 作如此執/18	3	13	0	1 (Zhiyi)	1

[a]This was translated as *pizhi/pizhifo* 辟支/辟支佛 or *yuanjue* 緣覺 before Paramārtha.

[b]Upaśūnya 月婆首那 originally lived in Ye (Yedu 鄴都, present Anyang 安陽, Henan 河南 province) in the north. He later went to the south to translate Buddhist scriptures. See Tang (1938: 285).

[c]Bodhiruci usually uses *qi shijian* 器世間 instead of *qi shijie* 器世界. *Qi shijie* is found only once in Bodhiruci's works.

Table 3.5 New Translation Terms Coined by Paramārtha's Group

Term/total	T2805	Paramārtha	Before P	Between P and X	X and After
wuliu dao 無流道/22	3	17	0	0	2
wuliu ding 無流定/12	1	11	0	0	0
wiliu jie 無流界/22	1	19	0	1 (T2806)	1
wuliu shan 無流善/15	4	8	0	0	3
youliu shan 有流善/36	5	12	5 (different senses: 有流, 善)	4 (Dharmagupta); 2 (T2809)	8
xinle wei 信樂位/13	3	3	0	1 (Zhiyan)	6

Table 3.6 Special Transliterations by Paramārtha's Group

Term/Total	T2805	Paramārtha	Before P	Between P and X	X and After
chihena 持訶那/26 (= Skt. *dhyāna*)	1	19	0	2 (Zhiyan); 1 (Daoxuan)	3
keluoluo 柯羅邏/43 or *keluoluo* 柯羅囉/2 (= Skt. kalala)	1	37	0	2 (Saṃghavarman)	5
polike 頗梨柯/23 (= Skt. *sphaṭika*)	3	18	0	0	2
qiehena 伽訶那/18 (= Skt. *ghana*)	2	4	0	0	12

Before Paramārtha, the Sanskrit term *dhyāna* was often transliterated as *chan* 禪 (as in the case of *chan boluomi* 禪波羅蜜). The Sanskrit term *sphaṭika* was translated as *shuijing* 水精, and Paramārtha uses this translation three times. But there were three different transliterations of *sphaṭika*, including *poli* 頗梨, *boli* 玻璃(瓈), and *pozhijia*頗胝迦, Xuanzang's usual choice.

Especially noteworthy in the second group are the Sanskrit terms *kalala* and *ghana*, each referring to one of the five stages of the fetus in the womb.[27] These two examples clearly show that T2805 is the only text (except for Paramārtha's own AKBh and *Sidi lun* 四諦論) before Xuanzang that discusses these five stages using Paramārtha's terminology.

Table 3.7 Various Transliterations of the Five Stages of the Fetus

	Paramārtha and T2805	Before Paramārtha	Xuanzang and After
kalala	柯羅邏or柯羅囉	歌羅羅 (Kumārajīva; Dharmakṣema, *Apitan piposha lun*)	羯剌藍
ghana	伽訶那	伽那 (Kumārajīva, Dharmakṣema, *Apitan piposha lun*)	鍵南
vyañjana	身分[a]	probably 出生 or 身具足	(色根)形相

[a]*Shenfen* 身分 (*vyañjana*) in Paramārtha and the *youse zhugen* 有色諸根 (*indriyāṇi rūpīṇi*) in Xuanzang refer to the "material organs with their supports" formed at the final stage of the fetus. See Pruden (1988), Vol. II: 400. According to de La Vallée Poussin, "The 'material organs' are the subtle parts of the eye, ear, nose, and tongue [= the eye properly so-called, that which sees . . .]; the *vyañjana*s are the visible supports (*adhiṣṭhāna*) of the eye thus defined, etc., for it is by reason of its support that the organ properly so-called is manifested (*abhivyajyate*). (The organ of touch exists from the very beginning)" (1988: 511, note 147).
If we search the word string "(*keluoluo* 柯羅邏 OR *keluoluo* 柯羅囉) AND *shenfen* 身分" in CBReader, then the only hits are from Paramārtha's *Abhidharmakośa-bhāṣya*, *Sidi lun* 四諦論, T2805, and the works of Wŏnch'ŭk.

Table 3.8 Newly Introduced School Names

Term/total	T2805	Paramārtha	Before P	Between P and X	X and After
Dazhong bu 大眾部/805	2	13	0	29 (Jizang); 1 (Zhiyan); 2 (Prabhākaramitra)	~758
Zhengliang (bu) 正量(部)/778	1	6	0	25 (Jizang); 2 (T2806); 1 (T2807); 5 (Prabhākaramitra);	738

Table 3.9 Special Technical Terms from Sanskrit

Term/Total	T2805	Paramārtha	Before P	Between P and X	X and After
dengliuguo 等流果/1188 (= Skt. *niṣyanda-phala*)	3	41	0	1 (Zhiyan)	~1143
feizemie 非擇滅 /2041 (= Skt. *aprati-saṃkhyā*)	2	25	0	1 (Zhiyan)	2013
zemie 擇滅 /4907 (= Skt. *prati-saṃkhyā*)	2	97	0	4 (Zhiyi); 6 (Zhiyan)	4798
guanxingren 觀行人 /217 (= Skt. *yogin*)	5	83	0	4 (Zhiyi); 2 (Jizang); 3 (T2809)	120
jitongjing 極通境 /12 (= Skt. *saṃbhinna-[dharma]*)[a]	5	5	0	1 (Zhiyan)	1
qing'an 輕安/2911 (= Skt. *prasrabdhi*)	2	23	1 (Buddhabhadra)	1 (Saṃghavarman); 1 (Huiyuan); 3 (Dharmagupta); 1 (Prabhākaramitra); 1 (Zhiyan)	2878
shi bianyi 識變異 /58 (= Skt. *vijñāna-pariṇāma*)	2	22	0	1 (Huiyuan's *Bashi yi*); 1 (Dharmagupta); 1 (Jizang)	31
ximei 細昧 /6 (= Skt. *abhisaṃkṣepa*)	1	2	0	0	3

[a]See Nagao (1994, Part II: 133).

Table 3.10 Special Concept Not Directly from Sanskrit

Term/total	T2805	Paramārtha	Before P	Between P and X	X and After
jingzhi wu chabie 境智無差別/6	1	5	0	0	0

Another example, not included in these five groups, is the term "cognition in its proper substance" (*zhengti zhi* 正體智). T2805 includes this concept three times, but the term is only indirectly hinted at in Paramārtha's *Shelun*.[28] On the other hand, according to Jizang's report, the concept of "cognition in its proper substance" was a distinct doctrine held by the Shelun masters.[29]

To conclude, it cannot be overemphasized that in the entire Chinese Buddhist canon no text is as similar in terminology to Paramārtha's Chinese translations as T2805. This suggests a close intimacy between the author of T2805 and Paramārtha. Next, I show that the author of T2805 may even have been Paramārtha's direct disciple.

3.5 Close Connection between T2805 and the *Suixiang lun*

In addition to the overlap of terminology between T2805 and Paramārtha's works, it is even more striking that a close relation exists between T2805 and the *Suixiang lun* 隨相論 (*Treatise on the Secondary Marks*,[30] T1641), attributed to Paramārtha. Since it has been included in Paramārtha's works since Fajing's *Zhongjing mulu* (594), and the attribution to Paramārtha has never been questioned, I think it is safe to treat the *Suixiang lun* as an authentic work of Paramārtha.

In establishing the connection between these two texts, I focus on several stylistically distinctive Chinese phrases rather than on technical terms, as shown in Table 3.11.[31]

A much stronger claim can be made on the basis of Table 3.11 than on the basis of Table 3.4 alone. The terms quoted here are not technical terms, but stylistic turns of phrase. Such phrases are more subconscious and individualized, and are only rarely transmitted from one author to another. In other words, it is easy for someone to adopt technical terms from a source text and then introduce them into their own writing, without also adopting these kinds of stylistic phrases.

3.5.1 The Phrase *Jiwufu* 既無復

Among these phrases, special attention should be paid to *jiwufu* ("now that it is no more"). A CBReader search of the entire Buddhist canon yields only fifteen hits for this phrase. Excluding the six cases in which the context would dictate a punctuation mark between *jiwu* and *fu*, the phrase occurs only nine times in the same sense as in T2805 and the *Suixiang lun* as shown in Table 3.12.

Here it is striking that *Suixiang lun* includes three of these occurrences and T2805 includes two but both texts are very short. The *Suixiang lun* consists of only one fascicle, and T2805 consists of only two incomplete fascicles. The phrase *jiwufu* seems to have been used in the south: all pre-Tang authors who used this phrase were located in the south. But it does not appear to be a common phrase even in southern China. The phrase is attested only once in the work of Daosheng 道生 but not in the work of other southern authors, such as Baoliang and Fayun 法雲 (467–529). And this phrase occurs only twenty-nine times (including some repetitions) in the *Siku quanshu* 四庫全書 (*A Complete Collection of Books in Four Stores*), a collection of all the books available in the imperial library edited from 1773 to 1784. All occurrences are in books later than the Song dynasty.[32]

Table 3.11 Terminology in T2805, *Suixiang lun* Compared to Others

	T2805	*Suixiang lun* by Paramārtha	*Lishi apitan lun* 立世阿毘曇論 by Paramārtha	Other P's Works	Before P	After P
budefu 不得復/295	1: 「亦不得復生起」	1: 「不得復還」	0	0	many	many
chuqi 出其/2808	3: 「此出其事」; 「出其有三義意」; 「次出其體相」	2: 「出其境界」 「無出其外」	1: 「吐出其骨」	0	many	many
chu zhengyi 出正義 or *chu yiyi* 出異義/65	1: 「破異解出正義」	1: 「前來皆是出異義」	0	0	0	~60
gukejian 故可見/44	1: 「故可見」	1: 「故可見」	0	0	19	23
huishi 迴施/425	1: 「迴施眾生」	2: 「隨所迴施」; 「迴施人非但無福」	0	0	~23	~399
jichu 極處/247	2: 「從法來至法本極處」; 「同是果上極處」	1: 「以生死為極處」	0	0	~16	~228
jijin 既盡/1073	1: 「諸生緣既盡」	1: 「現在報既盡」	1: 「血肉既盡吐出其骨」	0	~90	~980
jiwufu 既無復/9	2: 「從二定以上既無復覺觀」; 「真實本對相生既無復相生對。故成無性」	3: 「善既無復根本」; 「涅槃中既無復五陰」; 「既無復有勝涅槃者」	0	0	1 (Zhu Daoseng)	3: 1 (Jizang); 1 (Huijing); 1 (Puwan)
qifuyou 豈復有/109	1: 「於此定中豈復有惡」	1: 「此外豈復有別道耶」	0	0	14	93
yimu 以目/623	1: 「用緣極通境以目二智」	1: 「用盡不生義以目無為」	0	0	~20	~601
yuxiru 餘悉如/12	1: 「餘悉如釋論易見」	0	1: 「餘悉如剡浮」	0	0	10: 2 (Zhiyi)

Table 3.12 The Phrase *Jiwufu* in T2805, *Suixiang lun* and Other Works

Occurrence	Text	Author/ Translator	Date	Location
1	*Fahua jing shu* 法華經疏 (X577)	Zhu Daosheng 竺道生	355–434	Nanjing 南京--> Mountain Lu 廬山
3	*Suixiang lun*	Paramārtha 真諦	546–569 in China	Nanjing 南京--> Guangzhou 廣州
2	T2805	?	?	?
1	*Weimo jing lüeshu* 維摩經略疏 (X343)	Jizang 吉藏	549–623	Nanjing 南京→Kuaiji 會稽→Chang'an 長安
1	*Jin'gang jing zhu shu* 金剛經註疏 (X456)	Huijing 慧淨	578–c. 645	Hebei 河北→ Chang'an 長安
1	*Jin'gang jing xinyin shu* 金剛經心印疏 (X505)	Puwan 溥畹	Around Early Qing Dynasty (1644ff.)	Jiangsu 江蘇→Yunnan 雲南

Like *jiwufu*, the phrase *qifuyou* 豈復有 is also noteworthy, especially when it occurs together with *jiwufu*. *Qifuyou* occurs once in T2805 and once in the *Suixiang lun*, the only work by Paramārtha in which it is found. Moreover, if we search with CBReader 2007 for "*jiwufu* AND *qifuyou*," the only three texts in which both these phrases occur are *Suixiang lun*, Jizang's *Weimo jing lüeshu* (X343), and T2805, as shown in Table 3.13:

Table 3.13 The Phrases *Jiwufu* and *Qifuyou* in T2805, *Suixiang lun* and Jizang

	jiwufu 既無復	***qifuyou*** 豈復有
Suixiang lun	3	1
Jizang's *Weimo jing lüeshu*	1	1
T2805	1	1

3.5.2 T2805 and the *Suixiang lun*: Works by the Same Scribe

Based on the examples of *jiwufu* and other phrases, I suggest that the author of T2805 was probably the Chinese scribe (*bishou* 筆受) of the *Suixiang lun*, based on the high frequency of occurrences of the rarely used phrase *jiwufu* and its conjunction with *qifuyou*. Other evidence pointing to a relationship between T2805 and the *Suixiang lun* is the fact that T2805 is the only text before Xuanzang that explicitly mentions the "four kinds of wholesomeness" (*sizhong shan* 四種善) and, moreover, uses the same set of terms that Paramārtha uses in his AKBh and the *Suixiang lun* (The content of the "four kinds of wholesomeness" remains the same), as shown in Table 3.14.

3.5.3 Reflections and Disclaimers

To conclude, it is very likely that the author of T2805 was the scribe of the *Suixiang lun*. However, two caveats are necessary here. First, it is not impossible for readers to

Table 3.14 Translations of Four Kinds of Wholesomeness in T2805 and *Suixiang lun*

T2805 (T2805:85.983c1-4)	***Suixiang lun* (T1641:32.163a10-11)**	**AKBh (T1559:29.228c11-12)**	***Bore deng lun shi* 般若燈論釋 translated by Prabhākaramitra (T1566:30.79c22-23)**	**Xuanzang's AKBh (T1558:29.71a16-17)**
zhenshi shan 真實善	*zhenshi shan* 真實善	*zhenshi (shan)* 真實(善)	*diyiyi (shan)* 第一義(善)	*shengyi* 勝義
xingshan 性善	*zixing shan* 自性善	*zixing (shan)* 自性(善)	*zixing (shan)* 自性(善)	*zixing* 自性
xiangza shan 相雜善	*xiangza shan* 相雜善	*xiangza (shan)* 相應(善)	*xiangza (shan)* 相應(善)	*xiangying* 相應
faqi shan 發起善	*faqi shan* 發起善	*faqi (shan)* 發起(善)	*faqi shan* 發起(善)	*dengqi* 等起

adopt idiomatic phrases from a source text when they are sufficiently familiar with it. Therefore, I must admit the possibility that the author of T2805 was not the scribe of the *Suixiang lun*, although the two must have been closely related. The reason that I do not positively assert that the two texts have the same author is that my main concern is to show that T2805 preserves the authentic teaching of Paramārtha. For this purpose, it is not necessary to assert identity between the author of T2805 and the scribe of the *Suixiang lun*: proximity is sufficient.

Furthermore, the evidence I provide here, although extremely convincing, still needs to be taken with caution. One reason is that *jiwufu* was also used once by Jizang in the late sixth to early seventh centuries and once by Huijing in the mid-seventh century. My evidence would be completely conclusive only if I could prove that the phrase rarely appears in any other texts written in the sixth or seventh century. However, because many texts written in that period are no longer extant, the possibility that *jiwufu* was commonly used at that time cannot be excluded.

Thus, although the use of *jiwufu* in the two texts does not prove beyond a doubt that the author of T2805 was the scribe of the *Suixiang lun*, the evidence is strong enough, in the absence of any counter evidence, for my conclusion to be plausible.

3.6 The Northern and Southern Traditions of Chinese Buddhism in the Sixth Century

A comparison between the terminology of T2805 and the works of Paramārtha and other authors active before 440 and during the period from 444 to 589 can help us reach further conclusions about when and where T2805 may have been composed. First of all, T2805 contains, in addition to Paramārtha's characteristic terminology, several terms that Paramārtha never used, as shown in Table 3.15.

Here by "authors in the north," I mean authors/translators in the north from after the persecution of Buddhism in 444 until around 589. Foremost among them are Bodhiruci, Ratnamati, Tanluan 曇鸞 (476–?), and the translators of such texts as the *Zhengfa nianchu jing* 正法念處經 (T721) and the *Xianyu jing* 賢愚經 (T202).

By "authors of the south," I mean those who were educated and trained between 444 and 589 in the south, among them, Baoliang, Fayun 法雲, Huida 慧達 (d.u.), the author of the *Zhaolun shu* 肇論疏 (*A Commentary on the Zao lun*; X866), and Huiying 慧影 (d. 589–600), the author of the *Dazhidu lun shu* 大智度論疏 (*A Commentary on the Da zhidu lun*), who lived in Sichuan 四川 province. Zhiyi (538–97) seems to mark the end of this period, although he apparently had some knowledge about what was going on in the north.

As I have mentioned, both Jizang and Huijun were trained in the south but went to the north later in their respective careers; hence, their terminology should not be taken as independent evidence. But, as we shall see in Table 3.16, Jizang and Huijun share much more terminology with the southern authors than with the northern authors. For this reason, I tentatively classify them under the category of "authors in the south." Table 3.15 illustrates several important points.

Table 3.15 Terminology in T2805 Never Used by Paramārtha

Term	T2805	Paramārtha	Authors in the South between 444 and 589: Baoliang, Fayun, Zhiyi, Jizang, Huiying, Huida, Huijun	Authors in the North between 444 and 589: Bodhiruci, Fashang, Huiyuan, Tanyan (Excluding Sui Authors Dharmagupta, Jinagupta, and so on)	Authors before 440: Zhu Fonian, Kumārajīva, Dharmakṣema
daixiang 帶相/202	1	0	4	0	0
jiduan 既斷/356	3	0	35	3 (*Zhengfa nianchu jing*); 1 (Huiyuan); 1 (Fashang's *Shidi lun yishu*)	4
jiaming pusa 假名菩薩/141	1	0	20	0	17
jiande 兼得/410	1	0	39	1 (*Jin'gangxian lun*); 3 (Huiyuan)	12
jiecheng 結成/5548	1	0	334	1 (*Xianyu jing*); 10 (*Jin'gangxian lun*); 1 (Tanluan); 2 (Fashang's *Shidi lun yishu*); 135 (Huiyuan)	20
jieshi 結示/2410	4	0	9	0	0
jinluechu 今略出/63	1	0	22	0	1
jingshi 精識/130	3	0	22	0	3
jujing 舉境/140	2	0	32	1 (*Jin'gangxian lun*); 5 (Huiyuan)	0
keduan 科段/149	1	0	21	0	0
liyong 力用/1945	5	4	136	1 (*Piyesuo wenjin*); 1 (*Dasheng tongxing jing*); 1 (Lingbian's *Huayan jing lun*); 19 (Huiyuan)	36
liaojian 料簡/3307	1	1	>200	2 (*Jin'gangxian lun*); 3 (Fashang's *Shidi lun yishu*); 58 (Huiyuan)	10
piming 譬明/262	3	0	141 Includ. 68 (Baoliang)	0	0
xiangming 向明/319	1	0	37 Includ. 16 (Baoliang)	2 (*Jin'gangxian lun*); 1 (*Baoxing lun*)	15
zhangmen 章門/1803	3	0	>200 Include. 104 (Fayun); 20 (Baoliang)	29 (*Jin'gangxian lun*); 2 (Tanluan); 8 (Fashang's *Shidi lun yishu*); 88 (Huiyuan)	4 (*Apitan piposha lun*); 2 (*Bingposha lun*)
zishi 自釋/1207	3	0	63	123 (Huiyuan)	0
zongshi 總釋/1828	1	0	120	1 (*Jin'gangxian lun*); 4 (Tanyan); 52 (Huiyuan)	0

Table 3.16 (Table 3.15 modified) T2805's Connection with the Southern Tradition

Term	T2805	Paramārtha	Authors in the South, 440–600: Baoliang, Fayun, Zhiyi, Jizang, Huiying, Huida, Huijun	Authors in the North, 446–589: Bodhiruci, Ratnamati, *Zhengfa nianchu jing*, Tanluan, and so on.	Authors in the North around 589–600: Fashang, Huiyuan, Tanyan (Including *Jin'gangxian lun*, Narendrayaśas, Jīnagupta, and so on)	Authors before 440: Zhu Fonian, Kumārajīva, Dharmakṣema
daixiang 帶相/202	1	0	1 (Baoliang); 2 (Jizang); 1 (Huiying)	0	0	0
jiduan 既斷/356	3	0	35	3 (*Zhengfa nianchu jing*)	1 (Huiyuan) 1 (Fashang's *Shidi lun yishu*)	4
jiaming pusa 假名菩薩/141	1	0	20	0	1 (Jīnagupta); 1 (*Shi moheyan lun*)	17
jiande 兼得/410	1	0	39	0	4 (Jīnagupta); 3 (Huiyuan); 1 (*Jin'gangxian lun*);	12
jiecheng 結成/5548	2	0	334: 5? (Baoliang); 12 (Fayun); 263 (Zhiyi); 42 (Jizang); 1 (Huijun); 1 (Huiying); 1 (Huida)	1 (*Xianyu jing*); 1 (Tanluan);	10 (*Jin'gangxian lun*); 2 (Fashang's *Shidi lun yishu*); 135 (Huiyuan); 1? (*Dasheng zhiguan famen*)	20
jieshi 結示/2410	4	0	16	0	0	1
jinlüechu 今略出/63	1	0	22: 13 (Zhiyi); 8 (Jizang); 1 (Huijun)	0	0	1
jingshi 精識/130	3	0	22	0	0	3
jujing 舉境/140	2	0	32	0	1 (*Jin'gangxian lun*); 5 (Huiyuan)	0

(*Continued*)

Table 3.16 (Continued)

Term	T2805	Paramārtha	Authors in the South, 440–600: Baoliang, Fayun, Zhiyi, Jizang, Huiying, Huida, Huijun	Authors in the North, 446–589: Bodhiruci, Ratnamati, *Zhengfa nianchu jing*, Tanluan, and so on.	Authors in the North around 589–600: Fashang, Huiyuan, Tanyan (Including *Jin'gangxian lun*, Narendrayaśas, Jīnagupta, and so on)	Authors before 440: Zhu Fonian, Kumārajīva, Dharmakṣema
keduan 科段/149	1	0	21: 3 (Baoliang); 2 (Fayun); 9 (Zhiyi); 3 (Jizang)	0	0	0
liyong 力用/1945	5	4	136	1 (*Piyesuo wenjing*); 1 (*Dasheng tongxing jing*); 1 (Lingbian's *Huayan jing lun*)	19 (Huiyuan); 3 (Jīnagupta); 1 (Dharmagupta); 1 (*Dasheng zhiguan famen*); 1 (*Shi moheyan lun*)	36
liaojian 料簡/3307	1	1	>200	0	2 (*Jin'gangxian lun*); 3 (Fashang's *Shidi lun yishu*); 58 (Huiyuan)	10
piming 譬明/262	3	0	141 Include. 68 (Baoliang)	0	0	0
xiangming 向明/319	1	0	37 Includ. 16 (Baoliang)	1 (*Baoxing lun*)	2 (*Jin'gangxian lun*); 1 (*Shi moheyan lun*)	15
zhangmen 章門/1803	3	0	>200 Include. 104 (Fayun); 20 (Baoliang)	2 (Tanluan);	29 (*Jin'gangxian lun*); 8 (Fashang's *Shidi lun yishu*); 88 (Huiyuan)	4 (*Apitan piposha lun*); 2 (*Bingposha lun*)
zishi 自釋/1207	3	0	63	0	123 (Huiyuan)	0
zongshi 總釋/1828	1	0	120	0	1 (*Jin'gangxian lun*); 4 (*Tanyan shu*); 52 (Huiyuan)	0

3.6.1 A. The Affiliation of T2805 with Chinese Buddhism in the South

The best explanation for why T2805 contains several terms that are not found in Paramārtha's works is that its author was familiar with Buddhism in the south, as well as with Paramārtha. As far as we know from the XGSZ, all of Paramārtha's Chinese disciples had already been educated in the Buddhist scholarly tradition before they studied with Paramārtha and became his scribes and colleagues. This means his disciples were influenced both by their previous training in the indigenous (in this case, southern) Chinese Buddhist tradition and by their exposure to a new group of translated texts by Paramārtha. By his use of several terms that were popular in southern China, the author of T2805 reveals his educational background.

3.6.2 B. The Distinction between the South and the North

The use of terms and phrases in southern and northern China seems to have differed significantly. Regarding technical terminology, southern authors followed previous translation conventions to a greater extent than did the northern authors. For example, terms like *jiaming pusa* 假名菩薩 (bodhisattvas by designation) and *jingshi* 精識 (sharply observes) were used in the north before 440 but then completely disappeared. Only authors in the south continued using these two terms.

The transmission of Buddhist scholarship from the north to the south after the death of Kumārajīva (413) was probably the reason for this south–north distinction. At that time, Kumārajīva's disciples spread out to a few places in the south. After the persecution of Buddhism in 444 under Emperor Taiwu 太武 (reign 424–51) of the Northern Wei 北魏 dynasty (386–534), Buddhism declined in the north and recovered only around 500, when another great translator, Bodhiruci, came to the capital Luoyang 洛陽.

But Buddhism, after its revival in the north, went in a new direction with new translators, such as Bodhiruci and Ratnamati. Their terminology was quite different from the terminology of translators of the previous generation, such as Zhu Fonian 竺佛念 (d.u., active in Chang'an during 365–84), Kumārajīva, and Dharmakṣema.

In contrast, the scholarship in the south was more of a continuation and further development of the earlier tradition that had been established mainly in the north. One reason, I suspect, is that the southern Buddhist tradition was deeply involved in the study of the **Tattvasiddhi* translated by Kumārajīva and the *Mahāparinirvāṇa-mahāsūtra* (*Da boniepan jing* 大般涅槃經) translated by Dharmakṣema.[33] As a result, the terminology employed by Kumārajīva and Dharmakṣema was quite commonly followed by authors in the south.

3.6.3 C. The Confluence between the South and the North

A problem with this contrast between the northern and southern traditions is that some early northern Sui dynasty authors, such as Fashang 法上 (495–580), Huiyuan, and Tanyan, used some terms that seem to have been current only among southern authors.

The best explanation for this phenomenon I can suggest is that these northern authors already had access in the late sixth century to works composed in the south. Note that all three authors were active in the latter half of the sixth century, when the division between the north and the south was about to end, after more than 200 years. It is not unlikely that some communication between north and south had begun around this time. Chen (1987) notes that, at least during the reign of Yuwen Tai 宇文泰 (507–56), several Buddhist texts from the south were taken to the capital around 555, an event that might mark when Buddhist scholars in the north began to have access to texts from the south.[34] For this reason, although China was not reunified until the Sui dynasty in 589, it seems reasonable to assume that contact and interaction between the north and the south had started before reunification.

3.6.4 A Separate Category: Authors in the North around 589–600

It is for this reason that a separate category must be established in addition to the "authors in the north" and "authors in the south." I focus on authors who were influenced simultaneously by the south and the north. Given that most of them were active during 589–600, I call this group "authors in the north around 589-600." Foremost among them are Huiyuan, Fashang, and Tanyan, some translators, such as Narendrayaśas 那連提耶舍, Jīnagupta 闍那崛多(523–600), and Dharmagupta 達摩笈多, and the authors of a few apocryphal texts such as the *Jin'gangxian lun* 金剛仙論 (T1512),[35] the *Dasheng zhiguan famen* (T1924),[36] and the *Shi moheyan lun* 釋摩訶衍論 (T1668). Based on these observations, Table 3.15 can be modified slightly as Table 3.16.

In the next Table 3.17, we find more examples that highlight the distinction between the northern and southern traditions, based on the terminology in T2805.

3.6.5 Exegetical Tools in the South

Table 3.17 suggests that some terms exclusively employed in the south, for example, *zhengchu* 正出, *zhengming* 正明, and *zhengpo* 正破, are what can be called exegetical tools. That is to say, these terms were invented as exegetical tools for explaining what is going on in the text. Other exegetical tools frequently used in the south are included in Table 3.18.

Based on Table 3.18, I tentatively suggest that one of the factors that led to the marked difference in terminology between the northern and southern Buddhist traditions was the flourishing of indigenous exegetical works in the south.

Another noteworthy point here is that works of unknown authorship, such as the *Jin'gangxian lun* and the *Dasheng zhiguan famen*, were composed at the confluence of the northern and southern traditions. It is also intriguing that the *Awakening of Faith* does not use those terms that are characteristic of the southern tradition, which strongly suggests that it was not produced in the Buddhist environment of southern China where Paramārtha and his disciples lived.

Table 3.17 More Examples for T2805's Connection with the Southern Tradition

Term	T2805	Paramārtha	Authors in the South, 440–600: Baoliang, Fayun, Zhiyi, Jizang, Huiying, Huida, Huijun	Authors in the North, 446–589: Bodhiruci, Ratnamati, *Zhengfa nianchu jing*, Tanluan, and so on.	Authors in the North around 589–600: Fashang, Huiyuan, Tanyan (including *Jin'gangxian lun*, Narendrayaśas, Jīnagupta, and so on)	Authors before 440: Zhu Fonian, Kumārajīva, Dharmakṣema
aqietuo (*yao*) 阿伽陀(藥) [*agada*]/217	1	2	1	0	0	~19 [*agada*]; some in the sense of [*agata*]
buxiangguan 不相關/336	1	8	37	0	0	1
heyizhiran 何以知然/320	1	7	149	1 (*Xianyu jing*)	1 (*Jin'gangxian lun*)	0
huwei 呼為/1327	2	3	75	0	1 (Huiyuan)	23
huanju 還舉/112	1	1	33: including 5 (Baoliang); 2 (Fayun); 3 (Zhiyi); 5 (Jizang) 3 (Huiying);	1 (*Zhengfa nianchu jing*)	2 (*Jin'gangxian lun*); 3 (Huiyuan)	6
jiguo 極果/1570	1	6	113	1 (*Xianyu jing*)	1 (*Jin'gangxian lun*); 6 (Huiyuan); 1 (*Tanyan shu*)	1
jixie 即謝/118	1	6	20	0	1 (*Jin'gangxian lun*); 1 (*Dasheng zhiguan famen*)	0
jibuke 既不可/685	1	4	43	1 (*Za baozang jing*); 1 (*Zhengfa nianchu jing*); 1 (*Ye chengjiu lun*)	1 (Huiyuan) 1 (*Dasheng zhiguan famen*); 2 (*Tanyan shu*)	4

(*Continued*)

Table 3.17 (Continued)

Term	T2805	Paramārtha	Authors in the South, 440–600: Baoliang, Fayun, Zhiyi, Jizang, Huiying, Huida, Huijun	Authors in the North, 446–589: Bodhiruci, Ratnamati, *Zhengfa nianchu jing*, Tanluan, and so on.	Authors in the North around 589–600: Fashang, Huiyuan, Tanyan (including *Jin'gangxian lun*, Narendrayaśas, Jīnagupta, and so on)	Authors before 440: Zhu Fonian, Kumārajīva, Dharmakṣema
jijin 既盡/1073	1	2	82	20 (*Zhengfa nianchu jing*)	1 (*Jin'gangxian lun*); 1 (Fashang's *Shidi lun yishu*); 4 (Huiyuan)	35
jichang 計常/929	1	4	47	0	26(Huiyuan);	112
jiehuo 結惑/263	1	3	35	1 (Tanluan)	1 (Huiyuan)	1
jupi 舉譬/614	1	2	101	0	2 (Huiyuan)	0
juming 具明/1488	1	7	198	1 (*Xianyu jing*);	1 (*Jin'gangxian lun*); 23 (Huiyuan)	25
lunwen 論文/5998	4	2	186	0	54 (Huiyuan)	0
qide 豈得/3027	4	6	>200; Including 48 (Baoliang)	1 (Bodhiruci); 3 (Tanluan),	2 (Huiyuan); 1 (*Tanyan shu*)	53
qianshen 淺深/3908	5	4	>200	0	4 (Fashagn's *Shidi lun yishu*); 47 (Huiyuan)	1 (*Jiumoluoshi fashi dayi*); 7 (Sengzhao); 1 (Dharmakṣema);
renyun 任運/5747	1	1	>200	0	1 (Narendrayaśas' *Yuedeng sanmei jing*); 2 (Narendrayaśas' *Apitan xin lun jing*); 2 (Fashang's *Shidi lun yishu*); 19 (Huiyuan); 2 (*Tanyan shu*)	1 (Kumārajīva); 2 (Dharmakṣema)
shixing pusa 始行菩薩/88	1	1	43	2 (Pimuzhixian 毘目智仙);	5 (Huiyuan)	1 (*Pusa yingluo benye jing*); 1 (Sengzhao)

weipi 為譬/865	3	41	178 Include. Baoliang 59	1 (Bodhiruci); * 6 for "*wei piyu* 為譬喻" (*Zhengfanianchu jing* 4; Bodhiruci 1; *Baoxing lun* 1);	5 (Narendrayaśas); 7 [Huiyuan]);	120
weida 未達	3	2	60 Include. 19 (Baoliang);	1 (*Xianyu jing*)	5 (Narendrayaśas); 1 (Tanyan); 2 (*Fufazang yinyuan zhuan*); 4 (Huiyuan)	10
yuxian 欲顯/2333	2	92	>200	1 (*Xianyu jing*); 1 (Buddhaśānta); 1 (*Fangbianxin lun*)	1 (Narendrayaśas); 1 (*Jin'gangxian lun*); 5 (Huiyuan)	74 Include. 48 (*Apitan piposha lun*) 2 (Dharmakṣema); 1(*Bingposha lun*); 6 (*Shelifo apitan lun*); 4 (*Pusa dichi jing*)
zhengchu 正出/738	1	4	65 Include. 18(Fayun)	1 (*Sanjuzu jing youpotishe*)	9 (*Jin'gangxian lun*); 18 (Huiyuan)	
zhengming 正明/10858	5	5	>200 308 (Fayun); 28 (Baoliang)	0	355 (Huiyuan); 8 (Fashang); 5 (*Tanyan shu*)	0
zhengpo 正破/1752	3	1	>200	0	28 (Huiyuan); 1 (*Tanyan shu*)	1
zuoyi 作意/12807	10	110	>200 179 (Saṅghavarman); 2 (Fayun); 6 (Baoliang); 82 (Zhiyi); 18 (Jizang)	10 (*Zhengfa nianchu jing*); 1 (*Jietuojie jing*); 1 (*Sheng shanzhuyi tianzi suowen jing*); 2 (*Ye chengjiu lun*); 2 (*Baoxing lun*); 1 (Tanluan) "*zuo yiye* 作意業: 1 (Bodhiruci)	53(Huiyuan); 3 (Fashang) 1 (*Tanyan shu*); 1 (*Jin'gangxian lun*); 6 (Narendrayaśas)	72

Table 3.18 Exegetical Tools from the Southern Tradition

Term	T2805	Paramārtha	**Authors in the South, 440–600: Baoliang, Fayun, Zhiyi, Jizang, Huiying, Huida, Huijun**	**Authors in the North, 446–589: Bodhiruci, Ratnamati, *Zhengfa nianchu jing*, Tanluan, and so on.**	**Authors in the North around 589–600: Fashang, Huiyuan, Tanyan (including *Jin'gangxian lun*, Narendrayaśas, Jīnagupta, and so on)**	**Authors before 440: Zhu Fonian, Kumārajīva, Dharmakṣema**
biekai 別開/1286	1	0	1 (Baoliang); 1 (Fayun); ~10 (Zhiyi); 28 (Jizang); 1 (Huijun)	0	0 (Huiyuan in different senses such as "*fenbie kaishi* 分別開示"; Dharmagupta: "*fenbie kaijie* 分別開解"); 2 (*Shi moheyan lun*)	0
biepo 別破/978	1	0	2 (Baoliang); ~20 (Zhiyi); 86 (Jizang): 2 (Huiying); 1? (Huijun)	0	27 (Huiyuan); 1 (*Dichi yiji*)	0
bieshi 別釋/8343	7	81	5 (Baoliang); 4 (Fayun); 85 (Zhiyi); 164 (Jizang): 40 (Huiying); 2 (Huida); 1? (Huijun)	0	>50 (Huiyuan); 18 (*Tanyan shu*); 1 (Dharmagupta) ~15 (*Jin'gangxian lun*); 27 (*Shi moheyan lun*)	0
bingming 並明/264	1	0	1 (Baoliang) 5 (Zhiyi); 23 (Jizang): 1 (Huiying); 1 (Huijun)	0	1 (Huiyuan); 5 (*Jin'gangxian lun*)	0

chu deshi 出得失/11	1	0	1 (Zhiyi); 1 (Jizang):	0	0	0
chu qishi 出其事/32	1	0	2 (Baoliang); 1 (Zhu Daosheng); 3 (Jizang); 1 (Huiying); 1 (Huida)	0	2 (Huiyuan); 1 (Fashang); 1? (*Jin'gangxian lun*)	1 (Zhu Fonian)
chuzhengyi 出正義/57 or *chuyiyi* 出異義/8	1 ("chu zhengyi")	1 (Suixiang lun: "chu yiyi")	1 (Huida: "*chu yiyi*")	0	0	0
chuyijie 出異解/40	1	0	3 (Zhiyi); 3 (Huida)	0	0	0
chufan 初番/490	3	0	1 (Fayun); 26 (Zhiyi) 12 (Jizang); 1 (Huiying); 1 (*Hongming ji*)	0	40 (Huiyuan); 2 (Fashang); 1 (T2808)	0
chongju 重舉/564	1	0	14 (Baoliang); 3 (Zhiyi); 7 (Jizang);	0	14 (Huiyuan); 2 (Fashang); 10 (*Jin'gangxian lun*)	0
ci fanwei 此翻為/675	1	0	3 (Fayun); 23 (Zhiyi); 23 (Jizang)	0	0	0
ci fanming 此翻名/175	0	0	2 (Jizang)	0	107 (Huiyuan); 1 (*Tanyan shu*)	0
dangti 當體/2975	3	3	10 (Baoliang); 12 (Fayun); 32 (Zhiyi); 83 (Jizang); 2 (Huida); 3 (Huiying); 23 (Huijun)	0	15 (Huiyuan); 1 (Fashang); 1 (Dushun); 2 (T2806); 3 (T2807); 1 (T2808); 2 (Jīnagupta: in diff senses)	0

(*Continued*)

Table 3.18 (Continued)

Term	T2805	Paramārtha	Authors in the South, 440–600: Baoliang, Fayun, Zhiyi, Jizang, Huiying, Huida, Huijun	Authors in the North, 446–589: Bodhiruci, Ratnamati, *Zhengfa nianchu jing*, Tanluan, and so on.	Authors in the North around 589–600: Fashang, Huiyuan, Tanyan (including *Jin'gangxian lun*, Narendrayaśas, Jīnagupta, and so on)	Authors before 440: Zhu Fonian, Kumārajīva, Dharmakṣema
dieqian 牒前/2528	2	1 (*Jin qishi lun*)	14 (Zhiyi); 38 (Jizang)	0	460 (Huiyuan/ Only 3 in the *Dasheng yizhang*) 6 (*Tanyan shu*); 3 (Fashang); 23 (*Jin'gangxian lun*)	0
fuli 符理/67	1	1 (*Shelun*)	9 (Jizang)	0	0	0
hepi 合譬/1094	1	1 (*Rushi lun*)	22 (Baoliang); 77 (Fayun); 71 (Zhiyi); 126 (Jizang); 2 (Huiying); 1 (Huida)	0	2? (Huiyuan); 1 (T2806)	0
huju yibian 互舉一邊/55	1	0	3 (Fayun); 6 (Zhiyi); 2 (Jizang); 1 (Huijun)	0	2 (Huiyuan)	0
juming 具明/1488 (meaning "to show altogether")	1	7	1 (Baoliang) 2 (Fayun); 61 (Zhiyi); 135 (Jizang) 3 (Huijun); 1 (Huiying)	0	23 (Huiyuan); 1 (Dharmagupta); 1 (*Jin'gangxian lun*)	0

lunwen 論文/5998	4	7	5 (Baoliang); 2 (Fayun); 20 (Zhiyi); 140 (Jizang); 1 (Huijun); 10 (Huiying); 1 (Huida)	0	54 (Huiyuan); 6 (*Shi moheyan lun*)	0
tonglun 通論/1923	1	2 (*Suixiang lun* 1; AKBh 1)	2 (Baoliang); 94 (Zhiyi); 63 (Jizang); 3 (Huiying); 1 (Huida); 9 (Huijun)	0	141 (Huiyuan); 3 (T2808)	0
tongming 通名/2937 (meaning "general name")	3	19	7 (Baoliang); 1 (Fayun); 141 (Zhiyi); 62 (Jizang); 5 (Huiying); 3 (Huijun);	0	272 (Huiyuan); 2 (Fashang); 1 (*Jin'gangxian lun*); 2 (*Shi moheyan lun*)	~14 (Kumārajīva); 3 (*Apitan piposha lun*); 3 (Sengzhao)
tongming 通明/2156 (meaning "showing in general")	2	2 (*Shelun*)	2 (Baoliang); 2 (Fayun); 1 (*Gaoseng zhuan*); 143 (Zhiyi); 72 (Jizang); 5 (Huijun); 3 (Huiying)	0	29 (Huiyuan); 2 (Dushun); 3 (*Jin'gangxian lun*); 2 (T2808); 1 (*Dasheng zhiguan famen*);	1 (Dharmakṣema)
xianbiao 先標/1181	2	1 (*Shelun*)	1 (Baoliang); 1 (Fayun); 19 (Zhiyi); 5 (Jizang);	0	16 (Huiyuan)	0

(*Continued*)

Table 3.18 (Continued)

Term	T2805	Paramārtha	Authors in the South, 440–600: Baoliang, Fayun, Zhiyi, Jizang, Huiying, Huida, Huijun	Authors in the North, 446–589: Bodhiruci, Ratnamati, *Zhengfa nianchu jing*, Tanluan, and so on.	Authors in the North around 589–600: Fashang, Huiyuan, Tanyan (including *Jin'gangxian lun*, Narendrayaśas, Jīnagupta, and so on)	Authors before 440: Zhu Fonian, Kumārajīva, Dharmakṣema
yimu 以目/623 (meaning "to name; to aim at")	1	1 (*Suixiang lun*)	1 (Baoliang); 1 (Fayun); 7 (Zhiyi); 71 (Jizang); 1 (*Chu sanzang ji ji*); 1 (Huiying); 1 (Huijun)	0	1 (Huiyuan)	0
zongbiao 總標/5360	5	2 (*Shelun*)	17 (Zhiyi); 101 (Jizang); 3 (Huida)	0	30 (Huiyuan); 1 (*Tanyan shu*); 46 (*Shi moheyan lun*)	0
zongcheng 總成/775	1	0	1 (Zhiyi); 2 (Jizang);	0	1 (Jīnagupta)	0
zongjie 總結/8539	1	1 (*Xianshi lun*)	12 (Baoliang); 59 (Fayun); 119 (Zhiyi); 343 (Jizang); 25 (Huiying); 2 (Huida)	0	400 (Huiyuan); 4 (*Tanyan shu*); 1 (Jīnagupta); 20 (*Shi moheyan lun*); 1 (*Dasheng zhiguan famen*);	

zongming 總明/3762	4	1 (*Shelun*)	8 (Baoliang); 16 (Fayun); 57 (Zhiyi); 206 (Jizang); 10 (Huiying)	0	152 (Huiyuan); 2 (Fashang); 1 (*Tanyan shu*); 1 (T2809); 5 (*Dasheng zhiguan famen*)	0
zongwen 總問/1096	1	2 (*Shelun*, *Suixiang lun*)	4 (Fayun); 5 (Zhiyi); 27 (Jizang); 3 (Huiying)	0	15 (Huiyuan); 22 (*Shi moheyan lun*)	2 (Kumārajīva)

3.7 Unlikelihood That the Author of T2805 Came from the North

We have seen that some northern authors, like Huiyuan, adopted some vocabulary from the south after 589. Although it is possible that the author of T2805 also originated from the north, it is unlikely for three reasons. First, as mentioned earlier, the author of T2805 was probably the scribe of the *Suixiang lun*, and none of Paramārtha's Chinese colleagues is known to have come from the north. Second, T2805 includes several terms that never appear in works by northern authors. Third, some notions in T2805 are found only in works by southern authors.

3.7.1 Terms in T2805 That Are Never Used by Authors from the North

These terms in T2805, presumably peculiar to the south, never occur in northern works, including those of authors like Huiyuan, in the early Sui dynasty as shown in Table 3.19.

3.7.2 Notions in T2805 That Rarely Appear in Northern Works

Several notions in T2805 are seldom mentioned in northern works. I discuss three in detail.

3.7.3 Cause in Terms of Habituation and Cause of Retribution

As for the terms "cause in terms of habituation" (*xiyin* 習因) and "cause of retribution" (*baoyin* 報因), T2805 includes *xiyin* eight times, *baoyin* or *guobao yin* 果報因 three times, and *xibao yin* 習、報因 (i.e., the *xiyin* and the *baoyin*) four times. However, these two ideas do not seem to have been used as a contrastive pair in any known Indian source. Rather, they seem to have originated from different Indian sources and were later juxtaposed in this way only in China.

Searches with the CBReader 2007 suggest that the term "cause in terms of habituation" originated in the **Tattvasiddhi* as one of the three kinds of causal conditions (Skt. *hetupratyaya*; Ch. *yinyuan* 因緣). These three include cause in terms of production (Skt. **jananahetu*; Ch. *shengyin* 生因), cause in terms of habituation (Skt. **āsevana-hetu*; Ch. *xiyin* 習因) and cause in terms of being a basis (Skt. **niśraya-hetu*; Ch. *yiyin* 依因). Katsura translates the original explanation in the **Tattvasiddhi* as follows: "**janana-hetu* is that which causes a dharma to originate, as, e.g., karma causes results (*vipāka*), **āsevana-hetu* is as, e.g., greediness increases when one is accustomed to greediness, and **niśraya-hetu* is as, e.g., *citta* and (the so-called) *caitāsika* depend upon color, smell, etc. They are called *hetupratyayas*."[37]

On the other hand, the cause of retribution (Skt. *vipāka-phala*; Ch. *baoyin* 報因) is one of the six causes according to the Sarvāstivāda Abhidharma.[38] Originally, cause of retribution seems to refer to those wholesome, unwholesome, and indeterminate

Table 3.19 Terminology in T2805 Never Used by Authors from the North

Term	T2805	Paramārtha	Authors in the South, 440–600: Baoliang, Fayun, Zhiyi, Jizang, Huiying, Huida, Huijun	Authors in the North, 446–589: Bodhiruci, Ratnamati, *Zhengfa nianchu jing*, Tanluan, and so on.	Authors in the North around 589–600: Fashang, Huiyuan, Tanyan (including *Jin'gangxian lun*, and those in early Sui dynasty such as Dharmagupta; Jinagupta, and so on)	Authors before 440: Zhu Fonian, Kumārajīva, Dharmakṣema
aqietuo (*yao*) 阿伽陀(藥) [*agada*]/217	1	2	1	0	0	~19 [*agada*]; some in a diff. sense of [*agata*]
bu xiangguan 不相關/336	1	8	37	0	0	1
chu deshi 出得失/11	1	0	2	0	0	0
chu yijie 出異解/40	1	0	6	0	0	0
chu zhengyi 出正義/57 or *chu yiyi* 出異義/8	1	1	1	0	0	0
ci fanwei 此翻為/675	1	0	49	0	0	0
daixiang 帶相/202	1	0	4	0	0	0
fuli 符理/67	1	1	9	0	0	0
jiaming pusa 假名菩薩/141	1	0	20	0	0	17
jieshi 結示/2410	4	0	16	0	0	1
jin lüechu 今略出/63	1	0	22	0	0	1
jingshi 精識/130	3	0	22	0	0	3
keduan 科段/149	1	0	21	0	0	0
piming 譬明/262	3	0	141 Includ. Baoliang 寶亮 68	0	0	0

(i.e., neither wholesome nor unwholesome) deeds that would incur effects which are desirable or undesirable.[39] But the **Saṃyuktābhidharma-hṛdaya-śāstra* further specifies that the effect of retribution (*baoguo* 報果) specifically refers to effects that are dissimilar to the cause.[40] And for this reason, the cause of retribution becomes limited to only those causes that produce dissimilar effects. In contrast, the effect of dependence (*yiguo* 依果) refers to the effects that are similar to their causes and hence arise due to a cause of the same kind (Skt. *sabhāga-hetu*; Ch. *zifen yin* 自分因;),[41] another of the six causes. Thus, according to the **Saṃyuktābhidharma-hṛdaya-śāstra*, there are two contrasting pairs: the cause of the same kind and the cause of retribution; the effect of dependence, and the effect of retribution.

For some reason, the causal systems in the **Tattvasiddhi* and in the **Saṃyuktābhidharma-hṛdaya-śāstra* merged. According to Zhiyi,[42] the cause in terms of habituation in the **Tattvasiddhi* corresponds to the cause of the same kind in the **Saṃyuktābhidharma-hṛdaya-śāstra*, as is shown in Table 3.20 comparing the causal systems of the two texts.

Note that Zhiyi's usage of these terms is quite different from the **Tattvasiddhi*. The **Tattvasiddhi* stipulates only one cause that is responsible for the effect, namely, the cause in terms of production, and does not further distinguish between whether the effect is of the same kind as the cause or of a different kind. In other words, there are two differences between the **Tattvasiddhi* and the **Saṃyuktābhidharma-hṛdaya-śāstra*: the cause in terms of production in the **Tattvasiddhi* includes cause of the same kind as well as its cause of retribution as explained in the **Saṃyuktābhidharma-hṛdaya-śāstra*'s; the cause in terms of habituation in the **Tattvasiddhi* is not found in the **Saṃyuktābhidharma-hṛdaya-śāstra*.

Table 3.20 Causal Systems in **Tattvasiddhi* and **Saṃyuktābhidharma-hṛdaya-śāstra*

Tattvasiddhi	***Saṃyuktābhidharma-hṛdaya-śāstra***	***Saṃyuktābhidharma-hṛdaya-śāstra***
Three Causal Conditions	Six causes	Five Effects
cause in terms of habituation (*xiyin* 習因)	cause of the same kind (Ch. *zifen yin* 自分因; Skt. *sabhāga-hetu*)	effect of dependence (*yiguo* 依果)
cause in terms of production (*shengyin* 生因)	cause of retribution (Ch. *baoyin* 報因; Skt. *vipāka-hetu*)	effect of retribution (*baoguo* 報果)
cause in terms of being a basis (*yiyin* 依因)	cause in terms of efficiency (Ch. *suozuo yin* 所作因; Skt. *kāraṇa-hetu*) cause in terms of simultaneity (Ch. *gongyou yin* 共有因; Skt. *sahabhū-hetu*) cause in terms of pervasion (Ch. *yiqie bian yin*一切遍因; Skt. *sarvatraga-hetu*) cause in terms of association (Ch. *xiangying yin* 相應因; Skt. *saṃprayuktaka-hetu*)[a]	effect of disjunction (Ch. *jietuo guo* 解脫果; Skt. *visaṃyoga-phala*) effect of human effort (Ch. *gongyong guo* 功用果; Skt. *puruṣakāra-phala*) what contributes to the effect (Ch. *zengshang guo* 增上果; Skt. *adhipati-phala*)

[a]For the Sanskrit reconstruction of these six causes, see Willemen, Dessein, and Cox (1998: 28–9).

In any case, the pairing of the cause in terms of habituation and the cause of retribution seems to be a Chinese invention in the south resulting from a conflation of the **Tattvasiddhi* and the **Saṃyuktābhidharma-hṛdaya-śāstra*. A result of this conflation is another contrastive pairing of *xiyin* 習因and *baoyin* 報因 (the cause of retribution), with *xiyin* referring to causes leading to similar effects and *baoyin* referring to causes leading to dissimilar effects.[43]

The pair of the cause in terms of habituation and the cause of retribution was widely discussed and employed in the south after the Liang dynasty. It occurs several times in the works of Fayun, Zhiyi, and Jizang, and once in the work of Huida.[44] These terms occur especially frequently in the work of Huijun (*xiyin*: 40; *baoyin*: 7) and in the work of Huiying (*xiyin*: 7; *baoyin*: 25), both southern authors.

In a striking contrast, this pair is never found in the works of any northern author. Huiyuan uses the term *xiyin* in his introduction to the exposition of the three causes in the **Tattvasiddhi*, but not in the same context as it was used in the south.[45]

3.7.4 The Notion of the "Final Mind of the *Gotra* of the Path"

Another concept that appears in T2805 but only appears in southern works is the notion of the "final mind of the *gotra* of the Path" (*daozhong zhongxin* 道種終心). The "*gotra* of the Path" is a classification of practitioners before they enter the first bodhisattva stage (*bhūmi*). The term "the final mind of the *gotra* of the Path" refers to the practitioner's mental content just before entering the bodhisattva stage. In contrast, Huiyuan in the north refers to the same notion as "the final mind of resolute practice" (*jiexing zhongxin* 解行終心).

The problem here is that authors in the south and in the north divided the bodhisattva path in different ways based on different scriptures. In the south, the bodhisattva path was divided into six *gotras* (*zhongxing* 種性) on the basis of the *Renwang bore jing*[46] and the *Pusa yingluo benye jing*.[47] In this system, the *gotra* of the Path (*dao zhongxing* 道種性) refers to the stage immediately before the first bodhisattva stage. In contrast, authors in the north divided the bodhisattva path into seven stages (*di* 地) based on the *Pusa dichi jing* 菩薩地持經 (*The Scripture on the Stages of the Bodhisattvas*).[48] For them, it is the stage of *jiexing* (*jiexing di* 解行地) that immediately precedes the first bodhisattva stage.[49] The different stages that directly precede the bodhisattva stage according authors in the south and the north can be seen in Table 3.21 (the numbers in parentheses indicate the total number of occurrences by an author or in a text).

Table 3.21 Names of the Stage Immediately Preceding the First Bodhisattva Stage

	South	North	Author Unknown
daozhong zhongxin 道種終心	(4) Huijun; (2) Huiying; (2) Guanding		(1) T2805; (1) *Shidi yiji* 十地義記 (T2758)
jiexing zhongxin 解行終心	(2) Zhiyi	(8) Huiyuan; (1) Fashang	(2) T2807; (1) *Shidi yiji* 十地義記(T2758); (1) *Fahua jing shu* 法華經疏(T2749)

Thus, it seems as though authors in the south referred to the stage before the first bodhisattva stage as *daozhong zhongxin*, whereas the authors in the north identified it as *jiexing zhongxin* instead.

Here Zhiyi appears to be the only southern author to have used the term *jiexing zhongxin*. If we look more closely, however, we can see that Zhiyi actually uses the term differently from both the conventional usage based on the *Pusa yingluo benye jing* in the south and Huiyuan's usage in the north. The conventional usage, based on the *Pusa yingluo benye jing*, links the *gotra* of habituation (*xi zhongxing* 習種性) with the ten abidings (*shizhu* 十住) or ten understandings (*shijie* 十解), the *gotra* of nature (*xing zhongxing* 性種性) with the ten practices (*shixing* 十行), and the *gotra* of the Path with the ten merit-transfers (*shi huixiang* 十迴向).[50] In contrast, Zhiyi slightly reformulates this system by linking the *gotra* of habituation with the stage of understanding (*jie* 解), the *gotra* of nature with the stage of practice (*xing* 行), and the *gotra* of the Path with the stage of the final mind of resolute practice (*jiexing zhongxin* 解行終心).[51]

Two more things highlight the differences between Zhiyi and Huiyuan. For Huiyuan, the stage of *jiexing* refers only to the second stage (i.e., the *jiexing di* 解行地),[52] whereas for Zhiyi, the stage of *jiexing* includes the first three *gotras* (i.e., the *gotras* of habituation, nature, and the Path). In addition, Zhiyi does not use the typical names of the seven stages of the *Pusa dichi jing* when he discusses his stage/*gotra* theory; in contrast, Huiyuan also never refers to *miaojue xing* 妙覺性, the last of the six *gotras* that are accepted in the south.[53] The correspondences among the three different systems of *gotras* are mapped in Table 3.22.

To conclude, the inclusion in T2805 of the term "the final mind of the *gotra* of the Path (*daozhong zhongxin* 道種終心)," which predominantly appears in southern texts, suggests that the author of T2805 came from the south.

3.7.5 The Notion of *Jingzhi* 境智 (Cognitive Object and *Jñāna*)

Another indication of the southern provenance of T2805 comes from its use of the term *jingzhi* 境智 to refer to the cognitive object (*viṣaya*) and the cognition (*jñāna*) thereof. This had become a set term that was frequently used in southern China both before and after Paramārtha. For example, the term appears 12 times in Baoliang's *Da boniepan jing jijie*, 3 times in Fayun's *Fahua jing yiji* 法華經義記 (*A Record of the Meaning of the Lotus Sūtra*), 117 times in Huijun, 51 times in Huida, and a vast number of times in both Zhiyi and Jizang. With the exception of one occurrence in Fashang's *Shidi lun yishu* 十地論義疏 (*An Elucidation of the Daśabhūmika*), two occurrences in Huiyuan's *Da boniepan jing yiji* and possibly one occurrence in Huiyuan's *Dichi lun yiji* 地持論義記 (*A Record of the Meaning of the Scripture on the Stages of the Bodhisattvas*), this phrase does not appear in works by northern authors.

In the north, references to the cognitive object and the cognition thereof usually involve the terms *xinjing* 心境 or *xin jingjie* 心境界, although these terms are sometimes found in Paramārtha's works and in works from the south, including Bodhiruci's translations, where they appear more than twenty times. In the case of

Table 3.22 Three Systems of *Gotra*s in the South, North, and Zhiyi

South (Based on the *Pusa yingluo benye jing*)	**Zhiyi**		**North (According to Huiyuan Based on the *Pusa dichi jing*)**
(1) Ten confidences (*shi xin* 十信)	(1) outside worldlings (*wai fan*外凡)		
(2) *gotra* of habituation (*xi zhongxing* 習種姓) = Ten abidings (*shi zhu* 十住) or Ten understandings (*shi jie* 十解)	(2) [ten] understa-ndings (*jie* 解)	(2) inside worldlings (*nei fan* 內凡)	(1) the stage of *gotra* (*zhongxing di* 種性地) = Ten abidings (*shizhu* 十住)
(3) *gotra* of nature (*xing zhongxing* 性種姓) = Ten practices (*shi xing* 十行)	(3) [ten] practices (*xing* 行)	(3) inside worldlings	
(4) *gotra* of the Path (*dao zhongxing* 道種姓) = Ten merit-transfers (*shi huixiang* 十迴向)	(4) the final mind of resolute practice (*jiexing zhongxin* 解行終心) = ten merit-transfer	(4) inside worldlings	(2) the stage of resolute practice (*jiexing di* 解行地) Note: the end of this stage = the final mind of resolute practice (*jiexing zhong xin* 解行終心)
(5) *gotra* of the *ārya* (*sheng zhongxing* 聖種姓) = Ten bodhisattva stages (*shi di* 十地)	(5) ten bodhisattva stages		(3) the stage of purified mind (*jingxin di* 淨心地) =*1st bhūmi*; (4) the stage of the traces of practices (*xingji di* 行迹地) = *2nd - 7th bhūmi*;
(6) *gotra* of perfect enlightenment (*dengjue xing* 等覺姓) = *vajropamā-samādhi*	(6) the stage of the bodhisattva of the adamantine mind (*jin'gang xin pusa* 金剛心菩薩)		(5) the stage of the certitude (*jueding di* 決定地) =*8th bhūmi*;
(7) *gotra* of marvelous enlightenment (*miao juexing* 妙覺姓) = The stage of the Buddha	(7) the stage of the Buddha		(6) the stage of the certitude of practice (*jueding xing di* 決定行地) =*9th bhūmi*; (7) the stage of the ultimate goal (*bijing di* 畢竟地) =*10th bhūmi* & the stage of the Buddha

Huiyuan, *zhi* 智 (*jñāna*) is usually reserved to translate *prajñā* (wisdom) rather than to mean cognition in general. Thus, the use of the pair *jingzhi* 境智 in T2805 also supports my suggestion that its author came from the south.

3.8 Possible Objections to the Southern Origin of T2805

I have asserted that the author of T2805 came from the south and was possibly one of Paramārtha's scribes. Now I consider possible objections to my claim.

The basic principle underlying my assertion about T2805 is that its terminology must have been limited to what was accessible to the author. That is to say, if a term in the text was not available to a Buddhist author in southern China in the late sixth century who had studied with Paramārtha (e.g., a term that was attested only after Xuanzang), then my assertion can be disputed.

Earlier, I have shown that my assertion is not undermined by the inclusion in T2805 of terms that are not found in Paramārtha's works. Those terms were actually circulating in southern China and hence were readily available to a Buddhist scholar who was educated in that environment. I have also shown that, since a few of those terms and ideas were not circulating in the north, it is unlikely that the author was someone who had moved from the north to the south. Next, I consider two possible objections.

3.8.1 Objection A

Some terms are found in T2805 that do not appear elsewhere before 600, as shown in Table 3.23.

I first dismiss compounded terms such as *genben pin* 根本品. Although this phrase is rarely found in the Chinese Buddhist canon, it may simply be a combination of the adjective *genben* and the noun *pin*, both frequently used in the south. Following a similar logic, I can also dismiss *dingxin zhongzi* 定心種子 (the seeds for a concentrated mind) and *huoye zhongzi* 惑業種子 (the seeds from the karma out of delusion).

The term *duibing* 對竝/對並/對并 seems to be problematic, as the earliest example I could find of this term with an identical meaning is by Huizhao 惠沼/慧沼 (651–714) (one time), Zhizhou 智周 (668–723) (one time) and Zhanran 湛然 (711–82) (ten times). I have no good explanation for this anomalous case. However, I think we can basically ignore it for two reasons: first, it is a unique case; second, all internal clues suggest that T2805 could not possibly have been composed during or after Xuanzang's time.

Thus, these terms do not seem to undermine my claim. This leads me to the second possible objection.

3.8.2 Objection B

Some terms in T2805 are not found in late-sixth-century works from the south, but they do, in fact, appear in works composed in the north, as shown in Table 3.24.

Two things are worth noting in this table. First, although it is true that these terms raise some questions regarding my claim, it is noteworthy that most of these cases—except for *chongbian* 重辯, *danyou* 單有, and probably *yukejian* 餘可見—involve doctrinal notions, not habitually used stylistic terms and phrases. Since these doctrinal terms can be borrowed and shared among several authors with different background training, I suggest that they do not serve as counterexamples because their presence in T2805 can be explained as resulting from contact between the author and the north. Therefore, I do not think that these terms constitute evidence which would indicate that the author of T2805 came from the north.

Table 3.23 Terminology in T2805 Never Appeared before 600

Term	T2805	Paramārtha	South 440–600: Baoliang, Fayun, Zhiyi, Jizang, Huiying, Huida, Huijun	North 440–590: Bodhiruci, Huiyuan, Tanyan (Including Dharmagupta, Jinagupta, and so on)	Before 440: Zhu Fonian, Kumārajīva, Dharmakṣema	After 600 (Until the End of Tang in 900)
dingxin zhongzi 定心種子/9	1	0	0	0	0	8 (Xuanzang 5)
duibing 對竝/2	1	0	0	0	0	1 (Ming dynasty)
duibing 對並/42	0	0	0	0	0	10 (Zhanran);
duibing 對并/11	0	0	0	0	0	1 (Huizhao); 1 (Zhizhou)
genben pin 根本品 (meaning: "the basic element")/8	1	0	0	0	1 (in different sense)	5; 1 (in different sense)
huoye zhongzi 惑業種子/13	3	0	0	1 (T2807);	0	2 (Fazang); 1 (Xifu)

Table 3.24 Terminology in T2805 Never Appeared in the South but in the North

Term	T2805	Paramārtha	Authors in the South, 440–600: Baoliang, Fayun, Zhiyi, Jizang, Huiying, Huida, Huijun	Authors in the North, 440–590: Bodhiruci, Huiyuan, Tanyan (Including Narendrayaśas, Dharmagupta, Jinagupta, and so on)	Before 440: Zhu Fonian, Kumārajīva, Dharmakṣema	After 600 (Until the End of Tang Dynasty Only)
chongbian 重辯/56	1	0	0	9 (Huiyuan: *Niepan* 8, *Dichi* 1)	0	0
danyou 單有/84	1; "danyou 但有" appears few times	0	0	1 (*Zhengfa nianchu jing*); 8 (Huiyuan: *Niepan* 1; *Yizhang* 7)	0	0
huanxun 還熏/76	1	0	0	2 (Huiyuan's *Bashi yi*); 1 (*Tanyan shu*); 4 (*Dasheng zhiguan famen*); 2 (*Shi moheyan lun*)	0	1 (Xuanzang); 2 (Wŏnhyo)
lineng 力能 ("capability")	2	0	0	1 (*Yuedeng sanmei jing*)	0	
sanliang zhi 三量智/6	1	0	0	2 (Huiyuan); 2 (Fashang)	0	1 (Fazang)
sanzhong jingtu 三種淨土 (*zhen jingtu* 真淨土, *xiang jingtu* 相淨土, *shi jingtu* 事淨土)/2	1	0	0	1 (Huiyuan)	0	0
shengwen shidi 聲聞十地/15	1	0	0	1 (*Dasheng tongxing jing*)	0	1 (Zhiyan); 1 (Wŏnch'ŭk); 1 (Zhizhou); 1 (Xifu); 1 (Jiandengzhi)

Term	T2805	Paramārtha	Authors in the South, 440–600: Baoliang, Fayun, Zhiyi, Jizang, Huiying, Huida, Huijun	Authors in the North, 440–590: Bodhiruci, Huiyuan, Tanyan (Including Narendrayaśas, Dharmagupta, Jinagupta, and so on)	Before 440: Zhu Fonian, Kumārajīva, Dharmakṣema	After 600 (Until the End of Tang Dynasty Only)
suiwang sheng 隨妄生/5	1	0	0	1 (Huiyuan)	0	0
suiwang 隨妄/463	2	0	1 (Guṇabhadra); 4 (Zhiyi)	40 (Huiyuan); 5 (*Tanyan shu*); 1 (Bodhiruci); 1 (*Awakening of Faith*); 1 (*Shi moheyan lun*);	0	2 (Xuanzang); 1 (Wŏnhyo); 8 (Fazang)
yijie benyuan 依藉本願→ 依藉/9	1	0	0	1 (Huiyuan)	0	0
yijie benyuan 依藉本願→ (*yi* 依or *jie* 藉) before (5) *benyuan* 本願/64	1	0	0	5 (Bodhiruci: "*yi benyuan li* 依本願力"); 4 (Tanmoliuzhi 曇摩流支); 2 (*Zhancha shan'e yebao jing*)	0	54
yukejian 餘可見/14	2	0	0	1 (Fashang)	0	1 (Daoxian 道暹); 4 (Zhanran and Zhiyan 智嚴: "*li yu kejian* 例餘可見")

Second, it is striking that the terms in this table are so frequently used by both the author of T2805 and Buddhist figures such as Huiyuan, Tanyan, Fashang, and Narendrayaśas, who were all eminent monks in Chang'an at the end of the sixth century (approximately 580–600). This, I argue in the next section, is another crucial clue concerning the composition of T2805.

3.9 Possible Contact with Huiyuan

What is prominent from Table 3.24 is the close relation between T2805 and the works of Huiyuan. From the terminological perspective, it seems as though T2805 has adopted some vocabulary from Huiyuan. In particular, attention should be paid to three phrases.

3.9.1 The Notion of "Arising by Adjusting to Falsity" (*suiwang sheng* 隨妄生)

At first sight, it is not easy to tell whether the phrase *suiwang sheng* in T2805 originated in the south or the north, as the phrase *suiwang* appears in texts from both areas. The passage from T2805 reads:

> (Quotation 3.1)
> [*Shelun*:] "All dharmas have consciousnesses as their marks (*xiang* 相) and Thusness as their substance (*ti* 體)."
>
> [T2805:] The sentences beginning with "*he'yigu* 何以故" constitute the fourth paragraph. Here [it is shown that], although all dharmas are different from the Reality (*zhen* 真; i.e., Thusness) based on the conventional truth, [based on the ultimate truth] only consciousness exists. Because of this, if we take consciousnesses as the marks (i.e., appearance) [of all dharmas] and the perception (*zheng* 證) of the Reality as the realization (*wu* 悟) [into all dharmas], then the only thing that exists is Thusness, where there is no difference between object (i.e., Thusness) and *jñāna* (i.e., the *jñāna* about Thusness) (*jingzhi wu chabie* 境智無差別) Other than this (i.e., Thusness) no dharma exists. What is different from Thusness exists only at the conventional level, like an illusory rabbit,[54] which has no substance other than Thusness and hence is not different from Thusness. Hence they (i.e., those which are different from Thusness) have Thusness as their substance.
>
> Now if we follow (*ruozuo* 若作) the doctrine of "arising by adjusting to falsity" (*suiwang sheng* 隨妄生), then this means that, once the consciousnesses recede (*shixi* 識息) and falsity does not arise, such is Thusness. Therefore, all dharmas have Thusness as their substance. Nothing other than this Thusness can serve as the substance."[55]

The first thing to note here is that the phrase "*ruozuo* 若作 NEAR (within the range of 5 Chinese characters) *yi* 義" is not found in the north before the works translated by

Prabhākaramitra, who arrived in Chang'an in 627. In contrast, this phrase appears in the works of southern authors, such as Zhiyi (nineteen times), Jizang (thirteen times), and Huiying 慧影 (one time). This phrase is used typically when the author is referring to the doctrines of other masters. It means something to the effect of, "If we follow someone else's doctrine, then [what I said before] would mean so-and-so."[56]

Thus, when T2805 states, "If we follow the doctrine of 'arising by adjusting to falsity,'" this indicates that the author is citing the doctrine of another person. And here "someone else" is undoubtedly Huiyuan. I make this suggestion not because the *Dasheng qixin lun yishu*, traditionally attributed to Huiyuan, is the only text that uses the exact phrase *suiwang sheng*. In fact, a strong argument can be made against the attribution of this work to Huiyuan.[57] Rather, I attribute this doctrine to Huiyuan because he is the author who uses phrases similar to *suiwang sheng* the most frequently. These include: *suiwang zhuan* 隨妄轉 (at least five times), *suiwang liuzhuan* 隨妄流轉 (at least six times), *suiwang qi* 隨妄起 (one time), *suiwang jiqi* 隨妄集起 (one time). All these phrases suggest a similar sense of "arising/evolving by adjusting to falsity," which is exactly what *suiwang sheng* means in T2805. Moreover, the term *suiwang liuzhuan* 隨妄流轉 also appears twice in Tanyan. In contrast, none of these terms appear in any work composed in southern China.

Hence, it seems likely that there was some contact between the author of T2805 and Huiyuan. Given that T2805 appears to be citing the doctrine of others and that Huiyuan mentions this notion of "arising by adjusting to falsity" several times in at least four of his works, it is most likely that T2805 has borrowed this idea from Huiyuan, not the other way around. It is significant to note that T2805 employs this concept in a context different from Huiyuan's original notion.[58]

Note that the notion of *suiwang sheng* disappeared soon after Huiyuan, except in the writings of Huayan 華嚴 masters such as Li Tongxuan, Fazang, and Chengguan. Since T2805 ought to predate these authors, it cannot borrow the phrase *suiwang sheng* from them.

3.9.2 The Three Kinds of Pure Lands (*sanzhong jingtu* 三種淨土)

It is striking that, out of the whole Chinese Buddhist canon, only T2805 and Huiyuan's *Dasheng yizhang* 大乘義章 mention three kinds of pure lands. Comparing the two accounts, however, I find the two texts understand the three pure lands differently. Here I begin with T2805:

> (Quotation 3.2)
> A pure land of truth (*zhen jingtu* 真淨土) must have the enjoyment-body [residing] there. All the stages beginning with the first bodhisattva stage belong to the pure land of truth. The level before the first bodhisattva stage is the pure land of marks (*xiang jingtu* 相淨土). The level of "ten confidences" (*shixin* 十信) belongs to the pure land of matters (*shi jingtu* 事淨土). For example, the pure land of Maitreya (etc.), belongs to pure land of matters. This is because people such as the Hearers (Ch. *shengwen* 聲聞; Skt. *śrāvaka*), etc., have not [realized]

> equality, and hence still think about purity in terms of the differences among matters. Ordinary people, i.e., people of lower rank, see the defiled land (*huitu* 穢土).[59]

According to this passage, there are four types of lands: one defiled and three pure: (1) The defiled land, which ordinary people see and in which they dwell; (2) The pure land of matters, which practitioners at the lowest stages of the bodhisattva path (the ten stages of confidences [*shixin* 十信]), the Hearers (*śrāvaka*) and the Solitary Realizers (*pratyekabuddha*) see and in which they dwell; (3) The pure land of marks (*xiang jingtu* 相淨土), which bodhisattvas above the ten stages of confidences (between the stages of the ten abidings [*shizhu* 十住] and before the first bodhisattva stage) see and in which they dwell; (4) The pure land of truth (*zhen jingtu* 真淨土), which practitioners at or above the first bodhisattva stage perceive and in which they dwell.

In contrast, Huiyuan understands the correspondences between the three pure lands and the three vehicles differently: (1) Ordinary people in the pure land of matters; (2) The Hearers and the Solitary Realizers in the pure land of marks; (3) Bodhisattvas in the pure land of truth.[60] The differences between T2805 and Huiyuan are summarized in Table 3.25.

Postdating both T2805 and Huiyuan's lifetime, Zhiyan posits the existence of four pure lands. Although Zhiyan uses different terms for some of the three pure lands accepted by T2805 and Huiyuan, they are basically the same. Zhiyan adds a fourth, the pure land of transformation (*hua jingtu* 化淨土).[61]

Given that the three pure lands with the same names appear only in Huiyuan and T2805, there was probably some link between them. It is difficult to determine the direction of borrowing, although both Zhiyan and Daoshi 道世 (?–683) mention Paramārtha's *Shelun* when they discuss the four kinds of pure lands.[62] Therefore, it seems possible that it is Huiyuan who borrowed the notion of three kinds of pure lands from T2805. But, in any case, this indicates some contact between the author of T2805 and Huiyuan, as well as other Buddhist figures in northern China.

Table 3.25 Three Kinds of Pure Lands According to T2805 and Huiyuan

	T2805	**Huiyuan**
defiled land (*huitu* 穢土)	ordinary people	
pure land of matters (*shi jingtu* 事淨土)	The lowest stage of the bodhisattva path (the ten stages of confidences [*shixin* 十信]), the Hearers and the Solitary Realizers	ordinary people
pure land of marks (*xiang jingtu* 相淨土)	Bodhisattvas above the ten stages of confidences (between the stages of the ten abidings [*shizhu* 十住] and the first bodhisattva stage)	The Hearers and the Solitary Realizers
pure land of truth (*zhen jingtu* 真淨土)	Practitioners at or above the first bodhisattva stage	bodhisattvas

3.9.3 Reverse Permeation (*huanxun* 還熏)

"Reverse permeation" is a notion specific to Yogācāra philosophy that signifies the mutual relation between the base consciousness (i.e., the storehouse consciousness) and what arises from the base consciousness, that is, the mental representations that are mistaken as cognitive objects. Ordinary people are so deluded that they do not realize that what they regard as externally real objects are merely mental representations projected out of the base consciousness. But, for the very reason that these representations are mistaken as real, they arouse further attachments that can permeate their source in reverse, that is, the base consciousness, and produce further seeds. From these reversely permeated seeds, still further mental representations arise and cause further delusion and more reverse permeation, ad infinitum. And it is precisely this two-way movement—the representations arising out of the base consciousness and the reverse permeation of the base consciousness by those representations—that makes this cycle endless. As T2805 puts it:

> (Quotation 3.3)
> [*Shelun*:] Because of the existence of the defiled mentation (*ranwu shi* 染污識; i.e., the *kliṣṭa-manas*) and with their basis in self-view (*wojian* 我見), etc., the permeation of "I," "mine," etc., in the base consciousness (*benshi* 本識, i.e., the storehouse consciousness).
>
> [T2805:] Beginning with this, we have the brief explanation of the second *zhang* 章, namely, the *zhang* of "permeation by self-view."
>
> The self-view arises because the *tuona* 陀那 (i.e., the *atuona* 阿陀那, here referring to the seventh consciousness, i.e., the *kliṣṭa-manas*) grasps the *liye* 梨耶 (i.e., the storehouse consciousness) as the self, and from this arises the distinction between self and other. By this [seventh consciousness] the sixth consciousness becomes defiled so that the attachment to self also arises in the sixth consciousness. What defiles is the *atuona shi* 阿陀那識; and what is defiled is the mental consciousness (i.e., the sixth consciousness). After the sixth consciousness [is defiled,] the self-view then arises based on the [seventh and the sixth] consciousnesses and causes two kinds of mental representations (Ch.: *shi* 識; Skt. *vijñapti*)—i.e., the attachment to the self (*wozhi* 我執) and what is seen by the self (*wosuojian* 我所見) to arise from the base consciousness—and then permeates reversely the base consciousness. Because of these seeds in the base consciousness, the retribution of the different bodies between self and other ensues.[63]

This idea is not completely missing from Paramārtha's work.[64] But Paramārtha does not use the term "reverse permeation" in any of his translations. Moreover, the term *huanxun* is also found in the *Dasheng zhiguan famen* (four times) and the *Tanyan shu* (one time), both of which were composed in the north and are related to the *Awakening of Faith*. Furthermore, T2805 also uses the related phrase *huanfu xunxi* 還復熏習, while another similar phrase, *huanfu xun* 還復熏, appears, again, only in the *Dasheng zhiguan famen*.[65] Nevertheless, it is also true that T2805 does not always express this idea with the term *huanxun* or *huanfu xunxi*.[66]

To conclude, because T2805 includes a few particular notions that were prominent in Huiyuan's works, I suggest that it is likely that T2805, although its author was from the south, was composed after its author had some contact with Huiyuan.

3.10 Likelihood of Contact with the Buddhist Tradition in the North

In addition to its probable contact with Huiyuan in the north, T2805 also shows familiarity with some specifically northern notions and terms.

3.10.1 The Ten Bodhisattva Stages of the Hearers' Vehicle (*shengwen shidi* 聲聞十地)

T2805 quotes a list of the ten bodhisattva stages of the Hearers (*shengwen shidi* 聲聞十地) from the *Dasheng tongxing jing* 大乘同性經 (*The Scripture on the Coming Together [of All Sentient Beings]*, **Mahāyānābhisamaya-sūtra*; T673), translated in the north by Jīnagupta and Seng An 僧安 (d.u.) between 566 and 571.[67] T2805 appears to be the only text that quotes the complete list.[68] Although the *Dasheng tongxing jing* was translated in the north, we cannot be sure that it was circulated only in the north. Southern authors also refer to this scripture, for example, Zhiyi (one time) and Jizang (five times).

3.10.2 *Liushi xin* 六識心: T2805 and the Interpolated Explanation of the FXL

The compound "mind-mentation-consciousness" (*citta-manas-vijñāna*) occurs frequently in Yogācāra texts. The common interpretation of the compound is that "mind" refers to the storehouse consciousness, "mentation" to defiled mentation (*kliṣṭa-manas*), and "consciousness" to the six consciousnesses.[69] However, the interpolated explanation[70] in the FXL reverses the order:

> (Quotation 3.4)
> Explanation: "mind" refers to the mind as the six consciousnesses (*liushi xin* 六識心); "mentation" refers to the *atuona shi* 阿陀那識 (*ādāna-vijñāna*; the seventh consciousness); "consciousness" refers to the storehouse consciousness.[71]

Incidentally, T2805 also includes the term *liushi xin* 六識心.[72] A search of this term *liushi xin* 六識心 with CBReader 2007 shows that this term was popular exclusively around 590 in Chang'an, where it was used by Huiyuan, Tanyan, and Fashang. It is therefore not impossible that the interpolated explanation in the FXL was added to the original text in Chang'an, and that T2805 was composed there. Although the fact that some northern works include the term *atuona shi* with the same meaning as used by Paramārtha, thus proving that the connection between T2805 and Paramārtha is not exclusive, it indicates that the earliest spread of Paramārtha's distinctive teaching was in northern China. The term *liushi xin* in both T2805 and the interpolated explanation in FXL also seems to support this affiliation between T2805 and other Buddhist figures in the north.

3.10.3 *Lineng* 力能 ("Power and Capability")

Finally, the contact between T2805 and the north, especially with Huiyuan, can also be supported by the use in T2805 of the term *lineng* 力能 in the sense of "power and capability." This usage is extremely rare. More often, the meaning of capability is expressed in the south by the term *liyong* 力用 ("the functioning of power").[73] Thus, it seems likely that this term was borrowed by T2805 from elsewhere.

It is very difficult to trace this special usage of *lineng*, as almost all occurrences of this term, in which *neng* functions as an auxiliary verb instead of a noun, have a different meaning. As far as I can find, the only two examples of this usage of *lineng* appear in the *Yuedeng sanmei jing* 月燈三昧經 (*Samādhirāja-sūtra*, *The Scripture on the King of Samādhi*; T639),[74] translated by Narendrayaśas in 557.[75] Narendrayaśas was an Indian translator deeply involved in the northern Buddhist tradition from the middle of the sixth century until his death in 589. Throughout his long career in China, it is noteworthy that he stayed in Daxingshan Temple 大興善寺 in Chang'an from 582 to 589, a period when Huiyuan was also in Chang'an.

To conclude, all the aforementioned examples converge to form a coherent picture of the composition of T2805. It was composed when its author—apparently a southerner—had some contact with Buddhism in Chang'an around 590. In particular, the author shows familiarity with the writings of Huiyuan. This will be crucial to my discussion in Chapter 5 of the probable author of T2805.

3.11 Conclusion

In this chapter, based on a detailed investigation of the terms and phrases employed in T2805, I have made three important points. (1) T2805 is closely tied to Paramārtha's translations, especially to his *Suixiang lun*. (2) The author of T2805 came from southern China. (3) Nevertheless, a few anomalous details suggest that T2805 was composed after its author had some contact with Buddhism in northern China around 590, especially with Huiyuan.

In Chapter 5, I shall review all the available historical information about Paramārtha's Chinese disciples and Buddhism in Chang'an around 590. I shall suggest that T2805 was probably composed in Chang'an around 590–600 by one of Paramārtha's direct disciples, who was from southern China but later moved to Chang'an.

As I have suggested, the philological evidence is not conclusive because texts that are no longer extant may have contained contradictory testimonies. To compensate for this problem, I shall demonstrate in the following chapter that T2805 also has a very close doctrinal connection with other works by Paramārtha.

4

Doctrinal Coherence between T2805 and the Works of Paramārtha

In the previous chapter, through a comparison of the terminology in T2805 and contemporary works, I have shown that T2805 seems very similar to works by Paramārtha. In this chapter, I further investigate the doctrinal agreement between T2805 and the works of Paramārtha.

As I mentioned earlier, T2805 does not present an argument for particular theses but is instead a selective commentary on Paramārtha's *Shelun*. For this reason, specific doctrinal points are made here and there, without a systematic framework. We have to be careful when identifying its characteristic doctrines.

4.1 The Compound Mind-Mentation-Consciousnesses (*xinyishi* 心意識)

A piece of evidence that shows the affinity between T2805 and the works of Paramārtha is the peculiar use of the compound "mind-mentation-consciousness" (Ch. *xinyishi* 心意識; Skt. *citta-manas-vijñāna*). As Takeuchi points out,[1] Paramārtha, in his *Shelun*, seems confused about the notion of *atuona shi* 阿陀那識 (*ādāna-vijñāna*, grasping consciousness). In Asaṅga's MSg as well as in Vasubandhu's MSgBh, *atuona shi* is a synonym for the base consciousness (i.e., the storehouse consciousness). However, in the *Shelun*, Paramārtha sometimes follows Asaṅga and Vasubandhu in identifying the *atuona shi* with the base consciousness,[2] but at other times he identifies it with defiled mentation (Ch. *ranwu yi* 染污意; Skt. *kliṣṭa-manas*). The identification of the base consciousness with defiled mentation is characteristic of Paramārtha and deserves more attention.[3]

To begin, the following passages from the MSg and the MSgBh unequivocally claim that, for both Asaṅga and Vasubandhu, *atuona shi* is a synonym for the base consciousness:

(Quotation 4.1)
Asaṅga's MSg (Xuanzang's translation):
Furthermore, this consciousness (i.e., the storehouse consciousness) is also named the *atuona shi* 阿陀那識 (*ādāna-vijñāna*). . . . For what reason is this consciousness also taught to have the name *atuona shi*? Because it appropriates all

the corporeal sense faculties (Ch. *zhishou yiqie youse gen* 執受一切有色根; Skt. **sarvarūpīndriyopādāna*) and because it is the basis for all kinds of appropriation as one's own existence (Ch. *yiqie ziti qu suoyi* 一切自體取所依; Skt. **sarvātmabhāvopādānāśraya*).[4]
Vasubandhu's MSgBh (Xuanzang's translation):
Due to this sense, the *alaiye shi* (*ālayavijñāna*) is also named as the *atuona shi*.[5]

In the case of the *Shelun*, however, Paramārtha hesitates to identify *atuona shi* with the base consciousness. Sometimes, Paramārtha follows Vasubandhu's original text and asserts that *atuona shi* is a synonym for the storehouse consciousness:

(Quotation 4.2)
Paramārtha's *Shelun*:
Explanation: Now I shall make an argument to establish the name *atuona*. . . . Due to this sense, the *aliye shi* 阿梨耶識 (storehouse consciousness) is also named *atuona shi*.[6]

Just a few lines later, however, Paramārtha says something different. Here Asaṅga adduces the compound "mind-mentation-consciousness" (*citta-mano-vijñāna*) as evidence that "mind" (*citta*) is a synonym for the base consciousness (and hence for the *atuona shi*).[7] In this context, Paramārtha claims that *atuona shi* is a synonym for one of the two kinds of mentation, namely, defiled mentation:

(Quotation 4.3)
Asaṅga's MSg:
Second, there is the defiled mentation (*kliṣṭa-manas*) that always corresponds to four kinds of affliction.
Paramārtha's *Shelun*: (Paramārtha's interpolation)
This is where the author [of the MSg] wants to explain the *atuona shi*.[8]

As mentioned earlier, both Asaṅga and Vasubandhu explain that *atuona shi* is a synonym for storehouse consciousness, which is identified with the mind (*citta*) in the compound "mind-mentation-consciousness." Thus, it is obvious that Paramārtha here is deviating from both Asaṅga and Vasubandhu.

In fact, it is a distinctive feature of Paramārtha's translations that *atuona shi* stands for the seventh consciousness, that is, the consciousness between the storehouse consciousness and the six consciousnesses. According to classical Yogācāra teaching, the role of the seventh consciousness is to mistakenly "grasp" the storehouse consciousness as an enduring self. For this reason, the seventh consciousness is usually regarded as the origin of the false view about the existence of a self.[9]

Paramārtha is quite consistent in calling the seventh consciousness *atuona shi*.[10] In doing so, he changes the original sense of this term. Originally, Asaṅga explains that the storehouse consciousness is also called *ādāna-vijñāna* because it "can grasp all the corporeal sense faculties and because it is the basis for appropriating the entire basis of personal existence (i.e., the physical body)."[11] For Paramārtha, however, "grasping/appropriating" (*ādāna/upādāna*) refers instead to the grasping of the storehouse consciousness by the seventh consciousness, that is, defiled mentation. Here Paramārtha probably was reading a later development into the earlier term *ādāna-vijñāna* because the idea that the seventh consciousness "grasps" the storehouse consciousness is totally missing from the *Saṃdhinirmocana-sūtra*, where the term *ādāna-vijñāna* first appears as a synonym for the storehouse consciousness.[12] The idea that the seventh consciousness grasps the storehouse consciousness and mistakes it as the self can be found in later works such as the CWSL.[13]

As for T2805, it is striking that it depicts the *atuona shi* in exactly the same way as Paramārtha does in the *Shelun*. Quotation 3.3 testifies to this, and the following two passages also testify to this agreement:

(Quotation 4.4) (cf. quotation 3.3)
The self-view arises because the *tuona* 陀那 (i.e., the *atuona* 阿陀那, here referring to the seventh consciousness, i.e., the *kliṣṭa-manas*) grasps the *liye* 梨耶 (i.e., the storehouse consciousness) as the self, and from this arises the distinction between self and other. . . . By this [seventh consciousness] the sixth consciousness becomes defiled so that the attachment to self also arises in the sixth consciousness. What defiles is the *atuona shi* 阿陀那識; and what is defiled is the mental consciousness (i.e., the sixth consciousness):[14]

(Quotation 4.5)
Because the *tuona* (i.e., the *ādāna-vijñāna*) cannot fully penetrate into the Principle (*li* 理), it defiles the sixth consciousness by [defilements] such as the attachment to the self (*wozhi* 我執) [that arises due to the *ādāna-vijñāna*'s] grasping the *liye* (i.e., the storehouse consciousness) [as the self], and obstructs [the sixth consciousness] from penetrating into the Principle.[15]

It should be emphasized again that the ascription to *atuona shi* (as the seventh consciousness) of the role of grasping the storehouse consciousness is distinctive of Paramārtha's translation. Paramārtha seems to have been the first to introduce this idea to China. The fact that T2805 and Paramārtha in his *Shelun* agree about the meaning of *atuona shi* also reveals their affinity.

However, T2805 is not the only text that agrees with Paramārtha's *Shelun* about the meaning of *atuona shi*. This notion is found in a few other texts from northern China in the late sixth to early seventh centuries, including the *Bashi yi* in Huiyuan's *Dasheng yizhang*[16] and *Tanyan shu*.[17] Both texts accept Paramārtha's view of the *atuona shi*. In addition, the notion *atuona shi* also appears in T2807[18] and T2808.

4.2 The Disclosing Cause (*liaoyin* 了因)

In the *Shelun*, Paramārtha uses a special notion, "disclosing cause" (*liaoyin* 了因),[19] to describe the relationship between the path of [cultivating] antidotes (Ch. *duizhi dao* 對治道; Skt. **pratipakṣa-bhāvanā*[20]) and the transformation of the basis:

(Quotation 4.6)

Secondly, the antidote is the disclosing cause (*liaoyin* 了因) of the transformation of the basis. It is not the substance of the transformation of the basis (*zhuanyi ti* 轉依體). The antidote is the noble truth of the path (Ch. *daodi* 道諦; Skt. *mārga-satya*). The transformed basis is liberation and the dharma-body and hence is the noble truth of the cessation of suffering (Ch. *miedi* 滅諦; Skt. *nirodha-satya*). The destruction of seeds should be taken as the transformation of the basis.[21]

T2805 is the only extant text that comments on this passage using the same terminology and also an identical line of argumentation.[22] As it states:

(Quotation 4.7)

[*Shelun:*] "Secondly, the antidote is the disclosing cause."

[T2805:] This means: when the path of [cultivating] antidotes (Ch. *duizhi dao* 對治道; Skt. *pratipakṣa-bhāvanā*) in the sixth consciousness[23] arises, then the worldly (*shijian* 世間) sixth consciousness ceases. If the base consciousness does not exist, then there is no seed that can be destroyed. This is because originally (*ben* 本) we claim that, once the seeds in the base consciousness are destroyed, the base consciousness is transformed and have the dharma-body as its [new] basis. Hence the path of [cultivating] antidotes [*zhidao* 治道; a short form for *duizhi dao* 對治道] is the disclosing cause. The right [way] (*zheng* 正) is to take the base consciousness as the substance (*ti* 體) of the transformation of the basis. The right [way] is to take the correct meaning [of the "transformation of the basis" as follows]: when the unwholesome seeds are destroyed, the base consciousness becomes liberated and attains (*zhengde* 證得) the dharma-body and takes the dharma-body as its [new] basis. This is different from the case before [the transformation of the basis], when [the base consciousness] has the "dharmas of birth and death" (*shengsi fa* 生死法) as its basis. [Such a transformation from having the "dharmas of birth and death" as basis to having the dharma-body as the basis] is called the "transformation of the basis [of the base consciousness]."[24]

It is necessary to further explore the exact meaning of the term "disclosing cause," which is not very clear from the previous passage. The contrast between *liaoyin* 了因 and *shengyin* 生因 (generative cause)[25] was first introduced in China by Dharmakṣema in his translation of *Mahāparinirvāṇa-mahāsūtra*. Later, this contrast was current in both the south and the north, especially in the works of Baoliang and Huiyuan.

Paramārtha's understanding of the disclosing cause can be seen in his FXL, in a discussion of the "child of the Buddha."

(Quotation 4.8) (See quotation 5.4)

Such a person can be properly denominated as the child of the Buddha. Therefore, there are four aspects that can be discussed regarding this child of the Buddha: (1) cause; (2) condition; (3) basis; (4) accomplishment. First, what is meant by "cause" includes two: first, the *buddha-gotra* (*foxing* 佛性); second, the aspiration from confidence (*xinle* 信樂).[26] Between these two, the *buddha-gotra* is unconditioned;

> whereas the aspiration from confidence is conditioned. The aspiration from confidence serves as the "disclosing cause" (Ch. *liaoyin* 了因; Skt. **vyañjana-hetu* or **jñāpaka-hetu*) for the innate *buddha-gotra* (Ch. *xingde foxing* 性得佛性; Skt. *prakṛtistha-gotra*) because it discloses the *buddha-gotra* that is the cause proper (Ch. *zhengyin* 正因). The aspiration from confidence serves as the "generative cause" (Ch. *shengyin* 生因; Skt. *kāraṇa-hetu*) for applied practices (Ch. *jiaxing* 加行; Skt. *prayoga*) because it brings about various kinds of practices.[27]

Based on the contrast between disclosing cause and generative cause in this passage, we can infer that the disclosing cause is not the cause that gives birth to or produces the effect. Instead, it discloses what is either already there or what is produced by something else. According to this passage, the innate *buddha-gotra* that resides within one's consciousness is already there. It is unconditioned (*asaṃskṛta*) and hence is not generated by anything. The aspiration from confidence and the applied practices that it directly generates merely remove ignorance and afflictions, which hide the *buddha-gotra* that is already present.

The idea found in Paramārtha's *Shelun*, as well as in T2805, that the antidotes belong to the noble truth of the path (*daodi* 道諦) but not to the noble truth of the cessation (*miedi* 滅諦), is supported by another passage from the FXL, where it is said that three dharmas—purification, disclosing cause, and antidotes—all belong to the noble truth of the path:

> (Quotation 4. 9)
> Further, it should be known that the transformation of the basis (*zhuanyi* 轉依) of the Buddha is contained and maintained (*shechi* 攝持) by eight dharmas. These eight are: (1) being inconceivable; (2) being non-dual; (3) being without discrimination; (4) purification; (5) illuminating cause (*zhaoliao yin* 照了因; i.e., the disclosing cause); (6) antidote; (7) freedom from desire; (8) the cause for the freedom from desire. Taken together, these eight have two meanings: one is the freedom from desire (i.e., [7]), which is the noble truth of the cessation of sufferings; the other is the cause for the freedom from desire (i.e., [8]), which is the noble truth of the path. The first three items, "being inconceivable," etc. belong to the noble truth of the cessation of sufferings. The following three items, "purification," etc. belong to the noble truth of the path.[28]

The basic tenet here is the contrast between the noble truth of cessation and the noble truth of the path. As an unconditioned dharma, the noble truth of cessation is characterized by three attributes: (1) being inconceivable, (2) being non-dual, and (3) being without discrimination. It is permanent (*nitya*) and hence is not produced by anything. The noble truth of the path is conditioned, serving three functions: (4) purification, (5) illuminating cause, and (6) antidote. It leads to the noble truth of cessation and functions only to disclose the noble truth of cessation. Here the illuminating cause is obviously what is called the disclosing cause in both the *Shelun* and T2805.

To conclude, T2805 remains the only extant text from around the year 600, besides Paramārtha's *Shelun* and FXL, that asserts that the antidotes (i.e., the applied practices/cultivation) serve as the disclosing cause of the transformation of the basis.[29] This means that the practices only disclose the dharma-body, which serves as the new basis, but do not produce it.[30] The fact that T2805 is the only text other than the works of Paramārtha that makes this assertion again confirms the close relationship between T2805 and Paramārtha.

4.3 Realization of the Dharma-Body at the First Bodhisattva Stage

In addition to the examples given earlier, where T2805 agrees with Paramārtha's notions in the *Shelun* that were not widely shared by other texts, it is striking that T2805 agrees with Paramārtha's *Shelun* even when Paramārtha deviates from Asaṅga's original text. In this section, I first highlight two different views about the stages of practice, Asaṅga's and Paramārtha's,[31] that are discussed in Paramārtha's *Shelun*. Then I show that T2805 agrees with Paramārtha's own positions, and I argue for the affinity between T2805 and Paramārtha.

The disagreement between Asaṅga and Paramārtha concerns the attainment of the dharma-body. Asaṅga asserts that the dharma-body is attained at the end of the tenth bodhisattva stage, while Paramārtha states that it is attained upon entering the first bodhisattva stage.[32]

Asaṅga, in the last chapter of the MSg, explains how the dharma-body can be attained (*zhengde* 證得). According to passages in that chapter, the attainment of the dharma-body occurs at the end of the tenth bodhisattva stage, that is, when the practitioner has passed through all ten bodhisattva stages and achieved the diamond-like concentration (*vajropamasamādhi*), and when the ultimate "transformation of the basis" occurs:[33]

> (Quotation 4.10) Asaṅga's MSg: (Based on the Tibetan translation) (Cf. quotation 7.2)
> How, then, is this dharma-body initially attained through contact (Tib: *reg pas thog ma nyid du thob*; Xuanzang: *zuichu zhengde* 最初證得;)?[34] [It is attained] through the undiscriminating and subsequently-acquired *jñāna*. These have the unified doctrine of the Mahāyāna as their object; they have cultivated the five aspects well; and have properly accumulated the equipment in all the stages [leading to buddhahood]. [It is attained] by the diamond-like concentration, since [that concentration] destroys the subtle obstacles that are difficult to destroy. Because it is separated from all obstacles immediately after [attaining] that concentration, [the dharma-body] is thus attained through the transformation of the basis. (A modification of the translation of Griffiths et al. (1989): 93, section C)[35]

In contrast, some passages in Paramārtha's *Shelun* suggest that the dharma-body is attained at the first bodhisattva stage:

> (Quotation 4.11)
> At the Stage of Insight (*jianwei* 見位), a bodhisattva has already attained the dharma-body of the Tathāgatas.[36]

Here the "Stage of Insight" is apparently an abbreviation of "the stage of the Path of Insight" (Ch. *jiandao wei* 見道位; Skt. *darśana-mārga*), which is equivalent to the first bodhisattva stage according to Paramārtha's *Shelun*[37] and other Mahāyāna texts.

The conflict between these two different views can be resolved by comparing Paramārtha's *Shelun* with the other Chinese translations and the Tibetan translations. According to all three Chinese translations, the dharma-body is attained at the end of the tenth bodhisattva stage. Therefore, Asaṅga must have espoused this view in the original MSg. The alternate view, that the dharma-body is attained at the first bodhisattva stage, is peculiar to Paramārtha. Quotation 4.10 is found in all other translations and hence must belong to Asaṅga's original text, but quotation 4.11 is missing from other translations and was likely to have been inserted by Paramārtha. In other words, when Paramārtha follows Asaṅga's original text, the *Shelun* states that the dharma-body is attained at the end of the tenth bodhisattva stage, but Paramārtha also inserted his own ideas into his *Shelun*.

4.3.1 Paramārtha: Dharma-Body Includes Both Thusness and the Undiscriminating *Jñāna* about Thusness

Paramārtha's reason for stating that the dharma-body is attained at the first bodhisattva stage is closely tied to his definition of dharma-body.[38] According to Paramārtha, the dharma-body includes both Thusness and the undiscriminating *jñāna* about Thusness. For example, Paramārtha inserts a statement into his *Shelun* to the effect that Thusness and the undiscriminating *jñāna* about Thusness (*zhenru ji zhenzhi* 真如及真智)[39] are called the dharma-body.[40] Immediately following this, he also explains that the Buddha-dharmas (i.e., merits belonging to the Buddhas) have the dharma-body as their basis because they are not separated from purity and perfect undiscriminating *jñāna* (*qingjing ji yuanzhi* 清淨及圓智), which Paramārtha glosses as Thusness and the undiscriminating *jñāna* about Thusness (*ruru ruruzhi* 如如如如智).[41]

Here the undiscriminating *jñāna* about Thusness has Thusness as its sole cognitive object. This idea that the dharma-body includes both Thusness and the undiscriminating *jñāna* about Thusness is also found in Paramārtha's translation of the chapter on the Distinction among the Three Bodies (*Sanshen fenbie pin* 三身分別品) in the *Suvarṇaprabhāsottama-sūtra* (*Jin'guangming jing* 金光明經, T664), the Sanskrit text of which is lost. There it is also stated that only Thusness and the undiscriminating *jñāna* about Thusness (*ruru ruru zhi* 如如如如智) are called the dharma-body.[42]

The reason that the dharma-body includes both Thusness and the undiscriminating *jñāna* about Thusness is that the distinction between the subject (*grāhaka*) and object (*grāhya*) is eliminated there. In other words, Thusness and the undiscriminating *jñāna* about Thusness are necessarily undifferentiated, as Paramārtha says in his *Shelun*.[43]

Based on the definition of the dharma-body in terms of both Thusness and the undiscriminating *jñāna* about Thusness, we can now see why Paramārtha maintains that the dharma-body is attained at the first bodhisattva stage. This is because, according to Paramārtha, a bodhisattva attains the undiscriminating *jñāna* about Thusness upon entering the first bodhisattva stage.[44] As a consequence, Paramārtha also claims that one attains the insight into Thusness at the first bodhisattva stage.[45] All this explains why, for Paramārtha, one attains the dharma-body at the first bodhisattva stage.

In contrast, Asaṅga does not identify Thusness with the dharma-body. Asaṅga argues for the identity of Thusness and the Dharma-element, and, for this reason, he does not claim that the dharma-body is attained at the first bodhisattva stage.[46] It is true for both Asaṅga and Paramārtha that one acquires undiscriminating *jñāna* and hence attains the insight into Thusness at the first bodhisattva stage. The difference is that, for Asaṅga, Thusness is not identified with the dharma-body.

To summarize, two different views are found in Paramārtha's *Shelun* regarding the bodhisattva stage at which the dharma-body is attained: Asaṅga's original view is that the dharma-body is attained at the end of the tenth bodhisattva stage; Paramārtha's interpolated view is that it is attained at the first bodhisattva stage.

4.3.2 T2805: The Dharma-Body Is Attained at the First Bodhisattva Stage

Even more striking than Paramārtha's disagreement with Asaṅga's position in MSg is the fact that T2805 agrees with Paramārtha's contrary view that the dharma-body is attained at the first bodhisattva stage:

> (Quotation 4.12)
> At the first bodhisattva stage, [a bodhisattva] attains the dharma-body that is without the duality [of subject vs. object] in the aspect of Principle (*li* 理), and attains the permanent (Ch. *changzhu* 常住; Skt. *nitya*) dharma-body that is without the duality [of subject vs. object] in the aspect of undiscriminating *jñāna*. Only at this stage [does one attain the] stage of being truly noble (*zhen shengwei* 真聖位), which is different from [what he was before the first bodhisattva stage, i.e., being noble] only by designation (*jiaming* 假名).[47]

> (Quotation 4.13)
> At the first bodhisattva stage, a bodhisattva attains Thusness that is the dharma-body (*zhenru fashen* 真如法身). This is merely the accomplishment of the function (*yong* 用) of his benefits for oneself (Ch. *zili* 自利; Skt. *svārtha*). At the eighth bodhisattva stage, the effortless (Ch. *wugongyong* 無功用; Skt. *anābhoga*) benefits for oneself are attained. At the ninth bodhisattva stage, benefits for others (Ch. *lita* 利他; Skt. *parārtha*) are accomplished by means of the enjoyment-body. At the tenth bodhisattva stage, the function of benefits for others by means of the transformation-body, i.e., to convert the two vehicles, ordinary people, and people of low faculty, is accomplished for the first time. Even at this [tenth] stage, one still has tiny obstructions and attachments. He has not gained sovereignty and is still lower than the Buddhas. Regarding the inducement (*gan* 感) of [the bodies of] the Buddhas: ordinary people, the two vehicles, and the bodhisattvas who are in their beginning practices would induce the transformation-body [of the Buddhas]

(namely, they can only see the transformation-body). After this, [the bodhisattvas] after the [stage of] "Ten merit-transfers" (*shi huiqu* 十迴趣)[48] and above the first bodhisattva stage would induce the enjoyment-body [of the Buddha]. At the first bodhisattva stage, [one] attains (*zheng* 證) the dharma-body.[49]

Thus, T2805 clearly agrees with Paramārtha, even though Paramārtha's view conflicts with Asaṅga's original text. This agreement also confirms the close connection between T2805 and Paramārtha.[50]

However, the idea that the dharma-body is attained while entering the first bodhisattva stage is not found exclusively in T2805 and Paramārtha. It also appears in Huiyuan's *Dasheng yizhang*,[51] in *Tanyan shu*,[52] and in T2807.[53] Moreover, according to Jizang, it seems that both the masters in the north (*beidi lunshi* 北地論師) and the masters who lecture on the *Shelun* (*jiang Shedasheng lunshi* 講攝大乘論師) claim that the dharma-body is attained at the first bodhisattva stage.[54] This perhaps weakens my argument for the connection between T2805 and Paramārtha, although it supports the connection of T2805 to Huiyuan and Tanyan as indicated in 3.9-3.10.

4.4 The Attainment of Benefits for Oneself at the First Bodhisattva Stage

Quotation 4.13 from T2805 provides more support for the affinity between T2805 and Paramārtha because, again, both Paramārtha and T2805 deviate from Asaṅga's original text. Asaṅga says that one attains both benefits for oneself (Ch. *zili* 自利; Skt. *svārtha*) and benefits for others (Ch. *lita* 利他; Skt. *parārtha*) at the first bodhisattva stage.[55] But Paramārtha interpolates into his *Shelun* a few remarks asserting that the attainment of the dharma-body and undiscriminating *jñāna* results only in benefits for oneself, whereas attainment of the other two bodies—the enjoyment-body and the transformation-body—results in benefits for others.[56] Since, according to Paramārtha, the dharma-body and undiscriminating *jñāna* are attained at the first bodhisattva stage, it is clear that it is at this stage that the benefits for oneself are obtained. Similarly, quotation 4.13 from T2805 also claims that only benefits for oneself are attained at the first bodhisattva stage.

As for the idea that the dharma-body is associated with benefits for oneself while the enjoyment-body and transformation-body are associated with benefits for others, Paramārtha seems to have borrowed it from another of his works, the *Foshuo wushangyi jing*:

(Quotation 4.14)
Ānanda, what are the beneficial things (*liyi shi* 利益事) carried out via bodhi? [Bodhi] consists of two kinds of *jñāna*:[57] first, the undiscriminating *jñāna*; second, the subsequently acquired *jñāna* (Ch. *wufenbie houzhi* 無分別後智; Skt. *pṛṣṭha-labdha-nirvikalpa-jñāna*). These two kinds of *jñāna* have (i.e., carry out) two things: first, to attain benefits for oneself; second, to attain benefits for others.

> What does "benefits for oneself" mean? [It means] the perfection of the body of liberation (Ch. *jietuo shen* 解脫身; Skt. *vimukti-kāya*), the maintenance of the pure dharma-body, the destruction of the obstruction related to afflictions (Ch. *fannao zhang* 煩惱障; Skt. *kleśāvaraṇa*) and the obstruction to [the attainment of] omniscience (Ch. *yiqie zhi zhang* 一切智障; Skt. *sarvajñāvaraṇa*). Such are meant by "benefits for oneself." What does "benefits for others" mean? [It means: from the time when one attains] the subsequently acquired *jñāna* all the way till the end of birth and death (i.e., nirvana), without reflection (*buzuo siliang* 不作思量; i.e., spontaneously), manifests [himself] into two kinds of body (i.e., the enjoyment-body and the transformation-body), preaching endless kinds of teachings, without interruption, endlessly. This is for the purpose of liberating all sentient beings from the sufferings due to the birth and death in the three bad destinies (i.e., hell beings, hungry ghosts, animals), of settling them in the good destinies and having them dwell in the places of the three vehicles. This means "benefits for others."[58]

Here the *Foshuo wushangyi jing* clearly connects benefits for oneself to the dharma-body and undiscriminating *jñāna*, while it connects benefits for others to the enjoyment-body and the transformation-body and the subsequently acquired *jñāna*. Paramārtha interpolates this contrast into his *Shelun* when he claims that only benefits for oneself are attained at the first bodhisattva stage since the dharma-body and the undiscriminating *jñāna* are attained at this stage.

To conclude, Paramārtha's *Shelun* provides conflicting claims about whether only benefits for oneself or benefits for both oneself and others are attained at the first bodhisattva stage. Quotation 4.13 from T2805 clearly states that only benefits for oneself are obtained at the first bodhisattva stage. Here, T2805 again agrees with one of Paramārtha's positions that deviate from Asaṅga.[59] This again indicates the affinity between T2805 and Paramārtha.

4.5 The Enjoyment-Body of the Buddha

In addition to the examples given earlier, T2805 also sheds light on a puzzling passage in the *Shelun*, where Paramārtha deviates from Vasubandhu's original text. The issue here is the difference between the essence-body (*svābhāvika-kāya*) and the enjoyment-body. Asaṅga gives six reasons why they are different. Table 4.1 compares the different translations of the sixth reason (three Chinese and one Tibetan).

From all the other translations, it is clear that Vasubandhu originally said in MSgBh that the essence-body (*svābhāvika-kāya*) is attained after the transformation of the basis of the storehouse consciousness, and the enjoyment-body is attained after the transformation of the basis of the (six) evolving consciousnesses (Ch. *shengqi shi* 生起識 or *zhuanshi* 轉識; Skt. *pravṛtti-vijñāna*), as shown in Figure 4.1. The *Mahāyānasaṃgrahōpanibandhana* also confirms that this must have been Vasubandhu's original intent in MSgBh.[60]

Table 4.1 *Shelun* in Parallel with Other Translations of MSg and MSgBh X.35

Paramārtha	Xuanzang	Dharmagupta	Tibetan Translation
MSg: Sixth, because it is unreasonable that the transformations of the basis of the storehouse consciousness and the evolving consciousnesses (Ch. *shengqi shi* 生起識; Skt. *pravṛtti-vijñāna*) take place [as being identical with each other], hence it is unreasonable to assume that the enjoyment-body is the same as the essence-body. 六、阿黎耶識及生起識見[=現[a]]轉依非道理故，是故受用身無道理成自性身。(T1593:31.132a 23-25)	MSg: Sixth, because it is unreasonable that the transformations of the storehouse consciousness and of those evolving consciousnesses (*zhuanshi* 轉識) [are identical], it is unreasonable [to assume] that the enjoyment-body of the Buddhas is the essence-body. 六、阿賴耶識與諸轉識轉依非理可見故，佛受用身即自性身不應道理。(T1597:31.378c2-4)	MSg: Sixth, because the transformations of the basis of the storehouse consciousness and the evolving consciousnesses do not appear to be corresponding to each other, the thesis that the enjoyment-body is not the essence-body is established. 六、阿梨耶識及生起識等轉依不相應顯示故，是故受用身非自性身義成。(T1596:31.319c16-17)	MSg: (6) Because of the dissimilar appearance of the two transformations of the basis, that is, those of the base consciousness and the evolving consciousnesses, the enjoyment-body is different from the essence-body. (A modification of Griffiths et al.: 246, §O; For the Tibetan text, see Nagao [1982–7], Vol. II: *123*)
Shelun: Explanation: the storehouse consciousness and the evolving consciousnesses are the enjoyment-body (i.e., after the transformation of the basis, these two types of consciousness become the enjoyment-body). The basis [after the transformation of the basis] of these two is the dharma-body. If the essence-body were the enjoyment-body, then what Buddha-body would be attained after these two types of consciousnesses have transformed their basis? This is unreasonable, and therefore the enjoyment-body is not the essence-body. 阿黎耶識及生起識即是受用身，此二識轉依名法身。若自性身即是受用身，轉二識依復得何身？由此非道理故，受用身不成自性身。(T1595:31.267b27-c1)	MSgBh: In addition, after the storehouse consciousness is transformed, the essence-body is attained. Now if the enjoyment-body were the essence-body, then what Buddha-body would be attained after various evolving consciousnesses are transformed? Because this is unreasonable, the enjoyment-body is not the essence-body. 又轉阿賴耶識得自性身，若受用身即自性身，轉諸轉識復得何身？由此非理故，受用身非自性身。(T1597:31.378c19-21)	MSgBh: In addition, after the transformation of the basis of the storehouse consciousness, the essence-body is attained. Now if this essence-body were the enjoyment-body, then what Buddha-body would be attained after the transformation of the basis of the evolving consciousnesses? Therefore, the enjoyment-body is not the essence-body. 又復由阿梨耶識轉依已，即得自性身，若即此自性身是受用身者，生起識轉依已復得何身？是故受用身不即自性身。(T1596:31 .320a3-5)	MSgBh: (6) "The transformation of the basis of the storehouse consciousness" refers to the essence-body. If the enjoyment-body and the essence-body were one and the same, then this [transformation of the basis of the storehouse consciousness] would also refer to the enjoyment-body, and then what body would come to be supported upon the transformation of the basis of the evolving consciousnesses? Therefore, the enjoyment-body is not identical with the essence-body. (A modification of Griffiths et al. 1989: 247, §O; For the Tibetan text, see Griffiths et al. 1989: 369)

[a]Huizhao, in quoting this passage, substitutes 現 for 見 (T1863:45.424a28).

Vasubandhu's MSgBh:

Transformation of the basis

ālayavijñāna ---------------------------------- essence-body is attained

six evolving consciousnesses ---------------- enjoyment-body is attained

Figure 4.1 Before and after the transformation of the basis according to MSgBh

Hence Vasubandhu's rhetorical question is: Given that after the transformation of the basis of the storehouse consciousness, the essence-body is attained, now if the essence-body were the same as the enjoyment-body, then which Buddha-body would be attained after the transformation of the basis of the six evolving consciousnesses? The unsaid presupposition behind the rhetorical question is that after the transformation of the basis of the six evolving consciousnesses, the enjoyment-body is attained. Hence, if the essence-body were the same as the enjoyment-body, then the storehouse consciousness and the evolving consciousnesses would end up being the same thing after the transformation of the basis, a conclusion that Vasubandhu cannot accept. Vasubandhu's intent can be summarized in Figure 4.1.

This further suggests that, for Asaṅga and Vasubandhu, when the transformation of the basis takes place, the storehouse consciousness turns into the essence-body, and the six evolving consciousnesses turn into the enjoyment-body.

But here Paramārtha, apparently deviating from Vasubandhu's original text, says something very different. Paramārtha's text is actually quite puzzling, and even Nagao has difficulties making sense of it.[61] However, it is at least clear that Paramārtha links both the storehouse consciousness and the evolving consciousnesses with the enjoyment-body, not with the essence-body.

The following three passages from T2805 can help us understand what Paramārtha is saying:

(Quotation 4.15)

The base consciousness and the seeds from the karma out of delusion (*huoye* 惑業) were previously mutually dependent upon each other (meaning that the base consciousness had those seeds as its basis, and vice versa). But now the base consciousness attains the uncontaminated path of [cultivating] antidotes (*wuliu zhidao* 無流治道), which destroys the seeds [in the base consciousness], and becomes separated from the seeds. At this moment, the transformation of the basis takes place in relation to the base consciousness. The base consciousness [now] has the dharma-body as its [new] basis, and the base consciousness becomes the substance (*ti* 體) of the enjoyment-body. This is why this [transformation] is called the "transformation of the basis."[62]

(Quotation 4.16)

This shows that the base consciousness previously resides in birth-and-death by having the contaminated and polluted seeds as its basis. Now [the seeds] are destroyed by the path of [cultivating] antidotes and hence the base consciousness becomes purified, which means that the body of liberation (Ch. *jietuo shen*

> 解脫身; Skt. *vimukti-kāya*) and *tathāgatagarbha* (*rulaizang* 如來藏)[63] become one (*chengyi* 成一). The *tathāgatagarbha* attains the dharma-body—this is called liberation—and it becomes the substance (*ti* 體) of the enjoyment-body. Together with [the transformation of] the basis, all merits and wisdom (i.e., the two *saṃbhāra*) transform themselves into various kinds of merits (*de* 德; i.e., merits of the Buddhas). The path of the uncontaminated mental consciousness (*wuliu yishi dao* 無流意識道) arises so that it illuminates [the reality] that there are no seeds in the base consciousness. This is called "destroying the delusion" (*miehuo* 滅惑). Because the delusion is destroyed, the basis [of the base consciousness] is transformed and [the base consciousness] attains (*zheng* 證) the dharma-body (meaning that the base consciousness now has the dharma-body as its new basis).[64]

> (Quotation 4.17)
> The latter part shows the sense that the base consciousness becomes the enjoyment-body [after the transformation of the basis]. I shall explain this in an expanded way later.[65]

What do these three passages mean? First, quotation 4.15 suggests that T2805 has a distinctive understanding of the transformation of the basis that is different from that of Asaṅga and Vasubandhu. T2805 claims that, before the transformation of the basis, the defiled seeds are the basis for the base consciousness. After the transformation of the basis, the dharma-body becomes the new basis for the base consciousness. In other words, the transformation of the basis is understood as the replacement of the basis of the storehouse consciousness: the defiled seeds as the former basis are replaced by the dharma-body as the new basis. In contrast, according to Asaṅga and Vasubandhu, as we have seen earlier, transformation of the basis means that the storehouse consciousness turns into the essence-body (i.e., dharma-body), and the six evolving consciousnesses turn into the enjoyment-body.

In quotation 4.16, T2805 claims that the base consciousness becomes the enjoyment-body, which is endowed with all kinds of merits. According to T2805, the relationship between the enjoyment-body and the dharma-body is a relationship between a thing that bases itself upon something else (*nengyi* 能依) and the thing that serves as the basis (*suoyi* 所依). In other words, the enjoyment-body, into which the storehouse consciousness transforms, has the dharma-body as its basis. The idea that the base consciousness becomes the enjoyment-body is also confirmed in quotation 4.17.

4.5.1 Shedding Light on the Aforementioned Obscure Passage of the *Shelun*

This passage from T2805 can help us make sense of the aforementioned obscure passage of the *Shelun*, in which Paramārtha says that both the storehouse consciousness and the evolving consciousnesses are the enjoyment-bodies (*shouyong shen* 受用身) of the Buddhas. I repeat the passage from Paramārtha's *Shelun* cited earlier in Table 4.1.

(Quotation 4.18)

[*Shelun*:] Explanation: the storehouse consciousness and the evolving consciousnesses are the enjoyment-body (i.e., after the transformation of the basis, these two types of consciousness become the enjoyment-body). The basis [after the transformation of the basis] of these two is the dharma-body. If the essence-body were the enjoyment-body, then what Buddha-body would be attained after these two types of consciousnesses have transformed their basis? This is unreasonable, and therefore the enjoyment-body is not the essence-body.[66]

Regarding this passage, T2805 says that, after the transformation of the basis, the base consciousness has the dharma-body as its [new] basis and becomes the substance of the enjoyment-body (quotation 4.15). Therefore, when Paramārtha states that the storehouse consciousness and the evolving consciousnesses are the enjoyment-body, what he actually means is that the storehouse consciousness and the evolving consciousnesses become the enjoyment-body after the transformation of the basis. Before the transformation of the basis, the storehouse consciousness and the evolving consciousnesses have defiled seeds as their basis, but, after the transformation of the basis, they have the dharma-body as their new basis. Paramārtha's reasoning is that, if the enjoyment-body were identical with the dharma-body, then, after the transformation of the basis, the enjoyment-body would not have something beyond itself to rely upon as its basis. This would be an untenable consequence, so the dharma-body and the enjoyment-body must not be identical.

When we understand the passage from the *Shelun* in light of the passage from T2805, we can see the tremendous importance of the *Shelun* passage. As far as I know, this is the earliest passage in China that suggests that storehouse consciousness does not cease after the transformation of the basis. The only thing that changes is its basis, namely, from defiled seeds to the dharma-body.

This idea that the storehouse consciousness does not cease after the transformation of the basis is a radical new development within the post-Vasubandhu Yogācāra tradition. In *Thirty Verses* verse 5a, Vasubandhu says that the storehouse consciousness is extinguished at the stage of the arhat (i.e., buddhahood in this context).[67] It is precisely because the storehouse consciousness is regarded as fundamentally defiled that an arhat must adopt a new basis.

Strikingly, Paramārtha's idea here that the storehouse consciousness does not cease agrees with what later appears in works translated/compiled by Xuanzang. For example, the CWSL, following the FDJL,[68] explains that, after the transformation of the basis, the eighth consciousness becomes a special kind of *jñāna* that functions in accordance with mirror *jñāna* (Ch. *da yuanjing zhi* 大圓鏡智; Skt. *ādarśa-jñāna*;).[69] For this reason, the CWSL distinguishes between "the eighth consciousness" and the storehouse consciousness. The storehouse consciousness refers only to the defiled aspect of the eighth consciousness before the attainment of buddhahood.[70] Note that T2805 also endorses a similar line of thought by calling the eighth consciousness the "base consciousness" instead of the storehouse consciousness.

This agreement between Paramārtha and Xuanzang strongly suggests that both authors were aware of new doctrinal developments after Vasubandhu. Unlike

Xuanzang, who actually translated or compiled post-Vasubandhu texts, Paramārtha incorporated his knowledge of contemporary discussions into his translation of old texts. This is why, as I will show in Chapter 6, Xuanzang's works can actually help us understand the passages in which Paramārtha deviates from the original texts.

4.5.2 The Unconditioned Dharma-Body and the Conditioned Enjoyment-Body

The significant implication of the aforementioned passages of Paramārtha's *Shelun* and T2805 is that the base consciousness and the enjoyment-body are conditioned whereas the dharma-body (essence-body) is unconditioned. In the *Shelun*, Paramārtha continually tries to preserve the status of the dharma-body as being unconditioned, whereas the other two Buddha-bodies—into which the the storehouse consciousness and the six evolving consciousnesses metamorphose after the transformation of the basis—remain as conditioned. The distinction between the dharma-body and the other two bodies is emphasized in the following passage from *Shelun*:

(Quotation 4.19)
There are two kinds of body (i.e., Buddha-body): first, [the body] that is attained by [its own] nature (Ch. *ziran* 自然; Skt. *svabhāva*); second, [the body] that is attained through human efforts (Ch. *rengong* 人功; Skt. *puruṣakāra*). Regarding [the body] that is attained by [its own] nature, as it is said in a Scripture: "Whether a Buddha arises in this world or a Buddha does not arise in this world, the nature of dharmas (*faxing* 法性) always remain thus." This means that all dharmas are not empty (i.e., are not total non-existence) because the emptiness of the two (i.e., of subject and object) [exists], and the emptiness of the two is not empty (i.e., is not total non-existence) because [the emptiness of] falsity (*xüwang* 虛妄) [exists]. These two dharmas (i.e., the emptiness of the two and delusion) are attained due to their own nature, and hence are named "self-nature" (*svabhāva*). Regarding [the body] that is attained through human efforts, it means the body in the six destinies, which, due to delusion, produces karma—good, bad, or nonpropelling (*shan e budong ye* 善惡不動業)—acquires seven effects due to its karma, and creates even further delusion due to these effects. This is called [the body] attained through human efforts.

Regarding the body of the Tathāgata, there are also two kinds of attainment. First, [the body that is] attained by self-nature (*svabhāva*), i.e., the dharma-body; second, [the body that is] attained through human efforts, i.e., the enjoyment-body and the transformation-body. The essence-body (Ch. *zixing shen* 自性身; Skt. *svābhāvika-kāya*) is established in order to show that it is different from [the body that] is attained through human efforts. Based on the essence-body, one begins two practices [that aim at attaining] "merits" (*fude* 福德) and "wisdom" (*zhihui* 智慧). The effects produced from these two practices are the purity of the pure land and the great joy in dharmas (*da fale* 大法樂). The enjoyment-body is so named because it enjoys these two effects. For the other [sentient beings still] in the stages of cultivation (*xiuxing di* 修行地), due to the original vow (*benyuan* 本願) of the Buddha and his autonomous power (*zizai li* 自在力), his (i.e., the Buddha's) consciousness is transformed into the appearance of a sentient being (*si zhongsheng bianyi xian* 似眾生變異現). For this reason, this body is named the "transformation-body."[71]

An insistence like Paramārtha's—that the dharma-body must be unconditioned—can also be seen in T2805, which maintains that the dharma-body is identified with the Dharma-element, which is unconditioned:

(Quotation 4.20)
[The author] sees that although multiple Dharma-gates (*famen* 法門) are shown in the teachings of the Tathāgata, either in the Mahāyāna or the Hīnayāna, all aim at establishing the principle of Thusness that is of one taste (*yiwei* 一味) and is undifferentiated. The "one" here refers to the dharma-body which is the Dharma-element.[72]

To conclude, we find in T2805 information crucial to understanding an obscure passage in the *Shelun*, which clearly deviates from Asaṅga's and Vasubandhu's original texts. Both the *Shelun* and T2805 stress the strict distinction between the realms of the unconditioned (including the dharma-body) and conditioned (including the enjoyment-body and transformation-body). This agreement again suggests an intimate relation between T2805 and the *Shelun*.

4.6 Conclusion

In this chapter, I have shown that T2805 shares with other works of Paramārtha several doctrinal positions that were uncommon around the late sixth to early seventh centuries (Sections 4.1–4.2). It is particularly striking that, when Paramārtha's translation of the *Shelun* deviates and differs from the original texts of Asaṅga or Vasubandhu, T2805 consistently agrees with Paramārtha (Sections 4.3–4.4). T2805 also provides some insight into the obscure passages in the *Shelun* about the connection between the storehouse consciousness and the enjoyment-body (Section 4.5). Based on these points of agreement between T2805 and Paramārtha, I conclude that T2805 must have preserved the authentic teachings of Paramārtha, a conclusion that corroborates my observations in Chapter 3 regarding the relationship between Paramārtha and T2805.

5

Two Shelun Lineages and How the *Awakening of Faith* Came to Be Attributed to Paramārtha

5.1 Where and When the Dispute Regarding *Jiexing* Took Place

In Chapter 1, I showed that there are two competing interpretations regarding the notion of *jiexing*. The traditional Permanence Reading associated with the *Awakening of Faith* holds that *jiexing* is identified with original awakening and hence with the dharma-body of the Buddha. On the other hand, T2805 refutes this view outright and maintains an Impermanence Reading of *jiexing*. In Chapter 2, I pointed out a few reasons for skepticism concerning the Permanence Reading of *jiexing*, foremost among which is doubt about the traditional attribution of the *Awakening of Faith* to Paramārtha. In Chapters 3 and 4, I discussed the striking similarity, both philological and doctrinal, between T2805 and other works by Paramārtha. In this chapter, I try to locate the dispute regarding *jiexing* within a specific historical context in order to trace the Impermanence Reading of T2805 to Paramārtha and provide an explanation for why the *Awakening of Faith* came to be attributed to Paramārtha.

5.1.1 Date and Location of the Dispute Regarding *Jiexing*

Based on the evidence I have provided in previous chapters, I suggest that the dispute regarding *jiexing*—the Permanence Reading, associated with the *Awakening of Faith*, as opposed to the long-lost Impermanence Reading of T2805—probably took place in the Buddhist community in Chang'an around 590. The following evidence supports this suggestion.

First, the circulation of the *Awakening of Faith* is associated with Chang'an around 590. Tanqian (542–607), the earliest teacher in northern China of the *Awakening of Faith* and the *Shelun*, moved to Chang'an in 587 and stayed there until he died in 607. All later teachers of the *Awakening of Faith* are the disciples of Tanqian.

Second, as I pointed out in Chapter 1, the identification of *jiexing* with the dharma-body and original awakening appears as early as the *Tanyan shu*.[1] Regardless of whether Tanyan (516–88) himself was actually the author, this text, the earliest known commentary on the *Awakening of Faith*,[2] was definitely current in Chang'an around 590, along with the *Awakening of Faith* when it was first circulated.

Third, Huiyuan (523–92), in the *Dasheng yizhang*, expresses, but less explicitly, the same opinion regarding *jiexing* as the *Tanyan shu*. Huiyuan calls *jiexing* the "true mind" (*zhenxin* 真心) in fascicle 3[3] and defines the true mind as the dharma-body in fascicle 19.[4] Moreover, Huiyuan identifies the dharma-body with the concept of original awakening in the *Awakening of Faith*.[5] Huiyuan stayed in Chang'an from 587 until his death there in 592.[6] Hence, the fact that the *Tanyan shu* and Huiyuan both subscribe to the Permanence Reading of *jiexing* strongly suggests that the Permanence Reading was current in Chang'an around 590.

Fourth, in Chapter 3, I have shown that T2805 was probably composed in Chang'an around 590. T2805 includes some ideas that were exclusively limited to the Buddhism of Chang'an at that time.[7]

Based on the previous evidence, I suggest that the disputes between T2805 and its opponents probably took place in the Buddhist community of Chang'an around 590, the community within which the *Awakening of Faith* was first circulated. Although the *Awakening of Faith* itself does not include the term *jiexing*, both the *Tanyan shu* and Huiyuan interpret *jiexing* in terms of the idea of original awakening in the *Awakening of Faith*.

Next, I examine further evidence from contemporary authors concerning the Impermanence Reading in T2805 and the opposing view, which is closely associated with the *Awakening of Faith*.

5.2 Testimony about Two Theories of the Shelun Masters

So far, I have not found any testimony explicitly relating the debate between the masters of the *Awakening of Faith* and the masters linked to Paramārtha. After all, later Chinese Buddhists, except for Fajing and Chinkai,[8] were rarely aware that the *Awakening of Faith* might not have represented Paramārtha's authentic teachings. But sixth-century scholars, Jizang and Huijun in particular, mention disputes among the Shelun masters regarding two opposing theories. Next, I show that one theory described by Jizang and Huijun can be associated with the *Awakening of Faith*, the other theory with T2805.

Before I turn to Jizang's testimony, let me first summarize the view of T2805 and the opposing view regarding *jiexing* in Table 5.1.

5.2.1 Jizang on the Cessation of Permeation of Hearing

I begin with the testimony of Jizang, who says that some Shelun masters think that permeation of hearing (Ch. *wenxunxi* 聞熏習; Skt. *śrutavāsanā*) ceases after the practitioner becomes a Buddha, while others think that it does not cease. Permeation of hearing refers to the influence left on the consciousness by hearing the Buddha's teachings. According to classical Yogācāra theory, the fundamentally defiled consciousness gradually becomes purer as permeation of hearing accumulates in the consciousness. Now I quote Jizang's testimony.

Table 5.1 (= Table 1.1) Permanence vs. Impermanence Reading

Permanence Reading (*Awakening of Faith*)	Impermanence Reading (T2805)
Jiexing is permanent/unconditioned.	*Jiexing* is impermanent/conditioned.
Jiexing is the dharma-body.	*Jiexing* is not the dharma-body.
Jiexing (i.e., original awakening, Thusness, dharma-body) permeates ignorance.	*Jiexing* has yet to be permeated by the understanding arising from hearing and pondering.
Jiexing (i.e., original awakening, Thusness, dharma-body) functions as the cause/seed for liberation.	The dharma-body does not function as the cause/seed for liberation but is the final goal for the Buddhist path.

(Quotation 5.1)
After arriving in Chang'an, I witnessed that Shelun masters proposed two [opposing] theories. The first [theory] claimed that the permeation of hearing would not cease [after the transformation of the basis] and becomes the enjoyment-Buddha (*baofo* 報佛, i.e., the enjoyment-body of a Buddha). The second [theory] claimed that the permeation of hearing would cease and does not become the enjoyment-Buddha.

[I criticize both theories as follows:] The theory claiming that [permeation of hearing] becomes the enjoyment-Buddha commits the fault of [assigning] two [distinct] substances (*ti* 體) [to the same thing]. [This theory does this by holding two contradictory claims] (1) [It claims that] the permeation of hearing becomes the enjoyment-Buddha. This would mean that something impermanent (i.e., the permeation of hearing) becomes permanent (i.e., the enjoyment-Buddha). (2) [It claims that] the permeation of hearing is conditioned (Ch. *youwei* 有為; Skt. *saṃskṛta*), which would also require that it would cease (since conditioned things arise and cease by definition, contradicting his claim that permeation of hearing does not cease). Hence [this theory assigns] two [distinct] substances (i.e., one impermanent and the other permanent) to the single [substance] of the permeation of hearing.

Next, the theory claiming that [permeation of hearing] would cease was made because: all the merits [of the enjoyment-Buddha] arise from the substance, i.e., Thusness, while the permeation of hearing is considered merely as a contributory condition (Ch. *zengshang yuan* 增上緣; Skt. *adhipati-pratyaya*) to their arising. In reality, [the permeation of hearing] does not become the enjoyment-Buddha, and hence it would cease. This is like the human labor that is merely a condition for extracting gold from [its unrefined state of] a gold ore; it is from the gold ore that the gold is extracted [but not from human labor]. This theory commits the fault of "taking the cause to be non-existent" (*yinmieshi* 因滅失).[9]

According to this passage, there are two opposing theories held by the Shelun masters. One theory claims that permeation of hearing does not cease because it becomes the enjoyment-body of the Buddha, whereas the other holds that, after one becomes a Buddha, permeation of hearing ceases and does not become the enjoyment-body of the Buddha.

T2805 [Impermanence Reading] ←→ Opponent's View [Permanence Reading]
: ↓
: *Awakening of Faith*
: ↓
Jizang Theory (1) ←→ Jizang Theory (2)

Figure 5.1 Mapping between the two theories in Jizang onto T2805 and its opponent.

It is significant that, after he came to Chang'an, Jizang realized that the Shelun masters had two different opinions. In another passage, Jizang contrasts the opinion of the southern masters with the opinion of the Shelun masters.[10] We can infer that by "Shelun masters," Jizang meant those who taught the *Shelun* in the north, probably in Chang'an. Moreover, although in this passage Jizang does not explicitly say that there were two lineages of Shelun masters, in another passage he mentions two lineages in Chang'an.[11] This strongly suggests that there were disputes among the Shelun masters in Chang'an.

As shown later, the second theory mentioned by Jizang, that permeation ceases, seems to be in agreement with the Permanence Reading, which is further tied to the *Awakening of Faith*. The first theory, on the other hand, that permeation does not cease, is closely connected with the Impermanence Reading in T2805. In this case, it is likely that the disagreement regarding the Impermanence Reading in T2805 and the Permanence Reading, which is connected with the *Awakening of Faith*, arose in Chang'an around 590. My strategy of locating the view in T2805 and the opposing view can be illustrated in Figure 5.1.

5.2.1.1 *The Cessation of Permeation of Hearing (Awakening of Faith)*

With respect to the claim that permeation of hearing ceases, the *Awakening of Faith* mentions two kinds of permeation of hearing. Permeation of hearing in the primary sense is called "permeation by the substance and the characteristic marks of Thusness" (*zhenru zitixiang xunxi* 眞如自體相熏習); permeation of hearing in the secondary sense is called "permeation by the function [of Thusness]" ([*zhenru*] *yong xunxi* [眞如]用熏習). Permeation of hearing in the primary sense never ceases because it is permeation by Thusness itself, which refers to the Reality itself and never ceases. Since Thusness never ceases, according to the *Awakening of Faith*, permeation by Thusness likewise never ceases.[12]

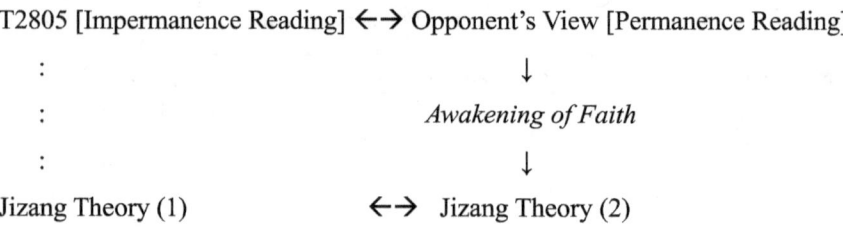

In contrast, "permeation of hearing in the secondary sense" refers to the permeation that one receives from the Buddha, teachers and good friends. After one becomes a Buddha, this permeation of hearing in the secondary sense ceases because it is no longer useful. This can best be illustrated by a simile in the *Awakening of Faith*: permeation of hearing in the secondary sense functions like a person who sets a piece of wood on fire. If there is no person to set the wood on fire, the wood cannot burn by itself.[13] But the wood can be kindled not because of the person but because wood has the nature of fire. This alone is the cause proper (*zhengyin* 正因) for the fire. Thus, after the wood has been set on fire, a person is not needed to set the fire again. In the same manner, after one becomes a Buddha, that is, after innate purity is fully disclosed, permeation of hearing is not necessary for further purifying oneself.

Permeation of hearing in the secondary sense in the *Awakening of Faith* accords well with the second theory mentioned by Jizang—that permeation of hearing ceases—because both accounts regard permeation of hearing as merely a contributory condition. The common point in both accounts is that the cause proper (i.e., innate purity) is disclosed through the help of the contributory condition. But once the cause proper has already come into play, there is no further need for the contributory condition.

5.2.1.2 The Non-Cessation of Permeation of Hearing (T2805)

On the other hand, the connection between the theory that permeation of hearing does not cease because it becomes the enjoyment-body of a Buddha and T2805 is less obvious. In Chapter 4 (Section 4.5), I pointed out that T2805 promotes the view that the storehouse consciousness (*ālayavijñāna*) becomes the enjoyment-body after the practitioner becomes a Buddha.[14] In order to understand the theory of non-cessation, we must understand the relationship between the storehouse consciousness and permeation of hearing.

In Yogācāra, the theory of the storehouse consciousness and the explanation of how to attain buddhahood are closely related. In Yogācāra, very simply speaking, the storehouse consciousness is where all the seeds resulting from positive and negative actions are deposited. But this consciousness is fundamentally defiled and cannot become liberated by its own power. Listening to the teachings of a Buddha, that is, the permeation of hearing, is necessary for liberation. As the permeation of hearing becomes stronger, fewer bad actions are performed. As a result, fewer seeds are deposited in the future and seeds resulting from bad actions are gradually destroyed. When all the seeds are destroyed, one becomes a Buddha.[15]

Thus, at the moment when one becomes a Buddha, what remains in the storehouse consciousness is the permeation of hearing deposited there, since all seeds for bad karma are destroyed. In other words, when T2805 explains that the storehouse consciousness becomes the enjoyment-body after one becomes a Buddha, it is the same as saying that the permeation of hearing becomes the enjoyment-body. In contrast, the *Awakening of Faith* does not mention anything about the relation between the permeation of hearing and the enjoyment-body.

The opinion described by Jizang, that the permeation of hearing becomes the enjoyment-body, is echoed in something else he explains:

> (Quotation 5.2) (= quotation 1.11)
> Seventhly, the Shelun masters (*Shedasheng shi* 攝大乘師) explain [as follows]: All sentient beings of the six destinies originate from the base consciousness.

> Because there are seeds for the six destinies in the base consciousness, the six destinies arise. Issuing from the pure Dharma-element, the twelve sections of scriptures arouse the permeation of hearing in just one thought (*yinian*一念), which then becomes attached to the base consciousness. This is the beginning of returning (Ch. *fanqu* 返去; Skt. *nivṛtti*) [to nirvana]. As the permeation of hearing increases, the base consciousness also decreases. Once the realization (*jie* 解) is perfectly established, the base consciousness ceases entirely. The enjoyment[-body of a] Buddha (Ch. *baofo* 報佛; Skt. *buddha-saṃbhoga-*[*kaya*]) is established by adopting the *jiexing* within the base consciousness. This *jiexing* will not cease [when the enjoyment-body is established]. The innate pure mind (Ch. *zixing qingjing xin* 自性清淨心; Skt. *prakṛtiprabhāsvara-citta*) is the dharma-body of a Buddha. When *jiexing* always agrees with (*changhe* 常合) the innate pure mind and reaches the ultimate stage, *jiexing* and the innate pure mind are associated with each other and become [united in] one substance (*yiti*一體). And hence not only is the dharma-body permanent but also the enjoyment-body is permanent.

In contrast to quotation 5.1, this passage says that it is *jiexing* within the base consciousness, not permeation of hearing, that becomes the enjoyment-body. This apparent conflict can be easily resolved if we recall that, according to Paramārtha's *Shelun*, when one hears the Buddhist teachings, the permeation of hearing is then deposited into the base consciousness through its mixture with *jiexing*.[16] In other words, since it is the mixture of permeation of hearing and *jiexing* that becomes the enjoyment-body, the two accounts are basically alluding to the same thing.

Thus, it seems likely that the opinions of the Shelun masters, according to Jizang, align doctrinally with T2805 and the *Awakening of Faith* as shown in Table 5.2.

This supports the existence of two Shelun lineages, as does Huijun's account, to which we turn now.

Table 5.2 Two Interpretations of Permeation of Hearing Attributed to Shelun Masters

Shelun Masters' Interpretation of Permeation of Hearing 1, According to Jizang	Shelun Masters' Interpretation of Permeation of Hearing 2, According to Jizang
The permeation of hearing does not cease when buddhahood is attained.	The permeation of hearing ceases when buddhahood is attained.
The permeation of hearing becomes the enjoyment-body.	The permeation of hearing does not become the enjoyment-body.
The permeation of hearing is a contributory condition for the dharma-body.[a]	The permeation of hearing is a contributory condition for the dharma-body.
Connected with T2805: the base consciousness becomes the enjoyment-body (see 4.5).	Connected with the *Awakening of Faith*.

[a]It is interesting that the idea that the permeation of hearing serves only as a "contributory condition" for the dharma-body also agrees with the authentic teaching of Paramārtha, which claims that the permeation of hearing does not serve as the cause proper for the dharma-body, while it does serve as the cause proper of the enjoyment-body and hence must not cease after the attainment of buddhahood.

5.2.2 Huijun's Account Regarding *Buddha-gotra*

We can now proceed to a passage from Huijun, which describes some differences between the two groups of Shelun masters concerning the *buddha-gotra* (*foxing* 佛性):

> (Quotation 5.3)
> Ninth, the Dilun masters say, "the eighth, i.e., the non-ceasing consciousness (*wumo shi* 無沒識) is the substance of the cause proper (*zhengyin ti* 正因體)." Tenth, the Shelun masters say, "the ninth, i.e., the spotless consciousness (Ch. *amoluo shi* 阿摩羅識; Skt. **amala-vijñāna*),[17] is the substance of the cause proper." Thus both masters (i.e., the Dilun masters and the Shelun masters) say that throughout the stage of ordinary people until the stage of the Buddha, the innate pure mind (Ch. *zixing qingjing xin* 自性清淨心; Skt. *prakṛti-prabhāsvara-citta*) is the substance that serves as the cause proper for buddhahood. And hence they (i.e., the Shelun masters) say: [throughout the stages there are] the innate *buddha-gotra* (Ch. *zixingzhu foxing* 自性住佛性; Skt. *prakṛtistha-gotra*), the drawn-forth *buddha-gotra* (Ch. *yinchu foxing*引出佛性; Skt. *samudānīta-gotra*), and the attained *buddha-gotra* (Ch. *deguo foxing* 得果佛性; Skt. **paripuṣṭa-gotra*[18]). *Those masters (i.e., the Shelun masters) have different interpretations with respect to the latter two buddha-gotra*s (i.e., the drawn-forth *buddha-gotra* and the attained *buddha-gotra*). According to one interpretation, all the three *buddha-gotra*s serve as the cause proper for buddhahood. According to the other, only the innate *buddha-gotra* serves as the cause proper for buddhahood, but the other two *buddha-gotra*s do not. Why? Because the *gotra* for the effect (*guo* 果) and the *gotra* for the effect of effects (*guoguo* 果果)[19] are the "attained *buddha-gotra*." The drawn-forth *buddha-gotra* is the *gotra* for "disclosing cause" (Ch. *liaoyin* 了因; Skt. **vyañjana-hetu* or **jñāpaka-hetu*) that observes [the dharmas] and cognizes (*guanzhi* 觀知) the [principle that] dharmas are produced based on the twelve links of causation. The innate *buddha-gotra* is the *gotra* that is the cause proper (Ch. *zhengyin xing* 正因性) for buddhahood, which is neither cause nor effect.
>
> The Dilun masters say: if we discuss them analytically, there are three kinds [of *buddha-gotra*]. The first is the *buddha-gotra* as principle (*li* 理); the second is the *buddha-gotra* as substance (*ti* 體); the third is the *buddha-gotra* as causation (*yuanqi* 緣起). When [the *buddha-gotra*] is hidden (*yin* 隱), it is *buddha-gotra* as principle. When [the *buddha-gotra*] is disclosed (*xian* 顯), it is the *buddha-gotra* as substance. When [the *buddha-gotra*] is functioning (*yong* 用), it is the *buddha-gotra* as causation. [Therefore,] the Dilun and Shelun [masters] agree at a deeper level. Both follow the doctrine of Master Tan Wuyuan 曇無遠 of old time. (My emphasis)[20]

This passage is very complicated and needs a great deal of unpacking. First, *gotra*, which literally means "family" or "lineage" in Buddhist texts, refers to categories of sentient beings and to the causes of belonging to these categories. For example, sentient beings are typically divided into three categories, and members of only one category can become Buddhas. This is because people in this category belong to the family (*gotra*) of the Buddha or because they have the "seed" for becoming a Buddha.[21] In order to preserve the ambiguity of this term, I chose not to translate it into English but to use the Sanskrit word *gotra* and *buddha-gotra*.

In this passage, Huijun contrasts the opinions of the Shelun masters with those of the Dilun masters. At first glance, it is not entirely clear whether he is talking about two different claims made by the Shelun masters when he says "those masters have different interpretations with respect to the other two *buddha-gotras*." But there are two good reasons for believing that he is. First, Huijun contrasts this with the opinion of the Dilun masters in the latter part of the text cited earlier. This suggests that the former views were held by the Shelun masters. Second, the notion of "three *buddha-gotras*" originated in the FXL of Paramārtha. It would make much better sense to ascribe the interpretations of this notion to the Shelun masters, namely, to those associated with Paramārtha.

If I am correct, this passage testifies that the Shelun masters held two different opinions about the three *buddha-gotras*. Some maintained that all three *buddha-gotras* are the cause proper (*zhengyin* 正因) for buddhahood, while others said that only the first, that is, innate *buddha-gotra*, is the cause proper.

Next, it is necessary to explain the distinction between *zhengyin* and *liaoyin* 了因 (disclosing cause).[22] Both terms come from the *Mahāparinirvāṇa-mahāsūtra*.[23] The stock scriptural example of the cause proper is the milk as the cause of thick sour milk. This cause proper is contrasted with the contributory cause (Ch. *yuanyin* 緣因; Skt. *pratyaya-hetu*), which is the enzyme and heat added to the milk to produce thick sour milk. A cause proper must be the same as the effect in substance, as in the case of milk and thick sour milk. Or the arising of the effect must involve the destruction of the cause, as in the case of a seed and the resulting tree.

The disclosing cause is easy to understand. In 4.2, I briefly discussed this idea. The stock scriptural example is a lamp or a candle that reveals an object in darkness. The object was already there. It is not newly created when the light illuminates it. Thus, the disclosing cause is usually understood as a kind of knowledge or cognition.[24]

5.2.2.1 *Three* **Buddha-gotras** *as the Cause Proper for Buddhahood*

The *Awakening of Faith* remains silent about *buddha-gotra* as the cause proper for buddhahood; in fact, it never mentions the idea of *buddha-gotra*. However, in light of Huijun's account, we can easily attribute the position that all three *buddha-gotras* are the cause proper to the Shelun masters who are associated with the *Awakening of Faith*. For the *Awakening of Faith*, the ultimate basis is the mind of all sentient beings (*zhongshengxin* 眾生心), which it explicitly identifies with the dharma-body of the Buddha. To this extent, the mind of all beings in its original calmness and purity is the innate *buddha-gotra*.[25] But when the mind is agitated, it becomes the mind of ordinary sentient beings, that is, the mind with the phenomenal world derived from it. Despite this, the mind still has the power of restoring its original purity through the help of the two kinds of permeation (i.e., "permeation by the substance and the characteristic marks of Thusness" and "permeation by the function of Thusness") mentioned earlier. To this extent, the mind itself is also the drawn-forth *buddha-gotra*. Finally, when the original purity is fully restored, the mind itself is the attained *buddha-gotra*. Under this scheme, no distinction among the three *buddha-gotra*s is required because it is the same mind that underlies all three *buddha-gotra*s.

5.2.2.2 The Innate Buddha-gotra Alone Is the "Cause proper" for Buddhahood

In contrast, for Paramārtha and T2805, there are differences among the three *buddha-gotra*s. The attained *buddha-gotra* refers to the state of having attained the ultimate effect (i.e., nirvana), and hence, it cannot act as a cause of anything because it points to the final state itself. The drawn-forth *buddha-gotra* acts as the disclosing cause, which is *jñāna* about the principle that all dharmas are produced based on the twelve links of causation. Only the innate *gotra* can serve as the cause proper for buddhahood.

To understand this, one should note that, for Paramārtha, buddhahood is regarded as being unconditioned,[26] and hence cannot be a cause proper of something else: it is not a cause proper of the Path of Cultivation. Nor is it an effect of something else: it is not something that is created by the Path of Cultivation. Since buddhahood is neither a cause proper of nor an effect of something else, buddhahood—or Thusness, dharma-body, innate *gotra*—itself alone is its own cause proper. The entire Buddhist path contributes to the disclosure of buddhahood but does not produce it. And this is why the path of the antidote is merely the disclosing cause. In the *Awakening of Faith*, however, there is no strict distinction between the unconditioned and the conditioned, and this is the main reason why there is no need to distinguish among the three *gotras*.

The position that only innate *buddha-gotra* serves as the cause proper is supported by Paramārtha's FXL:

> (Quotation 5.4) (See quotation 4.8)
> Firstly, what is meant by "the cause" includes two: first, the *buddha-gotra* (*foxing* 佛性); second, the aspiration from confidence (Ch. *xinle* 信樂; Skt. *adhimukti*). Between these two, the *buddha-gotra* is unconditioned; whereas the aspiration from confidence is conditioned. The aspiration from confidence serves as the "disclosing cause" (Ch. *liaoyin* 了因; Skt. **vyañjana-hetu* or **jñāpaka-hetu*) for the innate *buddha-gotra* (Ch. *xingde foxing* 性得佛性; Skt. *prakṛtistha-gotra*) because it discloses the *buddha-gotra* that is the cause proper (Ch. *zhengyin* 正因) (i.e., the innate *buddha-gotra*). The aspiration from confidence serves as the "generative cause" (Ch. *shengyin* 生因; Skt. *kāraṇa-hetu*) for applied practices (Ch. *jiaxing* 加行; Skt. *prayoga*) because it brings about various kinds of practices.[27]

Note from this passage that innate *buddha-gotra* alone is labeled as the "cause proper." Note also that when the FXL states that a *buddha-gotra* is unconditioned, it obviously refers to the innate *buddha-gotra*. The drawn-forth *buddha-gotra* is conditioned because it encompasses the whole Path of Cultivation.[28]

As the aforementioned quotation from the FXL indicates, the idea that only the innate *buddha-gotra* is the cause proper for buddhahood agrees with the FXL. This also implies that this is the authentic view of Paramārtha. I can now summarize the previous discussions in Table 5.3.

Table 5.3 Two Interpretations of *Buddha-gotra* Attributed to Shelun Masters

Three *Buddha-gotra*s Interpretation 1, according to Huijun	**Three *Buddha-gotra*s Interpretation 2, according to Huijun**
All the three *buddha-gotra*s are the cause proper for buddhahood.	Only the innate *buddha-gotra* is the cause proper for buddhahood.
	The innate *buddha-gotra* is unconditioned (*asaṃskṛta*).
Coheres with the *Awakening of Faith*.	Coheres with Paramārtha's FXL.

The contrast between the two Shelun groups described by Jizang and Huijun further indicates that the fundamental difference between Paramārtha's teaching and the *Awakening of Faith* is Paramārtha's dualism as opposed to the monism of the *Awakening of Faith*. For Paramārtha, the unconditioned (Thusness, dharma-body, innate *buddha-gotra*) and the conditioned (*jiexing*, drawn-forth *buddha-gotra*) are completely distinct. The unconditioned does not function as the substance of the conditioned, as is claimed by the *Awakening of Faith*. In the *Awakening of Faith*, the conditioned realm is regarded as a degenerated function (*yong* 用) of the unconditioned realm. Ultimately, there is only one substance (*ti* 體).

The distinction between the unconditioned and the conditioned can be confirmed by the mapping of innate *buddha-gotra* to dharma-body on the one hand and drawn-forth *buddha-gotra* to the enjoyment-body and the transformation-body, as is indicated in the FXL:

> (Quotation 5.5) (= quotation 6.9; also see quotation 7.24)
> There are two kinds of *buddha-gotra*s. First, the innate *gotra* (*zhu zixing xing* 住自性性) and second, the drawn-forth *gotra* (*yinchu xing* 引出性). The three bodies of the Buddhas are perfected (*chengjiu* 成就) as a result of these two *gotras*. . . . Regarding these two [*buddha-gotras* as] causes, the Buddha taught the three [Buddha-]bodies as effects. First, with the innate *buddha-gotra* as the cause, the Buddha taught the dharma-body. . . . Second, with the drawn-forth *buddha-gotra* as the cause, the Buddha taught the enjoyment-body (*yingshen shen* 應身; literally, the correspondence-body). . . .Third, with the drawn-forth *buddha-gotra* as the causes, the transformation-body (*huashen* 化身) is further derived.[29]

This passage implies that drawn-forth *buddha-gotra*—while acting as the disclosing cause of buddhahood or the dharma-body—is the cause proper of the enjoyment-body and the transformation-body. The positions of the two groups of Shelun masters are summarized in Table 5.4.

Based on this comparison between the different doctrinal views of two groups of Shelun masters, we can summarize their major differences in Figure 5.2.

5.3 The Shelun/T2805 Lineage and the Shelun/*Awakening of Faith* Lineage

In the previous section, I have reviewed accounts by Jizang and Huijun in order to argue that, in Chang'an around 590, two groups, both denominated as Shelun masters,

Table 5.4 Summary of the Two Interpretations Attributed to Shelun Masters

Shelun Masters Close to the Permanence Reading			**Shelun Masters Close to the Impermanence Reading**		
Jiexing	Permeation of hearing	Three *gotras*	*Jiexing*	Permeation of hearing	Three *gotras*
Jiexing is unconditioned.	The permeation of hearing ceases when buddhahood is attained.	All three *gotras* are the cause proper for buddhahood.	*Jiexing* is conditioned.	The permeation of hearing does not cease when buddhahood is attained.	Only innate *buddha-gotra* is the cause proper for buddhahood.
Jiexing is permanent.	The permeation of hearing does not become the enjoyment-body. The permeation of hearing is the contributory condition.		*Jiexing* is not permanent.	The permeation of hearing becomes the enjoyment-body.	The innate *buddha-gotra* is unconditioned.
Coheres with the *Awakening of Faith*.	Coheres with the *Awakening of Faith*.	Coheres with the *Awakening of Faith*.	T2805	T2805	Coheres with Paramārtha's FXL.

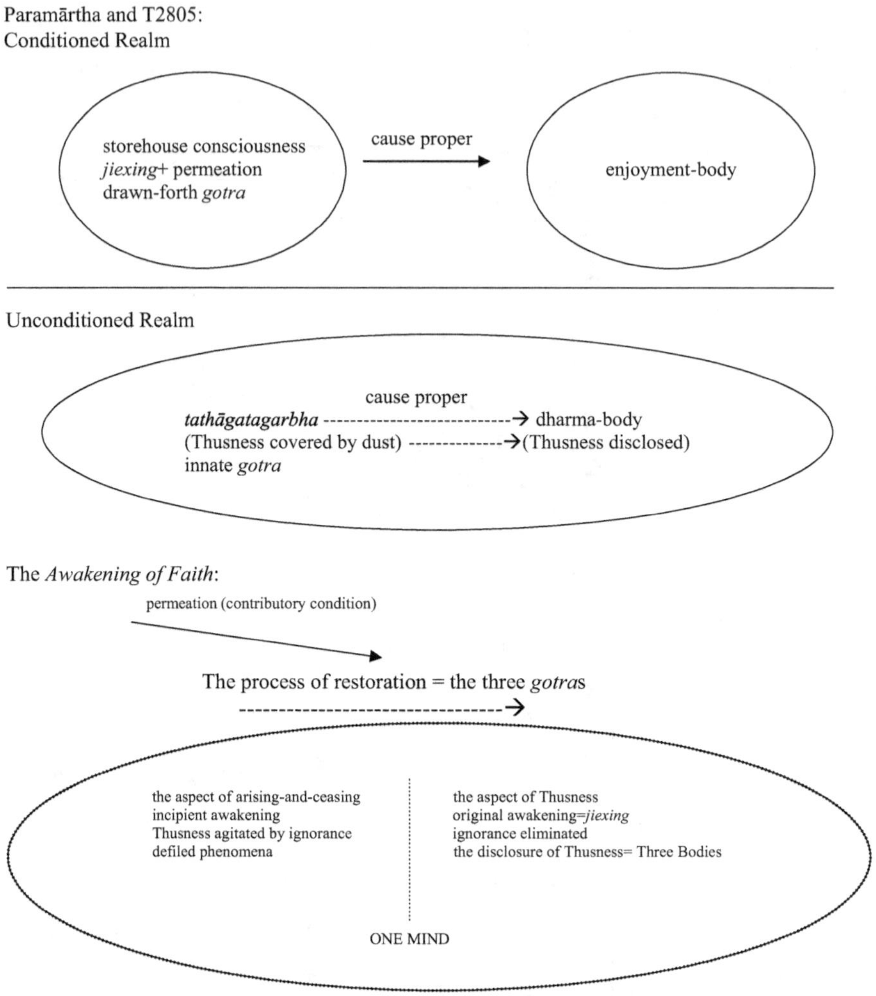

Figure 5.2 (= Figure 7.2) Doctrinal differences between the two Shelun lineages.

had differing views regarding the *buddha-gotras*. One view is in close accord with T2805 and Paramārtha's works in general; the other view is closely associated with the *Awakening of Faith*.

Next, I refer to the Shelun masters who were connected with T2805 as the Shelun/T2805 lineage. I refer to the ones who were connected with the *Awakening of Faith* as the Shelun/*Awakening of Faith* lineage. Now the next task is to identify the major figures in these two lineages. First, I briefly review the history of Paramārtha's disciples.

5.3.1 The Spread of Paramārtha's Legacy

According to the XGSZ, for more than twenty years during Paramārtha's stay in China, his translations and teachings did not spread widely.[30] After Paramārtha's death, his disciples spread out to promulgate his teachings, first in southern China and then in the north. The "Shelun Tradition (*Shelun zong* 攝論宗)" derives its name from Paramārtha's Chinese translation of the *Shelun*. The name was coined to refer to those who disseminated Paramārtha's teachings. The tradition was influential for the first eighty years after Paramārtha's death, but it later declined due to criticism from Xuanzang.

After Paramārtha died, "his disciples dwindled and were dispersed and his lineage was about to die out."[31] Among Paramārtha's disciples, his most beloved disciple Huikai died a year before him. His direct disciple, Fatai 法泰 (d.u., died after 571), went to Jiankang 建康 (present-day Nanjing) but was not initially successful in attracting followers.[32] Huikai's cousin, the layman Cao Pi 曹毘 (d.u.), stayed in Guangzhou and managed to invite someone else to teach the *Shelun* but had limited success in promoting the study of it. Later, he taught in Jiangdu 江都 (present-day Yangzhou 揚州).[33] Another monk, Zhijiao 智敫 (died in 601), began teaching Paramārtha's *Shelun* in 577 but had little success. His books and collections were burnt in 592. Around 598, he resumed teaching the *Shelun* on more than ten occasions and made some progress.[34] Finally, another disciple, Daoni 道尼 (d.u., died after 590), seems to have spent some time in Yangzhou before finally moving to Chang'an in 590 and staying there until his death.[35]

Instead of Paramārtha's direct disciples Fatai and Daoni, it was Tanqian (542–607) and Jingsong 靖嵩 (537–614) who were regarded by the later Chinese tradition as the actual promoters of Paramārtha's teachings in northern China.[36] Tanqian and Jingsong were the most important among a number of Buddhists who fled to the south because of the persecution of Buddhists in northern China between 573 and 578, a few years after Paramārtha's death. There they were exposed to Paramārtha's teachings. Tanqian did not study with any of Paramārtha's disciples, but he came upon Paramārtha's *Shelun* by accident and studied it by himself. Tanqian returned to Pengcheng 彭城 (present-day Xuzhou 徐州) to teach Paramārtha's works for a few years before he was summoned to Chang'an in 587. He is regarded as the first teacher of the *Shelun* in the north.[37] Jingsong fled to the south and stayed in Jianye 建業 (present-day Nanjing) sometime between 569 and 583. He regularly consulted with Fatai before returning to Pengcheng in 590 to spread Paramārtha's teachings. Jingsong was reported to have mastered Paramārtha's *Shelun* and had general knowledge about more than forty of Paramārtha's works.[38] Thus, Paramārtha's teachings and works almost disappeared and did not receive much attention until later, when Tanqian and Jingsong promoted them in the north.

Both Tanqian and Jingsong had already been well trained in the Dilun tradition before they were exposed to Paramārtha's teachings. With their Dilun background in mind, we cannot exclude the possibility that the teachings spread by Tanqian and Jingsong were actually a combination of Dilun and Paramārtha's ideas.[39]

Instead of supposing that Paramārtha's teachings were simply transmitted from the south to the north, we should think of Paramārtha's teachings as enmeshed in the interaction and confluence between the northern and southern Buddhisms, which had been developing separately for at least a hundred years. A complicated process of misquotation, reinterpretation, and appropriation was involved in the spread of Paramārtha's teachings by northern authors with strong Dilun backgrounds. Next, I demonstrate that Tanqian was probably the major figure of the Shelun/*Awakening of Faith* lineage among the Shelun masters.

5.3.2 The Shelun/*Awakening of Faith* Lineage—the Ninth Consciousness

The prominent doctrinal feature of the Shelun/*Awakening of Faith* lineage is its interpretation of the *Shelun* in light of the *Awakening of Faith*. *Jiexing* in the storehouse consciousness is identified with original awakening. Hence the storehouse consciousness is regarded as both pure and impure, a position that is consistent with the idea of the storehouse consciousness as a mixture between arising-and-ceasing (*shengmie* 生滅) and neither-arising-nor-ceasing (*busheng bumie* 不生不滅).

Another notable feature of this lineage is its peculiar interpretation of the **amalavijñāna* as the ninth consciousness. Jizang describes the position of the Shelun masters as follows:

> (Quotation 5.6) (Cf. quotation 1.8)
> The Shelun masters (*Shedasheng shi* 攝大乘師) regard the eighth consciousness as false (*wang* 妄) but the ninth consciousness as true. They also say (*youyun* 又云) that the eighth consciousness has two different senses: first, false; second, true. It is true in the sense that it has *jiexing*; it is false [in the sense] that it has the consciousness of retribution (Ch. *guobao shi* 果報識; Skt. *vipāka-vijñāna*). The mixture of arising-and-ceasing (*shengmie* 生滅) and neither-arising-nor-ceasing (*bushing bumie* 不生不滅) [as discussed] in the *Awakening of Faith* is taken to be the substance (*ti* 體) of the *aliye shi* (i.e., the storehouse consciousness)[40]

Here the Shelun masters, according to Jizang, cite the *Awakening of Faith*, so this should be taken as the position of the Shelun/*Awakening of Faith* Lineage. The term "the ninth consciousness" in this passage has created much confusion concerning Paramārtha. I agree with Yoshimura (2007) that Paramārtha nowhere proposes a system of nine consciousnesses.[41] Yoshimura suggests that the idea of the ninth consciousness was more likely a later interpretation.[42] But, based on Jizang's account, it is clear that the idea of the ninth consciousness was associated with the Shelun masters who were connected with the *Awakening of Faith*. As we shall see, based on a passage from Huiyuan, it seems that this interpretation was already in circulation in the early 590s.

The most likely parallel to the idea of the ninth consciousness in Paramārtha's works is the notion of "spotless consciousness" (Ch. *amoluo shi* 阿摩羅識; Skt. **amala-vijñāna*) since the ninth consciousness is understood to be true or undefiled. In Paramārtha's works, the spotless consciousness is definitely undefiled because its reconstructed Sanskrit name suggests that it is "spotless" (*a-mala*), and it is characterized in Paramārtha's works variously as "an unconditioned dharma,"[43] "Thusness,"[44] "the perfected nature,"[45] and "the innate pure mind" (Ch. *zixing qingjing xin* 自性清淨心; Skt. *prakṛti-prabhāsvara-citta*).[46] But all these characterizations of the spotless consciousness agree on one point: it is unconditioned. The term "consciousness" here should be understood as unconditioned, undiscriminating *jñāna* (*zhi* 智), which has unconditioned Thusness as its sole cognitive object. This *jñāna* is changeless because its cognitive object (i.e., Thusness) remains the same. Further, because the distinction between subject (*grāhaka*) and object (*grāhya*) is eliminated when the spotless consciousness is attained, Thusness must also be included in the definition of the "spotless consciousness."[47]

Although Paramārtha never calls the spotless consciousness the ninth consciousness, we know, as shown in quotation 5.7 by Huiyuan, the idea of the ninth consciousness was already current in the early 590s. Moreover, it was interpreted in connection with the *Awakening of Faith* and hence was understood very differently from Paramārtha's spotless consciousness. According to the *Awakening of Faith*, underlying the defiled eighth consciousness—from which all defiled phenomena arise—there is an undefiled basis, called "the aspect of Thusness of the Mind" (*xin zhenru men* 心真如門), "dharma-body," or "original awakening." It is this undefiled basis, which is located within the eighth consciousness, that is sometimes called the ninth consciousness. Huiyuan explains the ninth consciousness as follows:

(Quotation 5.7)
[The total number of the consciousnesses] can also be said to be nine. This is why the General Chapter (*zongpin* 總品; i.e., the beginning chapter) of the *Laṅkāvatāra-sūtra* states, "The eight or nine kinds of consciousnesses are like waves in water." What is the outlook of these consciousnesses? We can distinguish [their outlook] in two ways. First, [we can] distinguish the true [aspect] from the false [aspect] in order to make them nine kinds. The false [aspect] is divided into seven kinds, namely, six consciousnesses of matter (*shishi* 事識) and the false consciousness (*wangshi* 妄識; i.e., the grasping consciousness (Ch. *atuona shi* 阿陀那識; Skt. *ādāna-vijñāna*) The true [aspect] is divided into two kinds, namely, the *amoluo* 阿摩羅 (i.e., the spotless consciousness [**amala-vijñāna*]) and the *aliye* 阿梨耶 (i.e., storehouse consciousness). The meaning has been discussed before. With these [two] combined with the former [seven], we have nine in total.

Second, [we can first] separate the true from the false [aspects] and then combine them to make nine kinds. The true [aspect] alone counts one, namely, the so-called innately pure (*benjing* 本淨) *amoluo shi* 阿摩羅識. The combination between the true and the false [aspects] makes eight kinds [of consciousnesses] in total. The meaning has been discussed above. [These eight kinds] include: the base consciousness, the *atuona shi* 阿陀那識, and the evolving six consciousnesses (*qi liushi* 起六識). With these [eight] combined with the former [one], we have nine [consciousnesses].[48]

It is interesting that Huiyuan, in this passage, considers the storehouse consciousness to be true (i.e., undefiled). This is explained as follows:

(Quotation 5.8)
Third, [we may] divide both the true and the false [aspects] in order to make them four. The true [aspect] is divided into two: first, the *amoluo shi*, which means [consciousness] without dust (*wugou* 無垢) in Chinese. It is also called

> the [consciousness] that is innately pure. [If we] examine the truth of the true [consciousness], the true substance [of it] is permanently pure. Hence, it is said to be without dust. This is similar to the aspect of Thusness of the Mind previously [discussed].
>
> Second, the *aliye shi*, which means [consciousness] without cessation (*wumo* 無沒). This is just the true mind previously [discussed] that evolves by adjusting to falsity (*suiwang liuzhuan* 隨妄流轉). But because its substance becomes neither deceased nor decayed (*ti wu shihuai* 體無失壞), it is said to be [the consciousness] without cessation. Hence the *Awakening of Faith* states, "The *tathāgatagarbha*, which is a dharma of neither-arising-nor-ceasing, is combined with arising-and-ceasing, and is called the *aliye*." The false [aspect] is divided into two, namely, falsity (*wang* 妄, i.e., the seventh consciousness) and matters (*shi* 事; i.e., the six evolving consciousnesses). Since each true and false [aspect] consists of two, there are four in total.[49]

Here Huiyuan states that the storehouse consciousness is simply the spotless consciousness that evolves by adjusting to falsity (*suiwang liuzhuan* 隨妄流轉). Again, Huiyuan quotes the *Awakening of Faith* to assert that the storehouse consciousness, as the eighth consciousness, is a combination of the spotless consciousness and falsity, that is, ignorance. When the spotless consciousness is considered separately from its defiled state, in which it is combined with ignorance, it is called the ninth consciousness.

These two quotations from Huiyuan indicate that the theory of eight consciousnesses can readily be reformulated into a theory of nine consciousnesses. It merely depends on how one would like to consider the spotless consciousness. In the system of eight consciousnesses, the spotless consciousness is regarded as the pure aspect (the aspect of Thusness of the Mind) within the eighth consciousness. In the system of nine consciousnesses, on the other hand, the spotless consciousness is considered separately from the other eight consciousnesses and is regarded as the pure consciousness, which is completely free from impurity. In both quotations, we can see that the different systems described by Huiyuan are inspired by the *Awakening of Faith*.[50] Thus, we can confirm the connection between the idea of the ninth consciousness and the *Awakening of Faith*.

5.3.3 Tanqian: The Major Figure of the Shelun/*Awakening of Faith* Lineage

Earlier, I have suggested that the Shelun/*Awakening of Faith* lineage is important because of its association with the *Awakening of Faith* and its peculiar way of understanding *amoluo shi* as the ninth consciousness. On the basis of this association, I suggest that the Shelun/*Awakening of Faith* lineage was associated with (if not started by) Tanqian. My main reason is that, according to the XGSZ, Tanqian was the only person associated with all the texts relevant to the Shelun/*Awakening of Faith* lineage: the *Shelun*, the *Awakening of Faith*, and the *Chapter on the Nine Consciousnesses* (*Jiushi zhang* 九識章). According to the XGSZ, Tanqian wrote commentaries on the *Shelun* and the *Awakening of Faith*, and he was also the author of the *Chapter on the Nine Consciousnesses*.[51]

Tanqian was described in the XGSZ as well as in the later tradition as the first and most prominent promoter of the *Shelun* in the north even before he was summoned by the emperor to Chang'an in 587.[52] When Tanqian lectured on the *Shelun* in Chang'an, even the most eminent monks, such as Huiyuan, attended his lectures.[53]

Tanqian's close connection with the *Awakening of Faith* is also mentioned in the XGSZ, which reports that he studied the *Awakening of Faith* before fleeing to the south in 577 due to the persecution of Buddhists.[54] In addition, the XGSZ says that Tanqian lectured on the *Awakening of Faith* and Paramārtha's *Shelun* at Musheng Temple 慕聖寺 in Pengcheng sometime between 581 and 587.[55]

Finally, the question of Tanqian's association with the *Chapter on the Nine Consciousnesses* is somewhat more complicated. Modern scholars differ concerning Paramārtha's authorship of the text.[56] Here I first try to show that, according to a later account by Wŏnch'ŭk, the positions in the *Chapter on the Nine Consciousnesses* agree with the views maintained, according to Jizang, by the Shelun/*Awakening of Faith* lineage.

Before I cite Wŏnch'ŭk, I should note that although Wŏnch'ŭk did have access to Paramārtha's authentic works and T2805,[57] he was unaware that there were two lineages of Paramārtha's disciples; hence, he regarded this text as an authentic work by Paramārtha.[58] For this reason, his understanding of Paramārtha was distorted by the Shelun/*Awakening of Faith* lineage, and his criticism of Paramārtha may not be valid.[59] Here I quote the two passages from Wŏnch'ŭk in which he cites the *Chapter on the Nine Consciousnesses* in his discussion of original awakening:

> (Quotation 5.9)
> Secondly, The Tripiṭaka master Paramārtha posits the doctrine of nine consciousnesses based on his *Juedingzang lun*, as was discussed in its "Article on the Nine Consciousnesses" (*Jiushi pin* 九識品). About the nine consciousnesses, the six among them, eye-consciousness, etc., are similar to what is taught in the MSg. The seventh consciousness, i.e., the *atuona* 阿陀那 (**ādānavijñāna*), should be rendered as "grasper" here [in terms of Chinese language]. It grasps the eighth consciousness as the self and that which pertains to the self (*wo wosuo* 我我所). This [corresponds] only to the obstruction related to afflictions (Ch. *fannao zhang* 煩惱障; Skt. *kleśa-āvaraṇa*) but goes without the attachments to dharmas (*fazhi* 法執). This (i.e., seventh consciousness) will never lead one into becoming a Buddha. The eighth consciousness, the *aliye shi* 阿梨耶識 (i.e., the storehouse consciousness), has three [different aspects]: (1) The *liye* 梨耶 of *jiexing* 解性 (i.e., the *jiexing* within the *aliye*) which leads one into becoming a Buddha; (2) The *liye* of retribution (*guobao* 果報), which has the eighteen realms (*dhātu*) as its cognitive objects. Hence it is said in a verse of the *Distinction between the Middle and the Ends* (Ch. *Zhongbian fenbie* 中邊分別; Skt. *Madhyāntavibhāga*): "The base consciousness arises with an appearance (Ch. *si* 似; Skt. *pratibhāsa*) of sense faculties (*sattva*), objects (*artha*), the subject (*ātman*), and consciousness-and-representation (*vijñapti*)." Based on this and the other treatises, it is claimed

that the eighth consciousness has the eighteen realms as its cognitive objects. (3) The *aliye* of defilements, which produces four kinds of slander (*bang* 謗) when cognizing Thusness. This [corresponds] to the attachments to dharmas (*fazhi* 法執) rather than the attachments to selfhood (*renzhi* 人執). [Here] I am following the lineage of Sthiramati (*Anhui zong* 安慧宗) to make the above points. The ninth consciousness, i.e., the *amoluo shi* 阿摩羅識 (**amala-vijñāna*), is named here [in Chinese language] as the spotless consciousness (*wugou shi* 無垢識). It has Thusness as its substance (*ti* 體). There are two aspects with respect to the unitary Thusness (*yi zhenru* 一真如): (1) [Thusness as] a cognized object, which is named Thusness, the Apex of Reality (Ch. *shiji* 實際; Skt. *bhūtakoṭi*), etc.; (2) [Thusness as] a cognizer, which is named the spotless consciousness, also original awakening. For details, see the discussions by "Chapter on the Nine Consciousnesses" (*Jiushi zhang* 九識章), which cites "Article on the Nine Consciousnesses" in the *Juedingzang lun*.[60]

(Quotation 5.10)
What is said as the "consciousnesses of sentient beings" (*zhongsheng shi* 眾生識) is meant to be a general label for all consciousnesses. With respect to this, there are two different explanations. First, the Tripiṭaka master Paramārtha establishes [the doctrine] of nine consciousnesses. The first one [among nine] refers to the *amouluo shi* (**amalavijñāna*), which has Thusness and the original awakening as its nature. It (*amouluo shi*) is called *tathāgatagarbha* while being entangled (*zaichan* 在纏) [with defilements]; it is called the dharma-body after being liberated from the entanglement [with defilements]. The *amuoluo shi* is also named the spotless consciousness as in the *Chapter on the Nine Consciousness* (*Jiushi zhang* 九識章). For the remaining eight consciousnesses, it [the doctrine of Paramārtha] is similar to other masters.[61]

According to Wŏnch'ŭk, the *Chapter on the Nine Consciousnesses* maintains that Paramārtha's notion of the spotless consciousness is, in fact, the ninth consciousness, which is also identified in this text with original awakening. Hence, Wŏnch'ŭk's account should be taken as mainly representing the doctrines of the Shelun/*Awakening of Faith* lineage. The fact that Wŏnch'ŭk's account is based on Tanqian's interpretation in the *Chapter on the Nine Consciousnesses* gives us reason to believe that Tanqian must have been a central figure in the Shelun/*Awakening of Faith* lineage.[62]

Given the sources currently available, it is difficult or impossible to decide whether the *Awakening of Faith* was composed by Tanqian or a predecessor. The only work of Tanqian that has survived is too short to be compared with the *Awakening of Faith*.[63] For my purposes, it suffices that Tanqian is definitely closely connected with the Shelun/*Awakening of Faith* lineage.[64]

5.3.4 A Criticism of Ōtake's Proposal

Ōtake (2012) argues that the doctrines described by Wŏnch'ŭk can indeed be attributed to the historical Paramārtha. His main evidence is the parallel between Wŏnch'ŭk's quotations and, on the one hand, the lost fragments from the commentary on the

Renwang bore jing (*Renwang bore jing shu* 仁王般若經疏) attributed to Paramārtha, and, on the other hand, Sthiramati's doctrines in his *Triṃśikābhāṣya*. I reserve a more extensive criticism of Ōtake's claim for a separate work. Here I simply point out a few major shortcomings in his proposal.

1. Paramārtha's authorship of a text entitled *Jiushi zhang* 九識章 is dubious. I think Ōtake makes a serious mistake in regarding *Jiushi yiji* 九識義記 and *Jiushi zhang* 九識章 as variant titles of the same text. Ōtake (2017: 543) believes that *Jiushi zhang* was composed in 549 based on the record from the *Lidai sanbao ji* that *Jiushi yiji* was composed in 549.[65] Note, however, that the title *Jiushi zhang* 九識章 was first attributed to Paramārtha no earlier than the eleventh century, in the *Sinpyeon jejong gyojang chongnok* 新編諸宗教藏總錄, edited by the Korean monk Uicheon 義天 (1055–101). Among the earlier Chinese Buddhist catalogs, only the *Lidai sanbao ji*, which it is not completely reliable as mentioned earlier,[66] attributes to Paramārtha the title *Jiushi yiji* 九識義記 but not *Jiushi zhang* 九識章. In contrast, the XGSZ clearly attributes *Jiushi zhang* 九識章 to Tanqian. Since Tanqian was regarded by later tradition as an authentic heir of Paramārtha, it is quite likely that Tanqian's identification of the spotless consciousness with the ninth consciousness was later attributed to Paramārtha.
2. Again, only the *Lidai sanbao ji* attributes the *Commentary on the Renwang jing* to Paramārtha.[67] This attribution is even more dubious if we take into account the fact that most scholars now consider the *Renwang bore jing* to be an apocryphal text.[68]
3. Wŏnch'ŭk cites the MAV and refers to Sthiramati concerning only the *aliye* 阿梨耶 of retribution but not with regard to *jiexing* or the ninth consciousness. Therefore, the correspondence between Wŏnch'ŭk's report and Sthiramati's work that Ōtake points out completely fails to prove that the idea of the ninth consciousness should be attributed to Paramārtha, who was Sthiramati's contemporary.
4. Finally, all the accounts by Jizang (quotation 5.6), Huiyuan (quotation 5.8), and Wŏnch'ŭk cite the *Awakening of Faith* (or the notion of original awakening) to support their understanding of the spotless consciousness as the ninth consciousness. This reveals a close connection between this interpretation and the *Awakening of Faith*. Since Ōtake also agrees that the *Awakening of Faith* was composed in China,[69] it would seem unlikely that the identification of the spotless consciousness with the ninth consciousness originated from India.

5.3.5 Daoni, the Major Figure of the Shelun/T2805 Lineage

As for the Shelun/T2805 lineage, the major figure was Daoni. Daoni, furthermore, was probably also the author of T2805.

Let me first review my conclusions in Chapter 3 about the philological study of T2805. The author of T2805 must have come from the south because T2805 includes several terms that were never used in northern China. He must have been in Paramārtha's translation group because T2805 shares a few uncommon phrases with the *Suixiang lun* translated by Paramārtha. Finally, he must have been somehow connected with Buddhism in Chang'an around 590 because T2805 contains a few of Jingying Huiyuan's important ideas. If we consult the biographies of Paramārtha's disciples in the XGSZ, we find a monk, named Daoni, who meets all the aforementioned qualifications.

We know very little about Daoni's life. According to our main source, the XGSZ, Daoni was from Jiujiang 九江 (currently Jiangxi 江西 province) and hence was a southerner.[70] He was one of Paramārtha's most important disciples after his death. The XGSZ records that Daoni was one of the scribes when Huikai, Paramārtha's beloved disciple in his last years, lectured on his AKBh.[71] After Huikai's death, Paramārtha summoned Daoni and eleven other disciples to ask them to vow to propagate the *Shelun* and his AKBh.[72]

Daoni was summoned by imperial decree from Yangdu 楊都 (present-day Yangzhou 揚州) to Chang'an in 590.[73] Unfortunately, we know nothing about Daoni's study and career as a translator and scribe under Paramārtha's direction. We know only a little more about Daoni's later career of spreading the *Shelun* in Chang'an. When he first arrived in Chang'an in 590, he stayed in Daxingshan Temple,[74] where Huiyuan stayed at around the same time.[75] It is noteworthy that, when Tanqian first moved to Chang'an in 587, he also stayed in Daxingshan Temple.[76] A monk named Daoyue 道岳 studied with Daoni in Chang'an.[77] Furthermore, Daoni lectured on the *Shelun* around the same time as Tanqian.[78]

It is crucial for my purpose to note that Daoni and Tanqian lectured on the *Shelun* in Chang'an at the same time. According to the XGSZ, Tanqian was already teaching Paramārtha's works three years before Daoni moved to Chang'an in 590.[79] Thus, it seems as though the dispute regarding *jiexing* mentioned in T2805 could have been Daoni's refutation of Tanqian's interpretation of *jiexing*.

Based on all the information we have about Daoni, I suggest that he is the most likely author of T2805. Daoni, as a direct disciple and scribe of Paramārtha who later went to Chang'an in 590, perfectly fits the profile of the author of T2805 that is suggested by everything we can glean from philological and philosophical study. Daoni's stay at Daxingshan Temple also explains why T2805 displays a familiarity with Huiyuan's ideas.

I am fully aware that my attribution of T2805 to Daoni is somewhat speculative. We are not sure, for instance, that Daoni was the scribe when Paramārtha translated the *Suixiang lun*. Even if he was, we still cannot exclude the possibility that T2805 was composed by someone who was close to Daoni, rather than by Daoni himself. However, I argue that it is quite plausible that Daoni was the author of T2805. With this assumption, we can get a fairly coherent idea of the disputes regarding *jiexing* that are mentioned in T2805 and a clearer picture of how the *Awakening of Faith* came to be attributed to Paramārtha. In any case, readers should keep in mind that, even if Daoni later proves not to have been the author of T2805, it does not disprove my assertion that there were two disputing lineages of Shelun masters.

I have concluded that there were two Shelun lineages in Chang'an around 590: the Shelun/*Awakening of Faith* lineage headed by Tanqian and the Shelun/T2805 lineage presumably headed by Daoni (if he is the author of T2805). However, we still must explain why these two masters could have developed contrary interpretations of *jiexing*. After all, they both were spreading the teachings of the same Indian teacher, Paramārtha. At this point, we must carefully review the details of their biographies.

5.3.6 Why Daoni and Tanqian Had Different Views

It should be no surprise that T2805, if Daoni was its author, agrees with Paramārtha's corpus both in terminology and doctrine. Daoni was a direct disciple of Paramārtha, and we have no good reason to believe that he deviated very far from Paramārtha's original teachings. The biography of Tanqian can help to explain how Tanqian came to hold different opinions from those of Daoni. In contrast to the scanty information we have about Daoni, quite a detailed biography of Tanqian can be found in the XGSZ.[80] Tanqian came from the north and had already been well established as a scholar before he fled to the south during the persecution of Buddhists between 573 and 578. It was during his stay in the south that he received Paramārtha's *Shelun* by accident, and he regarded it as presenting the highest Buddhist teaching. He read the text carefully, and, when Buddhism was no longer banned in northern China, he returned to the north and devoted himself to teaching the *Shelun*. He first taught in a city in present-day northern Jiangsu province and was summoned to the capital in 587. According to the XGSZ, Tanqian, not Paramārtha's direct disciple Daoni, was regarded as the first teacher of the *Shelun* in north China.[81]

Although Tanqian was considered the first to teach the *Shelun* in north China, he never studied with Paramārtha nor did he ever meet him. Paramārtha had already died in 569 in Guangzhou when Tanqian fled to Jinling between 573 and 578. Nor is there any evidence that Tanqian ever studied with any of Paramārtha's direct disciples. Therefore, it is quite possible that Tanqian taught Paramārtha's texts based on his own interpretations rather than on Paramārtha's original teaching.

Hence, it is quite likely that Tanqian's view differed from Daoni's because Tanqian interpreted Paramārtha's *Shelun* from the standpoint of the *Awakening of Faith*. Earlier, I have discussed Tanqian's close connection with the *Awakening of Faith*.[82] Everything we know about Tanqian's opinions of Paramārtha's teachings is closely intertwined with the *Awakening of Faith*. For example, Tanqian, in his *Chapter on the Nine Consciousnesses*, identifies the spotless consciousness with the ninth consciousness, and he adopts the Shelun/*Awakening of Faith* view that *jiexing* is identified with original awakening, referring to the permanent and the pure aspects within the defiled storehouse consciousness.

To conclude, we now have a clear picture of the Shelun masters. The Shelun/T2805 lineage was headed by Daoni and should have preserved the original teachings of Paramārtha. The Shelun/*Awakening of Faith* lineage was headed by Tanqian and re-interpreted the *Shelun* based on the *Awakening of Faith*.

If I am correct about this, it should now be fairly clear that the *Awakening of Faith* came to be attributed to Paramārtha because the later Chinese tradition failed to recognize that Tanqian's Shelun/*Awakening of Faith* lineage did not preserve Paramārtha's original teachings. This failure is mainly due to the fact that Tanqian's lineage prospered, while Daoni's lineage ended prematurely.

5.3.7 The Success of the Shelun/*Awakening of Faith* Lineage

There are several reasons why Tanqian's lineage was successful.

First, Tanqian was politically influential. Tanqian appears to have been quite charismatic, and he was highly admired by his contemporaries. In 587, he was summoned to the capital and proclaimed one of the Six Great Meritorious Ones (*liu dade* 六大德) by Emperor Wendi 文帝 (ruled 581–604).[83] In 592, he was called one of the Ten Great Meritorious Ones (*shi dade* 十大德).[84] He was so greatly favored by Emperor Wendi that Wendi asked him to sleep in the same bed during Wendi's visit to Jinyang 晉陽 in 590[85] and to Qizhou 岐州 in 593.[86] More importantly, it was Tanqian who persuaded Emperor Wendi to "lift all restrictions on Buddhist ordination, which resulted in the rapid growth of the Saṅgha."[87] This contributed tremendously to the revival of Buddhism in northern China. In addition, Tanqian was well received by other eminent monks, such as Huiyuan, who is said to have often acknowledged Tanqian's talent.[88] Unlike Tanqian, Daoni, although he had already arrived in Chang'an and lectured in Daxingshan Temple, was not installed as one of the Ten Great Meritorious Ones.

Another important reason why Daoni's lineage was soon forgotten and overshadowed by Tanqian's *Shelun* lineage was that Daoni probably died only a few years after he moved to Chang'an.[89] Although Daoni's lineage may not have completely died out around 599,[90] its demise can be attested by the following facts:

1. Daoni disappears from history after he went to Chang'an in 590. As I mention earlier, we know very little about Daoni's career in Chang'an, who his disciples were, or when he died. Given the almost complete lack of information about Daoni's activity and lineage, it is reasonable to assume that his lineage did not prosper for long. In sharp contrast, a detailed biography of Tanqian is included in the XGSZ, and we also have several biographies of his disciples who were active before Xuanzang. To repeat, as Kashiwagi points out, all the teachers of Paramārtha's *Shelun* described in the XGSZ were at the same time teachers of the *Awakening of Faith*.[91]
2. A monk named Daoyue, the only one who studied with Daoni according to the XGSZ, claimed himself to be an expert on the AKBh, not the *Shelun*, even though he studied the AKBh on his own and not with Daoni. This strongly suggests that the authoritative teacher of the *Shelun* was Tanqian, not Daoni, despite the fact that Daoni was Paramārtha's direct disciple.
3. Another indication of the decline of Daoni's authority can be seen in the striking disagreement regarding the authorship of the *Awakening of Faith* between the *Fajing lu* and the *Lidai sanbao ji*, two Buddhist catalogs edited in the 590s. The *Fajing lu* (594) assigns the *Awakening of Faith* to the category of dubious authorship as it is missing from the list of Paramārtha's translations.[92] But in the *Lidai sanbao ji* (597), the *Awakening of Faith* is unreservedly attributed to Paramārtha.[93] This disagreement can be explained by the fact that, around 594, Daoni, or Daoni's lineage, was still strong enough to reject the attribution of the *Awakening of Faith* to Paramārtha. Readers may recall that Fajing says

that he consulted the list of Paramārtha's translations.[94] It was probably Daoni who provided such a list. But as Daoni's authority waned and Tanqian's became stronger, from 597 onward, the *Awakening of Faith* was recognized as an authentic work of Paramārtha.

5.3.8 Challenge to and Defense of Tanqian

There is some evidence that Tanqian's authority was challenged during the period of disagreement between the two groups of Shelun masters. To begin, the early diversity of the Shelun tradition is mentioned in the biography of Fachang 法常 (567–645).[95] In addition, we know something about how Tanqian was challenged.

1. According to the XGSZ, Tanqian was criticized for being addicted to worldly glory and royal favor:

    (Quotation 5.11)
    Now that Qian 遷 (i.e., Tanqian) has been paid honor by the emperor and invited by the high officials, some people protested against him and disputes arose. Some people said that he (i.e., Tanqian) was "content with honors and imperial favors," (*zhiyu rongchong* 滯於榮寵) etc. [Tanqian] then wrote the *Wang shifei lun* 亡是非論 to show to himself [that he should not be criticized in that manner].[96]

2. Tanqian's understanding of *jiexing* may have been disputed in T2805. As I mentioned in Chapter 1, T2805 cites a different reading of *jiexing* and tries to refute it. This different interpretation agrees with the *Awakening of Faith* in regarding *jiexing*, or original awakening, as an unconditioned dharma. Thus, it is possible that T2805 was challenging Tanqian's view about *jiexing*.
3. A defense of Tanqian's authority appears in the biography of Tanqian in the XGSZ. There the author of the XGSZ cites a prophecy from fascicle 1 of his own XGSZ biography of Paramārtha:

    (Quotation 5.12)
    Although sometimes he (i.e., Tanqian) made far-fetched (*chuanzao* 穿鑿) claims that resulted in heterodox opinions (*yiduan* 異端) against him, none of his understanding was not originally from the previous master (i.e., Paramārtha). Hence it is said in "The Biography of Paramārtha" [in the XGSZ]: "Soon, a man of great capability in a great kingdom that is neither far nor near will promote this treatise." Now I (i.e., the author of the XGSZ) look for such a figure in the present and in the past, who else could it be [except Tanqian]![97]

One significant point in this passage is that it mentions heterodox opinions that arose in protest against Tanqian. From this, we can infer that Tanqian met opposition while lecturing on the *Shelun*. At that time, there were people who realized that Tanqian might not be faithful to Paramārtha's works.

Second, the narrative of the XGSZ makes it obvious that the author regards Tanqian as teaching the authentic doctrines of Paramārtha and thus labels differing opinions as heterodoxies. Bearing this in mind, we should take the description in the XGSZ with a grain of salt when it gives full credit to Tanqian for the dissemination of the *Shelun* in the north.

Third, the author of the XGSZ seems to be citing as fact the prophecy story in his own biography of Paramārtha and then identifying Tanqian as the one whom the prophecy predicts. But I suggest it is more likely that the prophecy story in the biography of Paramārtha of the XGSZ is a fabrication. An attentive reading of the original passage from the biography of Paramārtha is in order:

> (Quotation 5.13)
> When thinking about the future, Paramārtha then drew a long breath [and sighed], bursting out breaths of anger three times (i.e., again and again). Kai (i.e., Huikai 慧愷, Paramārtha's favorite disciple in his later career) asked him why. Paramārtha answered, "You folks received the right Dharma (*zhengfa* 正法) whole-heartedly, but in fact you are only subordinates (*fu* 副) regarding the understanding and spreading [of the right Dharma]. I just regret that I am not promoting the Dharma at the right time. [This makes me feel that] the original intention of coming here [to China] is not fulfilled." Hearing these words, Kai felt like sobbing. After a long while, Kai burst out crying. He knelt down and replied, "The great Dharma is free from dust (i.e., not hindered by worldly affairs). It is spread as far as the Red County (*chixian* 赤縣; i.e., China). Although people do not respond, yet how could it just stay hidden?" Pointing in the direction of northwest, Paramārtha said, "To that direction there is a great country, neither near nor far. [The right Dharma] will be prosperously promoted after our death. [It is a pity that] we do not get to see the flourishing [of the right Dharma]. This is why I sighed." This [story] testifies to what happened in the remote past.[98]

It is hard to believe that this conversation ever happened or that Paramārtha once had a vision that his teachings would be promoted by someone whom he had never met. This is even more improbable when we realize that the capital Chang'an, where Tanqian lectured, is just to the northwest of the city of Guangzhou, where Paramārtha was living at that time. If Paramārtha actually had some mystical knowledge about the spread of his teachings in Chang'an, he would have known that his own disciple Daoni would also be promoting his teachings in the "great country to the northwest." Moreover, the fact that this story of a prophecy is intended to promote Tanqian by pointing to the northwest also betrays its lateness. Had the author of this story been aware that Daoni also spread Paramārtha's teachings in Chang'an, he would have added some more information in order to identify Tanqian alone without including Daoni as well. The fact that he thought that the phrase, "the person in Chang'an," would be enough to identify Tanqian betrays his unawareness of Daoni's presence in Chang'an at the same time as Tanqian.

I suggest that the best way to make sense of the story of the prophecy is to read it as a defense of Tanqian's lineage. The story may have been current for quite some time before the writing of the XGSZ around 645, so the author of the XGSZ regarded it as reliable. The fabrication and circulation of this story also supports my assertion that Tanqian's lineage was not unchallenged.

5.4 Implication: No Connection between the *Awakening of Faith* and Paramārtha

So far I have argued that there were two Shelun lineages: the Shelun/T2805 lineage, presumably headed by Daoni, and the Shelun/*Awakening of Faith* lineage headed by Tanqian. I have also discussed the possible reasons for the success of Tanqian's lineage and the decline of Daoni's lineage.

My uncovering of the connection between Daoni's lineage and T2805 provides strong evidence against the traditional attribution of the *Awakening of Faith* to Paramārtha. Next, I make this point by refuting the strongest argument for the traditional attribution, set forth by the Japanese scholar Kashiwagi.

5.4.1 Kashiwagi's Assertion of the Indian Provenance of the *Awakening of Faith*

In Chapter 2, I reviewed the arguments for and against the attribution of the *Awakening of Faith* to Paramārtha. My conclusion is that Kashiwagi (1981) has so far made the strongest case for the claim that the *Awakening of Faith* was indeed translated by someone who was associated with Paramārtha and hence the doctrinal claims made by the *Awakening of Faith* should be treated as "being constructed based on the direct extended line of Indian Buddhist thought."[99]

The major reason why Kashiwagi still believes in the connection between the *Awakening of Faith* and Paramārtha is the fact that Paramārtha's teachings were disseminated in northern China together with the *Awakening of Faith*. That is to say, the spread of the *Awakening of Faith* was closely related to the Shelun masters, that is, the people who taught Paramārtha's *Shelun*.

Having established the differences between these two Shelun lineages, we can return to the inconsistency, unresolved by Kashiwagi, regarding the relationship between Paramārtha and the *Awakening of Faith*. On the one hand, philological and philosophical evidence obviously reveals differences between Paramārtha and the *Awakening of Faith*. On the other hand, it is no less true that a close tie exists between the spread of the *Awakening of Faith* and the Shelun masters.

However, if we accept that there were two lineages of Shelun masters in Chang'an around 590, the inconsistency can easily be resolved. It is true that the *Awakening of Faith* was spread by the Shelun masters, but only by the ones belonging to the Shelun/*Awakening of Faith* lineage. That the Shelun/T2805 lineage did not promote the *Awakening of Faith* can be confirmed by the fact that it is never cited in T2805. The attribution of the *Awakening of Faith* to Paramārtha resulted from the fact that the later Chinese tradition was not aware of the existence of the Shelun/T2805 lineage and treated the Shelun/*Awakening of Faith* lineage as the only authentic lineage descended from Paramārtha.

5.5 The Debates between the Dilun and the Shelun Traditions

The history of Paramārtha's disciples and their interactions with the indigenous scholastic tradition in the north, that is, the Dilun tradition, is one of the most puzzling issues in the study of sixth-century Chinese Buddhism. At this stage, I cannot solve all the puzzles, but I would like to comment on some of the limitations of previous studies in this field.

As far as I can tell, no attention has ever been paid to Jizang's account of the two theories of the Shelun masters. For a long time, many scholars[100] have been quite misled by the following explanation by Zhanran (711–82):

> (Quotation 5.14)
> First, [the text, i.e., the *Fahua xuanyi* 法華玄義 of Zhiyi] explains that the teachings and the approaches are fraught with disputes. . . . Regarding the first [point], the text says, "As the Dilun [tradition is divided into] the two: [those in] the southern region and [those in] the northern region (*nanbei erdao* 南北二道)," [this means that] before the Chen 陳 and the Liang 梁 dynasties the masters spreading the *Dilun* were different in different areas. The [masters in the] northern region (*beidao* 北道) of the Province of Xiang (*Xiangzhou* 相州) held that the storehouse consciousness is the basis (Ch. *yichi* 依持; Skt. *āśraya*);[101] the [masters in the] southern region (*nandao* 南道) of the Province of Xiang held that Thusness is the basis. Both these masters of treatises based [their teachings] on Vasubandhu, but their teachings were different like water and fire. Moreover, as the *Shelun* became prosperous, it also held [that] the storehouse consciousness [is the basis] and hence [they] allied with [masters in] the northern region. In addition, the old and new translations of the *Shelun* (i.e., the old one by Paramārtha and the new one by Xuanzang) are different just as the two opinions held by the Dilun [masters]. The old translation stipulates the spotless consciousness (*anmoluo shi* 菴摩羅識, i.e., the *amoluo shi* 阿摩羅識), but the Tripiṭaka master of the Tang dynasty (i.e., Xuanzang) only stipulates the eighth consciousness [i.e., the storehouse consciousness].[102]

There are several problems here. First, Zhanran is probably too late to give a reliable historical account of the Shelun masters around 600. Second, Zhanran here is commenting on the original passage from Zhiyi, who says:

> (Quotation 5.15)
> As the Dilun [tradition is divided into] the two: [those in] the southern region and [those in] the northern region (*nanbei erdao* 南北二道). Moreover, the *Shelun* also became prosperous. All of them held their own views to be true and rejected the views of each other.[103]

Here Zhiyi's mention of two branches of the Dilun tradition, that is, those in the southern and those in the northern regions, seems to have been hinted at by Jizang[104] and hence is to be trusted. However, it must be noted that, in the original passage, Zhiyi does not mention that the Shelun tradition was allied to the northern branch of the Dilun tradition (and hence presumably antagonistic to the southern branch). Zhanran seems to have made up this part of his account. In fact, as I have shown, Tanqian maintained a very good relationship with Tanyan and Huiyuan, who both came from the southern branch of the Dilun tradition.[105]

The real problem here is that neither Zhiyi nor Zhanran were aware that there were two lineages of Shelun masters or knew about the debates between them. It should be noted that Zhiyi never traveled to Chang'an. Hence it is not clear whether *Shedasheng* 攝大乘 for Zhiyi refers to the Shelun teachers in the south, to Tanqian's lineage, or to Daoni's lineage.

In fact, it may be a mistake to read Zhiyi's report as an accurate historical description because he appears to have used the term *Shedasheng* in at least two different senses. When he contrasts the *Shedasheng* with the *Dilun* and says that the *Shedasheng* takes the storehouse consciousness as the basis (*yichi* 依持), whereas the *Dilun* takes the nature of dharma (Ch. *faxing* 法性; Skt. *dharmatā*) as the basis,[106] Zhiyi is referring to the original doctrine of the *Shelun*, which differs from the *Awakening of Faith*. But, on the other hand, Zhiyi also says, "The *Shelun* shows the meaning of the ten superior marks. All people agree that it is profound and ultimate to the extent that the Dilun (tradition) is converted (to the Shelun tradition)."[107] In this passage, he is apparently referring to the success of the Shelun tradition, presumably Tanqian's lineage.

There are two possible reasons for this confusion in Zhiyi's usage of the term *Shedasheng*. Zhiyi may have combined two different things: on the one hand, his understanding of the doctrinal contrast between the Dilun tradition and the teaching of Paramārtha's *Shelun*, and, on the other, what he learned via hearsay about the success of the Shelun tradition in Chang'an. Alternatively, he may have mentioned different things that he knew about what happened in Chang'an in his different works. Without further certainty about Zhiyi's knowledge of the Dilun and the Shelun traditions, we must remain cautious in referring to his account.

Suppose, as reported by Zhanran, as there were indeed disputes regarding the issue of basis (*yichi* 依持) between the northern and the southern branches of the Dilun tradition, it would not be difficult to speculate on why Tanqian's lineage as represented by the *Awakening of Faith* could have finally settled the debates. The scheme of "One Mind in Two Aspects" in the *Awakening of Faith* can incorporate both positions in this debate. On the one hand, the *Awakening of Faith* agrees with the northern branch that it is the storehouse consciousness that serves as the basis of defiled phenomena; on the other hand, it agrees with the southern branch that, ultimately speaking, Thusness—whether it is called *jiexing*, original awakening, dharma-body, *tathāgatagarbha*, the ninth consciousness, or the true mind—resides in the defiled storehouse consciousness and is the basis of everything, defiled or undefiled.

To conclude, we should not, as scholars used to, overly trust Zhanran's account. There seems to be no reason to believe that the Shelun tradition was an opponent of the southern branch of the Dilun tradition. It is imperative to reexamine all these accounts in light of my study of T2805 and Daoni's lineage in the Shelun tradition.

5.6 Conclusion

In this chapter, I draw on the two different interpretations of *jiexing* and on testimony from Tanqian's and Daoni's contemporaries to demonstrate that there were two different Shelun lineages: the Shelun/T2805 lineage and the Shelun/*Awakening of Faith* lineage. The Shelun/T2805 lineage was headed by a direct disciple of Paramārtha (i.e., the author of T2805, most probably Daoni) and probably better preserved Paramārtha's authentic teachings. The Shelun/*Awakening of Faith* lineage was headed by Tanqian as an indirect disciple of Paramārtha, who interpreted the *Shelun* by using the conceptual scheme of the *Awakening of Faith*. Based on this new observation of the history of the Shelun masters, I refute Kashiwagi's assertion that the *Awakening of Faith* was connected to Paramārtha and hence originated in India. The *Awakening of Faith* is connected only indirectly with Paramārtha through the Shelun/*Awakening of Faith* lineage. Because the Shelun/T2805 lineage died out prematurely, Paramārtha came to be known to later generations almost solely through the lens of the Shelun/*Awakening of Faith* lineage; thus, understanding of his ideas became distorted.

The kind of historical approach I have taken in this chapter is always somewhat speculative. I have done my best to draw a clear and plausible picture based on the currently available information. I may be mistaken in identifying Daoni as the author of T2805. However, the fact that there were two competing interpretations of *jiexing* in Chang'an in 590 supports my assertion that there were two groups of Shelun masters, one associated with T2805 and the other with the *Awakening of Faith*.

The traditional attribution of the *Awakening of Faith* to Paramārtha is a crucial part of what I call in the Introduction the "traditional image of Paramārtha." In this chapter, I have reinforced arguments against this attribution by offering an explanation of how the *Awakening of Faith* came to be attributed to Paramārtha. I hope this will help to dissociate the *Awakening of Faith* from Paramārtha and, moreover, to correct the distorted traditional image of Paramārtha.

Only by discarding this distorted image of Paramārtha can we begin to re-locate him in the development of Indian Yogācāra Buddhism, a task that I will take up in Chapter 7. But now that the traditional interpretation of *jiexing* has been questioned, I will move on to examine what exactly *jiexing* meant to Paramārtha.

6

What Exactly Is *Jiexing*?

In the previous chapter, I established that the traditional interpretation of *jiexing*—as being identical with original awakening and referring to the permanent and undefiled aspect within the defiled storehouse consciousness—is not the original teaching of Paramārtha. Now I will try to establish what Paramārtha originally meant by *jiexing*.

To do so, I start by considering *Shelun Jiexing* Passages (1) and (2) and T2805 *Jiexing* passages (1) and (2). Unfortunately, this comparison will not yield a sufficiently clear understanding of the original meaning of *jiexing*. Therefore, I turn to Xuanzang's FDJL and the CWSL. Surprisingly, it seems that Paramārtha and Xuanzang agree much more than what scholars have previously assumed. In other words, I believe that a more developed version of Paramārtha's theory of *jiexing* can be found in Xuanzang's works.[1]

Points gleaned from these four texts are discussed next.

6.1 Paramārtha's *Shelun*

A number of points become clear about Paramārtha's understanding of *jiexing* in the *Shelun* despite the fact that he only uses the term twice and neither defines nor explains it. I return to *Shelun Jiexing* Passage (1), where Paramārtha introduces the term *jiexing*, suggesting that it is an attribute of the storehouse consciousness:

> *Shelun Jiexing* Passage (1):
> [*Shelun*:] Commentary: Now [the author of the MSg] wants to prove the substance (*ti* 體) and the name of the storehouse consciousness by referring to the Āgama [i.e. the teachings of the Buddha]. Āgama here refers to the **Mahāyāna-abhidharma-sūtra*, in which the World-honored One says the verses. The term "this" [in the MSg] refers to the element (*dhātu*), i.e., the storehouse consciousness (*aliye shi jie* 阿黎耶識界), *which has jie as its xing*. (*yi jie wei xing* 以解為性). (My emphasis[2])

Point 1: *Jiexing* is an attribute of the storehouse consciousness.

In *Shelun Jiexing* Passage (2), Paramārtha suggests that *jiexing* is something located inside the storehouse consciousness:

> *Shelun Jiexing* Passage (2):
> The supramundane transformation of the basis (Ch. *chushi zhuanyi* 出世轉依; Skt. **lokōttarāśraya-parāvṛtti*) is also like this. As the power of the base consciousness

(Ch. *benshi* 本識; Skt. **mūla-vijñāna*) gradually diminishes and the permeation of hearing (Ch. *wenxunxi* 聞熏習; Skt. *śrutavāsanā*), etc., increase step by step, the basis for ordinary people (Ch. *fanfu yi* 凡夫依; Skt. **pṛthagjanāśraya*) is discarded and the basis for noble people (Ch. *shengren yi* 聖人依; Skt. **āryāśraya*) is made. What is called "the basis for noble people" comes from *the mixture between the permeation of hearing and jiexing* (*wenxunxi yu jiexing hehe* 聞熏習與解性和合). With this being the basis, all noble paths are born." (My emphasis[3])

On the basis of this passage, we can refine Point 1 as follows:

Point 1[a]: *Jiexing* refers to something inside the storehouse consciousness.

Next, *Shelun Jiexing* Passage (2) states that sentient beings are originally dependent upon the basis for ordinary people that resides in the storehouse consciousness. But due to the function of the permeation of hearing the Buddhist teachings, the defiled storehouse consciousness is weakened, and this basis for ordinary people is discarded and replaced by the basis for noble people. Thus:

Point 2: The mixture between *jiexing* and the permeation of hearing forms the basis for noble people. Before the basis for noble people is formed, the basis for ordinary people is operative.

It is very confusing that Paramārtha's *Shelun* actually mentions two different views concerning the stages at which nobility is attained: one becomes noble at the stage of ten understandings (*shijie* 十解), which refers to a stage before the first bodhisattva stage,[4] or at the first bodhisattva stage (*bhūmi*).[5]

To solve this ambiguity, we should note that, as Funayama points out, the standard Mahāyāna view is that nobility is attained upon entering the first bodhisattva stage.[6] More importantly, T2805 clarifies the situation by maintaining that the practitioner at the stage of ten understandings is merely a bodhisattva by designation (*jiaming pusa* 假名菩薩). Only upon entering the first bodhisattva stage can the status of true noble people (*zhensheng* 真聖) be attained.[7]

In addition, there are two other ways in which the *Shelun* suggests that nobility begins with the first bodhisattva stage.

1. The replacement of the basis for ordinary people by the basis for noble people is closely connected with the notion of "being supramundane" (Ch. *chushi* 出世; Skt. *lokōttara*). Furthermore, in the *Shelun,* "being supramundane" is often linked with the ten bodhisattva stages.[8]
2. The practitioner is said to be under the influence of permeation of hearing throughout the transformative stage of advancing the force and harming the power (Ch. *yili sunneng zhuan* 益力損能轉; Skt. **durbalīkaraṇōpabṛṃhaṇa-parāvṛtti*).[9] According to the *Shelun*, "advancing the force" here means "advancing the force of the permeation of hearing"; "harming the power" means "harming the power of the permeation by various kinds of delusion (*zhuhuo xunxi* 諸惑熏習).[10] At this stage, the permeation of hearing corresponds to understanding

> arising from hearing (Ch. *wenhui* 聞慧; Skt. *śrutamayī prajñā*), understanding arising from pondering (Ch. *sihui* 思慧; Skt. *cintāmayī prajñā*), and, finally, understanding arising from cultivating (Ch. *xiuhui* 修慧; Skt. *bhāvanāmayī prajñā*). After understanding arising from cultivating is formed, the previous basis (i.e., the basis for ordinary people) is transformed, and the practitioner advances to the transformative stage of penetration (Ch. *tongda zhuan* 通達轉; Skt. *prativedha-parāvṛtti*), i.e., entering the first bodhisattva stage.[11] This clearly indicates that the basis for ordinary people is discarded when one enters the first bodhisattva stage.

T2805 also confirms this point by saying that the transformative stage of advancing the force and harming the power corresponds to the stages before the first bodhisattva stage.[12] Interestingly, this passage is immediately followed by T2805 *Jiexing* Passage (1), where the notion of *jiexing* is extensively discussed. This also confirms the close connection between *jiexing*, permeation of hearing, and the transformative stage of advancing the force and harming the power. This close connection provides crucial information for the following discussion in 6.4.

For the aforementioned reasons, it is clear that the replacement of the basis for ordinary people by the basis for noble people occurs when one enters the first bodhisattva stage. This means that throughout the transformative stage of advancing the force and harming the power, the practitioner still has the basis for ordinary people. Thus:

> Point 2[a]: The mixture between *jiexing* and the permeation of hearing forms the basis for noble people. Before this basis for noble people is formed, the practitioner has the basis for ordinary people. The replacement of the basis for ordinary people by the basis for noble people takes place when the practitioner enters the first bodhisattva stage.

To conclude, in this section I draw attention to the two *jiexing* passages in the *Shelun*, where Paramārtha states that the mixture between *jiexing* and the permeation of hearing forms the basis for noble people. The process of mixing covers the transformative stage of advancing the force and harming the power. In addition, I argue that the replacement of the basis for ordinary people by the basis for noble people takes place when one enters the first bodhisattva stage, that is, at the end of the transformative stage of advancing the force and harming the power.

Even after examining the *Shelun*, we still do not have a clear idea of what *jiexing* is. We need to turn to T2805 for more information.

6.2 T2805 *Jiexing* Passages

> T2805 *Jiexing* Passage (1) (Abridged):
> [Commentary by T2805:] . . . when the understanding arising from hearing (Ch. *wen [hui]* 聞[慧]; *śrutamayī[-prajñā]*) and the understanding arising from

> pondering (Ch. *si [hui]* 思[慧]; *cintāmayī[-prajñā]*) permeate the impermanent (Ch. *wuchang* 無常; Skt. *anitya*) *jiexing* of the base consciousness (Ch. *benshi* 本識; Skt. **mūla-vijñāna*), [the practitioners] are still ordinary people (*pṛthagjana*) . . .
>
> Question: Regarding the *jiexing* that is permeated by the seeds of [the understanding arising from] hearing and [the understanding arising from] pondering, an explanation states that *jiexing* refers to the true and pure dharma-body (*zhenjing fashen* 真淨法身). How can you (my master) claim that it is an impermanent dharma?
>
> Answer: [This explanation] is arbitrary words (*manyu* 漫語) that, based on one's own [incorrect] thinking (*zigui shi xin* 自歸識心), arise from a dark discriminating mind (*fenbie anxin* 分別闇心). This is not the correct interpretation. A permanent dharma cannot be permeated, unlike an impermanent [dharma], which can be permeated in six contexts (*liuyi* 六義). The understanding arising from hearing and the understanding arising from pondering permeate [the storehouse consciousness], and only when they further reside in the sixth, i.e., the mental consciousness, and establish the understanding arising from cultivating, is the uncontaminated path (Ch. *wuliu dao* 無流道; Skt. *anāsrava-mārga*) established. . . .When afflictions are cut off completely, (i.e., when one attains the dharma-body) . . . only the merits from the effect [of liberation] are based on the dharma-body. [The dharma-body] does not have the further (*wufu* 無復) sense of being a seed or a cause.[13]

According to this passage, *jiexing* is conditioned and must not be understood in terms of the unconditioned dharma-body. As the true pure mind (*zhenjing xin* 真淨心), the dharma-body serves as the final goal of the noble path, where all the merits from the effects of liberation are manifest, but there is no sense that it is a cause or a collection of seeds. Moreover, T2805 also mentions that an unconditioned dharma cannot be permeated as a seed can in six different contexts.[14] Thus:

> Point 3: *Jiexing* is conditioned. It must not be identified with the dharma-body.

6.2.1 Understanding Arising from Hearing and Pondering as opposed to Understanding Arising from Cultivating

Furthermore, according to T2805 *Jiexing* Passage (1), it is clear that, before nobility, *jiexing* is permeated by understanding arising from hearing and pondering (Ch. *wensi hui* 聞思慧; Skt. *śruta-cintā-mayī prajñā*). This permeation leads to understanding arising from cultivating (Ch. *xiuhui* 修慧; Skt. *bhāvanā-mayī prajñā*).

The connection here between *jiexing* and the understanding arising from hearing and pondering confirms my assertion that, for Paramārtha, *jiexing* is related to the transformative stage of advancing the force and harming the power. We can see this in Paramārtha's reference to these two types of understanding in his explanation of this particular transformative stage.[15]

Furthermore, it is crucial to note that understanding arising from cultivating has undiscriminating *jñāna* (Ch. *wufenbie zhi* 無分別智; Skt. *nirvikalpa-jñāna*) as its substance (*ti* 體); that is to say, it is based on undiscriminating *jñāna*.[16] There is general agreement in the Yogācāra tradition that one attains this undiscriminating *jñāna* upon entering the first bodhisattva stage, which corresponds to the Path of Insight,[17] and the Path of Cultivation (Ch. *xiudao* 修道; Skt. *bhāvanā-mārga*) immediately follows. Moreover, there is an intricate reciprocal relationship between understanding arising from cultivating and the subsequently acquired *jñāna* (Ch. *houde* [*wufenbie*] *zhi* 後得 [無分別]智; Skt. *pṛṣṭha-labdha-jñāna*). Subsequently acquired *jñāna* is attained based on understanding arising from cultivating, while understanding arising from cultivating at a higher bodhisattva stage is based on this subsequently acquired *jñāna*.[18]

To conclude, T2805 *Jiexing* Passage (1) elaborates further on the basis for noble people. While the *Shelun* only states that the mixture between *jiexing* and the permeation of hearing constitutes the basis for noble people, T2805 adds that the basis for noble people is established after understanding arising from cultivating is attained. We have seen that the replacement of the basis for ordinary people by the basis for noble people takes place upon entrance to the first bodhisattva stage, where undiscriminating *jñāna* is attained. Thus, we also can conclude that *jiexing* is permeated by understanding arising from hearing and pondering but remains latent (i.e., does not become the basis for noble people) during the transformative stage of advancing the force and harming the power, that is, the stages before the first bodhisattva stage.

> Point 4: *Jiexing* is permeated, but the mixture between *jiexing* and the permeation of hearing does not become the basis for noble people during the transformative stage of advancing the force and harming the power, i.e., the stages before the first bodhisattva stage.

Next we turn to T2805 *Jiexing* Passage (2).

6.2.2 T2805 *Jiexing* Passage (2)

In T2805 *Jiexing* Passage (2), *jiexing* is mentioned in the context of a discussion of undiscriminating *jñāna*.

> T2805 *Jiexing* Passage (2):
> The undiscriminating *jñāna* has the Dharma-element (*dharmadhātu*) as its faculty (Ch. *gen* 根; Skt. *indriya*). Its substance (*ti* 體) is the faculty of having learned (Ch. *zhigen* 知根; Skt. *ājñātendriya*), because it is born from the faculty of resolving to come to know something unknown (Ch. *zhiweizhi gen* 知未知根 or *weizhi yuzhi gen* 未知欲知根; Skt. *ājñāsyāmīndriya*). It is also called "having a faculty" (*yougen* 有根) because it has the faculty of resolving to come to know something unknown, which is born from the *jñāna* of things as they really are (Ch. *rushi zhi* 如實智; Skt. *yathābhūta-parijñāna*). Moreover, from the perspective of the contributory cause (*yuanyin* 緣因) [for the undiscriminating *jñāna*], the arising of *jiexing* is also called "having a faculty." [Moreover, the undiscriminating *jñāna*] is also called "having a faculty" because it can bring about the subsequently acquired *jñāna* (Ch. *houzhi* 後智; i.e., 後得智; Skt. *pṛṣṭhalabdha-jñāna*) and advance to the applied

> *jñāna* (*jiaxing zhi* 加行智) at later stages (*bhūmi*). "Having a faculty" means having something that serves as the substance (*you dangti* 有當體). Why? Because once this [undiscriminating] *jñāna* is attained, the other kinds of *jñāna* will cease. Based on this [undiscriminating] *jñāna*, the merits and wisdom at higher stages will be born. For this reason, it [the undiscriminating *jñāna*] is a faculty.[19]

This passage is somewhat strange in that it characterizes undiscriminating *jñāna* as having a faculty (Ch. *yougen* 有根; Skt. *sendriya*), specifically, one of the three uncontaminated faculties (Ch. *wuliu gen* 無流根 or *wulou gen* 無漏根; Skt. **anāsrava-indriya*), namely, the faculty of resolving to know something unknown (Ch. *weizhi yuzhi gen* 未知欲知根; Skt. *ājñāsyāmīndriya*); the faculty of having learned (Ch. *zhigen* 知根; Skt. *ājñātendriya*); and the faculty of the perfect knowledge (Ch. *zhiyi gen* 知已根; Skt. *ājñātāvīndriya*). It is not clear which uncontaminated faculty, *ājñāsyāmīndriya* or *ājñātendriya,* is intended here.[20] Fortunately, the *Shelun* unequivocally states that undiscriminating *jñāna* corresponds to the faculty of resolving to know something unknown.[21] This interpretation is consonant with two other passages in the *Shelun*.[22]

6.2.3 The Arising of *Jiexing*

Next, I turn to a brief statement in T2805 *Jiexing* Passage (2) that is very difficult to understand:

> (Quotation 6.1) (Abridged from T2805 *Jiexing* Passage (2))
> Moreover, from the viewpoint of the contributory cause (*yuanyin* 緣因) [of the undiscriminating *jñāna*], [the undiscriminating *jñāna*] is also called "having a faculty" (*yougen* 有根) because of the arising of *jiexing*.[23]

One major problem with this statement is that, when T2805 says that undiscriminating *jñāna* is attained due to the arising of *jiexing* (*jiexing sheng* 解性生), the meaning of "arising of *jiexing*" is unclear. If it means that *jiexing* does not exist before the attainment of undiscriminating *jñāna*, then *jiexing* cannot be mixed with permeation of hearing before the first bodhisattva stage. If it means that *jiexing* is latent before the first bodhisattva stage, then, since *jiexing* already exists, it does not make sense to say that it arises.

In light of what has been said earlier, "arising of *jiexing*" probably refers to the fact that, when undiscriminating *jñāna* is attained upon entrance into the first bodhisattva stage, *jiexing* somehow becomes "active": namely, it stops being latent, and the mixture of *jiexing* and the permeation of hearing at this moment becomes the basis for noble people. Thus:

> Point 5: The arising of *jiexing* is related to the attainment of undiscriminating *jñāna* upon entrance into the first bodhisattva stage.

6.2.4 The Arising of *Jiexing* as a Contributory Cause

The second problem is that, when the passage states that undiscriminating *jñāna* is called "having a faculty" due to the arising of *jiexing* as the contributory cause (*yuanyin*

緣因), it is unclear why *jiexing* can be called a contributory cause. The cause proper (*zhengyin* 正因) is not mentioned.

I have found no solution to these problems in Paramārtha's *Shelun*, his other works nor in T2805. I have also looked at every passage found in CBETA in which the term *jiexing* appears, to no avail. Before moving on to Xuanzang's works, I summarize everything we know so far in Table 6.1.

6.3 The Legitimacy of Consulting Xuanzang's Translations

In what follows, I suggest that, although there seems to be no further information about the term *jiexing* in the sources currently available to us, other strikingly similar ideas can be found in later Chinese translations of Yogācāra texts and in the Chinese Yogācāra tradition. Therefore, it is both legitimate and fruitful to examine what is said about *jiexing* in later Chinese works.

Until now, modern scholars have not thought about *jiexing* in connection with Xuanzang's translations. The main reason is that later Chinese Buddhist thinkers were aware of the hostility between Xuanzang's school and the Chinese Tathāgatagarbha traditions (Huayan in particular) that were strongly influenced by the *Awakening of Faith,* and so they incorrectly thought that Paramārtha's Yogācāra thought was substantially different from that of Xuanzang. Modern scholars, in turn, have adopted this mistaken way of thinking.

In Chapter 5, I argued that the traditional attribution of the *Awakening of Faith* to Paramārtha should be rejected. If I am correct, there is no reason to think that Paramārtha and Xuanzang were entirely at odds with each other. Despite their occasional differences, we can assume that they had much in common.

Nevertheless, we must be very cautious not to read later developments into earlier texts. There is a gap of at least one hundred years between Paramārtha and Xuanzang. As we shall see next, Xuanzang's thought reflects a complicated development of Paramārtha's more prototypical theories. If we think that we have found something pertinent to Paramārtha in Xuanzang's works, it is always a good idea to return to Paramārtha to see if there is any counter-evidence.

6.4 CWSL: *Jiexing* and Uncontaminated Seeds

The CWSL refers to the idea of uncontaminated seeds (*jingzhong* 淨種) in a discussion of the transformative stage of advancing the force and harming the power:

> (Quotation 6.2)
> The "transformative stages" (*zhuanyi wei* 轉依位) are, in brief, of six kinds. First, the "transformative stage of harming the power and advancing the force" (Ch. *sunli yineng zhuan* 損力益能轉; Skt. **durbalīkaraṇopabṛṃhaṇa-parāvṛtti*). This refers to the first two stages (i.e., the Stage of Provision [Ch. *ziliang wei* 資糧位; Skt. *saṃbhārāvasthā*] and the Stage of Applied Practices [Ch. *jiaxing wei* 加行位; Skt.

Table 6.1 Summary of All the Information about *Jiexing* from *Shelun* and T2805

Before the 1st *bhūmi* (Bodhisattva Stage)	Upon Entering the 1st *bhūmi*	Having Entered the 1st *bhūmi* (Immediately Advancing to the 2nd *bhūmi*)[a]	From the 2nd Until the End of the 6th *bhūmi*	The 7th *bhūmi* and above Until the End of the 10th *bhūmi*	Buddhahood
The transformative stage of advancing the force and harming the power (Ch. *yili sunneng zhuan* 益力損能轉; Skt. **durbalīkaraṇopabṛṃhaṇa-parāvṛtti*)		The transformative stage of penetration (Ch. *tongda zhuan* 通達轉; Skt. **prativedha-parāvṛtti*)[b]		The transformative stage of cultivation (Ch. *xiuxi zhuan* 修習轉; Skt. *bhāvanā-parāvṛtti*)[c]	The transformative stage of the perfection of effects (Ch. *guo yuanman zhuan* 果圓滿轉; Skt. **phalaparipūri-parāvṛtti*)
The Path of Expedient Means (Ch. *fangbian dao* 方便道; Skt. *upāya-mārga*) [= the Path of Applied Practices (Ch. *jiaxing dao* 加行道; Skt. *prayoga-mārga*)][d]	Path of Insight (Ch. *jiandao* 見道; Skt. *darśana-mārga*)	Path of Cultivation (Ch. *xiudao* 修道; Skt. *bhāvanā-mārga*) (T2805)[e]		The Ultimate Point [of the Path] (*jiujing dao* 究竟道 or *jiujing wei* 究竟位; **niṣṭhāvasthā*) (T2805)	
		Path of Cultivation (Ch. *xiudao* 修道; Skt. *bhāvanā-mārga*) (*Shelun*)[f]			The Ultimate Point [of the Path] (*jiujing dao* 究竟道 or *jiujing wei* 究竟位; **niṣṭhāvasthā*) (*Shelun*)
Understanding arising from hearing and pondering (Ch. *wensi hui* 聞思慧; Skt. *śruta-cintā-mayī prajñā*)	Undiscriminating *jñāna* (Ch. *wufenbie zhi* 無分別智; Skt. *nirvikalpa-jñāna*) is attained	Understanding arising from cultivating (Ch. *xiuhui* 修慧; Skt. *bhāvanā-mayī prajñā*)			
Basis for ordinary people (Ch. *fanfu yi* 凡夫依; Skt. **pṛthagjanāśraya*)	The replacement of the basis for ordinary people by the basis for noble people.	Basis for noble people (Ch. *shengren yi* 聖人依; Skt. *āryāśraya*).			Enjoyment-body of the Buddha.[g]

Jiexing is permeated by the understanding arising from hearing and pondering but remains latent (i.e., does not become the basis for noble people).	The arising of *jiexing*	The mixture between *jiexing* and the permeation of hearing forms the basis for noble people.	Enjoyment-body of the Buddha.
	Faculty of resolving to come to know something unknown.	Faculty of having learned.	Faculty of the perfect knowledge.

[a]In some places, Paramārtha's *Shelun* (T1595:31.225b26-29) and especially T2805 (T2805:85.991b3-5) also suggest that the Path of Cultivation corresponds to the second bodhisattva stage. My tentative view is that after one attains the Path of Insight, one immediately advances to the Path of Cultivation.

[b]MSg IX.2: This stage covers the first to the sixth bodhisattva stage. See Nagao (1982–7, Vol. II: 303–4).

[c]MSg IX.2: This stage covers the seventh to the tenth bodhisattva stage. See Nagao (1982–7, Vol. II: 303–4).

[d]Also called "the Status Aspiration from Confidence" (Ch. *yuanle wei* 願樂位or *xinle wei* 信樂位; Skt. *adhimukti*) in the *Shelun* and T2805.

[e]There is complication and disagreement here since T2805 states that the Path of Cultivation begins at the second bodhisattva stage and continues through the seventh bodhisattva stage. The [Path of the] Ultimate Stage (*jiujing wei* 究竟位) is said to begin at the eighth bodhisattva stage because all efforts have reached their culmination (*gongyong jiujing* 功用究竟) (T2805:85.991b3-5).

[f]*Shelun*: T1595:31.209a4-5.

[g]See 4.5, and 5.2.2.

prayogāvasthā]). Due to the accustomization (*xi* 習) of aspiration from confidence (Ch. *shengjie* 勝解; Skt. *adhimukti*) and due to the sense of shame (Ch. *cankui* 慚愧; Skt. *lajjā*),[24] the power of the contaminated seeds (*ranzhong* 染種) in the base consciousness is harmed and the force of the uncontaminated seeds (*jingzhong* 淨種) in the base consciousness is advanced. Although the seeds of hindrance (*zhangzhong* 障種) are not cut off and the basis is not yet really transformed, it (i.e., this stage) is still named a "transformative stage" (Ch. *zhuan* 轉; Skt. *parāvṛtti*) because the manifest function (Ch. *xianxing* 現行; Skt. *samudācāra*) [of the seeds of hindrance] is gradually suppressed (*fu* 伏).[25]

This passage from the CWSL is strikingly similar to Paramārtha's explanation of the transformative stage of advancing the force and harming the power.[26] Both passages mention the sense of shame. Both mention harming the contaminated seeds within the storehouse consciousness.[27] More importantly, both regard this transformative stage as occurring before the first bodhisattva stage.[28] Although this passage does not explicitly mention permeation of hearing, it does mention "aspiration from confidence" (Ch. *shengjie* 勝解; Skt. *adhimukti*), which originates from permeation of hearing.

A clearer association between the idea of uncontaminated seeds and permeation of hearing can be seen in the following passage of the CWSL:

(Quotation 6.3)
Therefore, one should believe in this: from the beginningless time some sentient beings have uncontaminated seeds that are established naturally (Ch. *fa'er* 法爾; Skt. *dharmatā*) but not due to permeation. These seeds are caused to grow due to permeation at the stage of superior advancement (Ch. *shengjin wei* 勝進位; Skt. **viśeṣāvasthā*[29]) and become the cause of uncontaminated dharmas. When these uncontaminated dharmas arise, again [their] permeation leads to further [uncontaminated] seeds. The situation with contaminated dharmas is also similar to this. Although several noble teachings claim that the inner seeds must be permeated [in order to become manifestly functioning], yet they do not make a definitive claim that *all* seeds are born due to permeation. Do they ever entirely reject [the idea of] originally existent seeds (*benyou zhognzi* 本有種子)? [No, certainly not!] But even the originally existent seeds must be permeated in order to grow and to produce effects, and this is why it is taught that inner seeds must be permeated. However, the permeation of hearing does not merely [act upon] the [inner] contaminated [seeds]. When one hears the correct teaching, one's originally existent uncontaminated seeds (*benyou wulou zhongzi* 本有無漏種子) are also permeated and gradually caused to grow again and again till the supramundane mind (Ch. *chushi xin* 出世心; Skt. *lokōttara-citta*) is born. For this reason, this [permeation of hearing to the uncontaminated seeds] is also named "permeation of hearing."[30]

Most important here is the statement that uncontaminated seeds are possessed naturally (*fa'er chengjiu* 法爾成就); that is to say, they have existed from the beginning. Starting from the stage of superior advancement, permeation causes the seeds to grow.

Master Ji, in his commentary on the CWSL, explains the stage of superior advancement in terms of the Abhidharma concept of wholesome roots that are conducive to liberation (Ch. *jietuofen shan'gen* 解脱分善根; Skt. *mokṣa-bhāgīya kuśala-mūla*).[31] The CWSL later identifies wholesome roots conducive to liberation with the Stage of Provision (Ch. *ziliang wei* 資糧位; Skt. *saṃbhārāvasthā*),[32] which begins with the generation of the mind of enlightenment (*bodhicitta*).[33]

To put it simply, the CWSL claims that the uncontaminated seeds exist originally.[34] Beginning from the stage when the practitioner generates the mind of enlightenment or resolution to follow the Buddhist path, these uncontaminated seeds start to be permeated by hearing the Buddhist teachings, and so on, and are caused to grow. Although neither Paramārtha nor T2805 discusses the origin of *jiexing* or the stage at which *jiexing* begins to be permeated, it seems obvious that the entire discussion about the originally existent uncontaminated seeds in the CWSL is very similar to what we know about *jiexing*. The accounts in the CWSL and the *Shelun* regarding the transformative stage of advancing the force and harming the power are similar. Thus:

> Point 6: *Jiexing* seems to refer to the idea of originally existent uncontaminated seeds within the storehouse consciousness as discussed in the CWSL. Paramārtha and the CWSL agree that *jiexing* or originally existent uncontaminated seeds begin to be permeated before the first bodhisattva stage.[35]

However, as discussed next, this is not really correct.

6.4.1 *Jiexing* Is Not the Exact Equivalent of Uncontaminated Seeds

Despite the similarity that we have seen between the CWSL and Paramārtha's notion of *jiexing*, there is good reason not to consider *jiexing* to be the exact equivalent of the concept of originally existent uncontaminated seeds. Paramārtha was perfectly familiar with the idea of seed (*bīja*) and its Chinese rendering, *zhongzi* 種子, which he uses several hundred times in his works. If a Sanskrit term such as **anādi-anāsrava-bīja* underlies *jiexing*, he probably would have translated it as *wushi wuliu zhongzi* 無始無流種子. And the fact that he chose not to render the notion of *jiexing* in terms of *zhongzi* strongly suggests that the Sanskrit term underlying *jiexing* is something other than originally existent uncontaminated seeds (**anādi-anāsrava-bīja*). Thus:

> Point 6[a]: *Jiexing* is not equivalent to the uncontaminated seeds in the CWSL.

6.5 CWSL: *Jiexing* and *Gotra*

An examination of passages in the CWSL concerning uncontaminated seeds can give us more information about *jiexing*. In fascicle 2 of the CWSL, the origin of the uncontaminated seeds that lead to final liberation is discussed at length. The CWSL mentions three different views: (1) All uncontaminated seeds are originally existent and do not arise from permeation; (2) All uncontaminated seeds arise from permeation; (3) Some uncontaminated seeds are originally existent, and some arise from permeation.[36] The first and third views are most relevant. The first view is presented as follows:

> (Quotation 6.4)
> [First View:] In this connection there is a theory claiming that all seeds exist due to their own nature (*benxing you* 本性有) and are not produced due to permeation (*buyouxunsheng* 不由熏生). The force of permeation can only cause to grow (*zengzhang* 增長) those seeds. . . .As it is said in a relevant scripture (i.e., the **Mahāyāna-abhidharma-sūtra*): "From beginningless time this element (*dhātu*) is the basis for all dharmas." Here "element" means "cause." . . . Moreover, [as it is said in the *Yogācārabhūmi*, there exists] the innate *gotra* that is attained naturally (Ch. *fa'er* 法爾; Skt. *dharmatā*) and is passed on from one [reincarnation] to another [reincarnation] from beginningless time. All these quotations testify that the uncontaminated seeds come to exist naturally and are not produced due to permeation.[37]

On several points, originally existent seeds in this passage resemble Paramārtha's *jiexing* in the *Shelun*. First, the CWSL discusses originally existent uncontaminated seeds in exactly the same way that Paramārtha and T2805 discuss *jiexing*. The uncontaminated seeds, like *jiexing*, reside within the storehouse consciousness but are caused to grow by the force of permeation of hearing from the outside. Second, this passage quotes from the **Mahāyāna-abhidharma-sūtra* in its discussion of originally existent uncontaminated seeds. This is the same passage in the **Mahāyāna-abhidharma-sūtra* that Paramārtha quotes while introducing the idea of *jiexing* in *Shelun Jiexing* Passage (1).

The use of the term "innate *gotra*" (Ch. *benxingzhu xing* 本性住性; Skt. *prakṛtistha gotra*) is especially striking in this passage. This, I believe, helps explain why Paramārtha uses the word *xing* in the compound *jiexing*. The Sanskrit term *gotra* is, as far as I know, always translated as either *zhongxing* 種姓 or simply *xing* 性. Paramārtha's use of *xing* in the compound *jiexing* would be natural if, as I suspect, the concept of *jiexing* involves the idea of *gotra*.[38]

Here the CWSL refers to the idea of innate *gotra* at the beginning of the *Bodhisattvabhūmi* portion of the *Yogācārabhūmi*. In fact, the view that some uncontaminated seeds are originally existent, whereas others arise from permeation connects the originally existent uncontaminated seeds with innate *gotra* and the uncontaminated seeds originating from permeation with cultivated *gotra* (Ch. *xisuocheng zhongxing* 習所成種姓; Skt. *samudānīta gotra*), as indicated in the third view cited by the CWSL:[39]

> (Quotation 6.5) [Third View:]
> There is a theory claiming that seeds are of two kinds: one kind is originally existent (*benyou* 本有) . . . this is called the "innate *gotra*" (Ch. *benxingzhu zhong* 本性住

種; Skt. *prakṛtistha gotra*). Another kind is incipient (*shiqi* 始起) . . . this is called the "cultivated *gotra*" (Ch. *xisuocheng zhong* 習所成種; Skt. *samudānīta gotra*).[40]

Later in the CWSL, there is another explanation of these two *gotras*:

(Quotation 6.6)
[Question:] Who can be awoken to (*wuru* 悟入) the nature and the characteristics of consciousness-and-representation-only (*vijñapti-mātratā*) established above? And at what stages? [Answer:] Only those who are endowed with the two *gotra*s of the Mahāyāna can be awoken gradually in five stages. [Question:] What does it mean by the two *gotra*s of the Mahāyāna? [Answer:] The first is the "innate *gotra*" (Ch. *benxingzhu zhong* 本性住種; Skt. *prakṛtistha gotra*), that is, the cause of uncontaminated dharmas that has resided in (*yifu* 依附) the base consciousness since beginningless time and is attained naturally (*fa'er suode* 法爾所得). The second is the "cultivated *gotra*" (Ch. *xisuocheng zhong* 習所成種; Skt. *samudānīta gotra*), that is, [the *gotra*] that is established by permeation—i.e., [the permeation] consists of hearing [the Buddhist teachings] (Ch. *wensuocheng* 聞所成; Skt. *śrutamaya*), etc.—after one has heard the dharmas that flow from the Dharma-element (*dharmadhātu*). Only those who are endowed with these two *gotra*s can be gradually awoken to consciousness-and-representation-only.[41]

This passage clearly identifies the innate *gotra* with the cause of uncontaminated *dharmas*. Since the terms "cause" and "seed" are synonyms, innate *gotra* here is clearly identified with the originally existent uncontaminated seeds.

The similarity between the originally existent uncontaminated seeds in the CWSL and Paramārtha's *jiexing* having been established, *jiexing* seems to be a translation of innate *gotra* in the *Bodhisattvabhūmi*. Thus:

Point 7: *Jiexing* probably refers to the notion of innate *gotra* (*prakṛtistha gotra*) in the *Bodhisattvabhūmi*.

Point 8: The term *xing* 性 in *jiexing* is a translation of the Sanskrit *gotra*.

Next, we turn to the FDJL to investigate the connection between *jiexing* and the undiscriminating *jñāna*.

6.6 FDJL: *Jiexing* and Innate *Gotra*

In the FDJL and the CWSL, the idea of innate *gotra* is connected with the context of four kinds of *jñāna*[42] but not directly with undiscriminating *jñāna*. The following passage highlights this close connection:

(Quotation 6.7)
Moreover, regarding the various states of mind (*xinpin* 心品)[43] that are associated with these four kinds of *jñāna* (*sizhi xiangying* 四智相應) as discussed above, at

which stage are they first attained? At which stage do they become manifestly functional (Ch. *xianxing* 現行; Skt. *samudācāra*)? The uncontaminated *gotra* is innate (*benyou* 本有) from beginningless time. It continues (*xiangxu* 相續) by relying upon the arising-and-ceasing of the maturing consciousness (Ch. *yishu shi* 異熟識; Skt. *vipāka-vijñāna*, i.e., the storehouse consciousness). After one has generated the mind [of enlightenment] (*faxin* 發心), [this *gotra*] increases gradually by means of permeation from outside.[44]

The FDJL goes on to explain at which stage each of these *jñāna*s first becomes manifestly functioning (*xianxing* 現行)[45] and concludes as follows:

(Quotation 6.8)
In this way, the seeds of the various states of mind (*xinpin* 心品) that are associated with the four kinds of *jñāna* are innate (*benyou* 本有) from beginningless time. They came to exist naturally (Ch. *fa'er* 法爾; Skt. *dharmatā*) but not due to permeation. They are called "innate *gotra*" (Ch. *benxingzhu zhongxing* 本性住種性; Skt. *prakṛtistha gotra*). After one generates the mind of enlightenment, permeated (xun 熏) by external conditions (i.e., the permeation of hearing) and becoming active (fa 發), [those seeds] grow gradually and are called the "cultivated *gotra*" (Ch. *xisuocheng zhongxing* 習所成種性; Skt. *samudānīta gotra*). After the first bodhisattva stage, they become manifestly functioning (Ch. *xianqi* 現起; Skt. *samudācāra*) following what they are associated with (*suiqi suoying* 隨其所應). Due to repeated permeation, they are caused to grow and become superior, and all the way to the point of diamond-like concentration (Ch. *jin'gangyuding* 金剛喻定; Skt. *vajropama-samādhi*).[46]

Notably, this passage states that innate *gotra* becomes active and is called "cultivated *gotra*" after the first bodhisattva stage. We have seen (Point 4) that *jiexing* is permeated but remains latent until the first bodhisattva stage while, after the first bodhisattva stage, the mixture between *jiexing* and the permeation of hearing serves as the basis for noble people. Here, the FDJL calls the mixture between *jiexing* and permeation of hearing a "cultivated *gotra*."

The idea that the innate *gotra* becomes active after the first bodhisattva stage also helps to explain what T2805 means by "the arising of *jiexing*" (*jiexing sheng* 解性生). I suggest that the best way to understand the arising of *jiexing* is that *jiexing*, as innate *gotra*, becomes active at the first bodhisattva stage. Thus:

Point 9: *Jiexing* refers to the idea of innate *gotra* as discussed in the FDJL.[47] It becomes active after entrance into the first bodhisattva stage, at which point it is called "cultivated *gotra*" in the FDJL and "basis for noble people" in the *Shelun*.

6.6.1 The Four Kinds of *Jñāna* and Undiscriminating *Jñāna*?

An seeming inconsistency between T2805 and the FDJL remains: T2805 mentions the arising of *jiexing* in connection with undiscriminating *jñāna*, while the FDJL mentions innate *gotra* in connection with the four kinds of *jñāna*. However, there is a close relation between undiscriminating *jñāna* and the four kinds of *jñāna*. According to quotation 6.8 from the FDJL, each of the four kinds of *jñāna* becomes active after the first bodhisattva stage. Since undiscriminating *jñāna* is attained after the first bodhisattva stage, the connection between the four kinds of *jñāna* and undiscriminating *jñāna* is clear.[48]

Moreover, according to the FDJL, having Thusness (*tathatā*) as the cognitive object (*suoyuan* 所緣; *ālambana*) is a crucial part of the definitions of both mirror *jñāna* and equality *jñāna*.[49] This again is evidence of the close relation between these two kinds of *jñāna* and undiscriminating *jñāna*, which is also defined as having Thusness as its sole cognitive object.

It seems that the notion of the four kinds of *jñāna* was further developed only after Vasubandhu. In the MSg, Asaṅga simply mentions that the four kinds of *jñāna* are attained after the transformation of the basis of the consciousness-aggregate (*shiyunyi* 識蘊依), without any further explanation. In Vasubandhu's MSgBh, these four are merely treated as four kinds of supernatural knowledge (*ṛddhi*): for instance, mirror *jñāna* is characterized as the ability to remember everything.[50] There is no discussion of the stage at which the various *jñāna*s operate. Sthiramati's commentaries on the *Thirty Verses* and the MAV do not relate the four *jñāna*s to the eight consciousnesses. The MSA, one the earliest texts to do so, pairs mirror *jñāna* with the transformation of the eighth consciousness, equality *jñāna* with the transformation of the seventh consciousness, observing *jñāna* with the transformation of the sixth consciousness, and performing *jñāna* with the transformation of the first five consciousnesses.[51] Both the FDJL and the CWSL follow the MSA in this regard.

Similarly, the connection between *gotra* and the four *jñāna*s also seems to have been established only at a fairly late stage of Yogācāra. Thus, the association between *jiexing* and undiscriminating *jñāna* in T2805, presumably based on Paramārtha's original teaching, may be an earlier version of a theory later developed in the FDJL and the CWSL.

If *Jiexing*, which previously was in the state of seeds, becomes active at the first bodhisattva stage, when the practitioner's mind is ready to attain undiscriminating *jñāna*, this would seem to imply that *jiexing* acts as the cause proper (*zhengyin* 正因) for undiscriminating *jñāna*. However, if this were the case, something unconditioned (i.e., undiscriminating *jñāna*) would be caused by something conditioned (*jiexing*). T2805 deals with this contradiction by saying that *jiexing* is merely a contributory cause (*yuanyin* 緣因).

Before discussing the position of T2805 in detail, I examine what the FXL says about *jiexing* and innate *gotra*.

6.7 *Jiexing* and Innate *Gotra* in Paramārtha's FXL

So far we have investigated the *Shelun*, T2805, Xuanzang's translation of the CWSL, and the FDJL. I conclude that the idea of an innate *gotra* in the FDJL most closely resembles *jiexing*. However, I have not yet mentioned that Paramārtha extensively discusses the notion of innate *gotra* in the FXL. Now I turn to the FXL to see if it confirms my assertion. Furthermore, I hope we can learn more about why T2805 regards *jiexing* as merely a contributory cause.

The FXL explicitly declares that there are two kinds of *buddha-gotra*: the innate *gotra* (*zhu zixing xing* 住自性性) and the drawn-forth *gotra* (*yinchu xing* 引出性).[52] Both the *Shelun* and an interlinear note to the FXL, however, mention that there are three kinds of *buddha-gotra*: the innate *gotra* and drawn-forth *gotra*, as well as a third type, the attained *gotra* (*zhide xing* 至得性 or *zhiguo foxing* 至果佛性).[53] Basically, the third *gotra* refers only to the state of having ultimately attained the state of buddhahood and has nothing to do with the actual process of cultivating practices. For this reason, it is omitted from the following discussion.

With respect to the original Sanskrit underlying these two (or three) kinds of *buddha-gotra*, I agree with Takasaki (2005) that the first two are translations of *prakṛtistha gotra* (innate *gotra*) and *samudānīta gotra* (cultivated *gotra*)[54] as found in the *Bodhisattvabhūmi* portion of the *Yogācārabhūmi*. Takasaki reconstructs the Sanskrit for the third *buddha-gotra* as *phala-prāpta-gotra*.[55]

It is noteworthy that the FXL states that innate *gotra* is related to the dharma-body, while drawn-forth *gotra* is related to the enjoyment-body and, derivatively, to the transformation-body:

> (Quotation 6.9) (= quotation 5.5; also see quotation 7.24)
> There are two kinds of *buddha-gotras*. First, the innate *gotra* (*zhu zixing xing* 住自性性) and second, the drawn-forth *gotra* (*yinchu xing* 引出性) The three bodies of the Buddhas are perfected (*chengjiu* 成就) due to these two *gotras*. . . . Regarding these two [*buddha-gotras* as] causes, the Buddha taught the three bodies as effects. First, with the innate *buddha-gotra* as the cause, the Buddha taught the dharma-body. . . . Second, with the drawn-forth *buddha-gotra* as the cause, the Buddha taught the enjoyment-body (*yingshen shen* 應身; literally, the correspondence-body). . . . Third, with the drawn-forth *buddha-gotra* as the cause, the transformation-body (*huashen* 化身) is further derived.[56]

The connection between innate *gotra* and the dharma-body[57] cannot be overemphasized here.[58] This passage implies that innate *gotra* must be regarded as being unconditioned since, according to the FXL, the dharma-body is unconditioned. Several other passages in the FXL explicitly claim that the dharma-body is unconditioned. For example, it states that it would be a mistake to take the dharma-body as conditioned.[59] In addition, being unconditioned is said to be one of the characteristics of the dharma-body because it is devoid of four kinds of faults, that is, birth, old age, sickness, and death.[60] Furthermore, the entire chapter on Invariability (*wubianyi pin* 無變異品) of the FXL is devoted to explaining that the dharma-body is unchangeable (*avikāra*[61]) in six different ways.[62]

According to the FXL, the reason why the dharma-body is unconditioned is that it is the principle of Thusness (*zhenru li* 真如理).[63] It also states that there are four synonyms of *tathāgata-gotra* (*rulaixing* 如來性): (1) dharma-body; (2) Tathāgata; (3) Ultimate Reality (*paramārtha*); (4) nirvana:

(Quotation 6.10)
Moreover, what is meant by "postulating four synonyms [for the *tathāgata-gotra*]" is this: First, because all Buddha-dharmas (*fofa* 佛法) are not separated [from this *tathāgata-gotra*], it (*tathāgata-gotra*) is named "dharma-body"; second, because this *gotra* is same as Thusness everywhere, it is named "*tathāgata*"; third, because it is devoid of delusions and perversions (*xuwang diandao* 虛妄顛倒), it is named "Ultimate Reality" (*zhenshi di* 真實諦); fourth, because it is originally tranquil (*benlai jijing* 本來寂靜), it is named "nirvana." These four senses and four synonyms are not different from the *tathāgata-gotra*. And hence the characteristic of "non-difference" (*wuchabie xiang* 無差別相) is taught.[64]

Since Tathāgata, Ultimate Reality, and nirvana are all unconditioned, the FXL implies that the innate *gotra* is unconditioned and should not be identified with *jiexing*.[65] This distinguishes Paramārtha's FXL from all other Yogācāra texts, which invariably consider both *gotras* to be conditioned.[66]

Given the identification of the innate *gotra* with the dharma-body in the FXL, Point 9 must be modified. The FXL treats innate *gotra* as being unconditioned. Therefore, if Paramārtha belonged to the interpretative tradition associated with the FXL, *jiexing* could not be identified with innate *gotra*. Thus:

Point 9[a]: *Jiexing* does not refer to the innate *gotra* as defined in Paramārtha's FXL because the innate *gotra* therein is unconditioned.

6.7.1 *Jiexing* and the Drawn-forth *Gotra*

We have seen that *jiexing* cannot be identified with the innate *gotra* as defined in the FXL. However, we have also seen that the term *xing* in *jiexing* seems to refer to ideas such as seeds and *gotra*. The possibility remains that *jiexing* is equivalent to drawn-forth *gotra*. The drawn-forth *gotra* is defined in the FXL as follows:

(Quotation 6.11)
Second, the drawn-forth *buddha-gotra*: beginning from one's generation of the mind of enlightenment until the mind of diamond[-like concentration] (*jin'gang xin* 金剛心), the *buddha-gotra* in-between is named "drawn-forth." The reason why it is called "drawn-forth" includes [the sense of drawing one out from the following] five states: (1) out of the status of "*icchantika*"; (2) out of the status of "non-Buddhists"; (3) out of the status of the Hearers (*śrāvakas*); (4) out of the status of the Solitary Realizers (*pratyeka-buddhas*); (5) out of the status where a bodhisattva dwells in ignorance (*wuming zhudi wei* 無明住地位). [Based on this *buddha-gotra*], the shell of afflictions (*fannao ke* 煩惱[糓-禾+卵]) [that covers] the dharma-body can be broken and the substance [of the dharma-body] can be disclosed. Therefore, [the *Tathāgatagarbha-sūtra*] teaches the sixth simile, i.e., the sprout of the Āmra tree (*Anluo shu* 菴羅樹, i.e., the mango tree). It (the drawn-forth *buddha-gotra*) is like the sprout of that tree: it can penetrate through

> the skin and flesh and gives birth to the king among trees. For this reason, [the *Tathāgatagarbha-sūtra*] teaches that the drawn-forth *buddha-gotra* is like a sprout of the Āmra tree because it can give birth to the king among trees.[67]

Although the FXL does not mention *jiexing*, it is clear that the drawn-forth *gotra* applies to the whole path of Buddhist practice, which is undoubtedly conditioned. *Jiexing*, insofar as it is characterized as conditioned in T2805, is definitely related to drawn-forth *gotra*.

The relation between *jiexing* and drawn-forth *gotra* can be further corroborated with reference to the enjoyment-body. As we saw in the previous chapter, Jizang explains that, according to the Shelun masters, *jiexing* becomes the enjoyment-body after the transformation of the basis.[68] The FXL, too, states that the enjoyment-body is derived from drawn-forth *gotra*.[69]

But something in the FXL again prevents us from directly identifying *jiexing* with the drawn-forth *gotra*. In its definition, the FXL states that the drawn-forth *gotra* begins with the first generation of the mind of enlightenment and applies to the whole path. But in the *Shelun*, Paramārtha does not deny that *jiexing* can precede the permeation of hearing Buddhist teachings. In fact, he says that permeation of hearing from the outside mixes with internal *jiexing*. This strongly suggests that *jiexing* exists even before the generation of the mind of enlightenment, which takes place at least partly due to hearing the Buddhist teachings. Thus:

> Point 10: *Jiexing* is closely related to drawn-forth *gotra* since both are conditioned. But *jiexing* still cannot be identified with drawn-forth *gotra* as defined in Paramārtha's FXL.

6.7.2 *Jiexing*: A Further Development of the *Gotra* theory in the FXL

An examination of the definitions of the two *gotras* in the FXL makes it clear that its two-*gotra* theory is incomplete. Namely, the FXL remains silent about the relationship between the two *gotras*. Moreover, the FXL only explains that the drawn-forth *gotra* applies to the whole Buddhist path after the generation of the mind of enlightenment, but it says nothing about whether the drawn-forth *gotra* is newly established when the mind of enlightenment is generated or it is based upon something established earlier.

There is a dilemma here. If the drawn-forth *gotra* were newly produced at the generation of the mind of enlightenment, then there is no necessary connection between the drawn-forth *gotra* and innate *gotra*. This would further imply that the enjoyment-body is not related to the dharma-body because each of these bodies is linked to a single *gotra*. On the other hand, the drawn-forth *gotra* cannot somehow be a transformation of the innate *gotra* because the innate *gotra*, being unconditioned, cannot become something conditioned.

Thus, it seems that a necessary connection between the unconditioned innate *gotra* and the conditioned drawn-forth *gotra* is missing in the FXL. This leads to a weakness in FXL's explanation of *gotra*, namely that the drawn-forth *gotra* seems to have come from nowhere. Moreover, the entire concept of permeation of hearing and the way it causes the drawn-forth *gotra* to grow is also missing from the FXL. In light of this, the FXL seems to represent an earlier form of the *gotra* theory than the FDJL or CWSL.

According to my interpretation, *jiexing* acts as a bridge between the two *gotras* in the FXL. On the one hand, *jiexing* is the conditioned basis of the drawn-forth *gotra*. On the other hand, *jiexing* is the uncontaminated seeds of *jñāna*, which, when they become active at the first bodhisattva stage, lead to the attainment of undiscriminating *jñāna*, which has Thusness, that is, innate *gotra*, as its sole cognitive object. Thus, the connection between the drawn-forth *gotra* and innate *gotra* is established. Since ideas similar to *jiexing* can be found in later Yogācāra works, it appears that the notion of *jiexing* was not invented by Paramārtha but has an Indian textual precedent, which, unfortunately, we currently have no way to identify.

Failure to see the strict distinction between the unconditioned innate *gotra* and the conditioned drawn-forth *gotra* can lead readers of Paramārtha's FXL to the conclusion that innate *gotra*, after it is active, becomes drawn-forth *gotra*. In fact, it seems likely that some Shelun masters made this mistake.[70]

6.8 *Jiexing* as a Contributory Cause

The previous review of the two-*gotra* theory in the FXL helps answer the question of why T2805 maintains that *jiexing* is a contributory cause of undiscriminating *jñāna*. The two-*gotra* theory in the FXL implies that *jiexing* cannot be identified with the unconditioned innate *gotra*. Since it is the cognition of unconditioned Thusness, undiscriminating *jñāna* must also be unconditioned. Therefore, the cause proper of undiscriminating *jñāna* can only be undiscriminating *jñāna* itself because an unconditioned dharma cannot have a cause proper other than itself.[71]

As we have seen in 4.3.1, Paramārtha's definition of the unconditioned dharma-body includes both Thusness and the *jñāna* about Thusness. This implies that, like Thusness, the *jñāna* about Thusness must also be unconditioned. Therefore, neither the *jñāna* about Thusness nor undiscriminating *jñāna* is produced through cultivation. Strictly speaking, they cannot be produced, only disclosed. Undiscriminating *jñāna* already exists and has always existed because it is unconditioned. The attainment of unconditioned undiscriminating *jñāna* upon entrance into the first bodhisattva stage is actually the generation of a state of mind that is associated (i.e., functions in accordance) with unconditioned undiscriminating *jñāna*. This state of mind discloses unconditioned undiscriminating *jñāna* but does not produce it. This is precisely why the FDJL states that the four uncontaminated states of mind that are generated through the transformation of consciousnesses, when they are associated with (Ch. *xiangying* 相應; Skt. *saṃyukta*) the four kinds of *jñāna*, are nominally designated (*jiashuo* 假說) as the four kinds of *jñāna*.[72] Such states of mind can be generated, but unconditioned undiscriminating *jñāna* cannot.

Thus, when *jiexing* becomes active after the first bodhisattva stage, it discloses unconditioned undiscriminating *jñāna* for the first time. When the practitioner becomes a Buddha after the transformation of the basis, *jiexing* becomes the enjoyment-body, which functions in accordance with the undiscriminating *jñāna*, an essential part of the dharma-body.

The idea that undiscriminating *jñāna* is unconditioned seems strange. Cognition, by definition, must change whenever the cognitive object changes. Therefore, an unconditioned *jñāna* should not really be a form of cognition at all. A passage from Plato's *Meno* (84–5) might help us make sense of Paramārtha's idea of unconditioned *jñāna*. There Socrates explains how a slave boy without any mathematical training can be taught to solve a geometry problem. The point is that everyone has innate or a priori knowledge from a previous life. However, people forget what they knew in past lives, so a learning process is necessary to recall that innate knowledge.

This idea of innate knowledge can be applied to Paramārtha's idea of unconditioned undiscriminating *jñāna* as follows: for Paramārtha, all sentient beings share Thusness and dharma-body, as well as unconditioned undiscriminating *jñāna*. Therefore, everyone is originally endowed with unconditioned undiscriminating *jñāna*, and our shared unconditioned undiscriminating *jñāna* is a kind of innate knowledge. Despite this, due to beginningless ignorance, we are not aware that we have this knowledge. Hence, a mental process is required for us to come to realize that we have this knowledge. By means of this process, unconditioned undiscriminating *jñāna* becomes disclosed, and our cognitive state (i.e., conditioned undiscriminating *jñāna*) operates in accordance with that knowledge. After we become capable of cognizing in accordance with that knowledge, we can begin to teach others (in terms of subsequently acquired conditioned *jñāna*) based on conditioned undiscriminating *jñāna*.

Although this idea seems strange, we can find traces of a similar idea of unconditioned *jñāna*, for example, in the MSA:

> (Quotation 6.12)
> The mirror *jñāna* does not move (*acala*). It serves as the basis for the remaining three kinds of *jñāna* (i.e., the equality *jñāna*, the observing *jñāna*, the performing *jñāna*).[73]

The nature of mirror *jñāna* is also discussed in the FDJL, which mentions a disagreement concerning whether mirror *jñāna* is associated with the essence-body (*svābhāvika-kaya*) or the enjoyment-body.[74] As I understand it, the key issue there is whether mirror *jñāna* should be regarded as unconditioned or conditioned. If it is unconditioned, it would be associated with the essence-body, which is unconditioned; if it is conditioned, it would be associated with the enjoyment-body, which is conditioned. In the MSA and the FDJL, we can see the beginning of a debate among Buddhist scholars over issues such as the nature of *jñāna* after buddhahood is attained and the relation between the practitioner's level of cultivation and the four kinds of *jñāna*. The discussions in T2805 and the works of Paramārtha are representative of this debate.

Now we finally are better able to appreciate why T2805 insists that *jiexing* is not the cause proper of undiscriminating *jñāna*. Since undiscriminating *jñāna* is unconditioned, its cause proper can only be itself; strictly speaking, it cannot have a cause. *Jiexing* can only be the cause proper of the state of mind (i.e., conditioned undiscriminating *jñāna*) that functions in accordance with unconditioned undiscriminating *jñāna*. To the extent that *jiexing* brings about the state of mind via which unconditioned undiscriminating *jñāna* is disclosed, *jiexing* should be regarded as a contributory cause of the unconditioned undiscriminating *jñāna*.[75]

6.9 The Agreement between Paramārtha and Xuanzang's Disciples

Finally, a number of texts from Xuanzang's lineage support my interpretation of *jiexing* as uncontaminated seeds. The *Yugaron gi* edited by Doryun 遁倫 or 道倫 (d.u.) presents the views of various Indian masters about whether permeation originally exists or is only established after one has the chance to hear Buddhist teachings. Doryun records the opinions of three teachers according to Shentai 神泰 (d.u., active 645–57):

> (Quotation 6.13)
> Tai 泰 (i.e., Master Shentai 神泰) reports:
> Shengjun 勝軍 (i.e., Prasenajit or Jayasena) claims that only new permeations (*xin xunxi* 新熏習; i.e., the permeations which arise after hearing Buddhist teachings) exist. Hence [despite] Thusness is a cognitive object (*suoyuan* 所緣; *ālambana*), [it does not cause the arising of the uncontaminated mind]. The uncontaminated (*wulou* 無漏; *anāsrava*) [mind] first arises from the seeds produced by the correct *jñāna* (*zhengzhi* 正智) [that has Thusness as its sole object] alone. The first [thing which is] uncontaminated (*chu wulou* 初無漏; i.e., Thusness) does not arise from causes and conditions.
>
> Huyue 護月 (aka. Yuezang 月藏; Candragupta or Candrapāla), etc. claim that there is only originally existent permeation (*benyou xunxi* 本有熏習). The nature (*xing* 性) of the originally existent permeation is to realize (*zheng* 證; i.e., cognizes) Thusness, which is the cognitive object (*ālambana*) of the originally existent permeation. This permeation is called seeds [born from] having Thusness as the cognitive object (Ch. *zhenru suoyuanyuan zhongzi* 真如所緣緣種子; Skt. **tathatālambanabīja*).[76] From this the noble path (*shengdao* 聖道; *āryamārga*) arises for the first time.
>
> Jiexian 戒賢 (Śīlabhadra) claims that both new and old (i.e., originally existent) permeation exist. The old permeation is just the same as claimed by Huyue, etc. Although there is the old permeation, if there is no new permeation, the old permeation cannot generate the noble path. For this reason, only a mixture (*hehe* 和合) between the new and old [permeation] can give rise to the noble path. The nature (*xing* 性) of both permeations is *jñāna* (*zhi* 智), i.e., the *jñāna* that has Thusness as its cognitive object. The is why it is said [in the *Viniścayasaṃgrahaṇī* portion of the *Yogācārabhūmi*] that "Supramundane dharmas arise from the seeds [born from] having Thusness as the cognitive object"[77] and in the *Mahāyānasaṃgrahabhāṣya* (here referring to Paramārtha's *Shelun*) that "the mixture between the permeation of hearing and *jiexing* gives birth to all noble paths."[78]

The *Mahāyānasaṃgrahabhāṣya* cited here must be Paramārtha's *Shelun* because it alone includes the idea of *jiexing*. Therefore, the reference to the *Shelun* must have been made by Shentai rather than by Śīlabhadra, who could not have cited the *Shelun*, which existed only in Chinese. Shentai, in his interpretation of Śīlabhadra, compares the mixture between the old (i.e., originally existent) permeation and the new permeation (i.e., after one begins to hear the Buddhist teachings) to the notion in the *Shelun* of the mixture between permeation and *jiexing*. Obviously, Shentai takes *jiexing* to refer to Śīlabhadra's notion of "old permeation."

Shentai's interpretation supports my interpretation of *jiexing* in two aspects. First, according to Shentai's interpretation, *jiexing* should be regarded as being conditioned since it is identified with permeation, which has causes and effects and hence is conditioned. Second, Shengtai relates permeation to the arising of the noble path. The *Shelun* similarly says that the mixture between permeation of hearing and *jiexing* leads to the arising of the noble path.

A complication here, however, is that such notions as "originally existent uncontaminated seeds" and "innate *gotra*" are discussed in the CWSL under the context of five *gotras*.[79] That is to say, the existence of originally existent uncontaminated seeds does not imply that all sentient beings are endowed with these seeds, much less that all sentient beings will eventually become Buddhas. Now it is not clear whether for Paramārtha *jiexing* exists in all sentient beings or not with his much too brief statement that there is *jiexing* within the storehouse consciousness (*Shelun Jiexing* Passage [1]). Again, I think this indicates that Paramārtha's notion of *jiexing* predates those much more complicated discussions in the CWSL.

In addition, a passage from the CWSL, based on what it says about the great enlightenment attained after the transformation of the basis (i.e., buddhahood), also supports my interpretation of *jiexing*:

> (Quotation 6.14)
> Second, what is produced (*suo shengde* 所生得) [after the transformation of the basis], namely, the great enlightenment (*da puti* 大菩提). Although there are originally existent seeds that can produce it (i.e., the great enlightenment), it is not produced due to the obstructions related to cognitive objects (Ch. *suozhi zhang* 所知障; Skt. *jñeyāvaraṇa*). When the power of the noble path cuts off those obstructions, [that power] brings it (i.e., the great enlightenment) forth from its seeds, and as such it is called "attaining enlightenment." After it arises, it continues into the indefinite future. This [enlightenment] refers to the state of mind (*xinpin* 心品) that is associated (i.e., functions in accordance) with the four kinds of *jñāna*.[80]

Here the CWSL claims that there are originally existent seeds of the great enlightenment, and these seeds are activated to become the great enlightenment. This view of originally existent seeds is very close to my interpretation of *jiexing* as the seeds of a state of mind that functions in accordance with unconditioned undiscriminating *jñāna*. Further, the CWSL also states that the seeds of the four kinds of *jñāna* are originally existent. When they become active through permeation (*xunfa* 熏發), these seeds become manifestly functioning (*xianxing* 現行) and produce their effect, namely, the state of mind that functions in accordance with the four kinds of *jñāna*.[81] This again supports my interpretation of *jiexing* as the originally existent seeds of this state of mind.

Finally, I conclude my investigation about *jiexing* with the following passage from Master Ji, where he distinguishes two kinds of *buddha-gotra*: the unconditioned *gotra* (*wuwei xing* 無為性) and the *gotra* that has causes and conditions (*you yinyuan xing* 有因緣性):

> (Quotation 6.15)
> There are two kinds of *gotras*: first, uncontaminated; second, contaminated. Under uncontaminated there are two: first, the "unconditioned *gotra*" (*wuwei xing* 無為性). As is stated in the *Śrīmālādevīsiṃhanāda-sūtra*, "When it is entangled (*zaichan* 在纏; i.e., with defilements [*sa-mala*]), it is called *tathāgatagarbha*; when it is unfettered, it is called the dharma-body." The *Mahāparinirvāṇa-mahāsūtra* states, "What is said by means of the lion's roar is the definitive teaching (Ch. *jueding shuo* 決定說; Skt. *nītārtha*), namely, all sentient beings have *buddha-gotra*." *Second, the "gotra that has causes and conditions" (you yinyuan xing 有因緣性). When it is entangled, it is called the naturally-attained (fa'er 法爾) seeds that are to be permeated by much hearing; when it is unfettered, it is called the enjoyment-body.* The *Laṅkāvatāra-sūtra* states, "The storehouse consciousness is called the empty *tathāgatagarbha*. [But] in so far as it is completely endowed with undefiled dharmas of permeation, it is called non-empty *tathāgatagarbha*." [What is said in] the *Śrīmālādevīsiṃhanāda-sūtra* is based upon the sense of "unconditioned *gotra*": the afflictions are what cover and conceal (*neng fuzang* 能覆藏); the true Principle (*zhenli* 真理) is what is covered and concealed (*suo fuzang* 所覆藏). [What is said in] the *Laṅkāvatāra-sūtra* is based upon the sense of "conditioned *gotra*": the storehouse consciousness is what contains and conceals (*neng shezang* 能攝藏); the seeds are what are contained and concealed (*suo shezang* 所攝藏). Those two types which conceal and those two types which are concealed are all called *tathāgatagarbha*. (My emphasis[82])

This passage cannot be overemphasized because it supports the two observations I have made about *jiexing*. First, *jiexing* should be understood along the line of originally existent seeds, which corresponds to the idea of conditioned *gotra* (in Paramārtha's term: the drawn-forth *gotra*). Second, after one becomes a Buddha, the mixture of *jiexing* and the permeation from outside becomes the enjoyment-body (See 4.5). This agreement among Master Ji, Paramārtha's *Shelun*, and T2805 justifies my approach of finding clues about *jiexing* from the works of Xuanzang and his disciples.

6.10 A Note about *Jie* in *Jiexing*

Earlier, I have shown that the term *xing* in *jiexing* is a translation of the Sanskrit *gotra*. Reconstructing the Sanskrit underlying the term *jie* is more difficult. Based on T2805, I have argued that *jie* obviously has a close connection with the idea of undiscriminating *jñāna*. Despite the close doctrinal relation between *jie* and *nirvikalpa-jñāna*, *jie* is probably not based on the Sanskrit *jñāna* for the simple reason that Paramārtha always translates *jñāna* in the compound *nirvikalpa-jñāna* as *zhi* 智, not *jie* 解.

Another possible candidate for the Sanskrit original is the term *adhimukti*, but *adhimukti* is often translated by Paramārtha as *yuanle* 願樂 or simply *yuan* 願; *xinle* 信樂 or simply *xin* 信. In contrast, Xuanzang translates *adhimukti* as *shengjie* 勝解.[83] For this reason, I shall also exclude *adhimukti* as a likely candidate for *jie* in *jiexing*.

Thus, my tentative reconstruction of the original Sanskrit term for *jie* still is something like *vimukti* or *vimokṣa*, both meaning "release" or "liberation." As far as I know, however, neither **vimukti-gotra* nor **vimokṣa-gotra* (both meaning "having the *gotra* [that leads to] liberation") is attested in any extant Sanskrit text.

6.11 Conclusion: The Meaning of *Jiexing*

To conclude, the best way to make sense of *jiexing* is to consider what gives rise to the state of mind that functions in accordance with unconditioned undiscriminating *jñāna* (or more specifically the four kinds of *jñāna*). Based on the points discussed earlier, I explain *jiexing* as follows:

Jiexing is conditioned. It refers to the innate or originally existent uncontaminated *gotra* or seeds within the storehouse consciousness (Points 1, 3, 6, and 7). *Jiexing* is permeated by hearing the Buddhist teachings before the first bodhisattva stage (Points 2[a] and 4). *Jiexing* should not be identified with the innate *gotra* as described in the FXL (Point 9[a]); rather it is similar to what is called the drawn-forth *gotra* in the FXL (Point 10). Upon entrance into the first bodhisattva stage, the mixture of *jiexing* and the permeation of hearing arises, that is, becomes active as the state of mind that functions in accordance with the unconditioned undiscriminating *jñāna* (Points 5, 9, and 10). This mixture then serves as the basis for noble people until buddhahood is attained (Point 2). After buddhahood is attained, the basis for noble people becomes the enjoyment-body but not the dharma-body (Point 3; see also 4.5 and 5.2.1).

Regarding the term itself, *xing* in *jiexing* is a translation of the Sanskrit term *gotra* (Point 8). I have not come to a firm conclusion regarding the probable Sanskrit underlying the Chinese *jie*. I think that *vimukti-gotra* and *vimokṣa-gotra* are more likely than *jñāna-gotra* or *adhimukti-gotra*.

Finally, this chapter shows that Paramārtha and Xuanzang share many more doctrinal positions than scholars usually assume. This challenges the received wisdom that Xuanzang and Paramārtha are philosophically opposed. From the previous chapters, it should be clear that the seeming antagonism between Paramārtha and Xuanzang is largely due to the association of Paramārtha with the *Awakening of Faith* and the re-interpretation of Paramārtha's works (such as the notion of *jiexing*) through the lens of the *Awakening of Faith*. When we eliminate the *Awakening of Faith* from our consideration of Paramārtha, we can observe more agreement between the two great masters.

But even if we acknowledge the similarity between *jiexing* and ideas in Xuanzang's translations, we must address the long-standing view that Xuanzang's disagreements with Paramārtha mainly result from Paramārtha's insertion of Tathāgatagarbha ideas into his translations of Yogācāra works. Behind this view is the assumption that Yogācāra and Tathāgatagarbha hold substantially different, even contradictory, positions. In the next chapter, I question this assumption by demonstrating that long before Paramārtha, Vasubandhu, arguably the most important Yogācāra thinker, had already incorporated a weaker notion of *tathāgatagarbha* into his Yogācāra framework.

7

Paramārtha as a Successor to Vasubandhu

In Chapter 5, by showing that the Shelun/T2805 lineage and Shelun/*Awakening of Faith* lineage provided different interpretations of *jiexing*, I argued that the *Awakening of Faith* is not directly connected with Paramārtha. Since *jiexing* is traditionally regarded as a hallmark of Paramārtha's Tathāgatagarbha thought, now if the traditional interpretation of *jiexing* is not Paramārtha's authentic idea, would this not mean that Tathāgatagarbha is much less prominent in Paramārtha's works than we previously believed? To put it in another way, as an essential element of the traditional image of Paramārtha, the *Awakening of Faith* has long been regarded among the East Asian Buddhist traditions as the preeminent Tathāgatagarbha text, and, due to his association with the *Awakening of Faith*, Paramārtha was harshly criticized by Xuanzang's school for teaching heterodox Yogācāra, that is, Yogācāra mixed with Tathāgatagarbha thought. If it is now accepted that the *Awakening of Faith* is not directly related to Paramārtha, we must ask to what extent, if any, the authentic teaching of Paramārtha still reflects Tathāgatagarbha thought.

To answer this question, in this chapter I first show that Vasubandhu, in defining the dharma-body as Thusness, a definition shared by RGV and MSA, already subscribed to the Tathāgatagarbha assertion that all sentient beings are *tathāgatagarbha*s. Second, I show that Paramārtha's works similarly define the dharma-body as Thusness, and to this extent Paramārtha still agrees with the idea of *tathāgatagarbha* that was already accepted by Vasubandhu. Third, in other respects, Paramārtha's works show further development of Tathāgatagarbha thought beyond Vasubandhu and RGV; namely, they include the undiscriminating *jñāna* about Thusness in the definition of the dharma-body, and they provide a detailed account of the two kinds of *buddha-gotra*.

In the course of my argument, I make two important points. First, there is a distinction between a strong understanding of *tathāgatagarbha* and a weak understanding. The strong understanding (henceforth, "strong *tathāgatagarbha*") is the Sinicized concept of *tathāgatagarbha* found in the *Awakening of Faith*; the weak understanding (henceforth, "weak *tathāgatagarbha*") is the concept of *tathāgatagarbha* in India. The second point is that, surprisingly, Xuanzang's school, which has long been considered antagonistic to Paramārtha, also agrees that all sentient beings are *tathāgatagarbha*s in the weak understanding of the term, according to which *tathāgatagarbha* is not a sufficient condition for becoming a Buddha.

Before we begin, a methodological remark is in order. In my discussions here, I argue that Paramārtha followed a line of thought that had been initiated around a century earlier by Vasubandhu. Since Paramārtha's translations of Vasubandhu's works may reflect Paramārtha's own opinions, I avoid citing his translations and rely exclusively on Xuanzang's translations as well as the Tibetan translations.

7.1 Vasubandhu's Use of the Term *Tathāgatagarbha*

To understand the sense in which Paramārtha subscribes to Tathāgatagarbha thought, we must first reexamine what exactly is meant by the term *tathāgatagarbha*. As is well known, *tathāgatagarbha* does not appear at all in typical Yogācāra texts, such as the *Yogācārabhūmi*, the MAV, the MSg, the *Twenty Verses*, and the *Thirty Verses*. The most famous exception to this is the MSA (IX.37 and MSA-*bhāṣya*). But as far as I know, very little attention has been paid to the fact that the term *tathāgatagarbha* also appears once in Vasubandhu's MSgBh.[1]

Vasubandhu uses the term *tathāgatagarbha* in his explanation of the four dharmas of purity (*catur-vyavadāna-dharma*). I present Asaṅga's discussion of the four dharmas of purity followed by Vasubandhu's comments on the first, that is, the "innate purity" (*prakṛti-vyavadāna*):

(Quotation 7.1)
Asaṅga's MSg II.26.3 (Based on the Tibetan translation; Chinese terms from Xuanzang):

How should one conceive the perfected nature? One should conceive it through the teaching on the four dharmas of purity (*caturvidhavyavadānadharmadeśana*). These [four] are (1) the innate purity (Ch. *zixing qingjing* 自性清淨; Skt. *prakṛti-vyavadāna*), that is, Thusness, Emptiness, the Apex of Reality (Ch. *shiji* 實際; Skt. *bhūta-koṭi*), the Absence of Characteristic (Ch. *wuxiang* 無相; Skt. *animitta*), the Ultimate Reality (Ch. *zhenshi* 真實; Skt. *paramārtha*), the Dharma-element (Ch. *fajie* 法界; Skt. *dharmadhātu*); (2) the purity that is devoid of defilements (Ch. *ligou qingjing* 離垢清淨; Skt. *vaimalya-vyavadāna*), that is, the same purity (i.e., the innate purity) devoid of all kinds of obstructions (*sarvāvaraṇarahita*); (3) the purity of the path to the attainment of that [innate purity] (Ch. *decidao qingjing* 得此道清淨; Skt. *tatprāptimārga-vyavadāna*), that is, all the Dharmas of the factors leading to enlightenment (*bodhipakṣadharma*), all the perfections (*pāramitā*), etc.; and (4) the purity of the object that produces that [path] (Ch. *shengcijing qingjing* 生此境清淨; Skt. *tadutpādakālambana-vyavadāna*), that is, the correct teachings of the Mahāyāna (*deśita-mahāyāna-saddharma*). Because this teaching is the cause of the purity (*vyavadānahetutva*), it is not the imagined nature (*parikalpita-svabhāva*). Because it is an outflow (Ch. *dengliu* 等流; Skt. *niṣyanda*) from the pure Dharma-element, it is not the dependent nature (*paratantra-svabhāva*). All dharmas of purity are contained (*saṃgṛhīta*) in these four [dharmas of purity].[2] [My translation and modification of Lamotte (1973, Tome II: 121–2); also cf. Nagao (1982–7, Vol. I: 362–3)]

Vasubandhu's MSgBh on MSg II.26.3 (Based on the Tibetan Translation; Chinese terms from Xuanzang):

> What is meant by the "innate purity" is the self-nature (*svabhāva*) that is pure by its self-nature (Tib. *ngo bo nyid kyis*; Skt. *svabhāvataḥ?*); that is to say, the existence in accordance with Thusness. Because this exists as a common characteristic (Ch. *gongxiang* 共相; Skt. *sāmānya-lakṣaṇa*) among all sentient beings, it is taught that all dharmas have *tathāgatagarbha* (Ch. *yiqie fa you rulaizang*一切法有如來藏; Tib. *chos thams cad ni de bzhin gshegs pa'i snying po can*)[3]

Here Vasubandhu says that all dharmas have *tathāgatagarbha* in so far as they share Thusness (*tathatā*), which is a general characteristic for all sentient beings. In what follows, I argue that the reason why Vasubandhu makes this claim is that he has a distinctive idea about the dharma-body, namely, that it is identical with Thusness. Paramārtha also has a similar idea about the dharma-body, as does the MSA. As far as I know, this point has gone unnoticed in previous scholarship. However, recognizing that Vasubandhu and Paramārtha agree about the notion of dharma-body is important for understanding the development of Yogācāra thought in India.

Before we move on, a brief remark is in order about the meaning of *tathāgatagarbha* in the statement that all sentient beings are *tathāgatagarbha* (*sarvasattvās tathāgatagarbhāḥ*). The term *tathāgatagarbha* has been translated variously as "matrix of Tathāgata" (Takasaki 1966), "womb of the Tathāgata" (King 1991), "Embryonic Tathāgata" (King 1991), "Tathāgata-embryo" (Brown 1991), and simply "containing a Tathāgata" (Zimmermann 2002: 45).[4]

Underlying these various translations are quite different understandings of this key notion. Zimmermann (2014: 515–17) points out that the *Tathāgatagarbha-sūtra* includes at least two basic concepts of Buddha nature or *tathāgatagarbha*: the idea of disclosure ("Buddha nature as already present, and only requiring disclosure") and the idea of development ("Buddha nature as something which has to be developed"). Among the translations mentioned earlier, "Tathāgata-embryo" suggests the idea of development, while "containing a Tathāgata" suggests the idea of disclosure.

I agree with Kano (2020) and Zimmermann (2020), both of whom, though not focusing on the meaning of *tathāgatagarbha* specifically in the RGV, suggest that the term *tathāgatagarbha* has multiple meanings in early Tathāgatagarbha sources such as the *Mahāparinirvāṇa-mahāsūtra* and the *Tathāgatagarbha-sūtra*. As Zimmermann (2020: 41) notes, "it is impossible to reduce the genesis and meaning of the term *tathāgatagarbha* by way of a monoexplanatory model."

Kano's and Zimmermann's suggestion is valid, in my opinion, only for Tathāgatagarbha sources before the RGV. Next, I show that the RGV adopts the idea of disclosure and hence the translation "containing a Tathāgata" is preferable there. I also show that Vasubandhu interprets *tathāgatagarbha* in the same manner.

If we entertain the idea of development about *tathāgatagarbha* and adopt a translation like "Tathāgata-embryo," this would imply that sentient beings can develop or grow into full-blown Tathāgatas. The difficulty with this interpretation, however, is that it would lead to the conclusion that Tathāgatas are conditioned (*saṃskṛta*) because they are what ordinary sentient beings are transformed into via practice. This would be incompatible with the premise that Tathāgatas are permanent (*nitya*).

A way to avoid this difficulty is to suggest that *tathāgatagarbha* is a *Bahuvrīhi* compound meaning "[a sentient being] containing a Tathāgata." Namely, an unconditioned Tathāgata is already contained within every sentient being. It is covered by defilements and hence is not disclosed. Through Buddhist practice, one removes these defilements and discloses the innate Tathāgata. Throughout the whole process of disclosing the innate Tathāgata, the Tathāgata remains unchanged. The only difference is whether the defilements are removed or not. As indicated later, the RGV adopts this line of thought by identifying Buddha-body with unconditioned Thusness and hence considering it to be permanent.

In the next section, I show that, in the Yogācāra tradition, Vasubandhu adopts in the MSgBh the same line of thought by identifying the dharma-body with Thusness.

7.2 Vasubandhu: The Dharma-body Is Thusness

In the MSgBh, Vasubandhu tries hard to show that dharma-body is permanent because it is none other than Thusness itself. This may sound obvious, but in fact it was Vasubandhu's revolutionary claim within the Yogācāra tradition.[5] To show how Vasubandhu develops a distinct idea about dharma-body, I begin with a passage from the MSg, in which Asaṅga discusses the attainment of the dharma-body:

> (Quotation 7.2) (See quotation 4.10)
> Asaṅga's MSg X.4 (Based on the Tibetan translation; Chinese terms from Xuanzang):
> How, then, is this dharma-body initially attained through contact (Tib. *reg pas thog ma nyid du thob*; Ch. *zuichu zhengde* 最初證得)? [It is attained] by the undiscriminating (*nirvikalpa*) *jñāna* and subsequently-acquired (*pṛṣṭhalabdha*) *jñāna*. These have the unified doctrine of the Mahāyāna as their object; they have cultivated the five aspects well; and have properly accumulated the equipment in all the stages [leading to buddhahood]. [It is attained] by the diamond-like concentration (*vajropamāsamādhi*), since [that concentration] destroys the subtle obstructions that are difficult to destroy. Because it is separated from all obstructions immediately after [attaining] that concentration, [the dharma-body] is thus attained through the transformation of the basis (*āśrayaparāvṛtti*). [A modification of the translation by Griffiths et al. (1989: 93); section C][6]

Here Griffiths et al. have rightly pointed out a problem, namely that, if the dharma-body is identical with Thusness and is unconditioned, then it would be a mistake for Asaṅga to talk about its "attainment," let alone its "initial" attainment. As Griffiths et al. put it:

> There is, of course, a conceptual problem here. If all sentient beings already have (or, better, are) dharma-body, then it's difficult to see what sense it makes to speak of "attaining" it. This explains why all the commentaries (but especially Paramārtha's version of the MSgBh) attempt to make a distinction between "attainment" and "realization," or at least to distinguish among different senses of "attainment."[7]

According to Griffiths et al., this is why Vasubandhu in the MSgBh needs to make the distinction between "attainment" and "realization." Unfortunately, the Tibetan translation of this crucial passage is lost. The only texts we have are the three Chinese translations, which all agree on this point.[8] Here I quote the translation by Xuanzang:

(Quotation 7.3)
Vasubandhu's MSgBh (Based on Xuanzang's translation; Tibetan translation missing):
[The text] now explains how the dharma-body is initially realized (*zhengde* 證得). The line "it is initially realized" means that the dharma-body is not something that arises due to something [else] because *its substance (ti 體) is unconditioned (Ch. wuwei 無為; Skt. asaṃskṛta)*. For if it were, it would not be permanent. The term "diamond-like concentration" means that this concentration, just like a diamond, is able to destroy the minute obstructions that are difficult to destroy. The line "therefore it is attained through a transformation of the basis" means that, because of this diamond-like concentration, one is able to transform the basis [of consciousness] and rapidly attain the dharma-body.[9] (A modification of the translation by Griffiths et al. (1989: 94), section §C; my emphasis[10])

Here Vasubandhu makes it clear that, since the dharma-body is unconditioned and permanent, it cannot be said to arise. For this reason, according to Vasubandhu, the only way to make sense of what Asaṅga calls the "attainment of the dharma-body" would be to shift the sense of "attainment" (meaning to attain something that one has not attained) to "realization" (meaning to recognize the existence of something that one already has).

Contrary to what Griffiths et al. suggest, I propose that the difference between the MSg and the MSgBh actually shows that, for Asaṅga, it is not a problem to talk about the attainment of the dharma-body.[11] This becomes a problem only later, that is, when Vasubandhu posits that dharma-body is permanent and is identified with Thusness.[12] In short, only Vasubandhu and scholars after him feel the need to distinguish between "attainment" and "realization" in order to make sense of Asaṅga's statement about the attainment of the dharma-body.

Thus, Vasubandhu here is actually redefining the concept of the dharma-body. Next, I provide more textual evidence to show that Vasubandhu's reason for redefining the dharma-body as permanent is that he identifies the dharma-body with Thusness.

7.2.1 Vasubandhu: Thusness as the Self-nature (*svabhāva*) of All Buddhas

To begin, Vasubandhu claims that Thusness is the self-nature of all Buddhas:

(Quotation 7.4)
Vasubandhu's MSgBh on MSg X.27 (Based on Xuanzang's Chinese Translation; Tibetan translation missing):

> The line "you have accomplished the Ultimate Reality (*niṣpanna-paramārtha*)" refers to the self-nature (*zixing* 自性) of the dharma-body of all Buddhas, for *all Buddhas have as their self-nature purified Thusness that has accomplished the Ultimate Reality*. (My translation; my emphasis; cf. Griffiths et al. [1989: 170], §HH.[13])

This passage points out that Thusness is the self-nature of the dharma-body of all Buddhas. The term "self-nature" refers to what is essential. From this we can conclude that, according to Vasubandhu, Thusness is what is essential to the dharma-body of the Buddhas.

7.2.2 Vasubandhu: Dharma-body = Dharma-element (= Thusness)

Further, Vasubandhu's identification of dharma-body with Thusness is also demonstrated by his substitution of "dharma-body" for "Dharma-element" (*dharmadhātu*) in the following passage:

> (Quotation 7.5)
> Vasubandhu's MSgBh on MSg X.31 (Based on the Tibetan translation):
> "The Dharma-element of Buddhas" means the dharma-body. It is this that should be understood as exercising these five actions. [A modification of the translation by Griffiths et al. (1989: 223), §K[14]]

From the discussions of the "four dharmas of purity" in Asaṅga's MSg as well as in Vasubandhu's MSgBh (see quotation 7.1), it is clear that, according to both Asaṅga and Vasubandhu, Dharma-element is a synonym for Thusness. Based on this, we can infer that, according to Vasubandhu, the dharma-body is also synonymous with Thusness.

7.2.3 Vasubandhu: Thusness Is the Body of Tathāgatas

The strongest evidence for the identification between dharma-body and Thusness in MSgBh can be found in the following passage, in which Vasubandhu says that "Thusness . . . is the body of Tathāgatas":

> (Quotation 7.6)
> Vasubandhu's MSgBh on MSg X.29 (Based on the Tibetan translation; Chinese terms from Xuanzang)
> The line "the body of Tathāgatas is permanent (Tib. *rtag pa*; Skt. *nitya*)" means that uninterrupted (Tib. *rgyun mi 'chad pa*) *Thusness*, liberated from impurities, is permanent, and this *is the body of Tathāgatas* (Tib. *de bzhin gshegs pa'i sku yin te*; Ch. *xiancheng fashen* 顯成法身). Therefore, the body of Tathāgatas is permanent. (Translated by Griffiths et al. [1989: 201], §J2; my emphasis[15])

7.2.4 Vasubandhu: Dharma-body as the Disclosure of Thusness

Also noteworthy in Xuanzang's Chinese translation (quotation 7.6) is his use of the phrase *xiancheng* 顯成. Unfortunately, this phrase is not reflected in the corresponding

Tibetan translation. Griffiths et al. (1989: 202, §J2) translates *xiancheng* as "manifested and accomplished." A further example of Xuanzang's use of *xiancheng* can be found in the following passage from MSgBh, the Tibetan counterpart of which is again missing.

7.2.4.1 Thusness Discloses Itself to Be the Buddhas

(Quotation 7.7)
Vasubandhu's MSgBh on MSg X.3 (Based on Xuanzang's Chinese Translation; Tibetan translation missing):
The line "it is characterized by the purity of Thusness" means that the essence of pure Thusness is permanent. Because it is this (i.e., Thusness) that *discloses itself to be the Buddhas* (*xiancheng fo gu* 顯成佛故),[16] you should understand that a Tathāgata is characterized as being permanent. (A modification of the translation by Griffiths et al. (1989: 89), §B4; my emphasis[17])

This raises the question of the Sanskrit term underlying Xuanzang's *xiancheng*. The Tibetan translation of Vasubandhu's discussion of the second of "four dharmas of purity" in MSgBh may hold the answer:

7.2.4.2 Buddhahood Is Disclosed through Thusness

(Quotation 7.8) (Cf. quotation 7.1)
Vasubandhu's MSgBh on MSg II.26 (Based on the Tibetan translation; Chinese terms from Xuanzang):
What is meant by the "purity devoid of defilements" (*vaimalya-vyavadāna*) is the Thusness that is devoid of defilements (*gou* 垢), i.e., the obstructions related to afflictions and the obstructions related to cognitive objects (Ch. *fannao suozhi zhang* 煩惱所知障; Skt. *kleśa-jñeya-āvaraṇa*). It is through this Thusness, which is purity (*viśuddhi-tathatā*), that buddhahood is *disclosed*. (Tib. *rnam par dag pa'i de bzhin nyid kyis* rab tu phye ba*'i sangs rgyas nyid do*; Ch. *jiyou rushi qingjing zhenru xiancheng zhufo* 即由如是清淨真如顯成諸佛). (My emphasis[18])

In this passage, the Tibetan term corresponding to Xuanzang's *xiancheng* is *rab tu phye ba*, which, as far as I can trace, always renders the Sanskrit word *prabhāvita*.[19]

7.2.4.3 All Buddhas Are Disclosure of Thusness

Another passage that supports the correspondence between Tibetan *rab tu phye ba* and Chinese *xian* can be found in Xuanzang's translation of the MSgBh, where he says "disclosed" (*suoxian* 所顯) instead of "disclosure/discloses itself to be" (*xiancheng* 顯成):

(Quotation 7.9)
Vasubandhu's MSgBh on MSg X.28 (Based on the Tibetan translation; Chinese terms from Xuanzang):

> The line "[the Buddhas] are characterized (*rab tu phye; *prabhāvita*)[20] by the non-existence of existence" means that Thusness is the non-existence of existence. This means that the Buddhas are *disclosed through* (Tib. *rab tu phye ba*; Ch. *suoxian* 所顯) that [non-existence of existence which is Thusness]. (A modification of Griffiths et al. [1989: 182], §I3; my emphasis[21])

Here again, what lies behind Xuanzang's use of *suoxian* 所顯 is the Sanskrit term that is translated into Tibetan as *rab tu phye ba*. In addition to the aforementioned passages from MSgBh, three additional passages that corroborate the correspondence between *suoxian* 所顯 and *rab tu phye ba* in the context of the disclosure of Thusness can also be found in the *Nirupadhikā bhūmi* and the *Viniścayasaṃgrahaṇī* portions of the *Yogācārabhūmi*.[22] From these passages in the MSgBh and the *Yogācārabhūmi*, we can be confident that the Sanskrit term *prabhāvita* underlies Xuanzang's *xiancheng* 顯成 or *suoxian* 所顯 and the Tibetan *rab tu phye ba*.[23]

On the basis of the passages in MSgBh where the term *rab tu phye ba* (*xiancheng* 顯成 or *suoxian* 所顯 in Chinese) occurs together with the notions of Thusness and dharma-body or the Buddha's body, a formula can be reconstructed: *tathatayā prabhāvito dharmakāyaḥ* (the dharma-body is disclosed through Thusness).[24] This would also confirm that Vasubandhu uses the term *prabhāvita* intentionally to describe the identity between Thusness and dharma-body.

The identification between Thusness and the dharma-body can be found in other texts than the MSgBh, such as in the *Perfection of Wisdom in Eight Thousand Lines* (*Aṣṭasāhasrikā-prajñāpāramitā-sūtra*) and in the *Vajracchedikā-prajñāpāramitā-sūtra*.[25] A particularly interesting example can be found in a prose commentary on the *Vajracchedikā-prajñāpāramitā-sūtra*, preserved only in the Chinese translations by Bodhiruci (T1511) and Yijing (T1513), in which the dharma-body and Thusness are linked also via the term *prabhāvita*. In Keng (2013b), I draw on this unusual connection to suggest that this prose commentary on the *Vajracchedikā-prajñāpāramitā-sūtra* should be attributed to Vasubandhu, the author of the MSgBh.

7.3 Dharma-body as Thusness Disclosed

To explore the profound meaning of this peculiar usage of *prabhāvita* in connection with the dharma-body and Thusness, we must return to what Vasubandhu says about the first two of four dharmas of purity:

> (Quotation 7.10) (Cf. quotations 7.1 & 7.8)
> Vasubandhu's MSgBh on MSg II.26 (Based on the Tibetan translation; Chinese terms from Xuanzang):
> What is meant by the "innate purity (*prakṛti-vyavadāna*)" refers to the self-nature (Tib. *ngo bo nyid*; Skt. *svabhāva*) that is pure by its self-nature (Tib. *ngo bo nyid kyis*; Skt. *svabhāvataḥ?*); that is to say, the existence in accordance with Thusness. Because this exists as a common characteristic (*sāmānya-lakṣaṇa*) among all sentient beings, it is taught that all dharmas have *tathāgatagarbha*.

> What is meant by the "purity devoid of defilements" (*vaimalya-vyavadāna*) is the Thusness that is devoid of defilements, i.e., the obstructions related to afflictions and the obstructions related to cognitive objects (Ch. *fannao suozhi zhang* 煩惱所知障; Skt. *kleśa-jñeya-āvaraṇa*). It is through this Thusness, which is purity (*viśuddhi-tathatā*), that buddhahood is *disclosed*. (Tib. *rnam par dag pa'i de bzhin nyid kyis* rab tu phye ba*'i sangs rgyas nyid do*; Ch.: *jiyou rushi qingjing zhenru xiancheng zhufo* 即由如是清淨真如顯成諸佛). (My emphasis)

Here Vasubandhu juxtaposes innate purity and purity devoid of defilements. He means that Thusness in itself is innate purity and that, when the same Thusness is devoid of defilements, the dharma-body is disclosed (*prabhāvita*) through Thusness.

The implication here cannot be overemphasized. Given his identification of Thusness and the dharma-body, discussed earlier, what Vasubandhu claims is that sentient beings, who invariably share Thusness, are named differently depending on whether their defilements are removed: they are named *tathāgatagarbhas* when Thusness is still entangled with defilements; they are named "dharma-body" when Thusness is devoid of defilements.

Hence the "purity devoid of defilements" is the same as the "innate purity," both referring to the same Thusness. This point can be corroborated by Vasubandhu's claim that the first two dharmas of purity are "without change" (Tib. *mi 'gyur ba*; Ch. *wuyou bianyi xing* 無有變異; Skt. *avikāra*).[26] This means that the "purity devoid of defilements" itself is also unconditioned and never changes. When this purity is disclosed (and therefore the dharma-body is disclosed), nothing new is produced. Rather, it is only due to the removal of the defilements that Thusness is disclosed. Thusness remains unchanged before and after this disclosure. The Sanskrit term *prabhāvita* is *intentionally* employed to capture this subtle meaning: When the ultimate transformation of the basis takes place, that is, when the defilements are completely removed, Thusness is disclosed and yet it itself remains unchanged. I illustrate this point in Figure 7.1.

From this figure, it is obvious that Thusness, being unconditioned, remains unchanged, whether it is entangled with defilements or free from defilements. This is why it is called "innate purity," while the defilements covering it are regarded as

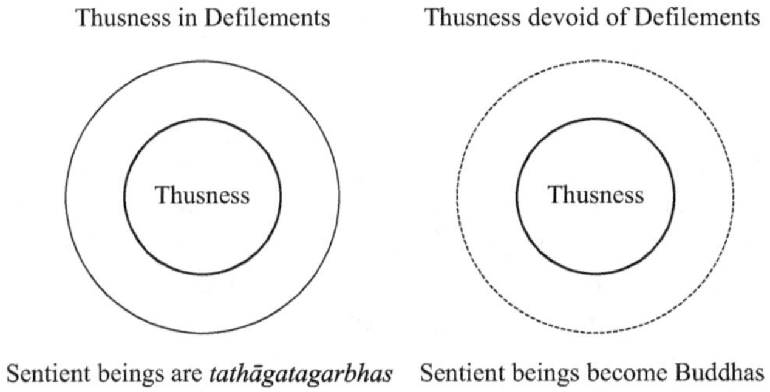

Figure 7.1 Dharma-body as Thusness disclosed.

adventitious (*āgantuka*), meaning that they never change the nature of Thusness. For this reason, Thusness is not different from the dharma-body: the dharma-body refers specifically to the manifested or disclosed state of Thusness.

Unfortunately, the profound meaning behind Vasubandhu's intentional choice of the term *prabhāvita* has been totally ignored by modern scholars, as far as I know. For example, Schmithausen (1969) gives four possible nuanced senses of the term *prabhāvita* in Yogācāra contexts, the second of which matches the particular sense in which Vasubandhu here uses the term in his MSgBh.[27] While recognizing that this specific meaning is reflected in Xuanzang's Chinese translation *suoxian* 所顯 and the Tibetan translation *rab tu phye ba*, Schmithausen overlooks Vasubandhu's peculiar use of the term by observing, "In the Yogācāra literature, I do not have at hand even one place that compels us to take it in this sense" (*Eine Stelle aus der Yogācāra-Literatur, die zu dieser Auffassung zwingt, habe ich allerdings nicht zur Hand*).[28]

Schmithausen's reading does not capture the subtle meaning of *prabhāvita* in the MSgBh. That is, Vasubandhu deliberately uses *prabhāvita* to express two things simultaneously: that Thusness and the dharma-body are identical and that the dharma-body refers specifically to the disclosed state of Thusness in which all the defilements are removed. To simply say that the dharma-body is "characterized by Thusness" (as Schmithausen does) does not adequately convey these two meanings.

7.4 Vasubandhu: Incorporating Tathāgatagarbha into Yogācāra

Vasubandhu's new way of understanding the dharma-body is significant in that it is compatible with Tathāgatagarbha thought. It is clear from the earlier discussion that for Vasubandhu, *tathāgatagarbha* refers to Thusness with defilements, and the same Thusness devoid of defilements is called the dharma-body. This also implies that all sentient beings are inherently endowed with the dharma-body, in the same way that Thusness is invariably shared by all sentient beings due to its pervasiveness (*parispharaṇa*).

Vasubandhu's interpretation of *tathāgatagarbha* in which Thusness is contained corresponds to the definition of *tathāgatagarbha* in the RGV, which is often regarded as the most doctrinally systematic Tathāgatagarbha text:

> (Quotation 7.11)
> RGV I.28 and RGVV:
> Now, with reference to "Thusness entangled with defilements" (*tathatā samalā*), it is said: "All sentient beings are *tathāgatagarbhas*." In what sense is this said?. . .[29] Because of the pervasion (*spharaṇa*) of the Buddha's body; because of the non-difference (*avyatibheda*) of Thusness [from the Buddha]; because of the [existence of *buddha*-] *gotra* [in sentient beings], all sentient beings are always *buddhagarbhas* (i.e., *tathāgatagarbhas*). | | I.28 | |
>
> In short, in three senses, it is taught by the Honored One that all sentient beings are always *tathāgatagarbhas*. Namely, in the sense of the pervasion (*parispharaṇa*)

> of the dharma-body of the Buddha; in the sense of there not being any difference between a Buddha and Thusness; and in the sense of the existence (*saṃbhava*) of the *buddha-gotra*.[30]

Here, like Vasubandhu, the RGV is discussing Thusness entangled with defilements (*samalā tathatā*). The RGV then gives three reasons why all sentient beings are *tathāgatagarbhas*: (1) The Buddha's body pervades everywhere; (2) Thusness is not different from a Buddha; (3) the *gotra* [of the Buddha] exists in all sentient beings.

All three reasons point to the identification among Thusness, dharma-body and *buddha-gotra* because they must all be understood as being unconditioned. First, Thusness is invariably treated as being unconditioned in the RGV, for example:

> (Quotation 7.12)
> RGV I.148:
> Being unchangeable (*avikāra*) by nature, sublime, and perfectly pure, Thusness is illustrated
> By the analogy with a piece of gold. (A modification of Takasaki 1966: 287)[31]

Here the term "unchangeable" (*avikāra*) and the analogy of gold strongly suggest that Thusness is unconditioned. In fact, Thusness is always treated in the Yogācāra sources as a synonym (*paryāya*) for Emptiness (*śūnyatā*), Dharma-element (*dharmadhātu*), Apex of Reality (*bhūtakoṭi*), and so on, all of which are unconditioned.[32]

Regarding dharma-body being unconditioned in the RGV, an example can be found in the following passage:

> (Quotation 7.13)
> RGVV on RGV I.6–8:
> The word "unconditioned" (*asaṃskṛta*) should be understood as being opposite to being conditioned (*saṃskṛta*). Here "being conditioned" means the thing, of which origination, lasting, as well as destruction are conceivable. Because of the absence of these characteristics, buddhahood (*buddhatva*) should be seen as having neither beginning, middle nor end, and being characterized by (*prabhāvita*) the unconditioned dharma-body (*asaṃskṛta-dharmakāya*). (A modification of Takasaki 1966: 156–7[33])

Here the RGVV suggests that buddhahood (*buddhatva*) has no beginning, middle, or end, and hence is the unconditioned dharma-body (*asaṃskṛta-dharmakāya*). This clearly asserts that dharma-body is unconditioned. Hence the term *saṃbuddhakāya* in verse I.28 must be read as referring to the dharma-body. And given that the dharma-body is unconditioned, we must conclude that the dharma-body is identical with Thusness, as Vasubandhu states in MSgBh.

Regarding *buddha-gotra*, it might sound odd to regard it as unconditioned because the notion of *gotra* itself seems to suggest some growth or development. I have two reasons for my assertion. First, the RGV I.28 appears to be giving three reasons here, but given that the first two—dharma-body and Thusness—are identical and hence the first two reasons actually boil down to one, it is reasonable to assume that the third reason also points to the same thing. In other words, the three reasons given in I.28 are all identical, and hence under this reading, *buddha-gotra* should be regarded as being unconditioned and identical with Thusness and the dharma-body.

In fact, the RGV later suggests that at least one kind of *buddha-gotra* is unconditioned:

> (Quotation 7.14) (Cf. quotation 7.23)
> RGV I.149:
> This *buddha-gotra* should be known as of two kinds, being like a deposited treasure (*nidhāna*) and being like a tree [grown] from a fruit (*phalavṛkṣa*). [The former] is innate (*prakṛtistha*) from beginningless [time]; the latter is cultivated (*samudānīta*).[34]

Here the first kind of *buddha-gotra* is compared to the treasure hidden underground from beginningless time; the second kind of *buddha-gotra* is compared to a tree grown from a fruit. The tree and fruit simile implies that *buddha-gotra* is conditioned. In contrast, the treasure simile suggests that *buddha-gotra* is unconditioned because the treasure remains the same whether it is hidden underground or is excavated.

My second reason is that, as I point out in Keng (2013a), the only way to justify the claim that "all sentient beings are *tathāgatagarbhas*" would be to define Tathāgatas as being unconditioned and to interpret *tathāgatagarbha* as "containing a Tathāgata." The reason here is that "all" in "all sentient beings" implies necessity. That is, anyone who is a sentient being must contain a Tathāgata. Given that Tathāgatas are unconditioned, then just as space (*ākāśa*) and Thusness pervade everywhere, Tathāgatas must also exist in all sentient beings. Hence, it would make no sense to think that only some sentient beings contain it while others do not. Conversely, if Tathāgatas are conditioned, then the sharing of Tathāgatas would depend upon specific causes. Hence, we would not be able to say that "all sentient beings are *tathāgatagarbhas*" because there is always a possibility that a certain sentient being lacks one or more among those specific causes.

The identification among the dharma-body, Thusness, and *buddha-gotra* in the context of the assertion that all sentient beings are *tathāgatagarbhas* is best summarized in the following sentence from the RGVV:

> (Quotation 7.15)
> RGVV on RGV I.149–52:
> Now, *tathāgatagarbha*, being united with the dharma-body, having the characteristics inseparable from Thusness, and being of the nature of the *gotra* properly fixed [towards the attainment of the buddhahood], exists everywhere, at whatever time and without exception among the living beings, this is indeed to be perceived in the light of the nature of dharmas (*dharmatā*) as the [highest] logical ground (*pramāṇīkṛtya*). (A modification of Takasaki 1966: 294[35])

Here the RGVV obviously defines *tathāgatagarbha* in terms of dharma-body, Thusness, and *gotra* (here understood as the first kind of *buddha-gotra*) in order to establish that all sentient beings are *tathāgatagarbhas*.

The same line of reasoning can also be found in the MSA:

(Quotation 7.16) MSA IX.37 and MSABh:
[MSA:] There is the very non-difference (*aviśiṣṭā*) among all beings. Thusness has come to purity, which is buddhahood, and therefore all bodily beings (*sarvadehin*) contain that [i.e., a Tathāgata] (*tadgarbha*). (IX.37)
[MSABh]: There is the non-difference (*nirviśiṣṭā*) of all beings. Thusness is the Buddha, whose nature is the purity of Thusness. Hence, it is taught that all sentient beings contain Tathāgatas (*tathāgatagarbha*):[36]

(Quotation 7.17)
MSABh on MSA XXI.60–1:
Here the Buddha's characteristics are explained in terms of six topics: essence, cause, result, activity, endowment, and functional mode. Purified Thusness (*viśuddhā tathatā*) is the Ultimate Reality that is accomplished (*niṣpannaḥ paramārthaḥ*). And it is the very essence (*svabhāva*) of the Buddhas.[37]

The MSA also gives two reasons why all sentient beings are *tathāgatagarbhas*: there is no difference among sentient beings (including Buddhas as well as ordinary people); all sentient beings have pure Thusness as their self-nature (*svabhāva*). Here the first reason is based on the second: because all sentient beings share Thusness, they are regarded as having no difference.

Another passage from the MSABh also uses the term *prabhāvita* to connect buddhahood and the purity of Thusness:

(Quotation 7.18)
MSABh on MSA IX.4:
All dharmas are buddhahood, because Thusness is not different [from them] and because [buddhahood] is disclosed (*prabhāvita*) through the purity of that [Thusness]. (A modification of Schmithausen 2014: 535[38])

Returning to Vasubandhu, we clearly see from his definition of *tathāgatagarbha* as "containing Thusness" how Vasubandhu's understanding echoes the RGV and MSA. At this point, it is very difficult to decide the direction of influence between Vasubandhu and the RGV and/or MSA. The relative chronology among these three is very difficult to determine, especially if we consider the possibility that, in the case of both the RGV and MSA, the verse and prose portions may have been composed by different authors and that, even with respect to the MSA, doubts have been raised concerning whether the verse portion itself is a homogeneous work or a layered compilation.[39]

Moreover, it may be misleading to consider RGV as a pure representative of the Tathāgatagarbha tradition. The RGV incorporates several key notions from Yogācāra, including the two obstructions (obstructions related to afflictions [*kleśāvaraṇa*] and obstructions related to cognitive objects [*jñeyāvaraṇa*]), and the transformation of the basis (*āśrayaparivṛtti*). More importantly, the definition of dharma-body in the RGV agrees with Vasubandhu's definition in the MSgBh and the MSA.

In this sense, I disagree with Takasaki, who claims that the RGV still is somewhat independent from Yogācāra in that it does not include the idea of the storehouse consciousness. According to Takasaki (1966: 60), the absence of storehouse consciousness in the RGV *garbha* theory was a weakness that later led to the introduction of the storehouse consciousness in texts such as the *Laṅkāvatāra-sūtra* and the *Awakening of Faith*. As a result, the *garbha* theory was incorporated into Yogācāra and was thus unable to be established as a separate school. But if my observation is correct, then the convergence of the RGV and Yogācāra (as exemplified in MSgBh and MSA) already began to take shape around the time of these three texts. So we must not think that Yogācāra and Tathāgatagarbha, at least during Vasubandhu's lifetime, were two independent traditions between which a boundary could easily be drawn.

To conclude, the efforts to introduce or incorporate the notion of *tathāgatagarbha* into the Yogācāra tradition began well before Paramārtha, at least as early as Vasubandhu's MSgBh. The lesson here is that the idea that Yogācāra and Tathāgatagarbha were two incompatible strains of thought must be abandoned or at least modified. This idea of incompatibility is the result of reading the disputes between the Chinese followers of Paramārtha and those of Xuanzang back into the earlier history of Indian Buddhism.

7.5 Strong and Weak Tathāgatagarbha

Now that the *Awakening of Faith* has been dissociated from Paramārtha, and Paramārtha's agreement with Vasubandhu regarding *tathāgatagarbha* has been established, we can distinguish at least two different meanings of *tathāgatagarbha*.

7.5.1 Strong Tathāgatagarbha

This refers to the notion of *tathāgatagarbha* according to the *Awakening of Faith*, in which Thusness as an unconditioned dharma is taken as the ontological basis of all conditioned dharmas, including the storehouse consciousness and all the illusory phenomena projected from it. By "ontological basis," I refer to the idea that the storehouse consciousness and the projected phenomena are a modification of Thusness. Alternatively, it is Thusness itself, when modified or agitated, that becomes the storehouse consciousness. In short, according to this interpretation, Thusness and the storehouse consciousness share the same ontological substance.

As far as I can tell, there was no clear sign of strong *tathāgatagarbha* in Indian Buddhist texts[40] because the idea of Thusness as an unconditioned dharma that can evolve into conditioned dharmas blurs or even totally obliterates the distinction between unconditioned dharmas and conditioned dharmas, a basic distinction that was established early on in the development of Abhidharma.[41]

Strong *tathāgatagarbha* can be taken as a distinctive feature of Sinicized Buddhism for three reasons. First, this idea of *tathāgatagarbha* had no evident precedent back in Indian Buddhist texts. Furthermore, it marks off indigenous Chinese Buddhist philosophy (the Huayan tradition at least)[42] from other major Buddhist philosophical systems. Finally, it resonates with the conceptual scheme of *ti-yong* 體-用 (substance and function), which plays an important role in the development of Chinese thought after the seventh century.[43]

In Keng (2014b), I show that Huiyuan, usually regarded as the most important and erudite scholar of the Dilun tradition, does not subscribe to strong *tathāgatagarbha*. The most striking feature of Huiyuan's thought is his strict distinction between natural purity (*xingjing* 性淨), which is unconditioned, and expedient means (*fangbian* 方便), which is conditioned. Neither of these ever directly transforms or evolves into the other. Huiyuan's most important idea is the adjustment of true consciousness (*zhenshi* 真識) to falsity (*suiwang* 隨妄), based on which true consciousness is interpreted as the substance (*ti* 體), that is, the basis, of defiled phenomena.[44] That is to say, when true consciousness adjusts to falsity and serves as the basis for defiled phenomena, it does not evolve into defiled phenomena. Instead, there is merely a superimposition (*samāropa*) of false conceptualization upon the true consciousness, which remains unchanged. Huiyuan compares this to the situation of mistaking a rope for a snake in darkness. The mistaken idea of a snake in this situation is a combination of two things: the perception of the image of a rope and the idea of a snake superimposed upon that perception. It is the superimposition of the idea of a snake (due to fear, anxiety, or a memory of snakes, for example) that distorts the final judgment, but even under false judgment, the rope itself remains the same and never changes into a snake. So when the dawn comes, the superimposition is gone, the rope can be correctly perceived as a rope, and one's correct judgment is restored.

Huiyuan cites the *Laṅkāvatāra-sūtra* several times in his works. However, except perhaps in the *Bashi yi* of his *Dasheng yizhang*, he does not cite it to justify strong *tathāgatagarbha*. Based on this, we can infer that Huiyuan (and probably the entire Dilun tradition) does not interpret the *Laṅkāvatāra-sūtra* from the perspective of strong *tathāgatagarbha*.[45]

7.5.2 Weak Tathāgatagarbha

Weak *tathāgatagarbha* refers to the notion of *tathāgatagarbha* found in the RGV and the works of Paramārtha and Vasubandhu, according to which *tathāgatagarbha* means "containing unconditioned Thusness, which is identical with the dharma-body of the Buddha." What underlies this weak understanding is a strict distinction between the unconditioned (i.e., Thusness, dharma-body, etc.) and the conditioned (i.e., *jiexing*, seeds, and the storehouse consciousness). Thusness can never be permeated,[46] nor can it serve as the ontological basis for conditioned dharmas, since this would violate the strict distinction between the two realms.

This sense of *tathāgatagarbha* cannot be overemphasized but, unfortunately, it has been neglected even by the most influential contemporary scholars. Takasaki in his seminal work (1966) was not aware of the importance of the distinction between unconditioned and conditioned. Regarding RGV I.27–8, where dharma-body, Thusness, and *buddha-gotra* are equated, Takasaki (1966: 196–8) does not realize that this would imply that the *buddha-gotra* in question, which is described in RGV I.149 as innate *buddha-gotra*, must be unconditioned. Similarly, regarding RGV I.149–52, where the two kinds of *buddha-gotra* are mapped onto the three Buddha-bodies, Takasaki (1966: 288–90) is not aware that the equation of the dharma-body, Thusness, and *buddha-gotra* would imply that the first *buddha-gotra,* which is mapped onto the dharma-body, must be unconditioned.

Ruegg, in his famous article (1976), was also unaware of this crucial distinction between conditioned and unconditioned *buddha-gotra*. For example, when discussing the two kinds of *buddha-gotra* in RGV I.149–52, Ruegg did not note that the first, which is linked to the dharma-body and Thusness in RGV I.27–8 and I.144, must be understood as being unconditioned. This is why, despite being aware of the coexistence of two metaphors for *gotra*, one biological and the other mineral, Ruegg (1976: 344–8) did not realize that the mineral metaphor is meant to emphasize that the first type of *buddha-gotra* and the first of the three Buddha-bodies (i.e., the dharma-body) are unconditioned.

Saitō, too, in his most recent article (2020), does not recognize the crucial difference between the dharma-body on the one hand and the other two Buddha-bodies on the other. He was not aware that, in RGV, dharma-body, Thusness and the first type of *buddha-gotra* are all unconditioned and hence are identical. In his discussion of RGV, Jones (2020a: 69) understands *tathāgatagarbha* as "a mental basis or foundation," and the explanation of *tathāgatagarbha* in the RGVV "was compatible with Buddhist discourse about the primacy of the mind (e.g. *prakṛtipariśuddhacitta; ālayavijñāna*), which could also account for continuity between transmigration and the liberated existence of a Buddha" (p. 72). Jones did not mention the distinction between unconditioned vs. conditioned. In addition, Jones (2020b: 160) was not aware that, based on RGV I.28, Thusness, dharma-body and *buddha-gotra* must all be understood as being unconditioned, as I have shown above in 7.4. As mentioned earlier, both Kano (2020) and Zimmermann (2020) suggest that the term *tathāgatagarbha* has multiple meanings in early Tathāgatagarbha sources such as the *Mahāparinirvāṇa-mahāsūtra* and the *Tathāgatagarbha-sūtra*. Their observation is valid regarding sources before RGV. In RGV and the works of Vasubandhu, however, *tathāgatagarbha* must be unconditioned; otherwise, it is impossible to prove that all sentient beings share *tathāgatagarbha* (see 7.4). For this reason, I distinguish between weak and strong *tathāgatagarbha*.

This sounds like a good solution, but unfortunately it would also lead to a fundamental soteriological difficulty, to which I now turn.

7.5.3 The Difficulty Inherent in Weak *Tathāgatagarbha*

In Keng (2013a), I point out that Thusness, being unconditioned, cannot actively lead to final liberation. Since Thusness is unconditioned, it cannot produce an effect in sentient beings. I argue that weak *tathāgatagarbha* in India would involve the following difficulty: in order to justify the Tathāgatagarbha assertion that all sentient beings are *tathāgatagarbha*s (containing Tathāgatas), Tathāgatas (i.e., the dharma-body) must be defined as Thusness, which is unconditioned and hence invariably shared by all sentient beings. But when dharma-body is thus defined, it becomes totally unable to act and can play no role in leading sentient beings toward ultimate liberation.

Given the strict distinction between unconditioned and conditioned inherited from Abhidharma, the RGV adopts the weak understanding of *tathāgatagarbha* and identifies dharma-body as Thusness, as seen in verse I.28. It follows that, although Thusness is shared by all sentient beings and thus all sentient beings are *tathāgatagarbhas*, one cannot become liberated simply by sharing Thusness. To become liberated, one must have uncontaminated seeds, whether inherent or acquired, in the storehouse consciousness. These seeds must then become active (i.e., become manifestly functioning) by hearing the Buddhist teachings. The person is then led onto the Path of Cultivation, which in turn implants more good seeds in the storehouse consciousness. These seeds eventually produce the two Buddha-bodies (the enjoyment-body and the transformation-body) which, unlike the dharma-body, can lead other sentient beings toward liberation. All elements in this cycle—seeds, storehouse consciousness, hearing the Buddhist teachings, the Path of Cultivation, the enjoyment-body and the transformation-body—are conditioned upon human volition and efforts. Sharing Thusness is not a sufficient ground for liberation. It is only the necessary condition for those conditioned practices to be able to generate effects. That is to say, if Thusness were not shared by sentient beings, then there would be no guarantee that, through those practices, one could eventually attain buddhahood, which is nothing but the disclosure of the originally endowed Thusness.

This distinction between the strong and weak understanding of *tathāgatagarbha* marks the fundamental difference between the *Awakening of Faith* on the one hand and Paramārtha's thought on the other. I have illustrated this difference in Figure 5.2. Based on this distinction, I believe it is now possible to resolve most of the difficulties in Paramārtha's thought as well as in the history of the Shelun tradition.

7.6 The Development of Tathāgatagarbha Thought in India after Vasubandhu and RGV: The Works of Paramārtha

Earlier, I have pointed out that Vasubandhu and the RGV define *tathāgatagarbha* as containing Thusness, which is identical with the dharma-body. Regarding this interpretation of *tathāgatagarbha*, I next examine two features in Paramārtha's work: a redefinition of dharma-body, and a further development of the mapping, first undertaken in the RGV, between the two *buddha-gotras* and the three Buddha-bodies.

Regarding the redefinition of dharma-body, I first note that, given the weak understanding of *tathāgatagarbha*, there is a problem with the concept of dharma-body, namely that it is insentient given that Thusness involves no consciousness or cognitive function. An insentient dharma-body as such, however, would be incompatible with the idea about the historical Buddha as a skillful and compassionate teacher. Moreover, under this line of thought, when sentient beings through practice become Buddhas, namely, when their inner Thusness is disclosed, they would suddenly become insentient.[47]

Faced with these difficulties, Paramārtha's FXL adopts the strategy of, so to speak, introducing sentience into the definition of dharma-body. That is, he redefines dharma-body as consisting of dual aspects: Thusness as a cognitive object and Thusness as the *jñāna* [about Thusness] (i.e., as unconditioned undiscriminating *jñāna*, discussed in Chapter 6), a concept not found in MSgBh or RGV.

Regarding the mapping between the two *buddha-gotra*s and the three Buddha-bodies, it is already found in RGV I.149–52, but it does not offer any further detail. Paramārtha provides more details and further develops this mapping in FXL, leading to a double-layered soteriological structure. The base layer is unconditioned: the dharma-body, which is identical with innate *buddha-gotra* (defined as both Thusness as a cognitive object and Thusness as undiscriminating *jñāna*). The upper layer is conditioned: the enjoyment-body and the transformation-body, which are identical with the drawn-forth *buddha-gotra*. The same idea has been outlined in Figure 5.2.

Now I turn first to the redefinition of dharma-body in Paramārtha's works.

7.6.1 Paramārtha's MAV: Faithful to Vasubandhu's Legacy

Earlier, I have shown that Vasubandhu defines dharma-body as Thusness in the MSgBh, as do the RGV and the MSA. Paramārtha also agrees with this definition. This is most clear in his interpolation of the notion dharma-body into his translation of the MAV:

> (Quotation 7.19)
> MAV I.14 (Based on Paramārtha's Chinese translation):
> What are the synonyms [for Emptiness]? It is said,
> Thusness, the Apex of Reality (*bhūtakoṭi*), the Absence of Characteristic (*animitta*), the Ultimate Reality (*paramārtha*), the Dharma-element (*dharmadhātu*), *the dharma-body* (*dharmakāya*), are, in brief, the synonyms (*paryāya*) for Emptiness (*śūnyatā*). (My emphasis[48])

Unlike in Paramārtha's translation, the term "dharma-body" is missing from both the extant Sanskrit text and Xuanzang's Chinese translation.[49] In addition to inserting the term "dharma-body" into the verse, Paramārtha goes even further by adding an explanation, again not found in the Sanskrit text or Xuanzang's translation.

> (Quotation 7.20)
> MAVBh on MAV I.14–15 (Based on Paramārtha's Chinese translation):
> Because it (i.e., Emptiness) has the sense of being the cause of noble dharmas (*āryadharmahetu*), it is named Dharma-element. Noble dharmas are born by having [Emptiness] as the cognitive object (*tadālambanaprabhava*). Here the sense of "cause" is the sense of "element" [in "Dharma-element"] *Because it (i.e., the element) has the sense of containing and maintaining the dharma-body (shechi fashen 攝持法身), it is also called the dharma-body*. (The *italicised* part is missing from the Sanskrit text and from Xuanzang's Chinese translation)[50]

Here Paramārtha's interpolation was caught and criticized by Master Ji, according to whose critique, "'Dharma-element, etc.,' was rendered as 'dharma-body, etc.,' in the old translation (i.e., Paramārtha's Chinese translation of the MAVBh). The term 'dharma-body' does not exist in the original text. It is an interpolation by the translator (i.e., Paramārtha)."[51]

Based on the insertion of the notion "dharma-body" into Paramārtha's translation, it is clear that Paramārtha was following an interpretative tradition under which dharma-body was regarded as synonymous with Thusness. To this extent, Paramārtha was faithfully following the legacy established by Vasubandhu.

7.6.2 Paramārtha's FXL: Redefinition of Dharma-body

The close connection between the FXL and the RGV has been pointed out by several Japanese scholars. Inspired by previous scholars such as TSUKINOWA Kenryu 月輪賢隆 and HATTORI Masaaki 服部正明, Takasaki argues that the FXL is a modification of the RGV, probably by Paramārtha himself, who, Takasaki speculates, was affiliated with a sub-tradition that promoted the RGV within the Yogācāra tradition.[52] Takasaki further argues for a close connection between the RGV and Paramārtha's *Shelun*[53] and his *Foshuo wushangyi jing* (T669).[54]

For the reason discussed in detail next, I think the FXL represents a further development of Tathāgatagarbha thought beyond Vasubandhu's MSgBh and the RGV, either by Paramārtha himself or by the hermeneutic tradition he inherited. In what follows, I simply focus on the FXL itself and label it as "Paramārtha's FXL" without trying to speculate about its probable author.

Similar to Paramārtha's MAVBh, Paramārtha's FXL also claims that the pure element of the mind (*xin qingjing jie* 心清淨界) is called *tathāgatagarbha* based on its three kinds of self-nature (Ch. *zixing* 自性; Skt. *svabhāva*), that is, the dharma-body, Thusness, and *buddha-gotra*:

(Quotation 7.21)
FXL:
Based on the three kinds of self-nature (*zixing* 自性), in order to show that the pure element of the mind (*xin qingjing jie* 心清淨界) is called *tathāgatagarbha*, [the *Tathāgatagarbha-sūtra*] teaches nine similes such as the [simile of the] lotus. The three kinds of self-nature refer to: first, dharma-body; second, Thusness; third, *buddha-gotra*. These nine similes taken together are intended for these three [types of self-nature]: the first three [similes] are for the dharma-body; the next one is for Thusness; and the last five are for *buddha-gotra*.[55]

From this we can infer that for the FXL, the following are all synonyms: the pure element of the mind, *tathāgatagarbha*, dharma-body, Thusness, *buddha-gotra*. This again clearly shows that Paramārtha faithfully followed Vasubandhu's MSgBh and RGV I.28 under my interpretation in 7.4.

Furthermore, Paramārtha in FXL goes beyond Vasubandhu and the RGV by redefining Thusness as containing dual aspects: Thusness as a cognitive object and Thusness as undiscriminating *jñāna*.[56] The FXL defines *tathāgatagarbha* as follows:

(Quotation 7.22)
FXL:
Further, one should know that there are three senses of the term *tathāgatagarbha*. What are those three? First, *garbha* in the sense of being contained (*suoshe zang*

> 所攝藏); second, *garbha* in the sense of being hidden (*yinfu zang* 隱覆藏); third, *garbha* in the sense of containing (*nengshe zang* 能攝藏). First, with respect to *garbha* in the sense of being contained, the Buddha says, "Due to the Thusness that remains innate (*zhu zixing ruru* 住自性如如), all sentient beings are *tathāgatagarbha*s."
>
> What is meant by "thus" (Ch. *ru* 如; Skt. *tathā*) [in the compound Tathāgata] here has two senses: first, "thus" (i.e., Thusness) as [undiscriminating] *jñāna* (*ruru zhi* 如如智); second, "thus" (i.e., Thusness) as a cognitive object (Ch. *rurujing* 如如境; Skt. **tathatālambana*). Both of these are not perverted (*dao* 倒) and hence are called "thus."
>
> What is meant by "come" (Ch. *lai* 來; Skt. *āgata*) [in the compound Tathāgata] is that one has come from its own nature (*zixing* 自性; or, from the innate *gotra*), i.e., coming from the ultimate attainment (*zhide* 至得). This is why [the Buddha] is called the "Thus-come [One]" . . .
>
> [*Tathāgatagarbha*] is called *garbha* because all sentient beings lie within the [scope of the] *jñāna* of the Thus-come [One] (*rulai zhi* 如來智), and therefore [sentient beings] are called *tathāgatagarbha*s. This is because Thusness as *jñāna* matches (*cheng* 稱) Thusness as a cognitive object. Given that all sentient beings do not lie outside Thusness as a cognitive object and all of them are contained (*suocang* 所藏) within the Thus-come One, all sentient beings are called *tathāgatagarbha*s.[57]

Regarding the first sense, that all sentient beings are contained in the Tathāgata, the FXL makes two points: (1) Thusness refers to both Thusness as *jñāna* and Thusness as a cognitive object; (2) All sentient beings can be contained in Thusness in the sense of being cognitive objects of the Thusness as *jñāna*, and hence are contained in the *jñāna* of the Tathāgata. This passage echoes RGV verse I.27, which states that all sentient beings are contained within the Buddha's *jñāna* (*buddhajñānāntargamāt sattvarāśes*).[58]

Here the idea of Thusness as *jñāna* should be understood in terms of unconditioned undiscriminating *jñāna* (see 6.8). Hence, the definition in the FXL of Thusness as having two aspects—Thusness as *jñāna* and Thusness as a cognitive object—also echoes Paramārtha's definition of the dharma-body as including both Thusness (i.e., Thusness as a cognitive object) and the undiscriminating *jñāna* about Thusness (see 4.3.1). This identification between Thusness and dharma-body implies that dharma-body is also defined as both Thusness as *jñāna* and Thusness as a cognitive object.

In his definition of dharma-body in the MSgBh, Vasubandhu does not identify Thusness with undiscriminating *jñāna*. According to the MSgBh, dharma-body refers only to Thusness as a cognitive object, which is cognized via undiscriminating *jñāna*. Later, either Vasubandhu himself[59] or someone else started to redefine dharma-body in terms of both Thusness as *jñāna* and Thusness as a cognitive object. Paramārtha's FXL reflects this later trend.

As mentioned earlier, the incorporation of Thusness as *jñāna* into the definition of dharma-body can be seen as an answer to the objection that the Buddhas are insentient. Because the dharma-body is unconditioned, sentience (or *jñāna*) is not suddenly produced when the dharma-body is fully disclosed. Rather, *jñāna* is an essential part of the dharma-body from beginningless time. It is always part of the dharma-body even before buddhahood is attained. On the attainment of buddhahood, the originally endowed *jñāna* simply becomes revealed because it is no more obscured by ignorance and defilements.

Although unconditioned undiscriminating *jñāna* is a kind of sentience, it cannot save sentient beings because it is unconditioned and cannot vary. It does not speak in Sanskrit or in Chinese; it does not employ concepts, similes, or metaphors to teach others. Therefore, the Buddhas also need conditioned undiscriminating *jñāna*, that is, a conditioned cognitive state that functions in accordance with unconditioned undiscriminating *jñāna*, from which the *jñāna* for teaching other sentient beings (i.e., the subsequently acquired *jñāna*) is derived.[60]

This also implies the connection between conditioned *jñāna* and the enjoyment-body and the transformation-body.[61] For our purpose, this explains why *jiexing* is connected with the enjoyment-body as explained by Jizang in quotation 1.11 (= quotation 5.2). *Jiexing* brings forth a state of mind that functions in accordance with unconditioned undiscriminating *jñāna* (*nirvikalpa-jñāna*) after entrance into the first bodhisattva stage, and after the transformation of the basis, *jiexing* becomes the enjoyment-body. Namely, both *jiexing* and the enjoyment-body are connected with conditioned *jñāna*, which functions in accordance with unconditioned undiscriminating *jñāna*, that is, Thusness as *jñāna*, which belongs to the dharma-body.

7.6.3 Two Kinds of *Buddha-gotra* in the RGV

In addition to redefining the dharma-body, Paramārtha in FXL develops the mapping between the two *buddha-gotras* and the three Buddha-bodies further than the RGV. Namely, Paramārtha makes it more explicit that the innate *buddha-gotra* (Ch. *zhuzixing foxing* 住自性佛性; Skt. *prakṛtistha gotra*) is unconditioned while the drawn-forth *buddha-gotra* (Ch. *yinchu foxing* 引出佛性; Skt. *samudānīta gotra*) is conditioned. The RGV maps the two *buddha-gotras* to the three Buddha-bodies as follows:

> (Quotation 7.23) (Cf. quotation 7.14)
> RGV I.149–52:
> This *buddha-gotra* should be known as of two kinds, being like a deposited treasure (*nidhāna*) and being like a tree [grown] from a fruit (*phalavṛkṣa*). [The former] is innate (*prakṛtistha*) from beginningless [time]; the latter is cultivated (*samudānīta*). It is held that the three Buddha-bodies are attained from these two *gotras*: from the former the first body [is attained], and from the latter the last two [bodies are attained]. The pure essence-body (*svābhāvika-kāya*; i.e., the dharma-body) is to be known as being like a precious icon (*ratnavigraha*) because it is the ground of the precious qualities by virtue of the non-artificiality of its nature (*akṛtrimatvāt prakṛter*); the enjoyment[-body] is like a universal monarch (*cakravartin*) because of sovereignty over the great Dharma (*mahādharmādhirāja*); and the transformation[-body] is like a golden image (*hemabimba*) because it has the nature of a reflected image. (A modification of Ruegg 1976: 345[62])

Table 7.1 Translations of the Five Similes by Takasaki and Ruegg

	Takasaki (1966: 289)	Ruegg (1976: 345)
1. *nidhāna*	a treasure	a deposited treasure
2. *phala-vṛkṣa*	a tree [grown] from a seed	a tree bearing fruit
3. *ratnavigraha*	a precious image	a precious icon
4. *cakravartin*	a Lord of the Universe	a universal monarch
5. *hemabimba*	a golden statue	a golden image

Here the RGV characterizes the two *buddha-gotras* with a simile (a treasure, a tree) for each, and gives three similes (a precious icon, a universal monarch, a golden image) for the three Buddha-bodies. By saying that the essence-body is attained through innate *buddha-gotra* while the other two bodies are attained through cultivated *buddha-gotra,* the RGV suggests that there is a mapping between the two *buddha-gotras* and the three Buddha-bodies, but it does not provide the exact correspondences for the last two Buddha-bodies.

At this point, the five similes require some clarification. Takasaki and Ruegg translate as shown in Table 7.1.

The exact significance of these five similes is not completely clear based on the RGV and RGVV, but I suggest that the point here is precisely the distinction between the unconditioned dharma-body, conditioned enjoyment-body, and transformation-body. As I have said earlier, the dharma-body and the innate *buddha-gotra* must be understood as being unconditioned and unchanging. This is suggested by the similes of a deposited treasure and a precious icon. Both the enjoyment-body and the transformation-body are conditioned and hence are compared to a tree grown from a fruit. Furthermore, the enjoyment-body is compared to a universal monarch because it is associated with the conditioned *jñāna* that can teach sentient beings. Finally, the transformation-body is not only conditioned but also illusory and hence is compared to a golden image.

Given the distinction between unconditioned and conditioned, there are problems with Takasaki's translations of the third and fifth similes, and Ruegg's are preferable although he never makes explicit such a distinction. The third simile maps onto the dharma-body; hence, an icon is more appropriate than an image, which is not ultimately real. Conversely, the fifth simile maps onto the transformation-body, which is illusory; therefore, an image is more apt here.

We thus summarize the mapping among the five similes, two *buddha-gotras* and three Buddha-bodies in Table 7.2.

The mapping that I have inferred from the RGV is supported in FXL, to which we now turn.

7.6.4 Two Kinds of *Buddha-gotra* in the FXL

Regarding the mapping between the two *buddha-gotras* and the three Buddha-bodies, we find in the FXL an explanation more detailed than the somewhat sketchy one in the RGV. According to the FXL, innate *buddha-gotra* maps onto the dharma-body

Table 7.2 Mapping among the Five Similes, Two Buddha-*gotra*s and Three Buddha-bodies

1. a deposited treasure	innate *buddha-gotra*	dharma-body
2. a tree grown from fruit	drawn-forth *buddha-gotra*	enjoyment-body and transformation-body
3. a precious icon	innate buddha-*gotra*	dharma-body
4. a universal monarch	drawn-forth *buddha-gotra*	enjoyment-body
5. a golden image	drawn-forth *buddha-gotra*	transformation-body

(which includes both Thusness as a cognitive object and Thusness as *jñāna*) and is unconditioned, whereas the drawn-forth *buddha-gotra* maps onto the enjoyment-body and the transformation-body and is conditioned:

> (Quotation 7.24)
> FXL:
> Regarding these two [*buddha-gotras* as] causes, the Buddha taught the three bodies as effects. First, with the innate *buddha-gotra* as the cause, the Buddha taught the dharma-body. The dharma-body has four kinds of merits (*gongde* 功德), therefore for the seventh [simile, the Buddha] brings forth the simile of "real gold wrapped in worthless cloth." Four kinds of merits include: (1) existing innately (*zixing you* 自性有): just like gold exists originally (*benyou* 本有) and is not manufactured; (2) being pure (*qingjing* 清淨): like how gold is originally pure, and is not defiled by any dust or stain; (3) serving as the basis for all merits (*yiqie gongde suoyichu* 一切功德所依處): like gold can bring about (*gan* 感) various things of value; (4) equally attained (*pingdeng suode* 平等所得): meaning all sentient beings equally ought to attain it. Just like how gold has no owner and is owned by all. One who cultivates [the practice of finding it] will attain it. Because of [the above four senses], the dharma-body is said to be like real gold.
>
> Second, with the drawn-forth *buddha-gotra* as the cause, the Buddha taught the enjoyment-body (*yingshen shen* 應身; literally, the correspondence-body). The enjoyment-body has four kinds of merits, therefore for the eighth [simile, the Buddha] brings forth the simile of "the embryo of a wheel-turning king in a poor woman." Four kinds of merits include: (1) [having] a basis (*yizhi* 依止): the basis refers to the thirty-seven factors of enlightenment, which is the basis of [the enjoyment-body]; (2) proper production (*zhengsheng* 正生): this refers to the desire to attain what one ought to attain, namely, the faculty of resolving to know something unknown (Ch. *weizhi yuzhi gen* 未知欲知根; Skt. *ājñāsyāmīndriya*); (3) proper abiding (*zhengzhu* 正住): this refers to the proper attainment, namely, faculty of having learned (Ch. *zhigen* 知根; Skt. *ājñātendriya*); (4) proper enjoyment (*zhengshouyong* 正受用): this refers to the faculty of the perfect knowledge (*zhiyi gen* 知已根; Skt. *ājñātāvīndriya*). These four senses taken together are called the enjoyment-body, just like the son in the womb who is going to be a wheel-turning king also has four senses: (1) The basis is his previous karma (*suye* 宿業); (2) his desire to attain the throne that he has not gained in the sense that the throne is first produced [for him]; (3) proper attainment of the throne in the sense of staying [on the throne]; (4) he will not lose it once he has attained it in the sense of enjoying

(*shouyong* 受用) [the throne]. Therefore, the enjoyment-body has its simile in the "wheel-turning king in the womb."

Third, with the drawn-forth *buddha-gotra* as the cause, the transformation-body is further derived. The transformation-body has three aspects (*shi* 事): (1) having an image (*youxiang* 有相): like the moon in water. This is because [the transformation-body] has image as its substance; (2) [coming to existence] due to efforts (*you gongli* 由功力), since [the transformation-body] is made by previous vows; (3) having a beginning and an end. For these reasons, the Buddha's statue in the mold is taken as a simile [for the transformation-body].[63]

Here in the FXL, we find an expression, more detailed than in the RGV, of the distinction between unconditioned and conditioned. The various ways in which the FXL characterizes innate *buddha-gotra* ("existing innately," "pure," "serving as the basis for all merits," "equally attained") all point to the fact that this *gotra* is unconditioned, and this is why it maps onto the dharma-body, which is unconditioned.

In contrast, the drawn-forth *buddha-gotra* is first characterized as being based upon the thirty-seven factors of enlightenment, which includes factors such as the four bases of mindfulness (*smṛtyupasthāna*) and four kinds of correct endeavor (*samyak-prahāṇa*), all referring to proper Buddhist practices. Then the drawn-forth *buddha-gotra* is characterized in terms of the "three uncontaminated faculties" (*ājñāsyāmīndriya, ājñendriya, ājñātāvīndriya*), which refer to mental functions ranging from desiring to know to having attained the perfect knowledge. For these reasons, the drawn-forth *buddha-gotra* clearly is related to actual practices for attaining conditioned undiscriminating *jñāna* and hence it is conditioned. It is even more obvious that the transformation-body is conditioned because it is compared to the image of the moon in water and is said to be produced by previous vows and to possess a beginning and an end.

To summarize, the mapping between the two *gotra* and the three Buddha-bodies supports my interpretation that innate *buddha-gotra* (identical with the dharma-body) is unconditioned while the drawn-forth *buddha-gotra*, from which the other two Buddha-bodies are derived, is conditioned.

7.6.5 Double-layered Soteriology in the FXL

Based on the redefinition of the dharma-body and the further development of mapping between the two *buddha-gotra*s and the three Buddha-bodies, Paramārtha's FXL sets forth a double-layered soteriological structure. The bottom layer consists of Thusness in its two aspects: Thusness as a cognitive object and Thusness as *jñāna* (i.e., unconditioned undiscriminating *jñāna*). When Thusness is obscured by ignorance and defilements, the mixture between Thusness and defilements is called *tathāgatagarbha*, that is, containing a Tathāgata (i.e., containing Thusness). When all defilements are eliminated, and Thusness is fully disclosed, it is called the dharma-body, hence the formula, "The dharma-body is disclosed through Thusness." Whether or not Thusness is disclosed, it is unconditioned and remains unchanged.

The top layer consists of causally conditioned mental processes. As a result of hearing Buddhist teachings, for example, people generate their mind of enlightenment and enter the path of Buddhist practice. In the course of practice, some people, due to the permeation of the originally existent uncontaminated seeds (*jiexing*), develop sufficiently for their minds to function, albeit sporadically, in accordance with the unconditioned undiscriminating *jñāna*. As a result, they begin to see that the world consists of phenomena that arise and cease based on the principle of dependent origination (*pratītyasamutpāda*) or Emptiness (*śūnyatā*). Seeing the world correctly gradually removes ignorance and defilements, and when they are completely eliminated, the transformation of the basis takes place, and the practitioner becomes a Buddha. The enjoyment-body and the transformation-body are derived from causally conditioned mental functions in the upper layers, which, after the transformation of the basis, function completely in accordance with the unconditioned undiscriminating *jñāna*.

These two layers appear most clearly in the discussion of three causes to buddhahood in the FXL. The first cause is the unconditioned principle of Thusness (the bottom layer); whereas the last two causes are vow and practice, which are conditioned (the upper layer):

(Quotation 7.25)
FXL:
The cause as attainability (*yingde yin* 應得因) refers to Thusness that is characterized by the two kinds of Emptiness (i.e., i.e., the Emptiness of the Self [*pudgala-nairātmya*] and of dharmas [*dharma-nairātmya*]). Due to this Emptiness, the mind of enlightenment (*bodhicitta*) and the preparatory practices (*jiaxing* 加行), and even the dharma-body after the Path (*daohou fashen* 道後法身) are to be attained. This is why [this Emptiness] is called [the cause as] attainability.

The cause to preparatory practice (*jiaxing yin* 加行因) refers to the mind of enlightenment. Because of this mind, one can attain the Dharmas that assist the Path (*zhudao zhi fa* 助道之法)—the thirty-seven factors, the ten stages (*bhūmi*), and the ten perfections (*pāramitā*)—and ultimately attain the dharma-body after the Path. This is called the "cause to preparatory practice."

The cause to perfection (*yuanman yin* 圓滿因) refers to those preparatory practices. Because of the preparatory practices, the perfection of cause (*yin yuanman* 因圓滿) and the perfection of effect (*guo yuanman* 果圓滿) are attained. The perfection of cause means the practices leading to merits and wisdom (*fuhui xing* 福慧行). The perfection of effect means the merits of wisdom, the merits of severing [affliction], and the merits of compassion (*zhi duan en de* 智斷恩德).

Among these three causes, the first one has the unconditioned principle of Thusness (*wuwei ru li* 無為如理) as its substance (*ti* 體). The latter two have the conditioned vow and practice (*youwei yuanxing* 有為願行) as their substance. As to the three kinds of *buddha-gotra*, the cause as attainability includes all three, namely, innate [*buddha-*]*gotra*, drawn-forth [*buddha-*]*gotra*, and attained [*buddha-*]*gotra*. (*zhide xing* 至得性)

Notes (*jiyue* 記曰): the innate [*buddha-*]*gotra* [belongs to those who are] at the stage of ordinary people before the Path (*daoqian fanfu wei* 道前凡夫位); the drawn-forth [*buddha-*]*gotra* [belongs to those who are] at the stages beginning

> with the stage of the generation of the mind [of enlightenment] all the way until the [highest] noble stage where one still needs practice (Ch. *youxue* 有學; Skt. *śaikṣa*); the attained [*buddha-*]*gotra* [belongs to those who are] at the noble stage where one needs no more practice (Ch. *wuxue* 無學; Skt. *aśaikṣa*).[64]

Some clarification is necessary here. First, the notes at the end of the main text, which seem to suggest that the innate *buddha-gotra* belongs only to ordinary sentient beings who have not yet entered the path, are somewhat misleading. As has been discussed, since innate *buddha-gotra* is unconditioned, it is shared by all sentient beings, regardless of the stage to which they belong. So what the notes mean to say is that one's innate *buddha-gotra* remains innate, that is, undisclosed, for sentient beings who have not trodden on the Buddhist path.

Some clarification is also required concerning the three *buddha-gotra*s mentioned here and the two kinds of *buddha-gotra* that we have been discussing. This is the only occurrence of three kinds of *buddha-gotra* in the FXL. I think that the three kinds can easily be reduced to two because the first and third types of *buddha-gotra*s refer to two different states of the same thing. According to the notes, the third *buddha-gotra* applies only to noble beings who need no further practice, namely, to the Buddhas. Hence, the third *buddha-gotra* simply refers to the complete disclosure of the first *buddha-gotra*. The relationship between the first and the third *buddha-gotra*s is parallel to the relationship between Thusness entangled with defilements (*tathatā samalā*) and Thusness not entangled with defilements (*tathatā nirmalā*) in the RGV, or the relationship between innate purity (*prakṛti-vyavadāna*) and purity devoid of defilements (*vaimalya-vyavadāna*) in MSg II.26.

The statement about the substance of each of the causes suggests that, among the three causes, the cause as attainability is unconditioned, while the cause to preparatory practice and the cause to perfection are conditioned. Thus, according to this passage, the cause as attainability corresponds to the bottom soteriological layer. Although it is called a cause, it is not a cause (*hetu*) in the proper sense because it is unconditioned and lies outside of the realm of causality. The upper layer consists of two stages: the generation of the mind of enlightenment and the preparatory practices. The preparatory practices include all Buddhist practices. They are caused by the mind of enlightenment and lead eventually to the perfection of causes and results, that is, the enjoyment-body and the transformation-body.

A potential problem with the aforementioned passage is its assertion that the cause as attainability includes all three kinds of *buddha-gotra*. This must not be understood to mean that the cause as attainability directly produces or leads to the drawn-forth and the attained *buddha-gotra*s. These two *buddha-gotra*s belong to the realm of conditioned dharmas. If the cause as attainability was able to directly produce the latter two *buddha-gotra*s, it would imply that Thusness could directly produce conditioned dharmas. This line of thinking is mistaken in the same way as the *Awakening of Faith*, and, as I have tried to show, it is unacceptable to Paramārtha.[65]

It is more likely that FXL is suggesting that all three *buddha-gotra*s are based on the cause as attainability. This means that innate *buddha-gotra* is identical with the cause as attainability, that is, Thusness/Emptiness, while the other two *buddha-gotra*s are merely based on the first *buddha-gotra*. If innate *buddha-gotra*—the cause as attainability, Thusness, Emptiness—did not exist in the first place, then the drawn-forth *buddha-gotra* would not be developed, and the attained *buddha-gotra* would not be disclosed. This is because without Thusness (in its two aspects) as innate *buddha-gotra*, the mind could not function in accordance with unconditioned undiscriminating *jñāna*. Hence, *buddha-gotra* could not be drawn forth and the attainment (when the mind functions totally in accordance with the unconditioned undiscriminating *jñāna*) could not be achieved.

The idea that the cause as attainability serves as the bottom layer also implies that it is possible for every sentient being to become a Buddha, but not that one will eventually become a Buddha. This point is stated in the following passage:

> (Quotation 7.26)
> FXL:
> Hence although the *tathāgata-gotra* (*rulaixing* 如來性; i.e., *buddha-gotra*) is called "attainability" (*yingde* 應得) [when it is at the state of being a] cause and is called "attainment" (*zhide* 至得) [when it is at the state of being an] effect, its substance is not different. [It is called differently] only because the difference with respect to its being pure or impure. When it is [at the state of being] a cause, it transgresses (*wei* 違) two kinds of Emptiness (i.e., the Emptiness of the Self [*pudgala-nairātmya*] and of dharmas [*dharma-nairātmya*]) and as a result ignorance arises. It therefore is mixed with afflictions and is called "defiled and turbid" (*ranzhuo* 染濁). Although it is not yet disclosed, it is called "attainability" because *it must be disclosable in the future (bi dang kexian* 必當可現*)*. When it is [at the state of being] an effect (i.e., when one has attained buddhahood), it is united with two kinds of Emptiness and is no more burdened by delusion (*huolei* 惑累). As it is not defiled by afflictions, it is called "pure" (*qing* 清). As the effect has been disclosed, it is called "attainment." (My emphasis[66])

Here, "it must be disclosable in the future" must not be understood as claiming that all sentient beings will eventually become Buddhas. The double-layered soteriology merely guarantees that all sentient beings must be able to become Buddhas. It does not guarantee that all sentient beings will eventually become Buddhas. The former concerns the mere possibility; but the latter concerns the actual reality. This difference will become clearer next when we discuss the issue of *icchantikas*.

To conclude, in the FXL we see a double-layered soteriology. The bottom layer is unconditioned innate *buddha-gotra,* which is Thusness consisting of two aspects; the upper layer is conditioned drawn-forth *buddha-gotra*, which is developed along the Buddhist path. At the stage of attainment, the mind functions in accordance with the unconditioned undiscriminating *jñāna* and becomes the enjoyment-body. Figure 5.2 explains the double-layered structure of soteriology, and I repeat it here as Figure 7.2.

7.6.6 The *Buddha-gotra* of Principle and the *Buddha-gotra* of Practice

The aforementioned distinction between innate *buddha-gotra* and drawn-forth *buddha-gotra* echoes a distinction that is significant in the Dilun tradition, namely, the

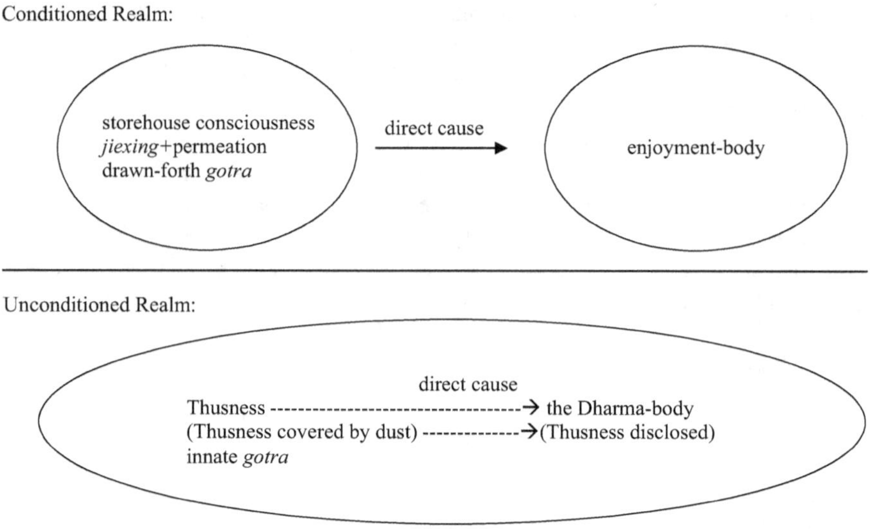

Figure 7.2 (= Figure 5.2) Doctrinal differences between the two Shelun lineages.

distinction between the *buddha-gotra* of principle (*li foxing* 理佛性) and the *buddha-gotra* of practice (*xing foxing* 行佛性).[67] According to Master Ji, these two kinds of *buddha-gotra* also suggest two different senses of *tathāgatagarbha*, as he explains in his commentary on the *Lotus Sūtra*:

> (Quotation 7.27)
> But [*buddha-*]*gotra* is of two kinds: first, the *gotra* of principle (*lixing* 理性) i.e., the idea of *tathāgatagarbha* in the *Śrīmālādevīsiṃhanāda-sūtra*; second, the *gotra* of practice (*xingxing* 行性), i.e., the idea of *tathāgatagarbha* in the *Laṅkāvatāra-sūtra*. The first kind is shared by all, but the second kind is shared only by some. *Even for those who claim that [all sentient beings] have [tathagata-]garbhas (you zang 有藏), they do not claim that [all sentient beings] will become Buddhas* (*wushuo jie zuofo* 無說皆作佛). According to the *Scripture of the Good Precepts* [of the Bodhisattvas] (*Shanjie jing* 善戒經) and the *Treatise of Proceeding the Stages* (*Dichi lun* 地持論),[68] only two kinds of sentient beings are mentioned: those who are endowed with *buddha-gotra* versus those who are not. That Scripture and that Treatise state, "The innate *gotra* (*prakṛtistha gotra*) refers to the distinction of the six sense bases (*ṣaḍāyatana-viśeṣa*) that exists from beginningless time by the nature of dharmas (*wushi fa'er* 無始法爾) and continues in one after another [reincarnations]." This refers to the sentient beings with *gotra* in the sense of the *gotra* of practice. [That Scripture and that Treatise further state,] "Those who are named 'without *gotra*' (*wuzhongxing ren* 無種姓人) do not have *gotra*. Hence even if they generate their mind of enlightenment, practice diligently and make efforts, still they would not attain the highest bodhi";[69] "The highest level he could culminate would be the good roots for the vehicle of human or heavenly beings."[70] This is what happens with sentient beings without *gotra*.[71] (My emphasis)

The point Master Ji makes here is this: When people talk about *tathāgatagarbha*, they are really talking about it in various different senses. One sense of *tathāgatagarbha*, prominent in the *Śrīmālādevīsiṃhanāda-sūtra*, is called the *buddha-gotra* of principle. This *buddha-gotra* of principle is unconditioned and hence is identical with innate *buddha-gotra* in the FXL. The other sense of *tathāgatagarbha*, prominent in the *Laṅkāvatāra-sūtra*, is called the *buddha-gotra* of practice, which is conditioned and is identical with drawn-forth *buddha-gotra* in the FXL.[72]

Significantly, Master Ji remarks: "Even those who claim that [all sentient beings] have *tathāgatagarbha* do not claim that [all sentient beings] will become Buddhas." This is because the assertion that all sentient beings have *tathāgatagarbha* is based on the *buddha-gotra* of principle, which is Thusness. It is true that all sentient beings share Thusness and hence in principle have the possibility of becoming Buddhas, which is none other than their originally endowed Thusness. But this simply suggests the theoretical possibility that everyone can become a Buddha; it does not guarantee the reality that all sentient beings will actually become Buddhas.

It is the *buddha-gotra* of practice that contributes to the fact that some sentient beings actually become Buddhas. This sense of *buddha-gotra* is synonymous with the notion of uncontaminated seeds and accounts for the actualization of practices along the Buddhist path: the accumulation of merits, the generation of the mind of enlightenment, the undertaking of the ten bodhisattva stages, the six perfections, and so on. The *buddha-gotra* of practice is not identified with Thusness because it is conditioned. Since the *buddha-gotra* of practice is conditioned by causes and conditions, it cannot be shared by all. It is noteworthy that innate *gotra* (*prakṛtistha gotra*) in the *Yogācārabhūmi*, defined as the "distinction of the six sense bases" (Skt. *ṣaḍ-āyatana-viśeṣa*; Ch. *liuchu shusheng* 六處殊勝),[73] also belongs to this *buddha-gotra* of practice.

According to Master Ji's distinction between the two kinds of *buddha-gotra*, the notion of *tathāgatagarbha* as discussed in MSgBh, RGV, MSA, and the *Śrīmālādevīsiṃhanāda-sūtra* belongs to the *buddha-gotra* of principle. This idea of *tathāgatagarbha* refers to Thusness and hence is shared by all sentient beings. The contrast between the unconditioned *buddha-gotra* and the conditioned *buddha-gotra* makes sense only if there is a strict distinction between the unconditioned and the conditioned realms. In contrast, these two *buddha-gotra*s are conflated into one according to the *Awakening of Faith* because it understands Thusness as both unconditioned and conditioned. This point can also be supported by what Huijun says in quotation 5.3.

7.6.7 The Issue of Icchantikas

With the two kinds of *buddha-gotra* and two senses of *tathāgatagarbha* clarified, now we are ready to answer a puzzling issue from the Tathāgatagarbha tradition: Why do some Tathāgatagarbha texts, including the RGV (e.g., verse I.33), while endorsing that all sentient beings are *tathāgatagarbha*s, also admit the existence of *icchantika*s? Probably with the original meaning "one who makes claims,"[74] this refers to those who will never be able to become Buddhas. But now the question is: When we say "will never be able to," do we mean theoretical impossibility or actual impossibility? The answer is that the idea that all sentient beings are *tathāgatagarbhas* rules out merely the former option but not the latter one. From the perspective of theoretical possibility, the *icchantikas* do share Thusness and *can* still become Buddhas. The issue here is that Thusness as the innate *gotra* or as the *buddha-gotra* of principle is merely a necessary condition but not a sufficient condition for one to become a Buddha.

Hence, the idea of *icchantikas* is *not* incompatible with the idea that all sentient beings share Thusness, on the condition that it is *actually* impossible for the *icchantikas* to become Buddhas. This means that, for example, *icchantikas* will never be exposed to Buddhist teachings due to their previous karma, and so on. For this reason, although Vasubandhu claims that all sentient beings have *tathāgatagarbha*, he still recognizes that some sentient beings are "without *gotra*" (*wu zhongxing* 無種姓), that is, without the actual cause to become Buddhas.[75]

Now since it is clear that sentient beings are *icchantikas* because they lack the *buddha-gotra* of practice, it would then imply a modification of the previous discussion. Since the *buddha-gotra* of practice is conditioned, its arising-and-ceasing depends upon causes and conditions. If we insist that an *icchantika* shall absolutely never become a Buddha, we would be endorsing determinism, which I think contradicts the Buddhist notion of dependent origination. To avoid this, we should not claim that an *icchantika* will never become a Buddha. Instead, we should only claim that an *icchantika* will not become a Buddha within a foreseeable future time.[76]

7.7 Paramārtha in the Post-Vasubandhu Yogācāra Traditions

To conclude my discussion of Paramārtha's FXL, to the extent that the FXL holds that the dharma-body and innate *buddha-gotra* are identical with Thusness (or the *buddha-gotra* of principle in Dilun tradition), the interpretative tradition behind the FXL still agrees with the legacy of Vasubandhu's MSgBh as well as the RGV.

But the FXL also shows significant further development beyond Vasubandhu and RGV. A major development concerns the re-definition of the dharma-body. As indicated earlier, Vasubandhu's MSgBh identifies the dharma-body with Thusness, and so does the RGV. FXL goes a step further to include under the dharma-body both Thusness as a cognitive object and Thusness as *jñāna*. It remains to be explored whether we can find this revised definition of FXL in any other Yogācāra texts.

Another major development concerns the notion of *gotra*. That is to say: in all the passages of the MSgBh where Vasubandhu talks about the notion of *gotra*, *gotra* is always understood as being of more than one type, shared by various types of sentient beings.[77] This implies that *gotra* is not common to all sentient beings for Vasubandhu. This also implies that the idea of innate *buddha-gotra* identical with Thusness as proclaimed by the FXL is not endorsed by Vasubandhu. In fact, Vasubandhu never talks about the two *gotras* (the innate *gotra* and the drawn-forth *gotra*) in his MSgBh. *Gotra* for Vasubandhu always seems to be conditioned. Thus, although both Vasubandhu and the FXL agree in the identification between Thusness and the dharma-body, FXL's adoption of the notion of "two *gotras*" clearly deviates from Vasubandhu's MSgBh.

FXL's interpretation of the two *buddha-gotras* obviously follows the RGV I. 149–52, where RGV proposes two *buddha-gotras* and the relation between the two *buddha-gotras* and the three Buddha-bodies. But note that even in the RGV itself, this is the only passage that discusses two *buddha-gotras* and their mapping onto the three Buddha-bodies. FXL clearly represents a further and more extensive development of the two-*buddha-gotra* theory that is in line with the RGV.

Further, the RGV-FXL lineage also shows marked difference from other Yogācāra texts. The fundamental disagreement is that RGV-FXL regards the innate *buddha-gotra* as unconditioned, whereas the *Bodhisattvabhūmi* defines this in terms of the "distinction of the six sense bases" and consider both *gotras* as conditioned.[78] This suggests that there existed more than one way of interpreting the idea of the two *buddha-gotras*: RGV-FXL stands on the one side against the *Yogācārabhūmi*, the MSA, the FDJL, and the CWSL.

In fact, the interpretation by the RGV-FXL lineage seems to be testified in Sthiramati's MAV-*ṭīkā*:

> (Quotation 7.28)
> There are some people who take *gotra* here to refer to Thusness (Tib. *de bzhin du*; Skt. *tathātvam*[reconstruction by Yamaguchi]) because they believe that in all sentient beings there exists the *tathāgata-gotra* (*tathāgatagotrika*).[79]

Here Sthiramati seems to allude to texts such as the RGV and the FXL. As early as Sthiramati, he already shows the enmity against or at least distance from RGV-FXL. Further background behind Sthiramati's report remains to be explored.

Now we have the following summary in Table 7.3.

There are several issues in the previous summary about the development of the Yogācāra Buddhist tradition.[80] The only point that I feel confident to make at the moment is this: the real difference between Paramārtha and Xuanzang does not lie

Table 7.3 Two-*gotra* Theory in Some Indian Buddhist Texts

		dharma-body ≠ Thusness	**dharma-body = Thusness**
No two-*gotra* theory		Asaṅga's works (except the *Yogācārabhūmi*)[a]	Vasubandhu
Two-*gotra* theory	Innate *gotra* = Thusness		RGV, Paramārtha's FXL
	Innate *gotra* ≠ Thusness	*Bodhisattvabhūmi*	MSA, FDJL[b], CWSL[c]

[a]Except for the *Yogācārabhūmi* (specifically, the *Bodhisattvabhūmi* within the *Yogācārabhūmi*), none of Asaṅga's works refer to the notion of two kinds of *gotra*.
[b]See, for example, T1530:26.326b16-19.
[c]Fascicle 10 of the CWSL cites two positions about how the five dharmas (namely, Thusness, correct *jñāna* [Ch. *zhengzhi* 正智; Skt. *samyag-jñāna*], conceptualization [Ch. *fenbie* 分別; Skt. *saṃkalpa*], names [Ch. *ming* 名; Skt. *nāma*], and images [Ch. *xiang* 相; Skt. *nimitta*]) map onto the three Buddha-bodies. Both positions agree that Thusness is included in the definition of the essence-body (Ch. *zixing shen* 自性身; Skt. *svābhāvika-kāya*), that is, the dharma-body. See T1585:31.58a6-22.

in their different notions of *tathāgatagarbha*. To the extent that at least one sense of *tathāgatagarbha* refers to Thusness, all Yogācāra texts after Vasubandhu accept that Thusness is shared by all sentient beings. Nor does their difference stem from whether there is a pure aspect within the defiled mind/consciousness. As long as no boundary can be set down upon Thusness, all Yogācāra texts after Vasubandhu accept that there is something pure—that is, Thusness—within the mind.[81] This pure aspect, however, must not be taken as an actual mental function or process because it is unconditioned. For the same reason, this pure aspect must not be taken as strong *tathāgatagarbha* as suggested by the *Awakening of Faith* because the former is unconditioned but the latter defies the strict distinction between unconditioned and conditioned. A crucial difference between Paramārtha and Xuanzang lies in their different characterizations of the notion of innate *gotra*, as mentioned earlier.

7.7.1 Tathāgatagarbha and Yogācāra Are Not Necessarily Incompatible

If my discussion earlier makes sense, then we can make a few concluding remarks. First, Paramārtha should not have been blamed for introducing heterodox Yogācāra teachings simply due to his endorsement of the notion of *tathāgatagarbha*. It was Vasubandhu who first opens the door to incorporating *tathāgatagarbha* into the Yogācāra tradition.[82]

Second, our idea about how the Yogācāra and the Tathāgatagarbha were two distinct or even antagonistic traditions must be put into serious doubt. As I discussed earlier, the sense in which Vasubandhu in the MSgBh employs the term *tathāgatagarbha* totally agrees with the way it is used in the RGV. If the RGV is regarded as the seminal text of the Tathāgatagarbha tradition, then we would have to admit that Vasubandhu also endorses the fundamental thesis of the Tathāgatagarbha tradition. Unless we would go so far as denying Vasubandhu as a genuine Yogācāra scholar, it would be a mistake to talk about the Tathāgatagarbha and Yogācāra (at least the Yogācāra after Vasubandhu) as two antagonistic or incompatible traditions. The idea that Yogācāra and Tathāgatagarbha are antagonistic to each other has a lot to do with reading the enmity between Xuanzang's and Paramārtha's disciples (the *Shelun/Awakening of Faith* lineage) retroactively back into the history of Indian Buddhism. A new map of the development of these two trends of thought is in need.

7.8 Conclusion

In this chapter, I show that Paramārtha's notion of *tathāgatagarbha* was not merely his own invention, nor some syncretism between his Yogācāra background and the indigenous Chinese materials. Rather, beginning with Vasubandhu's MSgBh, the notion of *tathāgatagarbha* was incorporated into the Yogācāra tradition. Vasubandhu did this by redefining the idea of the dharma-body, namely, by identifying the dharma-body with Thusness. Vasubandhu's move echoes the RGV as well as the MSA. I also suggest that Paramārtha's FXL represents a further development beyond Vasubandhu's MSgBh and RGV, in two aspects: (1) to redefine the dharma-body as including both Thusness as a cognitive object and Thusness as *jñāna*; (2) to follow the RGV and to provide more details about the mapping between the two *buddha-gotra*s and the three Buddha-bodies. In both aspects, Paramārtha's FXL sides with the RGV and deviates from other major Yogācāra texts. This not only teaches us about the diversity of the later Yogācāra tradition but also requires us to re-examine the relation between Yogācāra and Tathāgatagarbha in India.

8

Conclusion

8.1 What I Have Suggested in This Book

This book is mainly about the refutation of the traditional image of Paramārtha. This traditional image is actually the result of the reinterpretation of Paramārtha by his later Chinese interpreters (most probably Tanqian) *in the name of* his disciples, namely, the interpretation that goes hand in hand with the *Awakening of Faith*. The lineage of Paramārtha's direct disciples fell out of history only a few decades after his death. It is probable that T2805 was composed by one of Paramārtha's direct disciples, Daoni, and hence it is very likely that T2805 preserves the doctrines that are at least closer to Paramārtha's original teachings than those that are associated with the traditional image (Chapters 3–5).

This book focuses in particular on the notion of *jiexing* employed in Paramārtha's *Shelun*. The traditional account of *jiexing*, what I call the "Permanence reading," identifies *jiexing* with the notion of "original awakening" in the *Awakening of Faith* and hence with the dharma-body and Thusness. In contrast, T2805 unequivocally maintains an "Impermanence reading" and argues against the "Permanence reading" (Chapter 1). I argue that the "Impermanence reading" should have been close to Paramārtha's original teaching: the most likely approximation to *jiexing* is the notion of "originally existent uncontaminated seeds" mentioned in the CWSL. Paramārtha may have adopted this notion in order to build a bridge between the two *buddha-gotra*s, a theoretical difficulty that remains unresolved in his FXL (Chapter 6).

The major implications of my aforementioned claims are twofold. First, the *Awakening of Faith* is closely connected *only* with the indirect disciples of Paramārtha. The *Awakening of Faith* came to be attributed to Paramārtha because those indirect disciples were mistakenly regarded by the later Chinese Buddhist tradition as the true heirs of Paramārtha (Chapters 2 and 5). Second, I argue that the sense of *tathāgatagarbha* as employed by Paramārtha represents a further development of what had already been accepted by Vasubandhu. Both Vasubandhu and Paramārtha agree that all sentient beings have *tathāgatagarbha* because of the pervasiveness of Thusness in all sentient beings. To this extent, Vasubandhu was a major Yogācāra thinker who already incorporated Tathāgatagarbha into his Yogācāra theory well before Paramārtha. The fact that even Vasubandhu endorses the Tathāgatagarbha claim challenges the received wisdom that Yogācāra and Tathāgatagarbha were two antagonistic traditions in India (Chapter 7).

8.2 Re-evaluating the Three Dubious Assumptions about Paramārtha

Here I conclude by showing how my book contributes to the re-evaluation of what I call in the Introduction three dubious assumptions underlying the previous studies of Paramārtha.

8.2.1 The *Awakening of Faith* Was Related to Paramārtha in a Certain Way

As I discussed extensively in Chapter 5, the *Awakening of Faith* is connected with Paramārtha's indirect disciples headed by Tanqian, who taught Paramārtha's *Shelun* together with the *Awakening of Faith* in the capital Chang'an around 590. At the same time, Paramārtha's direct disciple Daoni, the most probable author of T2805, was also promoting Paramārtha's teachings. Daoni's lineage died out only a few years after he moved to Chang'an in 590. Tanqian's lineage remained as the only lineage of Paramārtha's disciples, a historical circumstance that contributes to the false attribution of the *Awakening of Faith* to Paramārtha.

The attribution of the *Awakening of Faith* to Paramārtha is a crucial part of the distorted traditional image of Paramārtha, which is also the deep root of why Paramārtha has remained a mysterious figure for modern scholars. The first step to recover the authentic teachings of Paramārtha, I believe, lies in the firm rejection of this false attribution with an explanation of why this attribution came to exist.

Following this, we can begin to take on three tasks that have not been systematically tackled. First, we could sort out Paramārtha's authentic teachings from later Chinese reports. We now have two solid criteria to determine the authenticity of the works traditionally attributed to Paramārtha or the later Chinese reports about Paramārtha's teachings: we have good reasons to doubt those reports that (1) do not follow the idiosyncratic terminology indicated in Chapter 3, or (2) go squarely against the points made in T2805 or owe much to the *Awakening of Faith*. With more studies in this field, we might arrive at a clearer understanding about how various lines of thought (e.g., various lines of Shelun masters, Dilun masters, or early Huayan masters) merge into the traditional image of Paramārtha.

Second, we could investigate the origin of the *Awakening of Faith* from a fresh perspective. The false attribution of the *Awakening of Faith* has obstructed scholars from investigating the real history behind the *Awakening of Faith*. Due to this false attribution, various conjectures about the *Awakening of Faith*—such as that it originated in Funan 扶南 (nowadays Cambodia)—have been proposed.[1] Once this attribution is refuted, we can join Mochizuki and Takemura in exploring how the *Awakening of Faith* grew out of the Chinese context, to study whether and how this text aimed at a reconciliation between the Dilun tradition on the one hand and the newly introduced teachings of Paramārtha's on the other hand, and so on.

Third, we may ask more meaningful questions regarding the sociopolitical milieu surrounding Paramārtha and the *Awakening of Faith*. The false attribution of the *Awakening of Faith* has also led scholars away from a deeper insight into the sociopolitical milieu leading to the prosperity of the traditional image of Paramārtha. For example, we may now ask: If the *Awakening of Faith* did not originate in India, then what was the historical and intellectual background behind the second "translation" of the *Awakening of Faith* in the beginning of the eighth century?[2] A deeper understanding of the doctrinal issues could have a huge impact on the exploration of sociohistorical issues, and vice versa.

8.2.2 Paramārtha Stood against Xuanzang

Once the *Awakening of Faith* is removed from the works of Paramārtha, we will see that Paramārtha's teachings are not so squarely against those of Xuanzang as the later Chinese tradition used to hold. In Chapter 6, I show that ideas very similar to Paramārtha's *jiexing* can also be found in Xuanzang's translations of the FDJL and the CWSL. Another striking similarity is that both T2805 and Master Ji agree that *jiexing* for Paramārtha, or the "originally existent uncontaminated seeds" for Master Ji, becomes the enjoyment-body after one becomes a Buddha (4.5). I firmly believe that, with more and more studies along this line, we shall find more and more agreements between Paramārtha and Xuanzang. The conjectures made by previous scholars—such as the idea that Paramārtha came from a minority Yogācāra school that was affiliated with Valabhī, which held different Buddhist teachings from Nālandā, where Xuanzang was trained[3]—must be subject to further investigation.

It is no doubt true that there are significant differences between Paramārtha and Xuanzang as was pointed out by Ueda (0.4.2). But rather than investigating whether Paramārtha or Xuanzang was more faithful to the early works by Asaṅga or Vasubandhu, I believe that it would be much more fruitful if we take Paramārtha and Xuanzang as representing two different phases in the development of the Yogācāra tradition(s).

Once we adopt a critically historical perspective on Paramārtha, we would come to appreciate the indispensable value of his works. Paramārtha represents a snapshot of the Yogācāra tradition(s) in India around the early sixth century. In other words, his deviation in the *Shelun* from Vasubandhu's original texts does not necessarily mean that he follows a heterodox Yogācāra lineage. Rather, it is more likely that this is because he represents a further development of Yogācāra after Vasubandhu.

A telling example in this vein is the different characterizations of the dharma-body by Vasubandhu and Paramārtha. In 7.2, I show how the idea of the dharma-body is identified with Thusness for Vasubandhu. This, however, is not the case for Paramārtha. Paramārtha consistently maintains that the dharma-body includes both Thusness and the unconditioned undiscriminating *jñāna* about Thusness (4.3.1 and 7.6). Moreover, in the later translations of Xuanzang, we do find reports of the debates in India about whether the undiscriminating *jñāna* of Thusness (i.e., the mirror *jñāna* [*ādarśa-jñāna*]) should be included in the definition of the dharma-body.[4] This teaches us that Paramārtha's characterization of the dharma-body might have represented a snapshot of the development within the Yogācāra tradition(s) between Vasubandhu and Xuanzang.

8.2.3 Yogācāra and Tathāgatagarbha Were Two Distinct and Antagonistic Traditions

With the disassociation of the *Awakening of Faith* from Paramārtha, we should be able to distinguish two different understandings of the notion of *tathāgatagarbha*: the strong *tathāgatagarbha* in the *Awakening of Faith* vs. the weak *tathāgatagarbha* in Paramārtha's works, in Vasubandhu's MSgBh, and in texts such as RGV and MSA (7.5). I have illustrated the difference between these two understandings in Figure 5.2: in Paramārtha's genuine works, the strict distinction between conditioned vs. unconditioned is maintained; whereas in the *Awakening of Faith* this very distinction is compromised.

Throughout the chapters of this book, the contrast between these two understandings of *tathāgatagarbha* remains a recurring theme in different forms: whether *jiexing* should be identified with the dharma-body (Chapters 1 and 6); whether Thusness can be permeated (2.4); whether *jiexing* would become the enjoyment-body of the Buddhas (4.5); whether the innate *buddha-gotra* alone or all the three *buddha-gotras* serve as the direct cause to buddhahood (i.e., the disclosure of the dharma-body) (5.2.2). This distinction is also embodied in the distinction made by Master Ji between the *buddha-gotra* of Principle vs. the *buddha-gotra* of Practice (quotation 7.27).

In Chapter 7, I have also shown that Paramārtha's weak *tathāgatagarbha* actually follows what had been endorsed by Vasubandhu. The confusion between the strong *tathāgatagarbha* of the *Awakening of Faith* and the weak *tathāgatagarbha* of Paramārtha and Vasubandhu has been a major reason leading us to believe that Yogācāra and Tathāgatagarbha were two incompatible trends of thought in Indian Buddhism. With this confusion cleared, we can now embark on a fresh investigation of the interweaving or confluence between Yogācāra and Tathāgatagarbha at least beginning with Vasubandhu.

8.3 General Remarks on Working with Chinese Buddhist Texts

I end this book with a few general remarks about how to make good use of the Chinese Buddhist texts to facilitate our understanding of Indian Buddhism. First, I argue for the usefulness of the Chinese sources because they alone can possibly provide clues to the development of Indian Buddhism before the seventh century. Second, I argue that the Chinese sources must be examined and contextualized first in the Chinese context, intellectual as well as sociopolitical. Third, I argue for the usefulness of the notion of Sinicization because this notion provides us with a perspective in which we may judge whether a Chinese source is relevant or not in reconstructing Indian Buddhism.

8.3.1 Chinese Buddhist Texts as Snapshots of Indian Buddhism

As I tried to show in this book, Paramārtha's Chinese translations together with all his commentarial interpolations, if used properly, can serve as snapshots for us to glimpse into what was going on in the Indian Yogācāra tradition around early sixth century. Given the paucity of the extant Sanskrit texts and the messy situation regarding the dating and authorship of those texts, it is nearly impossible to reconstruct the development of Indian Buddhism before the seventh century merely based on extant Sanskrit texts. Given the relative lateness of the Tibetan translations, all the snapshots that are preserved in the Chinese sources were almost forgotten by the time when those texts were translated into Tibetan. In other words, we have a lacuna if our work is based on extant Sanskrit texts; whereas we have snapshots of a much later scene if our work is based on the Tibetan sources. From this perspective, we would come to appreciate the unique value of the Chinese sources in providing at least some glimpses into the development of Indian Buddhism during the sixth to seventh centuries.[5]

8.3.2 To Examine Chinese Texts First in the Chinese Context

Given the potential usefulness of the Chinese sources, I would like to offer some reflections on how to employ the Chinese sources in a good way. My main point is: in order to avoid reading later Chinese reinterpretations retroactively back into the reconstruction of Indian Buddhism, the Chinese sources must first be contextualized and examined carefully within the Chinese context.

What I mean by the Chinese context naturally includes two dimensions: (1) the Chinese context before a Buddhist text was introduced and (2) the context in which this text was later received.

(1) A text must be examined against its Chinese context before this text was introduced. The examination includes aspects such as how a translator and his colleagues adopt available Chinese terms or craft new terms in order to make sense of the newly introduced texts. In Chapter 3, we see how Paramārtha's translations are embedded in the Buddhist context in southern China in the sense that they employ several Buddhist Chinese terms available only in the southern China. It is quite likely that in this process of translation some complicated interaction occurs: the introduction of a new text must adapt itself and make compromises in order to make sense to its contemporary and local Chinese audience; and conversely, the introduction of this text might also expand and reshape the Chinese milieu surrounding the people who received this text.

Regarding this complicated process of "translation," both Nattier and Funayama draw our attention to the issue of the mediation of the Chinese context in translation. For example, Nattier provides insightful observations about the presence of both a more vernacular style and a more elegant and classical style in early Chinese Buddhist translations; about the variance of style under "an" Indian translator probably due to the "shifting composition" of the translation committee; and about what Nattier calls "intertextuality," that is, "a common practice for Chinese translators to adopt terms that were already in circulation."[6] Fortunately, most of the issues that concern Nattier—such as what are the authentic works by a specific translator of Buddhist texts, and what are the criteria for making judgments about authenticity—can now be approached with the help of the digitalized Chinese Buddhist canon and hopefully at least some of the difficulties will be resolved in the near future.[7]

Funayama calls attention to the process through which a text comes into existence, namely, the mediation of editing. Funayama acutely points out that changes, such as omission and interpolation, were not uncommon in Chinese Buddhist translations before the Tang dynasty.[8] Based on this specific process involved in the editing of Chinese Buddhist texts, Funayama suggests that we should accept a special category of Chinese Buddhist texts that are neither literal translations of Indic texts nor purely Chinese compositions.[9] Prominent examples of this category, according to Funayama, include the lecture notes by Bodhiruci (a text entitled *Jin'gangxian lun*; T1512) and the lecture notes by Paramārtha.[10]

(2) A text must also be examined against its Chinese context after it was introduced. The examination includes all the aspects included earlier, plus an examination of later reception of this text. This would include questions like who were those authors who cited this text, who were manipulating this text for their own agenda, whether there existed later reinterpretations that might be different from the "original" sense of the text, and so on. These are no easy questions to answer indeed, but my book hopefully has shown how crucial it is to distinguish later reinterpretations from the "original teachings" of Paramārtha in our refutation of the traditional image of Paramārtha.

To sum up, I argue that the danger in utilizing the Chinese sources to reconstruct Indian Buddhism must *not* be avoided at the price of completely discarding Chinese sources. A more cautious way of dealing with this danger is to contextualize a Chinese text and carefully examine it first in its Chinese context.

8.3.3 Sinicization of Buddhism?

Finally, I would like to defend the usefulness of the notion of Sinicization in the efforts of reconstructing Indian Buddhism based on Chinese sources. In recent decades, the issue of the "Sinicization of Buddhism" has become quite unpopular. Part of the reason is because scholars sense a potential risk in employing this notion of Sinicization: it seems that we have to presuppose reified and essentialized entities such as India, China, Indian Buddhism, and Chinese Buddhism in order to talk about Sinicization of Buddhism. In what follows, I argue that the issue of Sinicization can also be examined with a case study in a specific historical context without necessarily stipulating any essentialized entities.[11]

In pursuing the issue of Sinicization, it would be useful to distinguish the weak sense of the term from its strong sense. Here I slightly modify the distinction between these two senses suggested by Michael Radich, and thereby define the weak sense of Sinicization as follows: any further development of or any change made in China to what was already present in Buddhism in India, regardless of the causes of that development or change. In contrast, the strong sense of Sinicization is defined as: any further development of or any change made in China to what is already present in Buddhism in India that can be traced at least partly to things that are characteristically Chinese, and are representative of them.[12] By "characteristically Chinese," I do not mean some sort of a priori psychological or linguistic structure belonging exclusively to "the Chinese people," but rather contingent historical factors that occurred only in China such as the influence of the Dilun tradition on the *Awakening of Faith* as indicated next.

Under this distinction, I consider the notion of *tathāgatagarbha* in the *Awakening of Faith* as an example of the Sinicization in the weak sense. The notion of *tathāgatagarbha* in the *Awakening of Faith* is apparently a continuation and further development of the notion of *tathāgatagarbha* in India.

Furthermore, I argue that the notion of *tathāgatagarbha* in the *Awakening of Faith* also qualifies as an example of Sinicization in the strong sense. In Chapters 5 and 7, I have demonstrated how the notion of *tathāgatagarbha* in the *Awakening of Faith* (strong *tathāgatagarbha*) deviates from the notion of *tathāgatagarbha* according to Indian authors, such as Vasubandhu and Paramārtha (weak *tathāgatagarbha*), by going against the strict distinction between unconditioned and conditioned. This distinction is so basic to the Abhidharmic taxonomy of dharmas[13] that it is almost inconceivable for a Buddhist scholar in India to violate this basic doctrine. A neglect of the aforementioned distinction—as an example of Sinicization in the strong sense—is likely to have occurred only in a Chinese setting.

This much being said, I certainly do not want to reach the conclusion that the factor leading to Sinicization in the strong sense is some sort of "Chinese mentality." I agree with Mochizuki and Takemura and suggest that the most likely cause behind this strong Sinicization in the *Awakening of Faith* is that its author was heavily influenced by his doctrinal background of an indigenous Chinese tradition, that is, the Dilun tradition.[14]

The point I want to illustrate here is that it is *not* necessary to stipulate essentialized entities such as the Chinese culture in order to talk about Sinicization. We can still work with this notion by focusing on a specific text (e.g., the *Awakening of Faith* compared to Paramārtha's original teachings that are preserved in T2805) in a particular historical context (e.g., the capital Chang'an around 590 CE). Of course, larger contexts such as the intellectual background in northern China and southern China must be taken into account to depict a more accurate picture of the historical context in question. But again, we do not have to reify any of those larger Buddhist contexts as a single, self-contained entity.

It should be clear that the notion of Sinicization serves as a benchmark against which the extent of the misunderstandings and (sometimes creative) reinterpretations by the Chinese audience can be measured. For the same reason, the notion of Sinicization can also serve as a criterion for whether a text should be closely consulted for the sake of reconstructing Indian Buddhism: it may not be a big problem if our reconstruction is based on those Chinese sources that are Sinicized in the weak sense, but it would be a serious problem to base our reconstruction on the Chinese sources that have been Sinicized in the strong sense.

Before we make use of a Chinese source to reconstruct Indian Buddhism, the sense and the degree of Sinicization of this source must be examined in both the Chinese and the Indian contexts. Of course, it is usually fairly difficult to judge in what sense and to what degree a Chinese source is Sinicized. Given the paucity of Indian sources and the lateness of the Tibetan sources, usually we could not find any reliable sources on the Indian side to compare in order to decide whether the Chinese text in question is Sinicized. The result is that more often than not we would end up being trapped in circular reasoning.[15] This goes back to my earlier point that a Chinese source must be examined first in the Chinese context, which I believe is usually the easiest way to tell in what sense a Chinese source is Sinicized.[16]

* * *

This book begins with the puzzle about the existence of two conflicting interpretations of *jiexing* and ends with a relocation of the great Indian teacher Paramārtha in the history of Chinese Buddhism as well as in the history of Indian Buddhism. Each part of my arguments might have its own weakness, but I believe that, taking arguments together, we can arrive at a fresh and coherent image about Paramārtha. With this new image, we are turning a new page with the studies of Buddhist thought during the sixth to seventh centuries.

Notes

Abbreviation

1 The Sanskrit title of this text has been constructed differently. John Keenan (1980) and Dan Lusthaus (2002) reconstruct the original Sanskrit title as the **Buddhabhūmy-upadeśa*, which is different from the Tibetan translation of the **Buddhabhūmi-vyākhyāna* attributed to Śīlabhadra (see Nishio 1982). The precise relation among these two commentaries on the **Buddhabhūmi-sūtra* and the *Cheng weishi lun* goes beyond the scope of this book (Cf. Lusthaus 2002: 400ff.). To avoid confusion, I choose to use Xuanzang's Chinese title throughout this book.

2 There are confusions regarding the title of the RGV. E.H. Johnston's Sanskrit edition puts it as "*ratnagotravibhāgo mahāyānottaratantraśāstram*" (Prasad 1991: 69). Based on the Tibetan translation of the commentary, E. Obermiller reconstructs the Sanskrit title of the commentary as "*Uttaratantra-vyākhyā*" (Prasad 1991: 220). Takasaki notes that "Being the explanation of the meaning of the *śloka* the commentary seems to be called the '*Ślokārthasaṃgrahavyākhyāna*'" (Takasaki 1966: 11).

Introduction

1 The *Awakening of Faith* is now considered by most scholars as a Chinese apocryphal text. See later for more details. For some general background information about the Chinese apocryphal texts, see Buswell (1989, 1990).

2 Aurel Stein Collection number 2747. I provide a more detailed introduction of T2805 in Chapter 3 (3.1).

3 Here I am intentionally using the term "tradition" in a somewhat vague sense, meaning something like "text tradition" or "doctrinal trend." In the earliest phase of the Yogācāra tradition, its followers might not have been an organized school. See Silk (2000) for details. However, it seems that sometime between Vasubandhu's era and the mid-seventh century, they became a more organized school. Master Ji 基法師 (632–82, also called Kuiji 窺基) reports that ten foremost masters composed commentaries on Vasubandhu's *Triṃśikā* before Xuanzang. In contrast, we know so little about Tathāgatagarbha that we are not even sure whether it was indeed a distinct tradition separated from Yogācāra. See Chapter 7 for more details.

4 I am aware that there are multiple types of Yogācāra and Tathāgatagarbha texts. Some Yogācāra texts may not endorse the idea of "acquired undiscriminating *jñāna*," whereas some Tathāgatagarbha texts may not endorse the idea of "innate undiscriminating *jñāna*." But for the sake of introducing how Paramārtha, according to the traditional image of him, represents a kind of syncretism between Yogācāra and Tathāgatagarbha, I deliberately contrast Yogācāra against Tathāgatagarbha along the

line of "acquired undiscriminating *jñāna*" vs. "innate undiscriminating *jñāna*." Here, by Yogācāra I am referring to the *Mahāyānasaṃgraha* of Asaṅga (*c.* fourth to fifth centuries), and by Tathāgatagarbha I am referring to Paramārtha's *Foxing lun* 佛性論. For the insistence in the *Mahāyānasaṃgraha* that liberation (including the seeds for acquiring undiscriminating *jñāna*) must come from outside, see Schmithausen (1987: section 4.8.5). For the idea that all sentient beings are innately endowed with undiscriminating *jñāna*, see my discussion in 7.6.2. Toward the end of the book, I will problematize such an oversimplistic picture that Yogācāra and Tathāgatagarbha were two antagonistic and incompatible traditions in Indian Buddhism.

5 The idealism of Yogācāra is most clearly and succinctly expressed in Vasubandhu's *Twenty Verses* (*Viṃśikā*). Some scholars in recent decades suggest that Yogācāra is not idealism but is a kind of Phenomenology, meaning that Yogācāra does not deny a reality external to mind. See Lusthaus (2002) for his proposal of "Buddhist Phenomenology." In this connection, I agree with the critique of Lusthaus by Schmithausen (2005) and regard Yogācāra as idealism in its strong sense.

6 By this I am referring to the doctrines held by the Chinese Yogācāra tradition (see later). This tradition insists that not all sentient beings can become Buddhas. Instead, there are five different "lineages" (*gotra*). Whether one can ultimately become a Buddha is determined by the lineage to which one belongs. Sentient beings belonging to three among these five lineages will not be able to attain buddhahood in the foreseeable future.

7 For an excellent detailed study of the etymological and contextual meaning of the term "*tathāgatagarbha*," mainly in the *Tathāgatagarbha-sūtra*, see Zimmermann (2002: 39–50). I will discuss the meaning of the term "*tathāgatagarbha*" in more detail in 7.1. For some general background information about the Tathāgatagarbha tradition and texts, see Hirakawa, Kajiyama, and Takasaki (1982b) and Radich (2015a). For a comprehensive study of the development of the Tathāgatagarbha tradition, see Takasaki (1974).

8 Here I give only a brief summary of Paramārtha's life. For a slightly more detailed version, see Keng and Radich (2019). Much more detailed versions of Paramārtha's biography can be found in Ui (1930: 1–130), Tang (1938: 618–26), and Su (1978). In addition, Diana Paul (1984: 11–37) provides a biography of Paramārtha in English.

9 T1559:29.161b11-12 and T237:8.766c6-7. On the usual circumstances surrounding the translation of Buddhist texts and the role played by the Chinese "interpreters," see Fukui (2003).

10 T2060:50.430a27-b3.

11 To the best of my knowledge, no Tibetan or Chinese Buddhist catalog attributes the MSgBh to any author other than Vasubandhu. Scholars since Frauwallner (1951b) have entertained the idea that there were two Vasubandhus: the older one composed mainly commentaries on the Mahāyāna texts, including MSgBh, MSABh, and MAVBh; the younger one composed the *Abhidharmakośa* (and *Abhidharmakośabhāṣya*), the *Twenty Verses* (*Viṃśikā*), and the *Thirty Verses* (*Triṃśikā*). A typical version of the division into two groups of the works traditionally attributed to Vasubandhu can be found in Schmithausen (1987: 262, footnote 101). Despite proposing his own theory of two Vasubandhus, Hartmut Buescher (2013: 370) also remarks, the theory of two Vasubandhus has become unpopular in recent years. The most up-to-date and reliable review of Vasubandhu and his works is Kritzer (2019). For the purpose of my discussion, I am concerned only with how the MSgBh

deviates from the MSg and how the MSgBh agrees with the RGV regarding the definition of the dharma-body (*dharmakāya*). For this reason, I do not deal with the issues of two Vasubandhus or with whether the author of the *Abhidharmakośa* and the author of the MSgBh were the same person. In this book, the name Vasubandhu is used to refer to the author of the MSgBh. I remain open whether this Vasubandhu also composed the important texts mentioned earlier.

12 See Chapter 2 for more details.

13 Funayama (2002) gives the most complete account of this procedure.

14 A similar situation is suspected in the case of the *Treatise from the Diamond-Sage* (Ch. *Jin'gang xian lun* 金剛仙論; T1512). See Ōtake (2001).

15 Although the original Sanskrit text of Vasubandhu's MSgBh is lost, we can still be sure that it did not include an idea of *jiexing* because this term does not appear in any of the other translations (two Chinese and one Tibetan translations).

16 The term "*Faxing zong*," as a contrast to *Faxiang zong*, appears to have been first adopted by the Huayan master Chengguan 澄觀 (738–839). *Faxing zong* means the same as what is called "*Rulaizang yuanqi zong* 如來藏緣起宗 (The Tradition of Dependent Origination on the Basis of *Tathāgatagarbha*)" (T1838:44.61c12) by the Huayan master Fazang 法藏 (643–712). In later Chinese Buddhist tradition, *Faxing zong* means pretty much the same thing as the Huayan tradition, whose doctrine is largely based on the *Awakening of Faith*.

17 Confounded by the various contradictory teachings current in China in the early seventh century, Xuanzang traveled to India (*c.* 629–45) and brought back to China what he claimed to be the "orthodox" Yogācāra.

18 See Mochizuki (1922).

19 See Demiéville (1929), Liebenthal (1958), Hirakawa (1990) and Takemura (1993). Kashiwagi (1981) provides a detailed review of the debate among Japanese scholars in the twentieth century.

20 See Aoki (1988, 1997, 2000), Aoki and Kŭmgang Taehakkyo Pulgyo Munhwa Yŏn'guso (2012, 2013), Ishii (1993, 1995), Ibuki (1999), and Kongō daigaku bukkyō bunka kenkyūjo 金剛大学仏教文化研究所 (2010, 2017a, b).

21 T1522:26.169a15.

22 The Sanskrit text reads: *cittamātraṃ bho jinaputrā yad uta traidhātukam iti sūtrāt*. See Lévi (1925: 3).

23 See the words of Huiyuan of the Jingying (Temple) 淨影(寺)慧遠 (523–92), for example: T1851:44.473b14-20, 551a4-5.

24 For more about the doctrinal background of the Dilun tradition and the doctrinal disputes between its two branches, see Gimello (1976: 294ff).

25 For more details about the idea that the storehouse consciousness is fundamentally negative (*dauṣṭhulya*), see Schmithausen (1987), Chapter 4 in particular, and Waldron (2003).

26 See Chapter 2, quotation 2.5 and quotation 2.6 respectively.

27 See 0.5 for more details.

28 See Nattier (2003).

29 See, for example, McRae (1986).

30 Note that this is not a complete list. For a detailed study of how different Chinese Buddhist catalogs attribute different works to Paramārtha, see Radich (2012).

31 The issue here is whether or not one enters the stage of "Path of Insight" (Skt. *darśana-mārga*; Ch. *jiandao* 見道). In his *Commentary on the Perfection of Wisdom Scripture for Humane Kings* (*Renwang jing shu* 仁王經疏), Wŏnch'ŭk lists three different

views, the third of which is not attributed to Paramārtha and is not relevant here. The first view is based on the "original notes" attributed to Paramārtha. This view claims that the stage of "Path of Insight" begins with the "ten merit-transfers" (*shi huixiang* 十迴向) (T1708:33.386c16-19). In contrast, the second view is based on Paramārtha's *Shelun* and holds that all practices—"ten confidences" (*shi xin* 十信), "ten understandings" (*shi jie* 十解) or "ten abidings" (*shizhu* 十住), "ten practices" (*shi xing* 十行), and "ten merit-transfers"—precede the stage of "Path of Insight" (T1708:33.386c19-387a3).

Briefly, "Ten Confidences," "Ten Understandings," "Ten Practices," and "Ten Merit-transfers" constitute the so-called forty mental (stages) (*sishi xin* 四十心) before the first bodhisattva stage. These terms do not exist in the works of Asaṅga, Vasubandhu, and Asvabhāva. Funayama (2000) points out that this notion of forty stages was based on Chinese apocryphal texts that were composed around the beginning of the sixth century in southern China. Based on Funayama's claim, there must have been a lively interaction between Paramārtha as an Indian master and his contemporary Chinese Buddhist context.

32 Paramārtha's idiosyncratic terminology (e.g., his rendering of the Sanskrit term *anāsrava* as *wuliu* 無流 in Chinese) is most prominent in his works such as *Shelun* and Paramārtha's AKBh, which all sources agree were translated in the last years of his career. Based on this, we can have some idea of which works he translated in his earlier career. The discovery of more such philological clues in the future may help us establish a chronology of Paramārtha's works.

33 See Ui (1930: 501–40).

34 See Ui (1930: 530).

35 Iwata gives a very brief review of the different evaluations of Paramārtha by the foremost Japanese Buddhologists: Ui Hakuju and Ueda Yoshifumi on the one side, who valued Paramārtha as representing the authentic teachings of the MSgBh, and Yūki Reimon and Nagao Gajin, on the other side, claiming that Paramārtha actually deviated from Vasubandhu's MSgBh. See Iwata (2004: x).

36 For Iwata, see Iwata (2004: xi). For Shengkai (2006), see his introduction, especially p. 3. Despite the fact that Iwata's book is the only comprehensive Japanese study of Paramārtha's thought so many years after Ui, it is basically a patchwork, with primary texts of Paramārtha listed one after another without a systematic structure. He sometimes simply follows Ui's account but more often comes up with his own interpretations without much consistency. In terms of seeking a new perspective on Paramārtha, Iwata's book is not quite useful.

37 See 2.3.3 for more details.

38 Ueda (1951: 295ff).

39 Ueda (1967: 156).

40 According to Ueda (1967: 161–2), "Dharmapala's understanding was different from that of Vasubandhu, whereas Sthiramati's was faithful to it. The interpretations of Sthiramati and Paramārtha concur with each other."

41 To be sure, I am not suggesting that there is no doctrinal difference between Paramārtha and Xuanzang. I agree with Ueda that they differ regarding the theory of the three natures. See my discussion in the following paragraph. My point here is that the differences between Paramārtha and Xuanzang should first be examined from a historical and diachronic perspective instead of an ahistorical and synchronic perspective.

42 Shengkai (2006: 3).

43 Shengkai (2006: 642).

44 Throughout his two-volume work, Shengkai does not devote even a single section to the relationship between Paramārtha and the *Awakening of Faith*. Obviously, he does not think the *Awakening of Faith* was translated by Paramārtha because he omits it from his list of Paramārtha's works. See Shengkai (2006: 21–6). He also makes scattered comments about the relation between the *Awakening of Faith* and the Dilun tradition and about how Shelun masters, such as Tanqian and Jingsong, may have interpreted Paramārtha's works from the point of view of the *Awakening of Faith*. See Shengkai (2006: 393–4).

45 Recall the doctrinal differences between Paramārtha and Xuanzang pointed out by Ueda. I believe that Paramārtha was closer to the earlier model whereas Xuanzang was closer to the later model.

46 In fact, if we go back to earlier Yogācāra texts such as the MAV, we also find ideas that are close to *tathāgatagarbha*, such as the notion of "innate pure mind" (*prakṛti-prabhāsvara-citta*).

47 For more detailed discussions of the history of the Shelun tradition, see Katsumata (1961) and Takamine (1963).

48 I will leave to later chapters a review of scholarship on the notion of *jiexing*—the central focus of this book—and a review of scholarship on Dunhuang fragment T2805—the crucial document on which my monograph is based.

49 Paul translates the title as "Evolution of Consciousness," which also suggests the same understanding with mine of the Sanskrit term "*pariṇāma*" behind the Chinese term "*zhuan*."

50 I revisit Funayama in my discussion about Sinicization in the Conclusion (8.3).

51 T2060:50.574b3-5.

52 T2146:55.142a16.

53 Johnston (1950: 99), lines 15–16; T1611:31.846a20-22.

54 Gimello (1976: 111). Gimello (1976: 93ff) offers an excellent discussion of Yūki's proposal. He shows how, in specific cases, Chinese Buddhism in the sixth century can be understood in light of Yūki's thesis. In my recent conversations with Professor Gimello, however, he expressed views about Sinicization that were somewhat different from what he wrote in his PhD dissertation.

55 See my discussion of the *Awakening of Faith* in the Conclusion (8.3.3) as an example of Sinicization in the strong sense.

56 In short, I argue that the significance of New Buddhism lay in the effort to eliminate the absolute dichotomy between the pure and the defiled. The idea that all things, pure or defiled, ultimately originate from the pure mind was most systematically expressed in the *Awakening of Faith*. I think this paves the way for New Buddhism in that even the worst defilements are somehow related to the original absolute purity. Thus, the claim, systematized later in the Tiantai and Huayan traditions, that the pure and the impure actually interpenetrate each other, makes sense.

57 See my discussion on Sinicization in the Conclusion.

58 A prominent example is the Japanese scholar Ui (see 1.1.4 for more details).

59 Examples include the suggestions of Higata, Ueda, Iwata, and Nagao. See Chapter 1, notes 6 and 21.

60 Kimura (1985). Ui (1935) also cites T2805 a few times.

61 Some particularly telling examples are the terms in compounds with *wuliu* 無流 (*anāsrava*). See 0.3.2.

Chapter 1

1 The precise meaning of this phrase is unclear. I leave the phrase untranslated at this stage, but in Chapter 6, I provide an explanation of the notion of *jiexing*.
2 The term "birth" in the context of the dharma-body seems dubious and is worth further exploration. In Chapter 7, I argue that for both Paramārtha and Vasubandhu, the dharma-body is unconditioned. It can only be disclosed and cannot be born.
3 T1595:31.156c9-22.
4 The notion of "transformation of the basis" is a complicated one that cannot be adequately discussed here. The basic idea is that, since the Yogācāra tradition insists that the storehouse consciousnesses of ordinary sentient beings are fundamentally negative (*dauṣṭhulya*) (see Introduction, note 25), when they become Buddhas, the defiled storehouse consciousness as the old basis (*āśraya*) must be replaced (*parāvṛtti*; literally, "turning, change") by an undefiled new basis. See Davidson (1985) and Sakuma (1990) for more details. Two different Sanskrit terms are found for "transformation of the basis": *āśraya-parāvṛtti* and *āśraya-parivṛtti*, but I agree with Schmithausen (1969: 90 ff.) that there is no clear distinction between these two terms in major Yogācāra texts such as the *Yogācārabhūmi*. For more discussion about "transformation of the basis," see 4.5.
5 T1595:31.175a23-26.
6 As far as I can tell, Iwata's reading follows the suggestion made earlier by Ueda (1951), where Ueda thanks HIGATA Ryūshō 干潟 龍祥 for proposing this reading. See Ueda (1951: 317ff, 342 note 97).
7 Iwata (2004: 14–16); see also his reading of the *Shelun Jiexing* Passage (2): 19–20.
8 See Chapter 6.
9 Here *y* can be either a noun or an adjective. Throughout Paramārtha's *Shelun*, there are 52 occurrences of *y* as a noun. One example, *yi hui wei yizhi* 以慧為依止, means "which has wisdom as its basis." There are two occurrences as an adjective, for example, *yi li wei sheng* 以理為勝, meaning "whose principle is supreme."
10 Ui (1935: 211–12, 341).
11 Etō (1932: 12).
12 Nagao (1982–7, Vol. I: 78, note 3).
13 For example, Iwata disagrees with Ui, and Nagao hesitates to agree with Ui. See notes 7 and 12 above.
14 See: *Shelun* fascicle 1 (T1595:31.156c16-22), *Shelun* fascicle 15 (T1595:31.264b7-17), Paramārtha's FXL (T1610:31.796b7-c8), the *Xianshi lun* (T1618:31.881c26-882a9) and the Chinese translation of the RGV (T1611:31.839a16-b15).
15 Ui (1935: 211–15), also see pages 340–3.
16 For a general review of the theory of the three natures, see Nagao (1991: 61–74), Sponberg (1983), Kitano (1999, 2001), Keng (2014a, 2015).
17 See Hirakawa, Kajiyama, and Takasaki (1982b: 119–38).
18 Ui (1935: 211–15).
19 T2269:128b13-15.
20 See T1666:32.576b7-14.
21 For example, Nagao criticizes Ui's reading but admits that he does not have a satisfactory alternative. See Nagao (1982–87, Vol. I: 78, note 3).
22 Kashiwagi (1981: 185ff). For a brief introduction to Tanyan and his commentary on the *Awakening of Faith*, see Jorgensen et al. (2019: 36–8).

23 T1666:32.576b11-14. See also Hakeda (1967: 37); Girard (2004: 29); Jorgensen et al. (2019: 72).
24 X755:45.159c18-21.
25 It is also called *xinle wei* 信樂位 (the status of aspiration from confidence).
26 That is: the understanding arising from hearing (*śrutamayī-prajñā*), the understanding arising from pondering (*cintāmayī-prajñā*), the understanding arising from cultivating (*bhāvanāmayī-prajñā*). Note that *prajñā* here should be understood as a mental concomitant (*caitta*), and hence is to be distinguished from the sense of "transcendental wisdom" as in *prajñāpāramitā*.
27 For a more detailed explanation of this "transformative stage of advancing the force and harming the power," see 6.1.
28 X755:45.161b15-19.
29 For the life and works of Huiyuan, see the works by YOSHIZU Yoshihide 吉津宜英.
30 See Chapter 2 (2.3.2).
31 Huiyuan is aware of the ambiguity of the term *xing* 性 in *foxing* 佛性. He explains *xing* in four different senses: (1) seed, cause, and basis (*zhongzi yin ben* 種子因本); (2) substance (*ti* 體); (3) unchanging (*bugai* 不改); (4) having a distinct nature (*xingbie* 性別). See T1851:44.472a8-b16. In view of this ambiguity, I translate *foxing* here as "Buddha nature" to keep it vague enough to accommodate all the above senses.
32 T1851:44.535a2-8.
33 A problem here is that, in Huiyuan's *Dasheng yizhang*, the chapter entitled "*Bashi yi* 八識義" ("On the Meaning of Eight Consciousnesses"), in which this passage is found, appears to have undergone later revision either by Huiyuan himself or by his disciples. Hence the exact date of the composition of this chapter is unknown. See Okamoto (2010: 176ff.) for more details.
34 See T32:1666.578b6-9.
35 For example, after assessing a few Japanese attributions of the *Dasheng zhiguan famen* to Tanqian, Paul Magnin (1979: 103–4) still is unconvinced and remains uncommitted to any definite conclusion regarding the authorship of *Dasheng zhiguan famen*. Thanks to Professor Robert Gimello, who drew my attention to Magnin's work.
36 Kashiwagi (1981: 235–7).
37 *Dasheng zhiguan famen* discusses *jiexing* in three other passages: T1924:46. 646b1-13, T1924:46.653b26-c11, T1924:46.661a15-27. For my discussion, see Keng (2009: 68–72).
38 T1924:46.653c25-654a3.
39 See Oda (1990).
40 Also see T2806:85.1000b10-20, T2806:85.1010a23-b11.
41 T2806:85.1003c28-1004a7. The topic of this passage is the storehouse consciousness (*ālayavijñāna*).
42 T1824:42.104c7-11.
43 In addition to the passages quoted here, there are several other passages by Fazang, as well as by later Huayan masters such as Chengguan, Li Tongxuan 李通玄 (635–730 or 646–740), and the Korean monk Taehyeon 太賢 (d.u.), in which *jiexing* was understood in the same manner. I do not include them here. For some more relevant passages from Fazang, see T1790:39.431c4-16; T1733:35.185a24-b6; T1733:35.456a20-b11; T1733:35.456c12-18.
44 Also see T1866.485c14-2.
45 T1866:45.487b29-c5.

46 In Chapter 2, I review the many convincing reasons advanced by other scholars to doubt the traditional attribution of the *Awakening of Faith* to Paramārtha.
47 The *Awakening of Faith* adopts the simile of waves from the *Laṅkāvatāra-sūtra* to highlight this point: the Mind is originally calm just like the water of the ocean. But when it is agitated by wind (ignorance), then waves (delusive representations) arise (T1666:32.576c9-16).
48 T1666:32.579a12-20. See also Hakeda (1967: 64–5); Girard (2004: 81–3); Jorgensen et al. (2019: 102–3).
49 The Taishō text reads *zhiyi* 之義. After consulting the scanned image of the original scroll of T2805, I believe that the character *zhi* 之 is a mistaken transcription of *liu* 六. Vasubandhu's MSgBh mentions that there are six contexts of the notion of "seeds" (T1595:31.165c15-166a5; the same point is made by the CWSL: T1585:31.9b7-28).
50 It seems that the idea of a "body of liberation" (*jietuo shen* 解脫身) is implied because this notion is often contrasted with the notion of dharma-body. See, for instance, Paramārtha's *Shelun* (T1595.174c10-21). See also passages from Paramārtha's works, including *Foshuo wushangyi jing* 佛說無上依經 (*The Scripture on the Supreme Basis Taught by the Buddha*, T669: 16.472c8-10) and *Zhuanshi lun* (T1587:31.63c4-10).
51 After examining the scanned image of the original scroll of T2805, I believe that the character *ye* 耶 in the Taishō canon should be emended to *na* 那.
52 T2805:85.982b22-c7.
53 T2805:31.999b12-17.
54 The major problem with Kimura's study is that he begins from a false assumption, namely that, according to Paramārtha, *jiexing* is close in meaning to *tathāgatagarbha*. As I point out in Chapters 6 and 7, *jiexing* and *tathāgatagarbha* are very different according to Paramārtha.
55 I think the best explanation of the term "agree with" (*he* 合) is: after one attains buddhahood, the enjoyment-body, which is associated with undiscriminating *jñāna*, takes the dharma-body, which is identified with Thusness, as its cognitive object. Thus, "agree with" in this context refers to the agreement or non-duality between the cognitive aspect (the enjoyment-body) and the cognized aspect (the dharma-body). See the following note.
56 T1824:42.54a18-26. A complication here, however, is Jizang's conclusion that both the enjoyment-body and the dharma-body are permanent. My interpretation is that, since the enjoyment-body is different from the dharma-body, both cannot be permanent in the same sense. Otherwise, the dharma-body and the enjoyment-body would both be primary at the same level, which, however, is impossible because the enjoyment-body should somehow be derived from the dharma-body. As said in the previous note, I think the best way to make sense of Jizang's remark is to understand the two Buddha-bodies in terms of the relation between "what cognizes" and "what is cognized." It's not so clear whether Jizang understands the enjoyment-body as unconditioned undiscriminating *jñāna* or conditioned undiscriminating *jñāna*. Based on his emphasis that the enjoyment-body is permanent, he seems to understand it as unconditioned undiscriminating *jñāna* that is permanent. But my discussion later suggests that the enjoyment-body is conditioned according to Paramārtha (4.5). Either way, here Jizang understands *jiexing* to be something different from the dharma-body. This suggests at least a distance from the Permanence Reading where *jiexing* is identified with the dharma-body and the original awakening.

57 The association between *jiexing* and the enjoyment-body can also be found in a fragmentary text entitled *Zhaolun shu* 肇論疏 (*A Commentary on the Zhaolun*): X866:54.49c19-50a8.

58 T1716:33.744b27-c2.

59 For example, a few lines before the passage quoted here, Zhiyi mentions the disputes between the Dilun and Shelun masters. See T1716:33.744b18-22. Also see my discussion in 5.5.

Chapter 2

1 Kashiwagi (1981: 184–97).

2 First, this commentary cites the opinion of "Yuan fashi 遠法師" (T1843:44.192b28-c2), presumably Huiyuan. Second, it is characteristic of Huiyuan's extant works that they are composed in four-character phrases. The *Dasheng qixin lun yishu* attributed to Huiyuan, however, deviates from this pattern. For more details, see Yoshizu (1972).

3 See the following section for more details.

4 T1846:44.246a15-b8.

5 For a detailed investigation of the classification of the *Awakening of Faith* in various Chinese Buddhist catalogs, see Kashiwagi (1981: 63–84) and Yoshizu (2003: 242 and 282ff).

6 T2146:55.142a16.

7 HAYASHIYA Tomojirō 林屋友次郎 was the first to voice skepticism regarding the reliability of the *Lidai sanbaoji* in his *Kyōroku kenkyū* 經錄研究 (1941). For a brief review of modern evaluations of the *Lidai sanbaoji*, see Nattier (2008: 14, note 25), and Radich (2019c).

8 Hirakawa (1990: 10). In other words, Hirakawa argues that the mistake made in the catalog edited in 594 was later corrected in 602.

9 Hirakawa (1990: 11).

10 Hirakawa (1990: 14–15).

11 For more details about the distinction between the terminology popular in the north and the terminology popular in the south, see my discussions of Mochizuki and Takemura, and also 3.6.

12 Hirakawa (1990: 22).

13 For example, see the entry on the *Awakening of Faith* in the *Encyclopedia of Buddhism* by Ding-Hwa Hsieh in Buswell (2004: 38).

14 Kashiwagi (1981: 152–3).

15 Radich (2014, 2015c) suggests that those chapters included in the *Hebu jinguangming jing* 合部金光明經 (T664) that are traditionally attributed to Paramārtha are not entirely straight translations but are texts between translation and composition. Even if this is true, as indicated later, I still think those chapters agree with Paramārtha's other works in terms of their terminology and doctrines.

16 This means to break the true body (*zhenshen* 真身) into two (i.e., the dharma-body and the enjoyment-body), and to keep the response-body (*yingshen* 應身) as one (i.e., the transformation-body). For Jizang's explanation, see, e.g., his *Commentary on the Lotus Sūtra* (T1721:34.603b19-22).

17 T1666:32.576b8-9.

18 See Kashiwagi (1981: 90–1).

19 For more details, see Kashiwagi (1981: 90–1). For Hirakawa's reservations about Chinkai, see Hirakawa: (1990: 15–16). Hirakawa distrusts what Chinkai says about Huijun because Huijun's statement cannot be found in the extant edition of the *Silun xuanyi*. A potential response to Hirakawa is that the extant edition is incomplete. Among the ten fascicles, the first, third, and fourth are missing. See Kashiwagi (1981: 91).

20 See Kashiwagi (1981: 135ff).

21 For example, see T1522:26.138b12-13. Bodhiruci also uses the terms *fafo* 法佛 *fashen fo* 法身佛, *baofo* 報佛 and *yinghua fo* 應化佛 in his translation of the *Laṅkāvatāra-sūtra* (T671:16.525b12-14).

22 In fact, the phrase *xiuduoluo (zhong) shuo* 修多羅(中)說 ("The Scripture says") was used a few times by authors in the south, such as Guṇabhadra. Nevertheless, Mochizuki's point is still valid, as this phrase never appears in any of Paramārtha's works.

23 See Takemura (1990: 337–41).

24 T1666:32.577b3-4. See also Hakeda (1967: 47), Girard (2004: 47), Jorgensen et al. (2019: 83).

25 In the AKBh, this compound occurs once, in verse II. 34; see Pradhan (1975: 61), Pruden (1988-1990, Vol. I: 205), and T1559:29.180c2-7. For the MSg, see Nagao (1994, Vol. II: 51–2).

26 T1666:32.582a12-15. Also cf. Hakeda (1967: 95); Girard (2004: 141); Jorgensen et al. (2019: 127).

27 The second character in Bodhiruci's rendering is *po* 婆 instead of *bo* 鉢.

28 For the corresponding Sanskrit, see Suzuki (1934: 270).

29 Takemura (1990: 338, note 28).

30 Kashiwagi (1981: 179).

31 Kashiwagi (1981: 182).

32 Kashiwagi (1981: 183ff.).

33 Kashiwagi (1981: 190ff.).

34 Kashiwagi (1981: 237).

35 Kashiwagi (1981: 197ff).

36 Kashiwagi (1981: 203–4).

37 Kashiwagi (1981: 236).

38 For example, the *Viniścayasaṃgrahaṇī* portion of the *Yogācārabhūmi* clearly says that Thusness is exclusively unconditioned. See T1579:30.697c5-7, 698a6-7.

39 Most prominently, it is sometimes said that an unconditioned dharma has itself as its own cause proper (*zhengyin* 正因). See Chapters 5 and 6 for details.

40 T1666:32.578a21-25. See also Hakeda (1967: 56–7); Girard (2004: 65); Jorgensen et al. (2019: 92).

41 T1666:32.578b6-10. See also Hakeda (1967: 58); Girard (2004: 67–9); Jorgensen et al. (2019: 95).

42 Lamotte (1973, Tome II: 41); Nagao (1982–1987, Vol. I: 162).

43 T1595:31.166a14-17.

44 Both Lamotte (1973, Tome II: 41) and Nagao (1982–1987, Vol. I: 162) reconstruct the Chinese term *jian* 堅 (Tib. *brtan*) in Asaṅga's MSg I.23 as *dhruva* in Sanskrit. But in the CWSL, Xuanzang uses the term *jianmi* 堅密, which in his translation of the AKBh renders *dṛḍha*. See Hirakawa (1973, Vol. II: 118). Therefore, it is possible that the original Sanskrit term was *dṛḍha*.

45 T1585:31.9c13-15. See de La Vallée Poussin (1928–29: 120).
46 T1585:31.9c19-21. See de La Vallée Poussin (1928–29: 121).
47 An example can be found in his *Zhuanshi lun* 轉識論 (T1587:31.63c3-6).
48 More examples can be found in: *Juedingzang lun* 決定藏論 (T1584:30.1020b8-19); FXL (T1610:31.795c23-28); *San wuxing lun* 三無性論 (T1617:31.873a23-24 & T1617:31.878a13-15); Paramārtha's AKBh (T1559:29.282b24-26); Paramārtha's MSg (T1593:31.128a23-24); *Shelun* (T1595:31.235b3-5, T1595:31.240a29-b2, and T1595:31.252c3-5).
49 T664:16.363c13-16.
50 T1599:31.456a26-29. Note that Paramārtha in his translation reversed the order between the second and the third, if we compare this to the Sanskrit text given in Nagao (1964: 41).
51 T1610:31.794b12-13.
52 I give a detailed explanation of this notion "*suoxian* 所顯" in Chapter 7.
53 T1617:31. 868a5-6.
54 For the Sanskrit terms for *nengyuan* and *suoyuan*, see Nagao (1982–1987, Vol. II: 48).
55 T1595:31.205b15-19.
56 T1584:30.1025c12-16. For the corresponding passage in Xuanzang's Chinese translation, see T1579:30.589a13-17. Xuanzang's translation has "遍行麁重" for Paramārtha's "遍一切處諸惡罪法." Schmithausen (1987, Vol. 1: 78) suggests "*sarvatragaṃ dauṣṭhulyam*" as the underlying Sanskrit.
57 See quotation 2.6. This constitutes another difference between the *Awakening of Faith* and Paramārtha's Chinese works in particular and the Indian Yogācāra texts in general. Namely, the *Awakening of Faith* mentions the notion of "inner permeation" by Thusness, whereas Paramārtha and Indian Yogācāra never make this claim. For Asaṅga, permeation is exclusively external due to the negativity of the storehouse consciousness. But it is both internal and external according to the *Awakening of Faith*.
58 For the example from Paramārtha's *Shelun*, see T1595:31.191c20-24. For the example from the FXL, see T1610:31.795c24-25.
59 For Thusness as a cognitive object in the *Yogācārabhūmi* and the intriguing notion of *zhenru suoyuanyuan zhongzi* 真如所緣緣種子(Tib. *de bzhin nyid la dmigs pa'i rkyen gyi sa bon*; Skt. **tathatālambanapratyaya-bīja*) discussed by Schmithausen (1987) and Yamabe (1990), see Keng (2009: 136–40).

Chapter 3

1 See Giles (1957: 178).
2 See Huang (1981, Vol. 23: 86–109).
3 Thanks to Dr. Susan Whitfield, Director of the International Dunhuang Project at the British Library during 1993–2017, who, upon my request, made the scanned image of T2805 available at the website of the International Dunhuang Project (IDP). To access this image, go to the IDP website (http://idp.bl.uk/) and type "S.2747" under "Search the IDP Database" at the left of the page (accessed April 23, 2021).
4 See note 1.
5 See Shengkai (2006: 55). Note that the quotations from the Chinese translation of Paramārtha's MSg and MSgBh in these two fragments do not always agree exactly

with the extant edition of Paramārtha's *Shelun*. The major reason behind the differences are the missing characters.

6 Shengkai (2006: 57–8).

7 T2808:85.1036a21-23.

8 Katsumata (1961: 789ff., esp. 796).

9 It should be noted here that T2805 is quoted word for word by in Wŏnch'ŭk's commentary on the *Saṃdhinirmocana-sūtra*. I was made aware of this by Dr. Ōtake Susumu at the Paramārtha Study Group led by Professor Funayama Tōru.

T2805:「相結即是分別執相，謂一切六識心所緣外境是有，未達此並是自心分別所作故。若見相並是識分別所作，欲瞋等則無從而生。」(T2805:85.988 b22-25);

Wŏnch'ŭk:「真諦解云：相結即是分別執相，謂一切六識心識[redundant word?]所緣外境是有，未達此並是自心分別所作故。若見相並是分別所作，欲瞋等則無從即生。」(X369:21.225a17-19).

However, Wŏnch'ŭk also attributes to Paramārtha certain works that are not authentic. For instance, Wŏnch'ŭk attributes Tanqian's *Jiushi zhang* 九識章 (*A Chapter on the Nine Consciousnesses*) to Paramārtha. See quotation 5.9 and Chapter 5 (5.3.4) for more details. For this reason, Wŏnch'ŭk's attribution of T2805 to Paramārtha is not reliable.

10 T1763:37.377b5-6.

11 In contrast, I am less certain about the origin of the division of the first chapter of the *Shelun* into five *pin*, since the portion of T2805 that comments on the first chapter is lost.

12 See the description in the XGSZ: T2060:50.430b11-16.

13 See Chapter 2 (2.3.3).

14 A note attached to the end of T2808 states that it was copied in the capital (Chang'an) in 601; thus, it must have been composed by that date. See T2808:85.1036a21-23.

15 T2806 refers to the title of **Tattvasiddhi* only once, with no reference to the **Saṃyuktābhidharma-hṛdaya-śāstra*. For more about the **Tattvasiddhi*, see Katsura (1974); about the **Saṃyuktābhidharma-hṛdaya-śāstra*, see Dessein (1999).

16 T2805:85.992b5-6. This does not seem to refer to Huiyuan's *Dasheng yizhang* 大乘義章. Only T2805 and the FXL equate the idea of *buddha-gotra* with the idea of aspiration from confidence (*xinle* 信樂).

17 T2805:85.995a18. According to the earliest catalog edited by Fajing, Paramārtha translated a certain *Da niepan jing lun* 大涅槃經論. See T2146:55.141a14. This may be the *Niepan ji* mentioned in T2805.

18 T2805:85.995a1-8. For the ten kinds of equality, see the translation of *Chapter of the Ten Stages* in the *Buddhāvataṃsata-sūtra* by Buddhabhadra 佛陀跋陀羅 (358–429), for example, T278:9. 558b1-10.

19 Ibuki (1997) is mainly concerned with reconstructing the original edition of a text by examining how a particular term is adopted, reshaped, substituted for, or even omitted in different recensions. Ibuki's goal, however, is different from mine. In terms of computer-assisted analysis of Chinese Buddhist texts, Radich (2019a, 2019b) is methodologically most sophisticated and effective. I hope he will soon apply his tool to Paramārtha's corpus.

20 There seem to have been few new translations between the time of Bodhiruci and Ratnamati in the early sixth century and the time of Paramārtha's activity in China (546–569).

21 For example, the XGSZ describes how, after studying Paramārtha's AKBh for five years, Daoyue 道岳 (568–636) could only understand the general gist but still not its obscure meaning, and hence he needed to consult Paramārtha's original commentary from the south. See the "Biography of Daoyue" in the XGSZ, especially T2060:50.527b12-c2.

22 A notorious example of this is the later replacement of the term *xing* 姓 with *xing* 性 in the term "*buddha-gotra*" (*foxing* 佛姓). See Lusthaus (2002: 370) and Keng (2011b).

23 See the "Biography of Shanzhou" in the XGSZ, esp. T2060:50.519b13-19. See also Feng (2006: 90).

24 Okamoto (2010) tries to build a chronology of Jingying Huiyuan's works.

25 Shengkai (2006: 57–8) thinks that T2807 and S.6715 are different parts of the same text. If so, since S.6715 mentions Xuanzang (see Huang (1981, Vol. 50: 632)), T2807 may be the only one of these fragments that was composed later than 645.

26 See Ono (1974–88, Vol. 7: 255–6).

27 Namely, (1) *kalala*, (2) *arbuda*, (3) *peśī*, (4) *ghana*, (5) *praśākhā*.

28 Paramārtha's *Shelun* distinguishes three kinds of undiscriminating *jñāna* and names the second one as "in its substance of the Path" (*dao zhengti* 道正體), see T1595:31.238c24-27.

29 Jizang reports that according to the Shelun masters, wisdom (*prajñā*) refers to the "[undiscriminating] *jñāna* in its substance," which is unconditioned. See T1824:42.115c1-3. Also compare Jizang's *Shengman baoku* 勝鬘寶窟 (*A Room of Treasures of the Śrīmālā-sūtra*): T1744:37.31b18-c7.

30 The four noble truths are called the primary marks, and the sixteen aspects (*ākāra*) of the four noble truths are called the secondary marks. See also Michael Radich, "*Suixiang lun* 隨相論" on *Digital Dictionary of Buddhism* (http://www.buddhism-dict.net).

31 The *Lishi apitan lun* 立世阿毘曇論 (*An Abhidharma Treatise on the Constitution of the World*), another translation by Paramārtha, also seems to share some phrases with T2805 and the *Suixiang lun*. But more study is required in this respect.

32 See *Siku Quanshu* (*Wenyuange* Edition) 文淵閣四庫全書 [Intranet Version]. Hong Kong: Digital Heritage Publishing.
http://www.sikuquanshu.com/product/main.aspx. (Accessed through the National Taiwan University Library on January 24, 2022)

33 A detailed investigation of the spread of the study of the **Tattvasiddhi* and the *Mahāparinirvāṇa-mahāsūtra* from the north to the south and their prevalence in the south is beyond the scope of this book. The most authoritative source is Tang (1938), especially Chapters 16–18. An excellent collection of recent studies in the southern Buddhist tradition is Aramaki (2000), especially the article by Funayama (123–78).

34 Chen (1987: 333). For the report in the XGSZ that, in the time of Yuwen Tai 宇文泰, more than fifty monks from Yizhou 益州 (modern Sichuan province) brought Buddhist texts as well as Buddhist statues to the capital; see T2060:50.558a9-13. According to the *Zizhi tongjian* 資治通鑒, Yuwen Tai conquered the provinces of Liang 梁 and Jing 荊 in 553–554 (see *Zizhi tongjian*, Fascicle 156, "Liang ji" 梁紀 21). Thus, the transmission of Buddhist texts and statues mentioned earlier took place around 555.

35 Ōtake (2001) has argued that the *Jin'gangxian* is one of Bodhiruci's lost works. But, as is shown in the following table, the *Jin'gangxian* uses several terms that never appear in Bodhiruci's works. Based on this, I think it is quite difficult to establish a historical relationship between the *Jin'gangxian lun* and Bodhiruci.

36 Yoshizu (2000) argues that *Dasheng zhiguan famen* might have been composed by Tanqian. See Chapter 1.
37 Katsura (1974: 90–1). For the original Chinese translation by Kumārajīva, see T1646:32.252c28-253a2.
38 Cox (1995: 86). Also see p. 102, note 21. For the Chinese translation in the **Saṃyuktābhidharma-hṛdaya-śāstra*, see T1552:28.883a3-5.
39 T1552:28.884c3-8.
40 T1552:28.897b3-8.
41 Cox translates this as the "homogeneous cause"; see Cox (1995: 92).
42 Zhiyi identifies the "cause in terms of habituation" in the **Tattvasiddhi* with the "cause of the same kind" in the **Saṃyuktābhidharma-hṛdaya-śāstra*. He also identifies the "effect in terms of habituation" with the "effect of dependence" in the **Saṃyuktābhidharma-hṛdaya-śāstra*. See T1911:46.112a18-21.
43 This identification between *xiyin* in the **Tattvasiddhi* and *zifenyin* in the **Saṃyuktābhidharma-hṛdaya-śāstra* is not undisputed. For example, Huiying points out that the scope of *zifenyin* is not the same as that of *xiyin*: sometimes one is broader; at other times, the other is broader. See X791:46.822b2-17. Other authors, such as Zhanran 湛然 (711–782), follow Zhiyi and suggest that the "cause in terms of habituation" can be identified with *zhifen yin* 自分因 and hence with *tonglei yin* 同類因 in Xuanzang's translation. See T1912:46.403b15-17.
44 For the single case in Huida's *Zhaolun shu*, see X866:54.50b21-c1.
45 T1851:44.516c7-13.
46 The *Renwang bore jing* mentions only the names of the first three *gotra*s, namely, the *xi zhongxing* 習種性, *xing zhongxing*,性種性, and *dao zhongxing*. 道種性. See T245:8.826b25-c11 and T245:8.831a29-b26.
47 For these six kinds of *gotra*, see Chapter 3 of the *Pusa yingluo benye jing*, esp. T1485:24.1012b25-1015c16. The issue becomes much more complicated and goes beyond the scope of this book if we take into consideration the possibility that the *Pusa yingluo benye jing* was a Chinese apocryphon (see Funayama [2000]). Nobody earlier than Zhiyi, Jizang, and Huijun (all from the south) quotes or refers to this text.
48 The *Pusa dichi jing* divides the path into seven stages: (1) *zhongxing di* 種性地: the stage of *gotra*; (2) *jiexing di* 解行地: the stage of resolute practice; (3) *jingxin di* 淨心地: the stage of purified mind; (4) *xingji di* 行迹地: the stage of the traces of practice; (5) *jueding di* 決定地: the stage of certitude; (6) *jueding xing di* 決定行地: the stage of the certitude of practice; (7) *bijing di* 畢竟地: the stage of the ultimate goal (T1581:30.954a8-11). According to Huiyuan's explanation (see the following note), the third stage corresponds to the first bodhisattva stage.
49 According to Huiyuan, the third stage (*jingxin di* 淨心地) of the seven stages mentioned in the *Pusa dichi jing* corresponds to the first bodhisattva stage according to the traditional theory of the ten bodhisattva stages. For this reason, Huiyuan also explains that the first stage (*zhongxing di* 種性地) and the second stage (*jiexing di* 解行地) precede the first bodhisattva stage. See T1851:44.716a24-b13.
50 The *Pusa yingluo benye jing* does not directly identify, for example, the *gotra* of habituation with the ten abidings. Instead, it states that the *gotra* of habituation includes ten kinds of people (T1485:24.1012c6-10). Later in the text, it explains that these ten kinds of people are included in the category of ten minds (i.e., ten abidings) (T1485:24.1013a15-18). The same situation applies to the identification, in the *Pusa yingluo benye jing*, between the *gotra* of nature and the ten practices and the

identification between the *gotra* of the Path and the ten merit-transfers. For a brief introduction about the forty mental stages, see Introduction, note 31.

51 See Zhiyi's explanation: X338:18.480b13-16.

52 For Huiyuan's interpretation of *jiexing di* 解行地, see T1851:44.716a24-b13 and above note 49 in this chapter.

53 Huiyuan never gives a list of six *gotra*s like the one in the *Pusa yingluo benye jing*. However, he does use the terms for the first four lineages, namely, *xing zhong* 性種, *xi zhong* 習種, *dao zhong* 道種, and *shengzhong* 聖種. See, e.g., T1851:44.651a7-b6.

54 T has 幻免, which is obviously a typo for 幻兔.

55 T2805:85.991c16-22.

56 This typical usage of "*ruozuo* 若作 NEAR (within the range of 5 Chinese characters) *yi* 義" can be found in Zhiyi's work several times. For two examples, see: T1716:33.694a15-17; T1716:33.737c9-14.

57 See Chapter 2, note 2.

58 A few examples of Huiyuan's use of the phrase "arising by adjusting to falsity" can be found in various texts: T1776:38.462a1-3; T1851:44.536c8-11; T1851:44.652b12-16. Comparing Huiyuan to T2805, I find that they do not understand the meaning of "arising by adjusting to falsity" in exactly the same way. According to Huiyuan, the characteristics of dharma (*faxiang* 法相), such as arising-and-ceasing and nirvana, come into being because the true consciousness, namely, Thusness, arises by adjusting to falsity. But T2805 does not explicitly stipulate what Huiyuan calls "true consciousness," nor does it identify Thusness with true consciousness. It only says that once consciousness recedes, what remains is Thusness. But if we consider Paramārtha's notion that the dharma-body is defined both in terms of Thusness and the *jñāna* about Thusness (see 4.3.1 and 7.6), then Paramārtha and T2805 may well accept the notion of "true consciousness" discussed by Huiyuan.

59 T2805:85.988a28-b3.

60 See T1851:44.834a25-835a13.

61 Zhiyan's four pure lands include the pure land of transformation (*hua jingtu* 化淨土), the pure land of matters (*shi jingtu* 事淨土), the pure land of real retribution (*shibao jingtu* 實報淨土), and the pure land of the nature of *dharmas* (*faxing jingtu* 法性淨土). See, for example, T1870:45.541a6-b7.

62 Zhiyan mentions the MSgBh when he discusses the pure land of transformation (T1870:45.576c21-25). In contrast, Daoshi specifically mentions Paramārtha's *Shelun* when he discusses three of the four kinds of pure lands (T2122:53.397b26-c21). He does not mention the pure land of transformation.

63 T2805:85.987a28-b5.

64 For two examples in the *Shelun*, see T1595:31.186c26-187a13; T1595:31.188b3-5. For an example in Paramārtha's *Xianshi lun* (*A Treatise on the Manifestation of the Consciousness*), see T1618:31.878c11-18.

65 For T2805, see T2805:85.987b6-9; for the *Dasheng zhiguan famen*, see T1924:46.643b10-13.

66 T2805 puts this idea differently: (1) the portion of air (*qifen* 氣分) of conceptual elaboration (Ch. *xilun* 戲論; Skt. *prapañca*) permeates the base consciousness (T2805:85.987a13-18); (2) what is desired (*suo'ai* 所愛) permeates the base consciousness (T2805:85.987a22-27); (3) the two kinds of karma (positive and negative) (*shan'e er ye* 善惡二業) permeate the base consciousness

(T2805:85.989a11-14); (4) action due to ignorance (*wuming xing* 無明行) permeates the base consciousness (T2805:85.987b26-28).

67 This date is given in Fajing's *Zhongjing mulu* (T2146:55.115b25) as well as in Yancong's *Zhongjing mulu* (T2147:55.151b22-23). *Lidai sanbao ji* gives further information, specifically that the *Dasheng tongxing jing* was translated in the fifth year of Tianhe, that is, 570 (T2034:49.100b13-14).

68 For T2805, see T2805:85.997c22-998a2; for the original passage in the *Dasheng tongxing jing*, see T673:16.650a6-13.

69 For examples in the Chinese translation of the *Yogācārabhūmi*, see T1579:30.280b6-9; T1579:30.651b19-24. For an example in the MSA, see Lévi (1907), Tome I: 174 (lines 16–17), Bagchi (1970: 167) (lines 3–4); for the Chinese translation, see T1604:31.656b5-13.

70 That is, the explanation later interpolated into the original text of the FXL. It usually begins with the phrase *shiyue* 釋曰 (explanation), and there are sixteen interpolated passages of this sort in the FXL.

71 T1610:31.801c14-15.

72 T2805:85.988b23.

73 The term *liyong* 力用 appears 5 times in T2805, 8 times in Baoliang, 1 time in Fayun, and 6 times in Huiying. In addition, it also appears in Paramārtha's works such as the *Suixiang lun* (2 times), *Shelun* (1), and the *Xianshi lun* (1).

74 See T639:15.562c27-28; T639:15.576b27-28.

75 *Lidai sanbao ji* reports that it was translated in the eighth year of the Tianbao period 天保八年, that is, 557 (T2034:49.87b26).

Chapter 4

1 Quoted from Kashiwagi (1981: 41, note 33). See also Hakamaya's article entitled "*Mahāyānasaṃgraha ni okeru shin i shiki setsu* 摂大乗論に於ける心意識説" in Hakamaya (2001: esp. 614ff).

2 See Paramārtha's *Shelun*: T1595:31.157b4-158a17.

3 See Master Ji's critique of Paramārtha's mistaken understanding of the *atuona shi* as defiled mentation (T1829:43.169b8-12).

4 T1594:31.133b25-c1. Cf. Lamotte (1973, Tome II: 14); Nagao (1982–7, Vol. I: 85).

5 T1597:31.325b3-4.

6 T1595:31.158a6-17.

7 See Xuanzang's translation, where Xuanzang makes it clear that here the MSg takes "mentation" (*manas*) in the compound "mind-mentation-consciousness" (*citta-mano-vijñāna*) as defiled mentation, not the storehouse consciousness (T1597:31.325b5-16).

8 T1595:31.158a27-28. In MSgBh, Vasubandhu discusses defiled mentation in his comment on this passage, but he does not call it *ādāna-vijñāna*.

9 See, for example, verses 5-6 of Vasubandhu's *Triṃśikā*.

10 For example, Paramārtha's *Shelun* (T1595:31.180c3-10); *Xianshi lun*: (T1618:31.879b3-11; T1618:31.880a2-7); *Zhuanshi lun*: (T1587:31.61c6-9). See also Jizang's identification of the seventh consciousness as the *tuona* 陁那 (X582:27.518c14-19).

11 See above quotation 4.1.

12 See Nagao (1982–7, Vol. I: 86–8).

13 T1585:31.21c17-18.
14 T2805:85.987b1-3.
15 T2805:85.990a15-17.
16 T1851:44.534c19-23.
17 X755:45.169b16-c1.
18 See T2807:85.1015b27-1016a14; 1017c22-29; 1020b16-20.
19 The *Digital Dictionary of Buddhism* gives the Sanskrit term as **jñāpaka-hetu* (*Digital Dictionary of Buddhism*, "*liaoyin* 了因" [article by C. Muller]). Radich (2008: 125, note 345) agrees with this reconstruction. Takasaki (2005: 157), however, gives the Sanskrit term as **vyañjana-hetu*. See also note 25 below.
20 This term appears in the *Madhyāntavibhāga* as the title of the fourth chapter: *prati pakṣa-bhāvanāvasthā-phala-pariccheda*. See Nagao (1964: 50).
21 T1595:31.178a8-10.
22 Also compare the following passage from T2805, where it is said that the path is the disclosing cause: T2805:85.986b27-c3.
23 The term *liushi* 六識 in this passage is ambiguous. It is not clear whether it refers to all six consciousnesses, or to the sixth consciousness, that is, the mental consciousness, alone. From another passage in T2805, however, it seems clear that what is referred to here as *liushi* is the sixth consciousness alone (T2805:85.986a5-9). Why the sixth consciousness is singled out here is still unclear.
24 T2805:986b8-14.
25 Takasaki (2005: 157) reconstructs the Sanskrit term for "generative cause" as **utpatti-hetu*. The *Digital Dictionary of Buddhism* agrees with this reconstruction. See *Digital Dictionary of Buddhism*, "*shengyin* 生因" (article by C. Muller). Radich (2008: 125, note 345), however, reconstructs it as *kāraṇa-hetu* and identifies it with the cause proper (Ch. *zhengyin* 正因; Skt. *kāraṇa-hetu*). I am not sure if the generative cause should be identified with the cause proper, although I agree with Radich that there is considerable overlap in meaning between these two terms. Radich also makes a very helpful observation that the generative cause refers to the ontological cause whereas the disclosing cause refers to the epistemological cause. See also above note 19.
26 The term *xinle* 信樂 is Paramārtha's translation of the Sanskrit *adhimukti*, "aspiration from confidence," that is, the aspiration to become a Buddha that is generated from the confidence that one has *buddha-gotra*.
27 T1610:31.798a5-10.
28 T1610:31.801b23-28.
29 Two other passages that discuss this idea can be found in Doryun's *Yuqie lun ji*.瑜伽論記 (*A Record [of the Doctrines of the] Yogācārabhūmi*). See T1828:42.604b1-6 and T1828:42.787b6-12.
30 The idea that Thusness as an unconditioned dharma cannot be produced but can only be disclosed is also clearly spelled out in T2809, although the context, namely the contrast between the noble truths of cessation and the path, is not the same as in the *Shelun* and T2805. If we accept that T2809 was composed by Daoji (see Chapter 3, note 8), then T2809 may have been inspired by Paramārtha's *Shelun* and T2805 because T2809 must date to a few decades after T2805. T2809 clearly claims that Thusness is unconditioned and therefore cannot be produced by a generative cause, but can only be disclosed by a disclosing cause (T2809:85.1045b14-19). Note that this passage from T2809 quotes from the *Bore lun* 般若論 (short for *Jin'gang bore boluomi jing lun* 金剛般若波羅蜜經論 [*Vajracchedikā-prajñāpāramitā-sūtropadeśa*] translated

by Bodhiruci, T1511), which also insists that Thusness does not have a generative cause (T1511:25.785a14-22).

31 Here I omit Vasubandhu's view on dharma-body because he does not completely agree with Asaṅga. See Chapter 7 for more details.

32 Paramārtha in the *Shelun* occasionally also appears to concur with Asaṅga's idea that the dharma-body is not attained until the transformation of the basis occurs, for example: "A bodhisattva still does not have the superior capability at the tenth bodhisattva stage and has not yet attained the pure and perfect dharma-body" (T1595:31.226c25-26). Two interpolated passages by Paramārtha also identify the dharma-body with the transformation of the basis (T1595:31.173c24-25; T1595:31.254c19-21), which does not occur until the end of the tenth bodhisattva stage.

33 See also Paramārtha's translation of this passage (T1595:31.252b11-253a4).

34 For the reconstruct Sanskrit as: *sparśena prathamam eva prāptiḥ*, see Griffiths et al. (1989: 289, note 128).

35 For the Tibetan text and Sanskrit reconstruction, see Griffiths et al. 1989: 289; § C; for Xuanzang's Chinese translation, see T1594:31.149b25-28.

36 T1595:31.206c5-6.

37 T1595:31.179b27-29. Huida's *Zhaolun shu* also confirms that Paramārtha held the view that the dharma-body is attained gradually (*fenzheng* 分證) beginning with the first bodhisattva stage (X866:54.56a4-8).

38 It should be noted that, according to Paramārtha, there is a sense in which every sentient being is endowed with the dharma-body; hence, the dharma-body is attained even before one enters into the first bodhisattva stage. Or better, one is originally endowed with the dharma-body, even before starting on the Buddhist path. Hence, what is meant here by the attainment of the dharma-body is actually the disclosure of the dharma-body, not its new creation. In Chapter 7, I go one step further to argue that even Vasubandhu already had the idea of the identification between Thusness and the dharma-body.

39 Here I read *zhenzhi* 真智 as *zhenru zhi* 真如智.

40 T1595:31.249c21.

41 T1595:31.249c26-28.

42 T664:16.363a4-6.

43 All mental activities cease in the dharma-body because there is no difference between object and *jñāna* (T1595:31.252b8-9). Interestingly, the CWSL also cites a position that includes undiscriminating *jñāna* in the definition of essence-body (Ch. *zixing shen* 自性身; Skt. *svābhāvika-kāya*; i.e., the dharma-body). The reason provided there is: given that (1) the self-natured body is attained by transforming (i.e., through the transformation of the basis of) the storehouse consciousness and that (2) the mirror *jñāna* is attained by transforming the storehouse consciousness, the mirror *jñāna* must be included in the self-natured body. See T1585:31.58a7-9.

44 See Paramārtha's *Shelun*: T1595:31.202b22-24, T1595:31.208c6-8.

45 See Paramārtha's *Shelun*: T1595:31.221a22-23, T1595:31.225c19, T1595:31.222a24-29, T1595:31.224b28-c1.

46 Asaṅga says instead that one penetrates into the Dharma-element (MSg V.3). For the Tibetan translation, see Lamotte (1973, Tome I: 66). For Xuanzang's Chinese translation, see T1594:31.146a2-3.

47 T2805:85.995b14-15.

48 See Introduction, note 31.

49 T2805:85.998a22-28.

50 Asvabhāva in his *Mahāyānasaṃgrahopanibandhana* provides yet another view concerning the attainment of the dharma-body by means of the commitment to and the practice of teaching. For the English translation, see Griffiths et al. (1989: 95–6).

51 T1851:44.825a21-23.

52 X755:45.160b22-24.

53 T2807:85.1014b10-17.

54 T1780:38.891a15-29. In this text Jizang also uses the term "*Dilun shi* 地論師" but never "*nan Dilun shi* 南地論師" and hence I think "*beidi lunshi* 北地論師" here refers to "masters in the north" rather than "the Dilun masters in the northern region" (*beidao dilunshi* 北道地論師). In an almost identical passage in another work of Jizang, we find *beitu lunshi* 北土論師 instead of *beidi lunshi* 北地論師 (T1853:45.62c7-18).

55 MSg V.2. For the Tibetan translation, see Lamotte (1973: 65). For Xuanzang's Chinese translation, see T1594:31.145c14-15.

56 See Paramārtha's *Shelun*: T1595:31.209b29-c2; T1595:31.261b3-4; T1595:31.242b29-c3. All of these passages are missing in the other two Chinese translations.

Paramārtha's *Shelun* occasionally also states that the dharma-body includes benefits for both oneself and others. This does not necessarily contradict what he states elsewhere suggesting that dharma-body is limited to benefits for oneself. The difference is that, when Paramārtha states that the dharma-body includes both kinds of benefits, he is referring to the dharma-body in the broader sense, that is, the dharma-body that includes both the enjoyment-body and the transformation-body. For example, see: T1595:31.255b11-15; T1595:31.246a4-10. Both passages are missing in the other two Chinese translations.

57 Read *erzhong shi* 二種事 as *erzhong zhi* 二種智 here.

58 T669:16.472c5-14.

59 It is not clear how Paramārtha tries to reconcile these two different views in his *Shelun*. He seems to claim that purity (dharma-body, undiscriminating *jñāna*, etc.) is first attained at the first bodhisattva stage, but this purity is not completely perfected (*jiujing* 究竟) until the end of the tenth bodhisattva stage (T1595:31.241b8-11; T1595:31.241b15-18).

60 See T1598:31.448a10-12 and Griffiths et al. (1989: 250).

61 Nagao (1982–7, Vol. II: 441–2, note 1).

62 T2805:85.986a25-27.

63 The exact meaning of *rulaizang* (*tathāgatagarbha*) is not clear. Judging from the context, I tend to regard it as referring to the base consciousness before the transformation of the basis.

64 T2805:85.986b17-23.

65 T2805:85.990a29-b1.

66 T1595:31.267b27-c3.

67 The Sanskrit text reads: "*tasya vyāvṛttir arhattve.*" See Lévi (1925: 22); Buescher (2007: 12).

68 T1530:26.302c1-3 and T1530:26.309a24-27.

69 T1585:31.56b2-3.

70 See T31.1585.9c12; T31.1585.13c3-7; T31.1585.20c27-28; T1585:31.21b3-4; T31.1585.24b8-9.

71 T1595:31.249c6-17.

72 T2805:85.999a21-23.

Chapter 5

1 See Chapter 1, quotation 1.3.
2 See Chapter 1, note 22.
3 T1851;44.535a4-5. Cf. quotation 1.5.
4 T1851:44.839b2-11.
5 T1851:44.525c20-25.
6 See Chen (2002: 17).
7 See 3.9-3.10.
8 See 2.3.2.1.
9 T1824:42.133b4-11.
10 Jizang says: "There are two masters offering [different] explanations of the notion of 'conditioned wisdom' (*youwei boruo* 有為波若): Southern (*nanfang* 南方) [masters] say, 'All the cognitions [attained during] the ten bodhisattva-stages (*shidi jie* 十地解) are conditioned. This is why they are called 'conditioned wisdom.' The Shelun masters say, 'Wisdom is cognition in its proper substance (*zhengti zhi* 正體智). It is unconditioned'" (T1824:42.115c1-3).
11 The passage by Jizang reads: "There are two [groups of] Shelun masters (*er Shelun shi* 二攝論師) in Chang'an. One claims that permeation of hearing ceases; the other claims it does not (note: the original Chinese text has no negative here, but it should be implied from the logical progression of the passage) cease. Besides, there is the view held by southern [masters] that it both ceases and does not cease" (X582:27.505c13-14).
12 As the *Awakening of Faith* states, "Moreover, Permeation by defiled dharmas does not cease from beginningless time. It ceases only after one has become a Buddha. Permeation by pure dharmas, on the other hand, never ceases even in the future [after one becomes a Buddha]. What does this mean? Due to constant permeation by the dharma of Thusness, the defiled mind ceases, and the dharma-body is disclosed (*xianxian* 顯現). [After this], permeation by the function (*yong xunxi* 用熏習) [of Thusness] arises, and this is why permeation [of Thusness] never ceases" (T1666:32.579a8-11). Here, the *Awakening of Faith* claims that the permeation by Thusness (in the primary sense) never ceases because even after the dharma-body is disclosed (i.e., after one becomes a Buddha), this permeation serves as the basis from which permeation by the function of Thusness is derived. The implicit presumption here is that the dharma-body will issue forth the "permeation by the function of Thusness" incessantly. Although permeation by the function of Thusness is unnecessary for one who has already become a Buddha, the dharma-body must always issue forth this permeation because there are always other sentient beings to be liberated.
13 The *Awakening of Faith* states, "Although the nature of burning in a piece of wood is the cause proper (*zhengyin* 正因) of the fire [in that piece of wood], it is impossible, if no one attends to that wood or if one does so without any means [such as implements for lighting a fire], that [the nature of burning in that wood] can burn the wood by itself" (T1666:32.578c4-6).
14 See quotations 4.15-17 for more details.
15 For a more precise version of this theory, see Chapter 3 of Paramārtha's *Shelun*.
16 See Chapter 1, *Shelun Jiexing* Passage (2).
17 I shall discuss this notion in 5.3.2.

18 For the Sanskrit reconstruction, see Takasaki (2005: 121).

19 Here, based on a passage from the *Da boniepan jing jijie* edited by Baoliang (444–509) in the south (T1763:37.547c3-5), I understand the term "effect" to mean "enlightenment" (*bodhi*), while the term "the effect of effects" means nirvana. Because Huijun was from the south, there is good reason to believe that he was following the conventional usage of these two terms prevalent in southern China.

20 X784:46.601c23-602a9.

21 Cf. Ruegg (1976).

22 I agree with Michael Radich's suggestion that it is helpful to consider the "cause proper" as the "ontological cause" and the "disclosing cause" as the "epistemological cause" (Radich 2008: 125, note 345). See also Chapter 4, note 25.

23 See T374:12.530b26-29.

24 It should be noted that, in the *Mahāparinirvāṇa-mahāsūtra*, the cause proper is contrasted with the contributory cause, while the disclosing cause is contrasted with the generative cause (*shengyin* 生因).

25 For the identification of the bodies of all sentient beings with the bodies of all Buddhas according to the *Awakening of Faith*, see T1666:32.582b1-3 and T1666:32.579b9-14.

26 To put it briefly, buddhahood is unconditioned because the essence of buddhahood is the dharma-body of the Buddha, and the dharma-body is identified with Thusness according to Paramārtha. In Chapter 7, I assert that the identification between the dharma-body and Thusness had already been made by Vasubandhu before Paramārtha. In FXL, Paramārtha adds one more item that is identical with Thusness and the dharma-body, namely, the innate *buddha-gotra*.

27 T1610:31.798a7-10.

28 See quotation 6.11.

29 T1610:31.808b15-c25.

30 T2060:50.501c14-16.

31 T2060:50.431c13-14.

32 See the biography of Fatai in the XGSZ, esp. T2060:50.431a19-25.

33 See the description of the career of Cao Pi in the biography of Fatai: T2060:50.431b24-c2.

34 See the description of the career of Zhijiao in the biography of Fatai: T2060:50.431c2-432a5.

35 See the description of the career of Daoni in the biography of Fatai: T2060:50.432a5-8. See also 5.3.5 for more details about Daoni's life and career.

36 The XGSZ regards Tanqian as the one who first spread of the *Shelun* in the north. See T2060:50.572b16-20. For Jingsong's great success in promoting the teachings of the *Shelun* and reference to Paramārtha as described in the XGSZ, see T2060:50.501c23-502a6.

37 See the biography of Tanqian in the XGSZ, esp. T2060:50.572a15-c28.

38 See the biography of Jingsong in the XGSZ, esp. T2060:50.501c14-502a3.

39 For more about the doctrinal background of the Dilun tradition, see Gimello (1976: 294ff). Gimello also gives more detailed information about Jingsong (Ching-sung) on pages 180–2 and briefly discusses Tanqian (T'an-Ch'ien) on page 191.

40 T1824:42.104c8-11.

41 Yoshimura (2007: 178).

42 Yoshimura (2003a: 241, note 28). I thank Michael Radich, who drew my attention to Yoshimura's significant note.

43 See Paramārtha's *Juedingzang lun*: "The storehouse consciousness is impermanent (Ch. *wuchang* 無常; Skt. *anitya*) and contaminated (Ch. *youlou* 有漏; Skt. *āsrava*), whereas the spotless consciousness is permanent and uncontaminated. The spotless consciousness is realized when the Path towards having Thusness as the cognitive object (*zhenru jingdao* 真如境道) is attained" (T1584:30.1020b12-14).
44 See Paramārtha's *San wuxing lun*: "Because of the permanent absence of the imagined nature (*parikalpita-svabhāva*), the dependent nature (*paratantra-svabhāva*) also ceases. The absence of both those two [natures] is the spotless consciousness. This spotless consciousness alone does not change, and hence it is called 'Thusness'" (T1617:31.872a5-7).
45 See Paramārtha's *Zhuanshi lun*: "This absence of both object and consciousness is just the perfected nature (Ch. *shixing* 實性 [should be *zhenshi xing* 真實性?]; Skt. *pariniṣpanna-svabhāva*). This perfected nature is the spotless consciousness (*amoluo shi* 阿摩羅識)" (T1587:31.62c18-19).
46 See Paramārtha's *Shiba kong lun*: "The spotless consciousness is the innate pure mind, but it is called impure because it is defiled by adventitious defilements (Ch. *kechen* 客塵; Skt. *āgantuka-kleśa*). It is considered to be pure when all adventitious defilements is removed" (T1616:31.863b18-21).
47 Lü (1982: 164) makes a similar suggestion. He asserts that the *amoluo shi* necessarily includes both the aspect of Thusness and the aspect of the *jñāna* of Thusness (*ruru zhi* 如如智).
48 T1851:44.530c3-16.
49 T1851:44.530b6-12.
50 Yoshimura (2003b: 27) rightly points out that the basic scheme of Huiyuan's theory of nine consciousnesses is not very different from the traditional Dilun theory of eight consciousnesses expounded by his teacher Fashang. See also Yoshimura (2003a: 226–32), although I do not agree with Yoshimura's understanding of Jizang's account (230–2). More importantly, Yoshimura (2003a: 208ff.) also points out that the ninth consciousness of the Shelun masters is the result of interpreting Paramārtha's notion of spotless consciousness in light of the *Awakening of Faith*.
51 T2060:50.574b1-5.
52 T2060:50.572b16-20.
53 T2060:50.572c21-24.
54 T2060:50.571c28-572a2.
55 T2060:50.572b16-20.
56 For example, Yinshun (1956: 269 ff.) points out the close relation between the *Chapter on the Nine Consciousnesses* and Tanqian. In contrast, Ōtake (2012) insists that this text was composed by Paramārtha himself.
57 Wŏnch'ŭk cites T2805 word for word at one point. See Chapter 3, note 9.
58 X369:21.271b11-14.
59 Having studied with Xuanzang, Wŏnch'ŭk harshly criticizes Paramārtha. For example, he finds faults with the lack of scriptural support for Paramārtha's teaching (as understood by the Shelun/*Awakening of Faith* lineage) on the spotless consciousness. Wŏnch'ŭk also points out that this teaching goes against the *Rulai gongde zhuangyan jing* 如來功德莊嚴經 (*Scripture on the Merits and Ornaments of the Tathāgatas*). Moreover, Wŏnch'ŭk also points out that there is no article on the nine consciousnesses (*Jiushi pin* 九識品) in the *Yogācārabhūmi*, on which the *Chapter on the Nine Consciousnesses* (*Jiushi zhang* 九識章) claims to be based. See X369:21.241a5-9.

60 X369:21.240b20-c7. A problem with this passage is that Wŏnch'ŭk did not provide any explanation of *jiexing*. I think this shows that Wŏnch'ŭk, just like his other contemporary scholars, simply assumed *jiexing* to be identical with original awakening (see Chapter 1) and hence no explanation was in need. Understood thus, then, *jiexing* refers to the ninth consciousness that resides within the eighth consciousness.
61 T1708:33.400b25-b29.
62 It should be noted that Jingsong 靖嵩, according to the XGSZ, composed a text entitled *Jiushi xuanyi* 九識玄義 (*Mysterious Teachings of the Ninth Consciousness*), not *Jiushi zhang* 九識章. See the biography of Jingsong: T2060:50.501c28-502a3.
63 The only extant work indisputably attributed to Tanqian is a short text called *Wang shifei lun* 亡是非論 (*A Treatise on Eliminating [the Attachments to the Distinction between] Right and Wrong*), which is quoted in full by Zhiyan in his *Huayan jing nei zhangmen deng za kongmu* 華嚴經内章門等雜孔目 (*Essays on Sundry Topics in the Avataṃsaka-sutra*). See T1870:45.580c14-581b19.
64 Like Tanqian, Jingsong 靖嵩 (537–614) was also from the north, traveled to the south, and disseminated Paramārtha's *Shelun*. Together with Tanqian, Jingsong was also regarded by the XGSZ as a major promoter of Paramārtha's teachings. Some evidence, however, prevents us from associating Jingsong with the Shelun/*Awakening of Faith* lineage of the *Shelun* masters. No record at all suggests that Jingsong was related to the *Awakening of Faith*, and Jingsong was not connected with Buddhism in Chang'an. Furthermore, during his stay in Jinling, Jingsong studied Paramārtha's works while occasionally consulting Paramārtha's direct disciple, Fatai 法泰. This suggests that Jingsong's understanding of the *Shelun* may not deviate very much from Paramārtha's original teachings. Finally, a monk named Fahu 法護 (born between 576 and 634, see Shengkai 2006: 40) studied the *Shelun* with Jingsong. XGSZ reports that Fahu lectured on the *Shelun* often. He also critically edited the MSgBh. (I suspect that this means that he compared the *Shelun* with Dharmagupta's Chinese translation of 590.) Moreover, according to the XGSZ, Fahu's interpretation accords very well with Xuanzang's retranslation of the MSgBh (T2060:50.530b20-c11.) This also suggests that Jingsong's reading of the *Shelun* does not deviate very much from Paramārtha's original teachings and that Paramārtha's original teachings on the *Shelun* are not very different from Xuanzang's understanding of the MSgBh. About Fahu, see also Shengkai (2006: 40), Yinshun (1956: 273).
65 Ōtake (2017: 479, 543).
66 See Chapter 2, note 7.
67 T2034:49.99a10.
68 See Orzech (1998).
69 See Ōtake (2017).
70 T2060:50.432a5. It is reported that Paramārtha traveled to Jiujiang around 553 or 554. If this is true, then it is possible that Daoni followed Paramārtha to Jiujiang after that.
71 T2060:50.431c9-10.
72 T2060:50.431c10-13.
73 T2060:50.527b8-10.
74 T2060:50.671b26-29.
75 Huiyuan was summoned to Chang'an as one of the Six Meritorious Ones and stayed in Daxingshan Temple from 587. He seems to have stayed sometimes in Daxingshan Temple and sometimes in Jingying Temple 淨影寺. See XGSZ: T2060:50.491a19-27.

76 T2060:50.572c18-19. Tanqian probably stayed in Daxingshan Temple for three years (587–90). See T2060:50.573a10-13 and Chen (2002: 18, note 24).
77 See later for more detail about Daoyue.
78 The XGSZ biography of Huixiu 慧休 states that Daoni and Tanqian lectured on the *Shelun* at the same time in Chang'an: T2060:50.544b28-c2. Here the term "*Ni lunshi* 尼論師" refers to Daoni.
79 Tanqian was summoned to Chang'an in 587. See XGSZ: T2060:50.572c4-14.
80 For a detailed account of the biography of Tanqian based mainly on the XGSZ, see Chen (2002: 11–50).
81 T2060:50.572b19-20.
82 See the section earlier, "Tanqian: The Major Figure of the Shelun/*Awakening of Faith* Lineage."
83 T2060:50.572c14-18. See also Chen (2002: 17).
84 T2060:50.434a29-b1. According to the chronological order of the narrative of the *Lidai sanbao ji*, Tanqian seems to have received this title in 592. See also Chen (2002: 17, note 21). Chen concurs with my assumption regarding the year 592.
85 T2060:50.572c28-573a1. See also Chen (2002: 18).
86 T2060:50.573b2-14. See also Chen (2002: 19–20).
87 Chen (2002: 18).
88 According to the XGSZ, Huiyuan often said, "The Chan master Qian [i.e., Tanqian] breaks people's attachments and penetrates into the correct logic. This talent of his surpasses mine" (T2060:50.574 a10-13).
89 I estimated that Daoni died during 593–603 based on the biography of Daoyue 道岳, see Keng (2009: 333–6).
90 Jizang arrived in Chang'an in 599 and reported that he learned that the Shelun masters had two different doctrines (Quotation 5.1).
91 See 2.3.3.
92 T2146:55.142a16. One objection to my trust in the *Fajing lu* might be that the *Fajing lu* does not list two of the three texts that are included in the so-called *Wuxiang lun* 無相論, namely, the *Zhuanshi lun* and the *Xianshi lun*, although the *Fajing lu* does list the *San wuxing lun*. My answer is that apparently these three texts were only later collected into a single work under the title *Wuxiang lun*, and the titles *Zhuanshi lun* and *Xianshi lun* were also assigned later. This is suggested by the fact that that none of the early catalogs lists the title *Wuxiang lun*, and only the later Dunhuang commentaries on the *Shelun*, that is, T2807 and T2809, refer to the *Wuxiang lun*.
93 T2034:49.99a5.
94 See Chapter 2, quotation 2.1.
95 T2060:50.540c23-26.
96 T2060:50.573a17-19.
97 T2060:50.572c25-28.
98 T2060:50.430c6-13. Cf. Diana Paul's (1984: 36) English translation.
99 Kashiwagi (1981: 182). For more details, see Chapter 2, the section on Kashiwagi (1981) and Yoshizu (2003). Both argue that the *Awakening of Faith* probably originated in India.
100 For example, Katsumata (1961: 680–1) struggles to make sense of this account by Zhanran.
101 The term *yichi* 依持 here should be understood as the basis due to which all conditioned dharmas are produced or derived. Zhiyi uses this term consistently in this sense. See also X909:55.673a19-22.

102 T1717:33.942c16-24. Hirakawa (1990: 21) points out the mistakes made by Mochizuki. See also Gimello (1976: 194ff).

103 T1716:33.792a13-14.

104 Jizang mentions that in 608 he lectured on the *Treatise of Hundred Verses* [*on the Mūlamadhyamaka-kārikā*] (Ch. *Bai lun* 百論; Skt. **Śata-śāstra*) to three groups of Treatise masters (*lunshi* 論師), namely, the masters of the *Shelun*, masters of the *Shidi* 十地 (i.e., *Daśabhūmika*), and masters of the *Dichi* 地持 (i.e., *Scripture on the Stages of the Bodhisattvas*, i.e., the *Bodhisattvabhūmi*) (T1827:42.302b4-6). A further question remains as to whether the *Shidi (shi)* 十地(師) and *Dichi (shi)* 地持(師) correspond to the so-called southern and northern branches of the Dilun tradition.

105 Zhiyi appears to be aware of the distinction between the Dilun masters in the northern and the southern parts of Xiang (for example, T1777:38.528b16-c5).

106 See T1911:46.54a23-29.

107 See T1716:33.704c3-4. It seems likely that the Dilun converted or merged into the Shelun tradition, as almost no record of Dilun masters who were active after 610 can be found. This seems to be confirmed by Jizang's use, in his *Zhongguan lun shu* 中觀論疏 (written in 608), of the terms *jiu dilun shi* 舊地論師 (T1824:42.7b4; T1824:42.104c7) or *xi dilun shi* 昔地論師 (T1824:42.54a17).

Chapter 6

1 Neither Asaṅga in the MSg nor Vasubandhu in the MSgBh mentions anything similar to the notion of *jiexing*, that is, something that resides within the storehouse consciousness and mixes with the permeation of hearing that comes from outside. In the discussion that follows, I show that it is reasonable to assume that the notion of *jiexing* is a further development beyond Asaṅga and Vasubandhu.

2 T1595:31.156c9-22. See my discussions of this passage in 1.1.1.

3 T1595:31.175a23-26. See my discussion of this passage in 1.1.2.

4 T1595:31.174c5-7. For a similar passage in Paramārtha's *Shelun*, see: T1595:31.177c18-19.

5 T1595:31.221b17-21. This is Paramārtha's interpolation into the MSgBh. Another example is that Paramārtha's *Shelun* claims that the "aspiration from confidence" after the first bodhisattva stage is called the "aspiration from confidence of the noble people" (*shengren xinle* 聖人信樂). See T1595:31.213b20-22 (Paramārtha's interpolation).

6 See Funayama (2005b: 378).

7 T 2805:85.995b9-15.

8 For example, the *Shelun* calls the ten bodhisattva stages "supramundane" (T1595:31.155c4) and states that dharmas before the first bodhisattva stage are worldly, while dharmas after the first bodhisattva stage are supramundane (T1595:31.208b22-23).

9 Asaṅga mentions six kinds of "transformation of the basis" (Ch. *zhuanyi* 轉依; Skt. *āśrayaparivṛtti*) in the ninth chapter of his MSg. Here I follow the CWSL and Nagao (1982–7, Vol. II: 306, note) in construing the first four as four transformative stages of practices instead of four kinds of transformation. For the reconstruction of the Sanskrit, see Lamotte (1973, Vol. II: 261–2) and Nagao (1982–7, Vol. II: 305–6). For the correspondence of the transformative stage of penetration to the first bodhisattva stage, see T1595:31.248a1-3.

10 T1595:31.247c16-19.

11 See T1595:31.247c15-20, which makes it clear that the "status of aspiration from confidence" corresponds to the stage before the first bodhisattva stage. In the *Shelun*, Paramārtha uses the Chinese terms *xinle wei* 信樂位 and *yuanle wei* 願樂位 interchangeably, both referring to the Sanskrit term *adhimukti*, that is, the stage before the first bodhisattva stage. See two passages in the *Shelun*: T1595:31.208c5-8; T1595:31.200a22-25.
12 T2805:85.982b18-21.
13 T2805:85.982b22-c7. See my discussions of this passage in 1.4.1.
14 Cf. my discussion of this point in 2.4.
15 See note 11.
16 See Paramārtha's *Shelun*: T1595:31.209b13-14. Here, undiscriminating *jñāna* should be understood as being unconditioned. See my discussion in 6.8.
17 See Asaṅga's MSg, III.9. For an example in the *Shelun*, see T1595:31.208c4-21. See also my discussion in Chapter 4 (Section 4.3).
18 See T1595:31.209b14-17. The Chinese term *cizhi* 此智 must refer to subsequently acquired *jñāna* in this passage.
19 T2805:85.999b12-17. See my discussion in 1.4.2.
20 On the one hand, T2805 states, "Its substance (*ti* 體) is the faculty having learned (*zhigen* 知根)" (T2805:85.999b12). On the other hand, it also states, "It has the 'faculty of resolving to know something unknown (*weizhi yuzhi gen* 未知欲知根),' which is born from the *jñāna* of things as they really are (*rushi zhi* 如實智)." (T2805:85.999b13-14).
21 Generally, the *Shelun* calls undiscriminating *jñāna* "having a faculty" because once this *jñāna* is attained, other kinds of *jñāna* cease. To be more specific, the *Shelun* associates undiscriminating *jñāna* with the first uncontaminated faculty, namely, the faculty of resolving to know something unknown, and it associates the three uncontaminated faculties with three things (*sanshi* 三事) concerning liberation (T1595:31.212b23-c4). Thus, the first faculty, *ājñāsyāmīndriya*, can produce liberation (*neng sheng jietuo* 能生解脫); this corresponds to the Path of Insight. The second faculty, *ājñātendriya*, can maintain liberation (*neng chi jietuo* 能持解脫); this corresponds to the Path of Cultivation. The third faculty, *ājñātāvīndriya*, can apply liberation (*nengyong jietuo* 能用解脫); this corresponds to the "Ultimate point [of the Path]."
22 The first passage calls the faculty of resolving to know something unknown "supramundane pure mind" (*chushi jingxin* 出世淨心). As we have seen, the idea of "being supramundane" is closely connected with undiscriminating *jñāna*. Moreover, the passage also states that the faculty of resolving to know something unknown arises after the stage of the understanding arising from hearing and pondering (*wensi hui* 聞思慧), which, as we have seen, corresponds to the stages before the first bodhisattva stage. This passage clearly implies that the faculty of resolving to know something unknown arises at the first bodhisattva stage, that is, the Path of Insight (T1595:31.174b3-4). The second passage states that understanding arising from pondering (*sihui* 思慧) produces the faculty of resolving to know something unknown (T1595:31.172c11-12). I also take this to mean that this faculty corresponds to the Path of Insight. Note also that the AKBh also associates *ājñāsyāmīndriya* with the stage of the Path of Insight (AKBh, II.9; Paramārtha's translation: T1559:29.174b11-18). This mapping of the three uncontaminated faculties to the three stages of Path of Insight, Path of Cultivation, and the Path of No Further Training (Ch. *wuxue dao* 無學道; Skt. *aśaikṣa-mārga*) is not uncommon in the Abhidharma literature.

23 T2805:85.999b14.
24 Paramārtha phrases this as *xiu . . . can* 羞 . . . 慚 in the *Shelun* (T1595:31.247c26), while Xuanzang phrases it as *canxiu* 慚羞 or *xiuchi* 羞恥 in his translation of the MSgBh (T1597:31.369b23).
25 T1585:31.54c1-4.
26 See note 9 above.
27 See T1595:31.247c17-19.
28 The CWSL states that this transformation refers to the "first two stages" (*chu er wei* 初二位), that is, the Stage of Provision (Ch. *ziliang wei* 資糧位; Skt. *saṃbhārāvasthā*) and the Stage of Applied Practice (Ch. *jiaxing wei* 加行位; Skt. *prayogāvasthā*). Both of these precede the first bodhisattva stage. See T1585:31.48b11-15.
29 de La Vallée Poussin (1928–9: 113).
30 T1585:31.9a7-17.
31 T1830:43.308a20-24.
32 T1585:31.48b11-15.
33 According to the CWSL, the arousal of the mind of enlightenment marks the beginning of the Stage of Provision. See T1585:31.48b24-26.
34 "Original" and "permanent" (*nitya*) are different. Later Yogācāra texts use the word "original" in order to justify the differences among the five *gotras*. The word "permanent" cannot be applied to conditioned *dharmas*, while "original" can, even though their beginning cannot be clearly traced.
35 This interpretation of *jiexing* also is consistent with what is said in the *Tanyan shu* 曇延疏; see Chapter 1, quotation 1.4.
36 According to Master Ji and the Chinese Yogācāra tradition, these three views are attributed to Huyue 護月 (Candrapāla or Candragupta), Nantuo 難陀 (Nanda), and Shengjun 勝軍 (Prasenajit or Jayasena), respectively. See de La Vallée Poussin (1928–29: 102ff). Yamabe (1989, 1991) also discusses this issue at length.
37 T1585:31.8a20-b5. Also cf. the discussion of the notion of originally existent seeds at the beginning of the *Yogācārabhūmi* (T1579:30.284b19-23).
38 Hakamaya and Arai (1993: 44) point out that, in the *Yogācārabhūmi*, the terms *gotra*, *dhātu*, *bīja*, and *prakṛti* are synonymous.
39 In the previous chapter, I translated the Sanskrit term *samudānīta gotra* as drawn-forth *gotra* because I was following Paramārtha's Chinese translation *yinchu xing* 引出性. In contrast, Xuanzang translates the same Sanskrit term as *xisuocheng zhongxing* 習所成種姓. In order to preserve the possible differences in their interpretations of this notion, I deliberately translate these two terms differently depending on which Chinese translation I am following in a given context.
40 T1585:31.8b23-c3.
41 T1585:31.48b5-11.
42 Namely, mirror *jñāna* (Ch. *dayuanjing zhi* 大圓鏡智; Skt. *ādarśa-jñāna*), equality *jñāna* (Ch. *pingdengxing zhi* 平等性智; Skt. *samatā-jñāna*), observing *jñāna* (Ch. *miaoguancha zhi* 妙觀察智; Skt. *pratyavekṣā-jñāna*), and performing *jñāna* (Ch. *chengsuozuo zhi* 成所作智; Skt. *kṛtyānuṣṭhāna-jñāna*). For an English translation of the passages on these four *jñānas* in the FDJL, see Keenan (2002: 75ff). See also *Digital Dictionary of Buddhism*, "*sizhi* 四智" (article by Charles Muller). The MSA includes an extensive discussion of these four kinds of *jñāna* (IX.67-IX.77).
43 De La Vallée Poussin (1928–9: 681) translates the term *xinpin* as "les diverses classes de pensée (huitième Vijñāna, etc.)." Keenan (1980: 559ff; 2002: 82ff) overlooks the importance of this term and simply does not translate it.

44 T1530:26.304a9-11. See also Keenan (1980: 586ff).
45 T1530:26.304a11-b2.
46 T1530:26.304b3-7. There is a passage similar to this in the CWSL, although the CWSL does not explicitly raise the issue of the stage at which the innate *gotra* becomes active (T1585:31.56c1-4). The diamond-like concentration refers to a deep concentration immediately before the attainment of buddhahood (*Digital Dictionary of Buddhism*, "*jin'gangyu ding* 金剛喻定" [article by Charles Muller]).
47 Note that, in Section 6.7, I point out that this point is incorrect.
48 The CWSL also discusses in detail the stage at which each of the various states of mind associated with the four kinds of *jñāna* become active. For example, it mentions two theories regarding the state of mind that is associated with the mirror *jñāna*: according to one, the state of mind associated with the mirror *jñāna* becomes active when a bodhisattva achieves the diamond-like concentration; according to the other, the state of mind associated with the mirror *jñāna* is acquired at the stage of the Path of Liberation (Ch. *jietuo dao* 解脫道; Skt. *vimokṣa-mārga*) (T1585:31.56b6-c4).
49 T1530: 26.302c12-303a13.
50 T1597:31.372a12-21.
51 For the MSA, see IX.67-76. For the Chinese translation, see T1604:31.606c22-607b2. For more details, see Sakuma (2006 [2008]).
52 T1610:31.808b15-16.
53 T1610:31.794a22-24; *Shelun*: T1595:31.200c23-24. See also the quotation in Chapter 5 from Huijun, who calls the third *buddha-gotra* "*deguo foxing* 得果佛性" (X784:46.601c23-602a9); T2806 (T2806:85.1000b28-c4) and Zhiyan (T1870:45.549b26-c1) call it "*zhideguo foxing* 至得果佛性."
54 See note 39.
55 Takasaki (2005: 33–4; 49). See also MAV III.11, Nagao (1964: 41). For Paramārtha's Chinese translation, see T1599:31.456a26-b2.
56 T1610:31.808b15-c25.
57 The FXL distinguishes two kinds of dharma-bodies: the dharma-body that is properly attained (*zhengde fashen* 正得法身) and the dharma-body that is properly teaching (*zhengshuo fashen* 正說法身). The dharma-body that is properly teaching refers to the Buddha's teachings and is divided into two (the profound for the Mahāyāna and the shallow for the two lesser vehicles) and, furthermore, these are conditioned. But the dharma-body that is properly attained is the dharma-body in its proper sense. It is described as "the purest Dharma-element, the 'object' of unconditioned undiscriminating *jñāna*, and the substance (*dangti* 當體) of all Buddhas, and it is obtained only by oneself" (*pratyātma-adhigamadharma* [Takasaki 2005: 234, note 4]). Moreover, the dharma-body that is properly attained is glossed as "having Thusness as its substance" (*ti shi zhenru* 體是真如 [FXL: T1610:31.808a17-b4]).
58 In Chapter 7, I demonstrate that the dharma-body is identified with Thusness and hence is an unconditioned *dharma* for both Vasubandhu and Paramārtha.
59 T1610:31.804c11-13.
60 T1610:31.809a4-5; see also FXL: T1610:31.802c18-23.
61 For the Sanskrit term, see Takasaki (2005: 222, note 5).
62 T1610:31.811c5-14. Here in this passage dharma-body is not mentioned in the explanation of the first way but it is clearly implied.
63 T1610:31.800c10-11.

64 T1610:31.812a13-17.
65 In contrast, according to the *Yugaron gi* 瑜伽論記 (*A Record of the Commentaries on the Yogācārabhūmi*), Dharmapāla says that the *prakṛtistha gotra* serves as the cause proper for the enjoyment-body. See T1828:42.487b2-4.
66 The FXL agrees with the RGV regarding the two-*gotra* theory. See my discussion in 7.6.
67 T1610:31.808c1-8.
68 See quotation 5.2 (= quotation 1.11). Jizang also reports that the Shelun masters considered the enjoyment-body to be conditioned (T1824:42.109b10-13).
69 See earlier, quotation 6.9.
70 See my discussion in Chapter 5 of Huijun's account (quotation 5.3).
71 See my discussion of the three *buddha-gotra*s in 5.2.2.
72 T1530:26.302b24-25.
73 MSA IX. 67. For the Sanskrit text, see Lévi (1907: 46); For the Chinese translation, see T1604:31.606c23.
74 See T1530:26.325c27-326b15.
75 For the same reason, Paramārtha argues in the *Shelun* that permeation of hearing together with correct reflection is only a contributory condition for correct view, that is, the unconditioned undiscriminating *jñāna*. See T1595:31.172b14-16; T1595:31.173c24-174a8.
76 For the notion of "seeds [born from] having Thusness as the cognitive object," see Chapter 2, note 59.
77 T1579:30.589a16-17.
78 T1828:42.614c27-615a8.
79 See, for example: T1585:31.8a20-9b6. Namely, sentient beings are divided into five groups, each group with its specific *gotra*s: Hearers, Solitary Realizers, bodhisattvas, those with an indefinite *gotra* (*buding zhongxing* 不定種姓), and those without *gotra*. (*wu zhongxing* 無種姓). Among these five, only those with the bodhisattva-*gotra* and indefinite *gotra* may eventually become Buddhas. For more details, see D'Amato (2003). As Delhey (2022) points out, this idea of five *gotra*s is in line with the orthodox Indian Yogācāra doctrine.
80 T1585:31.56a7-11.
81 See T1585:31.56c1-2.
82 T1782:38.1088a2-11.
83 See Nagao (1994, Part II: 6–7).

Chapter 7

1 For example, Suguro and Shimokawabe (2007) do not comment much about this.
2 For the Tibetan text, see Lamotte (1973, Tome I: 37–8); Nagao (1982–7, Vol. I: *86–7*); for the Sanskrit reconstruction, see Nagao (1982–7, Vol. 1: 364); for Xuanzang's Chinese translation, see T1594:31.140b4-12.
3 For the Tibetan text, see DT, Ri, 151a1-2 and Iwata (1981: 162). Iwata's text for some unknown reason omits *pa nyid kyi phyir, chos thams cad ni de bzhin gshegs pa'i snying po*; for Xuanzang's translation, see T1597:31.344a3-5. There is a problem here with the *can* in the Tibetan phrase *de bzhin gshegs pa'i snying po can*. Ruegg (1969: 510–11) suggests that *can* in this phrase (and *you* 有 in the Chinese *yiqie fa you rulaizang*

一切法有如來藏) is used only to indicate that this is a *Bahuvrīhi* compound, like the -*ka* ending that is sometimes found in *Bahuvrīhi* compounds. Zimmermann's (2002: 46) suggestion that the *can* is a later insertion might not be correct, since we find *can* in the Tibetan translation of Vasubandhu's MSgBh.

4 Zimmerman (2002) provides a detailed investigation of the meaning of the compound *tathāgatagarbha*. From the grammatical point of view, he argues that "the grammatically adequate interpretation serving as the basic one of the compound *tathāgatagarbha* is that of a *Bahuvrīhi* meaning 'containing a Tathāgata'" (45). But on the basis of the similes in the *Tathāgatagarbha-sūtra* itself, Zimmermann also admits that "the meaning 'embryo' would automatically acquire greater prominence, and possibly overshadow the first interpretation based on the lotus imagery" (loc. cit.). Hence, he concludes, "The richness of the term *garbha*, which means 'containing,' 'born from,' 'embryo,' '(embracing/concealing) womb,' 'calyx,' 'child,' 'member of a clan,' and even 'core' would from the very beginning tend to keep its semantic range from being reduced to a single word" (loc. cit.). Zimmermann also mentions that, according to Ruegg and Schmithausen, "the compound *tathāgatagarbha* can never mean 'matrix of the Tathāgata' in the Indian texts" (2002: 42). Recently, Saitō (2020: 12) also suggests that the term *tathāgatagarbha* in the RGV can be read both as a *tatpuruṣa* and a *Bahuvrīhi* compound. Saito's interpretation, which I shall discuss in more detail in 7.5.2, is based on his unawareness of the distinction between unconditioned and conditioned dharmas, and hence must be rejected.

5 A complete survey of the development of the idea of dharma-body within the Yogācāra tradition remains beyond the scope of this book, but, in Keng (2011a), I have suggested that, for Asaṅga in the MSg, the dharma-body has undiscriminating *jñāna* as its essential characteristic and hence it is conditioned. Briefly, for Asaṅga, dharma-body maps onto the pure aspect (*vyavadāna-aṃśika*) of the dependent nature (*paratantra-svabhāva*). The dharma-body therefore must be conditioned because it is the effect of the transformation of the defiled aspect of the dependent nature, that is, the transformation of the storehouse consciousness. For this reason, Asaṅga does not identify dharma-body with Thusness. As shown later, for Vasubandhu, dharma-body maps onto the perfected nature and is unconditioned. Thus, the fundamental difference between Asaṅga and Vasubandhu is that Asaṅga considers the dharma-body to be something attained only after one becomes a Buddha, while for Vasubandhu, the dharma-body is innate in the sense that it is identified with Thusness, which, like space, is shared by all sentient beings. A key implication, as we shall see later, is that Vasubandhu's move makes Yogācāra compatible with Tathāgatagarbha. It remains to be explored whether any other Yogācāra text before Vasubandhu ever made this identification.

6 For the Tibetan text and Sanskrit reconstruction, see Griffiths et al. (1989: 289); § C; for Xuanzang's Chinese translation, see T1594:31.149b25-28.

7 Griffiths et al. (1989: 93). Nagao (1982–7, Vol. II: 335) mentions that the commentators all distinguish two senses of "attainment" (Ch. *de* 得; Skt. *prāpti*). He thinks that the first refers to "original awakening" (*benjue* 本覺) and the second to "incipient awakening" (*shijue* 始覺), two key notions in the *Awakening of Faith*.

8 For Paramārtha's translation, see T1595:31.252b11-20; for Dharmagupta's translation, see T1596:31.313c20-24.

9 Asvabhāva's *Mahāyānasaṃgrahopanibandhana* also agrees with Vasubandhu's MSgBh that dharma-body is permanent. See Griffiths et al. (1989: 290); §C. For Xuanzang's Chinese translation, see T1598:31.437b25-27.

10 For Xuanzang's Chinese translation, see T1597:31.371c10-14.
11 See note 5 above.
12 The CWSL also cites a view that the dharma-body neither arises nor ceases because the essence-body (*svābhāvika-kāya*) is permanent. See T1585:31.58a15-18.
13 For Xuanzang's Chinese translation, see T1597:31.373c12-13.
14 For the Tibetan translation, see Griffiths et al. (1989: 360); DT Ri 186b1-2; for Xuanzang's Chinese translation, see T1597:31.377b21-22.
15 For the Tibetan translation, see Griffiths et al. (1989: 349), §J2; for Xuanzang's Chinese translation, see T1597:31.376b19-20. Note that here Asaṅga also claims that the body of the Tathāgatas is permanent for three reasons: [dharma-body] (1) has pure Thusness as its characteristic; (2) is under the impulse of former vows; (3) its activity is unending. From this we cạn infer that the main reason for Asaṅga's statement that the dharma-body is permanent is actually that it is constantly acting rather than being literally permanent.
16 Griffiths renders this as "Because it is this that manifests awakening," which I do not think reflects what Xuanzang is saying here.
17 For the Chinese translation, see T1597:31.371b18-20.
18 For the Tibetan text, see DT, Ri. 151a^{2}-a^{3}; Iwata (1981: 162); for Xuanzang's Chinese translation, see T1597:31.344a5-7.
19 I have checked all the entries of *rab tu phye ba* in Yokoyama's *Index to the Yogācārabhūmi* and also looked it up in the THL Translation Tool (http://www.thlib.org/reference/translation-tool/; accessed Apr. 20, 2021), and the Sanskrit term behind them is invariably *prabhāvita* (with a few related forms such as *pra-√bhū* and *prabhāvyate*). The only exception is one occasion on which *rab tu phye ba* renders the Sanskrit word *pravibhakta* (Yokoyama 1996: 832), which Xuanzang translates as *nengxian* 能顯. Therefore, when the Tibetan *rab tu phye ba* corresponds to Xuanzang's *xiancheng* 顯成 or *suoxian* 所顯, the underlying Sanskrit must be *prabhāvita*.
20 Here I translate *ra btu phye* as "characterized" instead of "disclosed" because Asaṅga does not identify Thusness with the dharma-body. (See note 5.) The term "disclosed" carries the sense of identity between the two when we say "the dharma-body is disclosed through Thusness."
21 For the Tibetan text, see Griffiths et al. (1989: 340); §I3; for Xuanzang's Chinese translation, see T1597:31.374c18-19.
22 For passage one, see Tibetan: DT, Tshi 282b4-5; Chinese: T1579:30.577b16-18; also see Schmithausen (1991: §2.2.0-2.2.1). For passage two, see Tibetan: DT, Tshi 283a3; Chinese: T1579:30.577c3-4; also see Schmithausen (1991): 1991: §2.2.4.1 d2. For passage three, see Tibetan: DT, Zi 122a7-122b1; Chinese: T1579:30.747c23-25.
23 In contrast, Asaṅga never uses the term *prabhāvita* to depict the relation between Thusness and the dharma-body.
24 I am grateful to Professor Parimal G. Patil for suggesting this English translation.
25 See Keng (2009: 412–14).
26 For the Tibetan translation, see DT, Ri, 151a6-7, Cf. Iwata (1981: 164); for Xuanzang's Chinese translation, see T1597:31.344a16.
27 Schmithausen (1969: 109–10) devotes a long footnote to the term *prabhāvita* by first indicating that its basic sense is "brought to light" (*zum vorschein gebracht*). He then proposes the rendering "constituted by" (*konstituiert durch*) in order to cover the four possible nuanced senses behind the term *prabhāvita*: (a) "brought to light" in the

sense of "indicated" (*zustandgebracht, gezeugt*); (b) "brought to light" in the sense of "made visible (through something)" (*sichtbar gemacht* [*durch etwas*]), "manifested (through something)" (*manifestiert* [*durch etwas*]); (c) "brought to light" in the sense of "(for a thinking subject) made visible (as something)" ([*vom denkenden Subjekt*] *sichtbar gemacht* [*als etwas*]), "characterized as" (*gekennzeichnet als*), "defined as" (*bestimmt als*); (d) "brought to light" in the sense of "essentially characterized as" ([*wesentlich*] *gekennzeichnet als*).

Kim (2007) reviews various uses of the term *prabhāvita* in the *Madhyāntavibhāgaṭīkā* by Sthiramati. Unfortunately, Kim also overlooks the crucial use of *prabhāvita* in relation to Thusness and dharma-body discussed here.

28 Makransky's (1997: 373, note 6) reading of *prabhāvita* is influenced by Harrison (1992: 56, and reference to Schmithausen on 81), who is in turn influenced by Schmithausen (1969). Thus, it seems to me that these three scholars all overlooked the significance of the use of the term *prabhāvita* to connect the dharma-body and Thusness.

More recently, Schmithausen (2014: 507) has undertaken an extensive investigation of the meaning of *prabhāvita*, but again he does not focus on Vasubandhu's special usage of *prabhāvita* in the MSgBh. There he mainly engages in a debate against Matsumoto about the meaning of *prabhāvita* in the *Saṃdhinirmocanasūtra*. Matsumoto holds that *prabhāvita* is used in a causal sense of "produced by/from" whereas Schmithausen himself insists that "essentially/specifically characterized by/as" is the better reading. For this reason, Schmithausen's detailed discussion is not directly relevant to my point here.

29 The RGV contains two verses (I.27 and I.28) that answer this question. Of these two, I.27 belongs to the oldest layer of the RGV according to Takasaki (1966: 10–19, and Appendix I). Takasaki takes I.28 to be a commentary on I.27 (1966: 14). I agree with Takasaki and think I.28 represents the final systematization of the Tathāgatagarbha doctrine in the RGV, the most distinct feature of which is, as I argue here, the identification of Buddha-body, Thusness, and *buddha-gotra* in verse I.28. Since this identification is missing in I.27, I do not cite it here.

30 For the Sanskrit text, see Johnston (1950: 26); Prasad (1991: 94); for the English translation, see Takasaki (1966: 196–8).

31 For the Sanskrit text, see Johnston (1950: 71); Prasad (1991: 139); for the Chinese translation, see T1611:31.838c12-13.

32 E.g., MAV I.14; MSg II.26.

33 For the Sanskrit text, see Johnston (1950: 8); Prasad (1991: 76); for the Chinese translation, see T1611:31.822c14-17.

34 For the Sanskrit text, see Johnston (1950: 71); Prasad (1991: 139); for the English translation, see Takasaki (1966: 288). See also my discussion in Chapter 6 (Section 6.7).

35 For the Sanskrit text, see Johnston (1950: 73); Prasad (1991: 141); for the Chinese translation, see T1611:31.839b6-9.

36 For the Sanskrit text, see Bagchi (1970: 43); for the Chinese translation, see T1604:31.604c8-15. Sthiaramati's *Vṛttibhāṣya* comments on IX.37 (c) as follows: "Although Thusness is in all things, when the [two kinds of] selflessness are free from adventitious defilements (*āgantuka-kleśa*) of the afflictive and cognitive obstructions, it becomes purified and is called Tathāgata." He comments on IX.37 (d) as follows: "Thus, because Thusness exists in all sentient beings, they are said to be embryos of Tathāgatas (*tathāgatagarbha*)." See Nguyen (1990: 396).

37 Quoted from Makransky (1997: 50). Note that these verses are also quoted in MSg X.27 discussed earlier.

38 For the Sanskrit text, see Lévi (1907: 34). Schmithausen's (2014: 535) translation reads: "buddhahood is all dharmas, because Suchness is not different [from them] and because buddhahood is essentially characterized by the [accomplished] purification of Suchness (i.e., is essentially just Suchness in the state of accomplished purification from all adventitious impurities)." As discussed earlier, Schmithausen insists on translating *prabhāvita* here as "essentially characterized," which I think does not adequately capture its subtle meaning. See also Makransky (1997: 43). In another passage (MSABh on MSA IX.65), however, the term *prabhāvita* does appear but is used in a different sense in a different context.
39 For the stratification of RGV, see Nakamura (1961: 16–17), Takasaki (1966: 10ff.) and Schmithausen (1971: 123ff.). For the stratification of MSA, see Hakamaya (1993: 17–27). Also cf. Odani (1984: 9–14); Keng (2015).
40 Whether the *Laṅkāvatāra-sūtra* is an exception to this rule requires a separate study. Lü (1980) argues that the *Laṅkāvatāra-sūtra* is no exception to this rule. The problem, according to Lü, is that the *Awakening of Faith* follows the mistakes made in Bodhiruci's Chinese translation and misinterprets the *Laṅkāvatāra-sūtra*. See also my discussion about Huiyuan's interpretation of the *Laṅkāvatāra-sūtra* below.
41 For example, Vasubandhu's AKBh divides all dharmas into five categories: (1) physical dharmas (*rūpa*); (2) mental dharmas (*citta*); (3) dharmas related to mind (*caitta*); (4) dharmas separate from both physical and mental dharmas (*cittaviprayukta-saṃskāra*); (5) unconditioned dharmas. Among these five, the first four are conditioned (*saṃskṛta*). See Potter (1999: 50).
42 The Huayan philosophy as culminated in Fazang 法藏 (643–712) and Zongmi 宗密 (780–841) is heavily influenced by the "One Mind in Two Aspects" (*yixin ermen*一心二門) scheme of the *Awakening of Faith*. See, for example, the article "Huayan School" by Mario Poceski included in Buswell (2004: 341–7).
43 For an overview of the importance of this scheme of *ti-yong* in the development of Chinese thought and in the *Awakening of Faith*, see Gong (1995: 105–32). On the other hand, Funayama argues that the origin of the conceptual scheme of *ti-yong* can be traced to around the year 500 in the southern dynasty, especially to Baoliang 寶亮 (*c*. 444–509). See Funayama (2005c: 126ff). See also my discussion of the issue of Sinicization in the Conclusion.
44 In Chapter 3 (Section 3.9.1), I suggest that *suiwang* 隨妄 is a key term in Huiyuan's work, a term that is also found in T2805.
45 It is still necessary to investigate whether Huiyuan subscribes to strong *tathāgatagarbha* in any of his works. In Keng (2014b), I suggest that, even if it is true that Huiyuan subscribes to strong *tathāgatagarbha*, it was only after Huiyuan came under the influence of the *Awakening of Faith* in his later career. Based on his distinction between the aspect [established by] the natural purity (*xingjing* 性淨) and the aspect [established by] expedient means (*fangbian* 方便), a distinction that is prevalent in his works, he must have interpreted the *Laṅkāvatāra-sūtra* according to the weak understanding of *tathāgatagarbha* in his earlier career, namely, when he was not yet influenced by the *Awakening of Faith*.
46 See my discussion in 2.4.
47 In his *Shelun*, Paramārtha directly addresses this question. His answer there, which I find unsatisfactory, is that the Buddha is neither sentient nor insentient. See T1595:31.259c7-12.
48 For Paramārtha's Chinese translation, see T1599:31.452b23-25. This point is discussed in Ui (1930: 187–8); Ye (1975: 47–51) (Appendix).

49 For the Sanskrit text, see Nagao (1964: 23); for Xuanzang's Chinese translation, which agrees with the Sanskrit text, see T1600:31.465c11-14. For D'Amato's English translation of the Sanskrit, see D'Amato (2012: 126). For Kotyk's English translation of Xuanzang, see Kotyk (2021: 24).
50 For Paramārtha's Chinese translation, see T1599:31.452c3-5.
51 See T1835:44.7a14-15.
52 See Takasaki (2005: 19–31), esp. p. 30.
53 See Takasaki's article in Takasaki (1989: 141–68).
54 See Takasaki's article "『無上依經』*Anuttarāśraya sūtra* の構造" in Takasaki (1989: 131–40).
55 For the Chinese text, see T1610:31.808a13-17.
56 The term *rulaizang* 如來藏 (*tathāgatagarbha*) occurs only eight times in Paramārtha's *Shelun*. Of those eight occurrences, seven are interpolated by Paramārtha, and their exact meanings are hard to pinpoint. In contrast, *rulaizang* occurs eighteen times in the FXL, and its meanings are much easier to unpack (see later). For this reason, I explore Paramārtha's Tathāgatagarbha thought based mainly on his translation of the FXL. The task of investigating Paramārtha's uses of the term *rulaizang* and the term *foxing* 佛性 in his various works remains to be done.
57 For the Chinese text, see T1610:31.795c23-796a14.
58 RGV I.27: Johnston (1950: 26); Prasad (1991: 94).
59 In Keng (2013b), I drew on a similar use of *prabhāvita* in the prose portion of *A Commentary on the Vajracchedikā-prajñāpāramitā-sūtra* (i.e., T1511 [see also T1513]) and in MSgBh to suggest that the author of the two texts was the same Vasubandhu. Strikingly, this commentary also claims that the dharma-body is a body that has *jñāna* as its mark (*zhi xiang shen* 智相身) or has *jñāna* as its self-nature (*zhi zixing* 智自性). Whether or not Vasubandhu was the author of this commentary, my thesis still holds: namely, in Vasubandhu's MSgBh and RGV, the dharma-body is defined merely as Thusness.
60 For exactly how this subsequently acquired *jñāna* works, see Tzohar (2020).
61 This is a complicated issue that remains outside the scope of this book. Readers can refer to fascicle 10 of the CWSL (T1585:31.58a6-b16), which offers two kinds of correspondences among the three Buddha-bodies and the five dharmas, namely, Thusness and the four *buddhajñāna*s.
62 For the Sanskrit text, see Johnston (1950: 72); Prasad (1991: 140); for the Chinese translation, see T1611:31.839a1-10. See also 6.7.
63 T1610:31.808c8-28.
64 For the Chinese text, see T1610:31.794a13-24.
65 Takasaki's (2005: 119, note 11) explanation, however, does not clearly avoid this mistake. He still says that Thusness is the "fundamental power" (原動力) to generate the mind of enlightenment, to cultivate, and to attain the ultimate effect of buddhahood.
66 For the Chinese text, see T1610:31.795c28-796a4.
67 The exact origin of these two *buddha-gotra*s remains to be explored. Jizang was the first to ascribe these two *buddha-gotra*s to the Dilun Masters. See T1853:45.39b15-17. Also see Liu (2005).
68 Namely the *Pusa dichi jing* 菩薩地持經 (T1581) by Dharmakṣema and the *Pusa shanjie jing* 菩薩善戒經 (T1582, T1583) by Guṇavarman. The two texts are different Chinese translations of the *Bodhisattvabhūmi* portion in the *Yogācārabhūmi*.
69 T1581:30.888a23-25.

70 T1581:30.900a19-20.

71 T1723:34.656a25-b4.

72 See also another similar passage from Master Ji's commentary on the *Śrīmālādevīsiṃhanāda-sūtra*. In this passage, Master Ji repeats the distinction between the *Śrīmālādevīsiṃhanāda-sūtra* and the *Laṅkāvatāra-sūtra*, but here he claims that there are four senses of *tathāgatagarbha*: "But there are four senses of *tathāgatagarbha*. There are two senses according to the *Laṅkāvatāra-sūtra*: [L1] the storehouse consciousness that is called the empty *tathāgatagarbha* (*kong rulaizang* 空如來藏); [L2] the [storehouse consciousness] that is perfectly containing uncontaminated permeation. This is called non-empty *tathāgatagarbha* (*bukong rulaizang* 不空如來藏). According to this *sūtra* (i.e., the *Śrīmālādevīsiṃhanāda-sūtra*), there are two senses of [*tathāgatagarbha*]: [S1] various afflictions cover the *gotra*, i.e., Thusness (*zhu fannao fu zhenru xing* 諸煩惱覆真如性); [S2] the *gotra* of principle, i.e., Thusness (*zhenru lixing* 真如理性). If the base consciousness contains uncontaminated seeds, at a later time [when one attains buddhahood those seeds give birth to] the enjoyment-body; If the Reality (*zhenli* 真理; i.e., the *gotra* of principle, Thusness [*zhenru lixing* 真如理性] mentioned above) covered by afflictions becomes disclosed in the future, the dharma-body is attained. [In the case of L1] *tathāgatagarbha* refers to the base consciousness that is to be discarded (*suoshe* 所捨); [In the case of S1], *tathāgatagarbha* refers to the afflictions that are to be separated from (*suochu* 所出); [In the case of L2] *tathāgatagarbha* refers to the permeation of hearing that is to be born (*suosheng* 所生) [as the enjoyment-body]; [In the case of S2] *tathāgatagarbha* refers to Thusness that is to be disclosed (*suoxian* 所顯) [as the dharma-body]." (X352:19.918b9-15.) Among these four, L1, L2 and S1 are conditioned, but S2 is unconditioned. It is striking to note that, again, Master Ji states that uncontaminated seeds (which are close to Paramārtha's notion of *jiexing*) become the enjoyment-body after the attainment of buddhahood. Also see Chapter 6, quotation 6.15, where Master Ji distinguishes between two kinds of *gotra*: "unconditioned *gotra*" (*wuwei xing* 無為性) and "*gotra* that has causes and conditions" (*you yinyuan xing* 有因緣性).

73 For the Sanskrit text, see Wogihara (1930: 3); for Xuanzang's Chinese translation, see T1579:30.478c13-15.

74 See Karashima (2007), see also *Digital Dictionary of Buddhism*, "*yichanti*一闡提" (article by C. Muller).

75 See, for example, the following passage in Vasubandhu's MSgBh: "If some sentient beings lack the dharmas for nirvana, they are called 'lacking the cause.' This means that they do not have the causes for nirvana because they are without the [*buddha-*]*gotra* (*wu zhongxing* 無種性). All Buddhas do not have [total] control over those people" (T1597:31.376b12-14). For an interesting proposal for how to employ modal concepts of necessity, possibility and contingency to resolve the tension in the MSA between "all sentient beings have the potentiality for attaining complete awakening" and "some beings are excluded from acquiring a *gotra*," see D'Amato (2003). An issue with D'Amato's view is that he thinks "all sentient being are *tathāgatagarbha*s (*tad-garbha*)" implies "all sentient beings have the potentiality for attaining complete awakening." If by "potentiality" he means something like "causes" or "seeds," then I disagree for the reason stated earlier.

76 This is precisely the position held by the *Laṅkāvatāra-sūtra*, which claims that, due to the power of the Tathāgatas (*Tathāgatādhiṣṭhāna*), all good roots can still arise for the *icchantika*s who have abandoned all wholesome roots (*sarvakuśalamūlotsarga*). See T670:16.487b29-c3.

77 Vasubandhu only talks about the notion of *gotra* in three passages in his MSgBh, in all of which the notion of *gotra* always implies its plurality. See T1597:31.371b5-7; T1597:31.367a1-6; T1597:31.378a5-6.
78 See note 73.
79 For the Sanskrit reconstruction, see Yamaguchi (1934: 56). For the Tibetan translation, see DT, Bi, 216b2-3. As Delhey (2022: 7, note 36) points out, Yamaguchi emends *de bzhin du* as *de bzhin nyid du* and reconstructs it as *tathātvam*, whereas Delhey (2022: 7) prefers to reconstruct it simply as *tathā* as an adverb and translates this sentence as follows, "Others state that because all sentient beings are endowed with the spiritual disposition [to become a] *buddha*, here the term *gotra* should be understood accordingly." Based on my interpretation of the *buddha-gotra* in RGV-FXL, I disagree with Delhey's reading.
80 For example: (1) If Asaṅga was the author/editor of the whole *Yogācārabhūmi*, then why in his own works did he not refer to the notion of the two kinds of *gotra*, which is prominent in the *Bodhisattvabhūmi*? (2) Should we doubt the traditional account that the current edition of the *Bodhisattvabhūmi* predated Asaṅga and Vasubandhu and had exerted much influence on both of them?
81 The ideas that the dharma-body is identified with Thusness and that no boundary can be set for Thusness are universally accepted after Vasubandhu in the Yogācāra tradition. But the problem is that later texts, for example the FDJL and the CWSL, avoid adopting the term *tathāgatagarbha* as well as the claim that "all sentient beings are *tathāgatagarbhas*." I cannot explain this intriguing anomaly. A possible reason is that the term *tathāgatagarbha* might have been picked up as one of the hallmarks of a certain rival tradition/school in later Yogācāra.
82 More studies must be done to examine the *gotra* theory in the development of the Yogācāra tradition in order to trace the history behind the idea that the innate *buddha-gotra* is Thusness. A key in this history could be the MAV because it reads "*gotrasya ca viśuddy-artham*" ("for the purpose of the complete purification of the spiritual lineage") (MAV I.19a) and its *Bhāṣya* comments "*gotraṃ hi prakṛtiḥ svābhāvikatvāt*" ("spiritual lineage means nature because it has the quality of an inherent nature"). For the Sanskrit text, see Nagao (1964: 26); for the English translation, see D'Amato (2012: 128). Whether this might be related to the idea of the innate *gotra* of the RGV and the FXL, and whether the author was the same Vasubandhu as the author of MSgBh, remain to be explored.

Chapter 8

1 For example, Yinshun (1995). Kashiwagi (1981: 182) also makes speculations on this, although only in passing.
2 In the Chinese Buddhist canon, a second version of the *Awakening of Faith* in two fascicles is included, which is not too different from the earlier version attributed to Paramārtha. All later Chinese Buddhist catalogs agree that this second version was translated by a Khotan monk named Śikṣānanda (arrived in China around 695 CE). According to the preface to this second version, it was translated in 700 CE (the third year of the sacred calendar of the Great Zhou [*dazhou shengli san nian* 大周聖曆三年]; see T1667:32.583c13). Kashiwagi (1981: 266–366) did an extensive comparison of the stylistic patterns of the passages in these two versions of the *Awakening of Faith* (also

see Kashiwagi [2005]), but because he believes that the *Awakening of Faith* originated from Paramārtha's group, he failed to explore the sociopolitical milieu behind this second "translation" of the *Awakening of Faith*.

3 For example, Frauwallner (1951a: 638ff) (original pagination 149ff.).
4 See Chapter 6, note 73.
5 The preciousness of the Chinese sources has been emphasized again and again by scholars of early Mahāyāna Buddhism, most prominently Paul Harrison, Jan Nattier, and the late KARASHIMA Seishi 辛嶋靜志. I fully concur with their view that, given the limitation of the Sanskrit, Tibetan, and other early Indic sources such as those in Gāndhārī, it is almost impossible to reconstruct the development of early Mahāyāna without making good use of the Chinese sources.
6 Nattier (2008: 17–24).
7 Michael Radich's works are noteworthy in this regard.
8 See Funayama (2007).
9 See Funayama (2002).
10 Funayama (2002: 21ff). Under Paramārtha's lecture notes, Funayama cites later Chinese Buddhist catalogs and includes several works that are allegedly attributed to Paramārtha. While agreeing with Funayama's overarching thesis—the existence of the category of neither literal translation nor purely Chinese translation–I do have doubts about whether these texts allegedly attributed to Paramārtha by later Chinese Buddhist catalogs were really composed by Paramārtha and his group.
11 Sharf (2002: 19) adopts an even stronger position suggesting that to a large extent the transmission of Buddhism was as if the Chinese audience encountered an *already* Sinicized Buddhism—Sinicized in the sense of being mediated through Chinese language and hence indigenous Chinese concepts, and so on. For this reason, Sharf (2002: 21) denies that there were real dialogues between India and China as two discrete cultural traditions when Buddhism was introduced to China. I found Sharf's claim unacceptable because of his over-polemical tone, as Ng (2007: 10) puts it "Sharf's polemical arguments run the risk of implying a Chinese Buddhism that is culturally self-contained, impermeable, and relatively isolated from other Buddhist geographical regions." It is no doubt true, as Sharf points out, that most ancient Chinese Buddhist scholars did not learn Sanskrit and could only read Buddhist texts through Chinese translations. But this does not imply, as Sharf claims, that they could never understand what those Buddhist texts say. In my limited experience, I have not found any concrete example that unmistakably endorses Sharf's extreme linguistic relativism. If Sharf wants to defend such a radical position, the burden of proof is on him: he needs to provide convincing examples to support his claim that, through translation, *all* the Chinese readers did not at all understand Indian Buddhist texts.
12 The original definition of Radich reads: "weak" Sinicization is any change that results in a Buddhism unique to China, regardless of the cause of that change (thus including changes resulting from chance vicissitudes of the translation process, translation errors, and a host of other factors); "strong" Sinicization refers to change resulting in aspects of Buddhism unique to China, caused by factors themselves already unique to China or characteristically Chinese (most typically, Chinese culture, thought or a Chinese "worldview")." See Radich (2008: 164), footnote 490.
13 Cf. Chapter 7, note 41.
14 Cf. 0.2.3 for a brief introduction of the Dilun tradition and 2.3.2 for the close relation between the *Awakening of Faith* and the Dilun tradition pointed out by Mochizuki and Takemura. We may also push the question further back to ask where the doctrinal

background of the Dilun tradition came from. Does the Dilun doctrine that false (i.e., defiled) phenomena are based on the true mind (i.e., Thusness) come from another Sinicization in the strong sense? Lü (1980) suggests that this Dilun doctrine was based on a misunderstanding of the *Laṅkāvatāra-sūtra* that was mainly due to Bodhiruci's problematic Chinese translation of the *Laṅkāvatāra-sūtra* (see Chapter 7, note 40). If Lü was right, then the Dilun doctrine would qualify as another example of strong Sinicization.

15 For example, a scholar who supports the traditional image of Paramārtha might first gloss Paramārtha's notion of *jiexing* in terms of the original awakening of the *Awakening of Faith*, and then employ the notion of original awakening to justify his reading of *jiexing*.

16 For example, the existence of two conflicting interpretations of *jiexing*—one in the *Awakening of Faith* and the other in T2805—gives us an easy clue that at least one of these two cannot be traced to Paramārtha himself.

Bibliography

Aoki, Takashi 青木隆, 1988. "Chūgoku Jironshū ni okeru enjū setsu no tenkai." 中国地論宗における縁集説の展開. *Philosophia*, vol. 75, pp. 147–161.

Aoki, Takashi 青木隆, 1997. "Jironshū nandōha no shinshū enshū setsu to shin'nyo ichi setsu." 地論宗南道派の真修・縁修説と真如依持説. *Tōhōgaku* 東方学, vol. 93, pp. 30–43.

Aoki, Takashi 青木隆, 2000. "Jironshū no yūsoku ron to engi setsu." 地論宗の融即論と縁起説. In Aramaki (2000), pp. 179–204.

Aoki, Takashi 青木隆 and Kŭmgang Taehakkyo Pulgyo Munhwa Yŏn'guso 金剛大學佛教文化研究所, 2012. *Changoe Chironjong Munhŏn Chipsŏng* 藏外地論宗文獻集成. Kŭmgang Haksul Ch'ongsŏ; 8. Sŏul T'ŭkpyŏlsi: Ssiaial.

Aoki, Takashi 青木隆 and Kŭmgang Taehakkyo Pulgyo Munhwa Yŏn'guso 金剛大學佛教文化研究所, 2013. *Changoe Chironjong Munhŏn Chipsŏng Sokchip* 藏外地論宗文獻集成續集. Kŭmgang Haksul Ch'ongsŏ; 18. Sŏul T'ŭkpyŏlsi: Ssiaial.

Aramaki, Noritoshi 荒牧典俊, ed., 2000. *Hokuchō Zui Tō Chūgoku Bukkyō shisōshi* 北朝隋唐中国仏教思想史. Kyōto: Hōzōkan.

Aramaki, Noritoshi 荒牧典俊, 2000. "Hokuchō kōhanki bukkyō shisōshi josetsu." 北朝後半期仏教思想史序説. In Aramaki (2000), pp. 13–85.

Bagchi, S., 1970. *Mahāyānasūtrālaṃkāra of Asaṅga*. Darbhanga: The Mithila Institute.

Brown, Brian E., 1991. *The Buddha Nature: A Study of the Tathāgatagarbha and Ālayavijñāna*. Delhi: Motilal Banarsidass Publishers.

Buescher, Hartmut, 2007. *Sthiramati's Trimśikāvijñaptibhāṣya. Critical Editions of the Sanskrit Text and its Tibetan Translation*. Wien: VÖAW.

Buescher, Hartmut, 2013. "Distinguishing the Two Vasubandhus, the Bhāṣyakāra and the Kośakāra." In Ulrich Timme Kragh (ed.), *The Foundation for Yoga Practitioners: The Buddhist Yogācārabhūmi Treatise and its Adaptation in India, East Asia, and Tibet*. Harvard Oriental Series 75, Cambridge, MA: Harvard University Department of South Asian Studies & Harvard University Press, pp. 368–396.

Buswell, Robert E., 1989. *The Formation of Ch'an Ideology in China and Korea: The Vajrasamadhi-Sutra, a Buddhist Apocryphon*. Princeton, NJ: Princeton University Press.

Buswell, Robert E., 1990. *Chinese Buddhist Apocrypha*. Honolulu: University of Hawai'i Press.

Buswell, Robert E., editor in chief, 2004. *Encyclopedia of Buddhism*. New York: Macmillan Reference USA/Thomson/Gale.

Chen, Jinhua 陳金華, 2002. *Monks and Monarchs, Kinship and Kingship: Tanqian in Sui Buddhism and Politics*. Kyōto: Scuola Italiana di Studi sull'Asia Orientale.

Chen, Yinke 陳寅恪, 1987. *Chen Yinke Wei Jin Nanbeichao shi jiangyan lu* 陳寅恪魏晉南北朝史講演錄. Ed. Wan Shennan 萬繩楠. Hefei: Huangshan shushe.

Cox, Collett, 1995. *Disputed Dharmas, Early Buddhist Theories on Existence: An Annotated Translation of the Section on Factors Dissociated from Thought from Saṅghabhadra's Nyāyānusāra*. Tōkyō: The International Institute for Buddhist Studies.

D'Amato, Mario, 2003. "Can All Beings Potentially Attain Awakening? *Gotra*-theory in the *Mahāyānasūtrālaṃkāra*." *Journal of the International Association of Buddhist Studies*, vol. 26, no. 1, pp. 115–138.

D'Amato, Mario, 2012. *Maitreya's Distinguishing the Middle from the Extremes (Madhyāntavibhāga) : Along with Vasubandhu's Commentary (Madhyāntavibhāga-bhāṣya) : A Study and Annotated Translation*. New York: American Institute of Buddhist Studies, Columbia University's Center for Buddhist Studies and Tibet House US.

Davidson, Ronald M., 1985. "Buddhist Systems of Transformation: *Āśraya-parivṛtti/parāvṛtti* among the Yogācāra." PhD diss., University of California, Berkeley.

Delhey, Martin, 2022. "The *Gotra* Theory in the *Madhyāntavibhāgaṭīkā*." *Journal of Indian Philosophy*, vol. 50, pp. 47–64.

Demiéville, Paul, 1929. *Sur l'authenticité du Ta tch'eng k'i sin louen*. Tōkyō: Maison franco-japonaise.

Dessein, Bart, 1999. *Saṃyuktābhidharmahṛdaya (Heart of Scholasticism with Miscellaneous Additions)*. Delhi: Motilal Banarsidass Publishers.

Etō, Sokuō 衛藤即応, 1932. *Daijō kishinron kōgi* 大乗起信論講義. Tōkyō: Tōhō Shoin.

Feng, Huanzhen 馮焕珍, 2006. *Huigui benjue: Jingying si Huiyuan de zhenshixin yuanqi sixiang yanjiu* 回歸本覺：淨影寺慧遠的真識心緣起思想研究. Beijing: Zhongguo shehui kexue chubanshe.

Frauwallner, Erich, 1951a. "*Amalavijñānam* und *Ālayavijñānam*." Reprinted in Erich Frauwallner, Gerhard Oberhammer and Ernst Steinkellner, 1982. *Kleine Schriften*. Wiesbaden: F. Steiner, pp. 637–648.

Frauwallner, Erich, 1951b. *On the Date of the Buddhist Master of the Law, Vasubandhu*. Roma: Is. M.E.O.

Fukui, Fumimasa 福井文雅, ed., 2003a. *Tōhōgaku no shinshiten* 東方学の新視点. Tōkyō: Goyō shobō.

Fukui, Fumimasa 福井文雅, 2003b. "Indo chūgoku kan no yakujin no jittai." インド・中国間の「訳人」の実態. In Fukui (2003a), pp. 573–589.

Funayama, Tōru 船山徹, 2000. "Jironshū to nanchō kyōgaku." 地論宗と南朝教学. In Aramaki (2000), pp. 123–153.

Funayama, Tōru 船山徹, 2002. "'Kan'yaku' to 'Chūgoku senjutsu' no aida: Kanbun butten ni tokuyū na keitai o megutte." 「漢訳」と「中国撰述」の間——漢文仏典に特有な形態をめぐって. *Bukkyō shigaku kenkyū* 仏教史学研究, vol. 45–1, pp. 1–28.

Funayama, Tōru 船山徹, 2005a. "Shindai sanzō no chosaku no tokuchō—Chū-In bunka kōshō no rei toshite." 真諦三蔵の著作の特徴——中印文化交渉の例として. *Kansai daigaku tōzai gakuzutsu kenkyūsho kiyō* 関西大学東西学術研究所紀要, vol. 38, pp. 97–122.

Funayama, Tōru 船山徹, 2005b. "Seija kan no ni keitō—Riku chō Zui Tō Bukkyōshi chōkan no ichi shiron." 聖者観の二系統——六朝隋唐仏教史鳥瞰の一試論. In Mugitani Kunio 麥谷邦夫 (ed.), *Sankyōkōshō ronsō* 三教交渉論叢. Kyōto: Kyōto daigaku Zinbun kagaku kenkyūzo, pp. 373–408.

Funayama, Tōru 船山徹, 2005c. "Taiyū shōkō." 体用小考. In Usami Bunli 宇佐美文理 (ed.), *Rikuchō Zuitō seishinshi no kenkyū* 六朝精神史の研究. Kyōto: Kyōto daigaku daigakuin bungaku kenkyūka, pp. 125–135.

Funayama, Tōru 船山徹, 2006. "Masquerading as Translation: Examples of Chinese Lectures by Indian Scholar-Monks." *Asia Major, Third Series*, vol. 19, no. 1–2, pp. 39–55.

Funayama, Tōru 船山徹, 2007. "Rikuchō butten no hon'yaku to henshū ni miru chūgokuka no mondai." 六朝仏典の翻訳と編輯に見る中国化の問題. *Tōhō gakuhō* 東方学報, vol. 80, pp. 1–18.

Funayama, Tōru 船山徹, ed., 2012. *Shindai sanzō kenkyū ronshū* 真諦三藏研究論集. Kyōto: Kyōto daigaku jinbun kagaku kenkyūjo.

Giles, Lionel, 1957. *Descriptive Catalogue of the Chinese Manuscripts from Tunhuang in the British Museum*. London: Trustees of the British Museum.

Gimello, Robert M., 1976. "Chih-yen (602–668) and the Foundations of Hua-yen Buddhism." PhD diss., Columbia University.

Girard, Frédéric, 2004. *Traité sur l'acte de foi dans le Grand Véhicule*. Tōkyō: Keio University Press.

Gong, Jun 龔雋, 1995. *Dasheng qixin lun yu foxue zhongguohua* 《大乘起信論》與佛學中國化. Taipei: Wenjin chubanshe.

Griffiths, Paul J. et al., 1989. *The Realm of Awakening: A Translation and Study of the Tenth Chapter of Asaṅga's Mahāyānasaṅgraha*. New York: Oxford University Press.

Hakamaya, Noriaki 袴谷憲昭, 2001. *Yuishiki shisō ronkō* 唯識思想論考. Tōkyō: Daizō Shuppan.

Hakamaya, Noriaki 袴谷憲昭 and Arai Hiroaki 荒井裕明, 1993. *Daijō shōgon kyōron* 大乘莊嚴經論. Tōkyō: Daizō shuppan.

Hakeda, Yoshito S., trans. with commentary, 1967. *The Awakening of Faith*. New York: Columbia University Press.

Harrison, Paul, 1992. "Is the Dharma-kāya the Real 'Phantom Body' of the Buddha?" *Journal of the International Association of Buddhist Studies*, vol. 15, no. 1, pp. 44–94.

Hayashiya, Tomojirō 林屋友次郎, 1941. *Kyōroku kenkyū* 經録研究. Tokyo: Iwanami shoten.

Hirakawa, Akira 平川彰, 1973. *Abidatsuma kusharon sakuin* 阿毘達磨俱舎論索引. Tōkyō: Daizō Shuppan.

Hirakawa, Akira 平川彰, 1990. *Nyoraizō to Daijō kishinron* 如来蔵と大乗起信論. Tōkyō: Shunjūsha.

Hirakawa, Akira 平川彰, Kajiyama Yuichi 梶山雄一, and Takasaki Jikidō 高崎直道, 1982a. *Nyoraizō shisō* 如来蔵思想. Tōkyō: Shunjūsha. In Chinese: *Rulaizang sixiang* 如來藏思想, trans. Li Shijie 李世傑. Taipei: Huayu chubanshe, 1986.

Hirakawa, Akira 平川彰, Kajiyama Yuichi 梶山雄一, and Takasaki Jikidō 高崎直道, 1982b. *Yuishiki shisō* 唯識思想. Tōkyō: Shunjūsha. In Chinese: *Weishi sixiang* 唯識思想, trans. Li Shijie 李世傑. Taipei: Huayu chubanshe, 1986.

Huang, Yongwu 黄永武, ed., 1981. *Dunhuang baozang* 敦煌寶藏 (also "*Tun-huang pao tsang*"). Taipei: Xinwenfeng publisher.

Ibuki, Atsushi 伊吹敦, 1997. "*Kongōkyō kaigi* no shohon no keitō to kokei no fukugen." 『金剛経解義』の諸本の系統と古形の復元. *Ronshō: ajia no bunka to shisō* 論叢アジアの文化と思想, vol. 6, pp. 63–218 (L).

Ibuki, Atsushi 伊吹敦, 1999. "Jironshū nandōha no shinshiki setsu ni tsuite." 地論宗南道派の心識説について. *Bukkyōgaku* 仏教学, vol. 40, pp. 23–59 (L).

Ikeda, Masanori 池田將則, 2009. "Tonkō bon *Shō daijō ron shō* no genpon (Moriya korekushon bon) to kōzoku bubun (Sutain 2554) to ni tsuite: honkoku to kenkyū (zenpen)." 敦煌本『攝大乘論抄』の原本守屋コレクション本）と後續部分（スタイン 2554）とについて——翻刻と研究（前篇）. *Bukkyōshi kenkyū* 仏教史研究, vol. 45, pp. 1–75.

Ikeda, Masanori 池田將則, 2010. "Tonkō bon *Shō daijō ron shō* no genpon (Moriya korekushon bon) to kōzoku bubun (Sutain 2554) to ni tsuite: honkoku to kenkyū (kōhen)." 敦煌本『攝大乘論抄』の原本守屋コレクション本）と後續部分（スタイン 2554）とにについて——翻刻と研究（後篇）. *Bukkyōshi kenkyū* 仏教史研究, vol. 46, pp. 1–73.

Ikeda, Masanori 池田將則, 2012. "Kyō'u shōku shozō Tonkō bunken *Daijō kishin ron sho* (gidai, Hane 333V) ni tsuite." 杏雨書屋所藏敦煌文獻大乘起信論疏 (擬題, 羽333V) について, *Bulgyohak ribyu* 불교학리뷰 (*Critical Review for Buddhist Studies*), vol. 12, pp. 45–167.

Ishii, Kōsei 石井公成, 1993. "Tonkō shutsudo no jironshū shobunken." 敦煌出土の地論宗諸文献. *Indogaku bukkyōgaku kenkyū* 印度学仏教学研究, vol. 84, no. 42–2, pp. 53–57.

Ishii, Kōsei 石井公成, 1995. "Tonkō bunkenchū no jironshū shobunken no kenkyū." 敦煌文献中の地論宗諸文献の研究. *Komazawa daigaku bukkyō gakubu ronshū* 駒沢大学仏教学部論集, vol. 1, pp. 91–96.

Ishii, Kōsei 石井公成, 2003. "*Daijō kishinron* no yōgo to gohō no keikō: NGSM ni yoru hikaku bunseki." <大乘起信論>の用語と語法の傾向 NGSMによる比較分析. *Indogaku bukkyōgaku kenkyū* 印度学仏教学研究, vol. 103, no. 52–1, pp. 202–208 (L).

Ishii, Kōsei 石井公成, 2012. "Shindai kanyo bunken no yōgo to gohō: NGSM ni yoru hikaku bunseki." 真諦關與文獻用語語法--NGSMによる比較分析." In Funayama (2012), pp. 87–120.

Iwata, Taijō 岩田諦静, 1981. *Shoki Yuishiki shisō kenkyū: Seshin-zō "Shōdaijōronshaku"-shōchisō shō no kanzō taishō* 初期唯識思想研究——世親造『摂大乘論』所知相章の漢蔵対照. Tōkyō: Daito Shuppansha.

Iwata, Taijō 岩田諦静, 2004. *Shindai no yuishikisestu no kenkyū* 真諦の唯識説の研究. Tōkyō: Sankibō Busshorin.

Johnston, E. H., ed., 1950. *Ratnagotravibhāga Mahāyānottaratantraśāstra*. Patna: Asaṅga, Bihar Research Society, Museum Buildings.

Jones, Christopher V., 2020a. "Reconsidering the 'Essence' of Indian Buddha-Nature Literature." *Acta Asiatica*, vol. 118, pp. 57–78.

Jones, Christopher V., 2020b. *The Buddhist Self: On Tathāgatagarbha and Ātman*. Honolulu: University of Hawaii Press.

Jorgensen, John, John Makeham, Dan Lusthaus and Mark Strange, trans., 2019. *Treatise on Awakening Mahāyāna Faith*. New York: Oxford University Press.

Kano, Kazuo 加納和雄, 2020. "A Syntactic Analysis of the Term *Tathāgatagarbha* in Sanskrit Fragments and Multiple Meanings of Garbha in the *Mahāparinivāṇamahāsūtra*." *Acta Asiatica*, vol. 118, pp. 17–40.

Karashima, Seishi 辛嶋静志, 2007. "Who Were the Icchantikas?" *Annual Report of The International Research Institute for Advanced Buddhology at Soka University (ARIRIAB)*, vol. 10, pp. 61–80.

Kashiwagi, Hiroo 柏木弘雄, 1981. *Daijō kishinron no kenkyū: Daijō kishinron no seiritsu ni kansuru shiryōronteki kenkyū* 大乘起信論の研究：大乘起信論の成立に関する資料論的研究. Tōkyō: Shunjūsha.

Kashiwagi, Hiroo 柏木弘雄, 2005. *Daijō kishinron: kyū shin yaku* 大乘起信論：旧・新二訳. In *Shin kokuyaku daizōkyō* 新国訳大蔵経, *Ronshu* (2) 論集部 2. Tokyō: Daizō shuppan, pp. 336–589.

Katsumata, Shunkyō 勝又俊教, 1961. *Bukkyō ni okeru shinshiki setsu no kenkyū* 仏教に於ける心識説の研究. Tōkyō: Sankibō Busshorin.

Katsura, Shōryu 桂紹隆, 1974. "A Study of Harivarman's *Tattvasiddhi*." PhD diss., University of Toronto.

Kawamura, Kōshō 河村孝照, ed., 1975–1989. *Shinsan Dai Nihon zoku Zōkyō* 新纂大日本續藏經. Tōkyō: Kokusho Kankōkai.

Keenan, John, P., 1980. "A Study of the *Buddhabhūmyupadeśa*: The Doctrinal Development of the Notion of Wisdom in Yogācāra Thought." PhD diss., University of Wisconsin-Madison.

Keenan, John, P., trans., 2002. *The Interpretation of the Buddha land (BDK English Tripiṭaka 46–II)*. Berkeley, CA: Numata Center for Buddhist Translation and Research.

Keenan, John, P., trans., 2003. *The Summary of the Great Vehicle (BDK English Tripiṭaka 46–III)*. Berkeley, CA: Numata Center for Buddhist Translation and Research.

Keng, Ching 耿晴, 2009. "Yogācāra Buddhism Transmitted or Transformed? Paramārtha (499–569) and His Chinese Interpreters." PhD diss., Harvard University.

Keng, Ching 耿晴, 2011a. "Zai jietuoxue mailuo xia de foshen lun: yi *Shedashenglun* wei zhongxin de tantao." 在解脫學脈絡下的佛身論——以《攝大乘論》為中心之探討. *Monthly Review of Philosophy and Culture* 哲學與文化, vol. 38, no. 3, pp. 119–145.

Keng, Ching 耿晴, 2011b. "Foxing yu foxing gainian de hunyao: yi *Foxing lun* yu *Dasheng qixin lun* wei zhongxin." 「佛性」與「佛姓」概念的混淆：以《佛性論》與《大乘起信論》為中心. In Wang Wensheng 汪文聖 (ed.), *Hanyu zhexue xin shiyu* 漢語哲學新視域. Taibei: Taiwan xuesheng shuju, pp. 69–98.

Keng, Ching 耿晴, 2013a. "Lun Rulaizang sixiang zai jietuoxue shang de genben kunnan: yi *Baoxing lun* wei zhongxin de tantao." 論如來藏思想在解脫學上的根本困難—以《寶性論》為中心的探討. *Hanyu foxue pinglun* 漢語佛學評論, vol. 3, pp. 201–231.

Keng, Ching 耿晴, 2013b. "Fashen wei zhenru suoxian: lun *Nengduan jingang banruo boluomiduo jing shi* duiyu fashen de jieding." 法身為真如所顯 —論《能斷金剛般若波羅蜜多經釋》對於法身的界定. *Taida foxue yanjiu* 臺大佛學研究 (*Taiwan Journal of Buddhist Studies*), vol. 26, pp. 1–56.

Keng, Ching 耿晴, 2014a. "*Bianzhongbianlun* songweng zhong de liangzhong weishi sanxingshuo moxing." 《辯中邊論》頌文中的兩種唯識三性說模型. *Taida foxue yanjiu* 臺大佛學研究 (*Taiwan Journal of Buddhist Studies*), vol. 28, pp. 51–104.

Keng, Ching 耿晴, 2014b. "A Re-examination of the Relationship between the *Awakening of Faith* and Dilun School Thought, Focusing on the Works of Huiyuan." In Lin Chen-kuo and Michael Radich (2014), pp. 183–215.

Keng, Ching 耿晴, 2015. "*Dasheng zhuangyan jing lun* de liangzhong weishi sanxingshuo moxing." 《大乘莊嚴經論》的兩種唯識三性說模型. *Taida foxue yanjiu* 臺大佛學研究 (*Taiwan Journal of Buddhist Studies*), vol. 30, pp. 1–64.

Keng, Ching 耿晴 and Michael Radich, 2019. "Paramārtha." In Jonathan Silk, Richard Bowring, Vincent Eltschinger, and Michael Radich (eds.), *Brill's Encyclopedia of Buddhism, Volume Two: Lives*. Leiden: Brill, pp. 752–758.

Kim, Jaegweon 金才權, 2007. "The Term '*prabhāvita*' in Yogācāra Texts, with Special Reference to the *Madhyāntavibhāgaṭīkā*." *Indogaku bukkyōgaku kenkyū* 印度學佛教學研究, vol. 110, no. 55–2, pp. 75–78 (L).

Kimura, Kunikazu 木村邦和, 1985. "Tonkō shutsudo *Shōdaijōron shoshō* ni mirareru yuishikisetsu (ni)." 敦煌出土『摂大乗論疏章』に見られる唯識説(二). *Indogaku bukkyōgaku kenkyū* 印度學佛教學研究, vol. 67, no. 34–1, pp. 236–241.

King, Sallie B., 1991. *Buddha Nature*. Albany: State University of New York Press.

Kitano, Shintarō 北野新太郎, 1999. "Sanshō setsu no hensen ni okeru Seshin no ichi: Ueda, Nagao ronsō o megutte." 三性説の変遷における世親の位置　上田・長尾論争をめぐって. *Kokusai bukkyōgaku daigakuin daigaku kenkyū kiyō* 国際仏教学大学院大学研究紀要, vol. 2, pp. 69–101.

Kitano, Shintarō 北野新太郎, 2001. "Vijñānapariṇāma: sono jikomujunteki nijū kōzō: sanshō setsu to no kankei o chūshin to shite." Vijñānapariṇāma一その自己矛盾的二重構造 一三性説との関係を中心として一. *Kokusai bukkyōgaku daigakuin daigaku kenkyū kiyō* 国際仏教学大学院大学研究紀要, vol. 4, pp. 262–291.

Kongō daigaku bukkyō bunka kenkyūjo 金剛大学仏教文化研究所, ed., 2010. *Jiron shisō no keisei to henyō* 地論思想の形成と変容. Tōkyō: Kokusho Kankokai.

Kongō daigaku bukkyō bunka kenkyūjo 金剛大学仏教文化研究所, ed., 2017a. *Tonkō shahon "Daijō kishinron sho" no kenkyū* 敦煌寫本「大乘起信論疏」の研究. Tōkyō: Kokusho Kankōkai.

Kongō daigaku bukkyō bunka kenkyūjo 金剛大学仏教文化研究所, ed., 2017b. *Jironshū no kenkyū* 地論宗の研究. Tōkyō: Kokusho Kankokai.

Kotyk, Jeffrey, 2021. *Analysis of the Middle and Extremes*. Moraga, CA: BDK America.

Kritzer, Robert, 2019."Vasubandhu." In Jonathan Silk, Richard Bowring, Vincent Eltschinger, and Michael Radich (eds.), *Brill's Encyclopedia of Buddhism, Volume Two: Lives*. Leiden: Brill, pp. 492–506.

de La Vallée Poussin, Louis, 1928–29. *Vijñaptimātratāsiddhi: La siddhi de Hiuan-Tsang*. Paris: Paul Geuthner.

Lamotte, Étienne, 1973. *La somme du Grand Véhicule d'Asanga (Mahayanasamgraha)*. Louvain-la-Neuve: Université de Louvain Institut orientaliste.

Lévi, Sylvain, 1907. *Mahāyāna-Sūtrālaṃkāra: exposé de la doctrine du Grand Véhicule selon le système Yogācāra*. Paris: H. Champion.

Lévi, Sylvain, 1925. *Vijñaptimātratāsiddhi: Deux traités de Vasubandhu: Viṁśatikā (La vingtaine) accompagnée d'une explication en prose/ et Triṁśikā (La trentaine) avec le commentaire de Sthiramati*. Paris: H. Champion.

Li, Zijie (Ri, Shishō) 李子捷, 2020. *Kukyō ichijō hōshōron to higashiajia bukkyō : go nanaseiki no nyoraizō shinnyo shushōsetsu no kenkyū* 「究竟一乗宝性論」と東アジア仏教 : 五-七世紀の如来蔵・真如・種姓說の研究. Tōkyō: Kokushokankōkai.

Liebenthal, Walter, 1958. "New Light on the *Mahāyāna-śraddotpāda śāstra*." *T'oung Pao*, vol. XLVI, pp. 155–216.

Lin, Chen-kuo 林鎮國 and Michael Radich, eds., 2014. *A Distant Mirror: Articulating Indic Ideas in Sixth and Seventh Century Chinese Buddhism*. Hamburg Buddhist Studies Series 3, Hamburg: Hamburg University Press.

Liu, Ming-wood 廖明活, 2005. "Li xing liangzhong foxing shuofa de xingcheng he yanbian 理、行兩種佛性說法的形成和演變." *Journal of the Center for Buddhist Studies* 佛學研究中心學報, vol. 10, pp. 119–150.

Lü, Cheng 呂澂, 1980. "*Qixin* yu Chan—dui *Dasheng qixin lun* laili de tantao." 起信與禪--對《大乘起信論》來歷的探討. In Zhang Mantao 張曼濤 (ed.), *Dacheng qixin lun yu Lengyan Jing kaobian. Xiandai Fojiao xueshu congkan* 大乘起信論與楞嚴經考辨 現代佛教學術叢刊, no. 35. Taibei: Dacheng wenhua chubanshe, pp. 299–314.

Lü, Cheng 呂澂, 1982. *Zhongguo foxue sixiang gailun* 中國佛學思想概論. Taipei: Tianhua Publication.

Lusthaus, Dan, 2002. *Buddhist Phenomenology: A Philosophical Investigation of Yogacara Buddhism and the Ch'eng Wei-shih Lun*. London; New York, NY: Routledge Curzon.

Magnin, Paul, 1979. *La vie et l'œuvre de Huisi* 慧思: *515–577: les origines de la secte bouddhique chinoise du Tiantai*. Paris: École française d'Extrême-Orient: dépositaire, Adrien-Maisonneuve.

Makransky, John, 1997. *Buddhahood Embodied: Sources of Controversy in India and Tibet*. Albany, NY: SUNY Press.

McRae, John R., 1986. *The Northern School and the Formation of Early Ch'an Buddhism*. Honolulu: University of Hawai'i Press.

Mochizuki, Shinkō 望月信亨, 1922. *Daijō kishinron no kenkyū* 大乗起信論の研究. Tōkyō: Kanao Bun'endō.

Muller, A. Charles, ed., 2021. *Digital Dictionary of Buddhism*. http://buddhism-dict.net/ddb (accessed March 31, 2021).

Nagao, Gajin 長尾雅人, 1964. *Madhyāntavibhāga-bhāṣya: A Buddhist Philosophical Treatise*. Tōkyō: Suzuki Research Foundation.

Nagao, Gajin 長尾雅人, 1982–1987. *Shōdaijōron: Wayaku to chūkai* 摂大乗論：和訳と注解. Tōkyō: Kōdansha.

Nagao, Gajin 長尾雅人, 1991. *Mādhyamaka and Yogācāra: A Study of Mahāyāna Philosophies: Collected Papers of G.M. Nagao*. Ed. Collated, and Trans. L. S. Kawamura in collaboration with G. M. Nagao. Albany: State University of New York Press.

Nagao, Gajin 長尾雅人, 1994. *An Index to Asaṅga's Mahāyānasaṃgraha*. Tōkyō: The International Institute for Buddhist Studies.

Nakamura, Zuiryū 中村瑞隆, 1961. *Kukyō ichijō hōshōron kenkyū: bon kan taishō* 究竟一乗宝性論研究：梵漢対照. Tōkyō: Sankibō Busshorin.

Nattier, Jan, 2003. *A Few Good Men: The Bodhisattva Path according to The Inquiry of Ugra (Ugraparipṛcchā)*. Honolulu: University of Hawai'i Press.

Nattier, Jan, 2008. *A Guide to the Earliest Chinese Buddhist Translations: Texts from the Eastern Han* 東漢 *and Three Kingdoms* 三國 *Periods*. Tokyo: The International Research Institute for Advanced Buddhology, Soka Univ.

Nishio, Kyōo 西尾京雄, 1982. *The Buddhabhūmi-sūtra. The Buddhabhūmivyākhyāna of Śīlabhadra*. Tōkyō: Kokusho Kankokai.

Ng, Zhiru, 2007. *The Making of a Savior Bodhisattva: Dizang in Medieval China*. Honolulu: University of Hawai'i Press.

Nguyen, Cuong Tu, 1990. "Sthiramati's Interpretation of Buddhology and Soteriology." PhD diss., Harvard University.

Oda, Akihiro 織田 顕祐, 1990. "Tonkō bon *Shōdaijōron shō* ni tsuite." 敦煌本『摂大乗論抄』について. *Indogaku bukkyōgaku kenkyū* 印度学仏教学研究, vol. 76, no. 38–2, pp. 223–229.

Odani, Nobuchiyo 小谷信千代, 1984. *Daijō shōgon kyōron no kenkyū* 大乗荘厳経論の研究. Kyōto: Bun'eidō.

Okamoto, Ippei 岡本一平, 2010. "Jōyō-ji Eon no chosaku zengo kankei ni kansuru shiron." 浄影寺慧遠の著作前後関係に関する試論. In Kongō daigaku bukkyō bunka kenkyūjo (2010), pp. 162–183.

Ono, Genmyō 小野玄妙, 1974–1988. *Bussho kaisetsu daijiten* 仏書解説大辞典. Tōkyō: Daitō Shuppansha.

Orzech, Charles D., 1998. *Politics and Transcendent Wisdom: The Scripture for Humane Kings in the Creation of Chinese Buddhism*. University Park, PA: Pennsylvania State University Press.

Ōtake, Susumu 大竹晋, 2001. "Bodairushi no ushinawareta san chosaku." 菩提留支の失われた三著作. *Tōhōgaku* 東方学, vol. 102, pp. 34–48.

Ōtake, Susumu 大竹晋, 2012. "Shindai *Kushiki shō* o megutte." 真諦『九識章』をめぐって. In Funayama (2012), pp. 121–153.

Ōtake, Susumu 大竹晋, 2017. *Daijō kishinron seiritsu mondai no kenkyū: Daijō kishinron wa kanbun bukkyō bunken kara no pacchiwāku* 大乗起信論成立問題の研究：『大乗起信論』は漢文仏教文献からのパッチワーク. Tōkyō: Kokusho Kankōkai.

Paul, Diana Y., 1984. *Philosophy of Mind in Sixth-century China: Paramartha's "Evolution of Consciousness."* Stanford, CA: Stanford University Press.

Potter, Karl H., 1999. *Buddhist Philosophy from 100 to 350 A.D. Encyclopedia of Indian Philosophies*. Vol. 8. Delhi: Motilal Banarsidass.

Pradhan, Prahallad, ed., 1975. *Abhidharmakośabhāṣyam*. Pātaliputram: Kāśīprasadajāya savāla-Anuśīlan-Samsthānam.

Prasad, H. S., 1991. *The Uttaratantra of Maitreya*. Delhi: Sri Satguru Publications.

Pruden, Leo M., trans., 1988–1990. *Abhidharmakośabhāṣyam*. From Louis de La Vallée Poussin's French version. Berkeley, CA: Asian Humanities Press.

Radich, Michael, 2008. "The Doctrine of **Amalavijñāna* in Paramārtha (499–569), and Later Authors to Approximately 800 C.E." *ZINBUN* 人文, vol. 41, pp. 45–174.

Radich, Michael, 2012. "External Evidence Relating to Works Ascribed to Paramārtha, with a Focus on Traditional Chinese Catalogues." In Funayama (2012), pp. 39–102 (L).

Radich, Michael, 2014. "On the Sources, Style and Authorship of Chapters of the Synoptic *Suvarṇaprabhāsottama-sūtra* T664 Ascribed to Paramārtha (Part 1)." *Annual Report of The International Research Institute for Advanced Buddhology*, vol. 17, pp. 207–244.

Radich, Michael, 2015a. "*Tathāgatagarbha* Scriptures." In Jonathan Silk, Oskar von Hinüber, and Vincent Eltschinger (eds.), *Brill's Encyclopedia of Buddhism, Volume One: Literature and Languages*. Leiden: Brill, pp. 261–273.

Radich, Michael, 2015b. *The Mahāparinirvāṇa-mahāsūtra and the Emergence of Tathāgatagarbha Doctrine*. Hamburg Buddhist Studies 5. Hamburg: Hamburg University Press.

Radich, Michael, 2015c. "Tibetan Evidence for the Sources of Chapters of the Synoptic *Suvarṇa-prabhāsottama-sūtra* T664 Ascribed to Paramārtha." *Buddhist Studies Review*, vol. 32, no. 2, pp. 245–270.

Radich, Michael, 2019a. "Was the *Mahāparinirvāṇa-sūtra* 大般涅槃經 T7 Translated by 'Faxian'? An Exercise in the Computer-Assisted Assessment of Attributions in the Chinese Buddhist Canon." *Hualin International Journal of Buddhist Studies: E-journal*, vol. 2, no. 1, pp. 229–279.

Radich, Michael, 2019b. "Zhu Fahu shifou xiuding guo T474?" 竺法護是否修訂過 T474? *Foguang xuebao* 佛光學報, vol. 5, no. 2, pp. 15–38.

Radich, Michael, 2019c. "Fei Changfang's Treatment of Sengyou's Anonymous Texts." *Journal of the American Oriental Society*, vol. 139, no. 4, pp. 819–41.

Ruegg, David Seyfort, 1969. *La théorie du tathagatagarbha et du gotra: études sur la sotériologie et la gnoséologie du bouddhisme*. Paris: École Française d'Extrême-Orient.

Ruegg, David Seyfort, 1976. "The Meaning of the Term '*Gotra*' and the Textual History of the '*Ratnagotravibhāga*,'" *Bulletin of the School of Oriental and African Studies*, vol. 39, no. 2, pp. 341–363.

Saitō, Akira 齋藤明, 2020. "Buddha-Nature or Buddha Within? Revisiting the Meaning of *Tathāgata-garbha*." *Acta Asiatica*, vol. 118, pp. 1–15.

Sakuma, Hidenori 佐久間秀範, 1990. *Die Asrayaparivrtti-theorie in der Yogacarabhumi*. Stuttgart: F. Steiner Verlag Wiesbaden.

Sakuma, Hidenori 佐久間秀範, 2006 (2008). "On Doctrinal Similarities Between Sthiramati and Xuanzang." *Journal of the International Association of Buddhist Studies*, vol. 29, no. 2, pp. 357–382.

Schmithausen, Lambert, 1969. *Der Nirvana-Abschnitt in der Viniscayasamgrahani der Yogacarabhumih*. Wien: Böhlaus.

Schmithausen, Lambert, 1971. "Philologische Bemerkungen zum *Ratnagotravibhāga*." *Wiener Zeitschrift für die Kunde Südasiens*, vol. XV/1971, pp. 123 ff., esp. 123–130.

Schmithausen, Lambert, 1987. *Ālayavijñana: On the Origin and the Early Development of a Central Concept of Yogacara Philosophy*. Tōkyō: International Institute for Buddhist Studies.

Schmithausen, Lambert, 1991. "*Yogācārabhūmi: Sopadhikā* and *Nirupadhikā Bhūmiḥ*." In Li Zheng 李錚 and Jiang Zhongxin 蔣忠新 (eds.), *Papers in Honour of Prof. Dr. Ji Xianlin on the Occasion of His 80th Birthday (II)*. Jiangxi: Jiangxi renmin chubanshe, pp. 687–710.

Schmithausen, Lambert, 2005. *On the Problem of the External World in the Ch'eng wei shih lun*. Tōkyō: The International Institute for Buddhist Studies.

Schmithausen, Lambert, 2014. *The Genesis of Yogācāra-Vijñānavāda: Responses and Reflections*. Tōkyō: International Institute for Buddhist Studies.

Sharf, Robert, 2002. *Coming to Terms with Chinese Buddhism: A Reading of the Treasure Store Treatise*. Honolulu: University of Hawai'i Press.

Shengkai, 聖凱, 2006. *Shelun xuepai yanjiu* 攝論學派研究. Beijing: Zongjiao wenhua chubanshe.

Silk, Jonathan A., 2000. "The Yogācāra Bhikṣu." In Jonathan A. Silk (ed.), *Wisdom, Compassion, and the Search for Understanding: The Buddhist Studies Legacy of Gadjin M. Nagao*. Honolulu: University of Hawai'i Press, pp. 265–314.

Sponberg, Alan, 1983. "The *Trisvabhāva* Doctrine in India and China." *Ryūkoku Daigaku Bukkyō Bunka Kenkyūjo Kiyō* 龍谷大学仏教文化研究所紀要, vol. 22, pp. 97–119.

Su, Gongwang 蘇公望, 1978. "Zhendi sanzang nianpu." 眞諦三藏年譜. In Zhang Mantao 張曼濤 (ed.), *Zhongguo fojiaoshi zhuan ji. Xiandai Fojiao xueshu congkan* 中國佛教史傳記 現代佛教學術叢刊, no. 13. Taibei: Dacheng wenhua chubanshe, pp. 339–400.

Suguro, Shinjō 勝呂信静, 1989. *Shoki yuishiki shisō no kenkyū* 初期唯識思想の研究. Tōkyō: Shunjūsha.

Suguro, Shinjō 勝呂信静 and Shimokawabe Kiyoshi 下川邊季由, 2007. *Shōdaijōron shaku* 摂大乗論釈. Tōkyō: Daizō Shuppan.

Suzuki, Daisetsu T., 1934. *An Index to the Lankavatara Sutra*. Second revised and enlarged edition. New Delhi: Mushiram Manoharlal Pvt. Ltd.

Takakusu, Junjirō 高楠順次郎 and Watanabe Kaigyoku 渡辺海旭, 1940. *Taishō shinshū Daizōkyō* 大正新修大蔵経. Tōkyō: Daizō Shuppan.

Takamine, Ryōshū 高峯了州, 1963. *Kegon shisōshi* 華厳思想史. Kyōto: Hyakkaen.

Takasaki, Jikidō 高崎直道, 1966. *A Study on the Ratnagotravibhaga (Uttaratantra), Being a Treatise on the Tathagatagarbha Theory of Mahayana Buddhism*. Roma: Istituto italiano per il Medio ed Estremo Oriente.

Takasaki, Jikidō 高崎直道, 1974. *Nyoraizō shisō no keisei: Indo Daijō Bukkyō shisō kenkyū* 如来蔵思想の形成：インド大乗仏教思想研究. Tōkyō: Shunjūsha.

Takasaki, Jikidō 高崎直道, 1989. *Nyoraizō shisō (II)* 如来蔵思想 (II). Kyōto: Hōzōkan.

Takasaki, Jikidō 高崎直道, 2005. *Busshō ron* 仏性論. In *Shin kokuyaku daizōkyō* 新国訳大蔵経, *Ronshu* (2) 論集部 2. Tokyō: Daizō Shuppan, pp. 1–332.

Takemura, Makio 竹村牧男, 1990. "Jiron shū to *Daijō kishinron*." 地論宗と大乗起信論. In Hirakawa Akira 平川彰 (ed.), *Nyoraizō to Daijō kishinron* 如来蔵と大乗起信論. Tōkyō: Shunjūsha, pp. 335–375.

Takemura, Makio 竹村牧男, 1993. *Daijō kishinron dokushaku* 大乗起信論読釈. Tōkyō: Sankibō Busshorin.

Tang, Yongtong 湯用彤, 1938. *Han Wei liang-Jin Nanbeichao Fojiao shi* 漢魏兩晉南北朝佛教史. Reprint. Beijing: Beijing daxue chubanshe; Xinhua shudian jingxiao, 1997.

Tzohar, Roy, 2020. "Turning Earth to Gold: The Early Yogācāra Understanding of Experience Following Non-conceptual Cognition." In Mark Siderits, Ching Keng and

John Spackman (eds.), *Buddhist Philosophy of Consciousness: Tradition and Dialogue*. Leiden and Boston: Brill-Rodopi, pp. 89–112.

Ueda, Yoshifumi 上田義文, 1951. *Bukkyō shisōshi kenkyū: Indo no Daijō Bukkyō* 仏教思想史研究：インドの大乗仏教. Kyōto: Nagata Bunshodō.

Ueda, Yoshifumi 上田義文, 1967. "Two Main Streams of Thought in Yogācāra Philosophy." *Philosophy East and West*, vol. 17, no. 1/4, pp. 155–165.

Ui, Hakuju 宇井伯寿, 1930. *Indo tetsugaku kenkyū (6)* インド哲学研究 (第六). Tōkyō: Kōshisha Shobō.

Ui, Hakuju 宇井伯寿, 1935. *Shōdaijōron kenkyū* 摂大乗論研究. Tōkyō: Iwanami Shoten.

Waldron, William S., 2003. *The Buddhist Unconscious: the Ālaya-vijñana in the Context of Indian Buddhist Thought*. London; New York: Routledge Curzon.

Willemen, Charles, Bart Dessein, and Collett Cox, 1998. *Sarvāstivāda Buddhist Scholasticism*. Leiden; New York: Brill.

Wogihara, Unrai 荻原雲來, 1930. *Bodhisattvabhūmi; A Statement of Whole Course of the Bodhisattva (Being Fifteenth Section of Yogācārabhūmi)*. Reprint. Tōkyō: Sankibō, 1971.

Yamabe, Nobuyoshi 山部能宜, 1989. "Shūji no hon'u to shinkun no mondai ni tsuite." 種子の本有と新熏の問題について. *Nihon bukkyō gakkai nenpō* 日本仏教学会年報, vol. 54, pp. 43–58 (L).

Yamabe, Nobuyoshi 山部能宜, 1990. "Shinnyo shoennen shūzi ni tsuite." 真如所縁縁種子について. *Nihon no Bukkyō to bunka: KITABATAKE Tensei kyōju kanreki kinen* 日本の仏教と文化：北畠典生教授還暦記念, pp. 63–87 (L).

Yamabe, Nobuyoshi 山部能宜, 1991. "Shūji no hon'u to shinkun no mondai ni tsuite (II)." 種子の本有と新熏の問題について(II). *Bukkyōgaku kenkyū* 仏教学研究, vol. 47, pp. 93–112.

Yamaguchi, Susumu 山口益, 1934. *Madhyantavibhagatika; exposition systématique du Yogacaravijnaptivada*. Nagoya: Librairie Hajinkaku.

Yeh, Ah-yueh (Yō, Agetsu) 葉阿月, 1975. *Yuishiki shisō no kenkyū: konpon shinjitsu to shite no sanshō setsu o chūshin ni shite* 唯識思想の研究: 根本眞實としての三性説を中心にして. Tōkyō: Kokusho Kankōkai.

Yinshun 印順, 1956. *Yi fofa yanjiu fofa* 以佛法研究佛法. Taibei: Shandaosi fojing liutongchu.

Yinshun 印順, 1995. "*Qixin lun* yu Funan Dasheng." 起信論與扶南大乘. *Zhonghua foxue xuebao* 中華佛學學報, vol. 8, pp. 1–16.

Yokoyama, Kōitsu 横山紘一, and Hirosawa Takayuki 広沢隆之, 1996. *Index to the Yogācārabhūmi*, Chinese-Sanskrit-Tibetan. Tōkyō: Sankibō Busshorin.

Yoshimura, Makoto 吉村誠, 2003a. "*Shōron* gakuha no shinshiki setsu ni tsuite." 摂論学派の心識説について. *Komazawa daigaku bukkyō gakubu ronshū* 駒沢大学仏教学部論集, vol. 34, pp. 223–242.

Yoshimura, Makoto 吉村誠, 2003b. "Chūgoku yuishiki shogakuha no tenkai." 中国唯識諸学派の展開. In Fukui (2003a), pp. 201–230.

Yoshimura, Makoto 吉村誠, 2007. "Shindai no amara shiki to Shōron gakuha no kushiki setsu." 真諦の阿摩羅識と摂論学派の九識説. *Indogaku bukkyōgaku kenkyū* 印度学仏教学研究, vol. 112, no. 56–1, pp. 177–183.

Yoshimura, Makoto 吉村誠, 2013. *Chūgoku yuishiki shisōshi no kenkyū: Genjō to Yuishiki gakuha* 中国唯識思想史研究: 玄奘と唯識学派. Tōkyō: Daizō Shuppan.

Yoshizu, Yoshihide 吉津 宜英, 1972. "Eon no *Kishinronsho* o meguru shomondai." 慧遠の『起信論疏』をめぐる諸問題. *Komazawa daigaku bukkyō gakuburonshū* 駒沢大学仏教学部論集, vol. 3, pp. 82–97.

Yoshizu, Yoshihide 吉津 宜英, 2000. "*Daijō shikan hōmon* no saikentō." 『大乗止観法門』の再検討. *Indogaku bukkyōgaku kenkyū* 印度学仏教学研究, vol. 96, no. 48–2, pp. 12–18.

Yoshizu, Yoshihide 吉津 宜英, 2003. "Shindai sanzō yakushutsu kyōritsuron kenkyūshi." 真諦三蔵訳出経律論研究誌. *Komazawa daigaku bukkyō gakubu kenkyū kiyō* 駒沢大学仏教学部研究紀要, vol. 61, pp. 225–286.

Zimmermann, Michael, 2002. *A Buddha Within: The Tathāgatagarbhasūtra: The Earliest Exposition of the Buddha-nature Teaching in India*. Tōkyō: International Research Institute for Advanced Buddhology, Soka University.

Zimmermann, Michael, 2014. "The Process of Awakening in Early Texts on Buddha-Nature in India." In Lin Chen-kuo and Michael Radich (2014), pp. 513–528.

Zimmermann, Michael, 2020. "A Multi-associative Term: Why *Tathāgatagarbha* Is Not One and the Same." *Acta Asiatica*, vol. 118, pp. 41–55.

Index

NOTE: Page references in *italics* refer to tables; page numbers followed by n. indicates notes.

Ueda's interpretation of (*see under* Ueda)
Ui's interpretation of (*see under* Ui)
aspect of arising-and-ceasing [of the mind] 29–31, *134*
aspect of Thusness [of the mind] 30, *134*, 137–8, 240 n.47
āśrayaparivṛtti/*āśrayaparāvṛtti* (*zhuanyi* 轉依) 22, 32, 151, 180, 189, 224 n.4, 243 n.9. *See also* transformation of the basis
Asvabhāva 221 n.31, 237 n.50, 248 n.9
Aśvaghoṣa 38, 42
attained buddha-gotra (*deguo foxing* 得果佛性, *zhide xing* 至得性, *zhiguo foxing* 至果佛性) 129–31, 202–3
atuona shi 阿陀那識
Asaṅga and Vasubandhu (*Shelun*) on *atuona shi* 107–8
synonym for 7th consciousness 103–4, 108–9, 137, 139, 234 n.3
synonym for 8th/base consciousness 107
avikāra (unchangeable) 14, 166, 185, 187
Awakening of Faith (*Awakening of Faith in Mahāyāna*)
authorship of 3, 5, 16, 37–46
and Bodhiruci 42–4, 56, 251 n.40, 255 n.14
deviation from Indian Buddhism 46–7
and Dilun (*see under* Dilun (tradition))
as example of strong Sinicization 217
and *jiexing* (*see under jiexing*)
and *Laṅkāvatāra-sūtra* 15, 42, 44, 190, 226 n.47, 251 n.40, 251 n.45
no reference in T2805 55
and Paramārtha 1, 3–19, 37–51, 56, 123–50, 157, 174, 177, 190, 211–4, 217, 223 n.44, 229 n.57, 240 n.50, 254 n.2
second "translation" of 42, 254 n.2
and Shelun masters (*see under* Shelun masters)
as strong *tathāgatagarbha* 7, 14, 177, 190–3, 208, 214, 217
and Tathāgatagarbha 3–5, 10–15, 157, 177, 190–3, 208, 214, 217
tenet of 3–4, 6, 24, 30, 226 n.47 (*see also* One Mind in Two Aspects; original awakening)

Bahuvrīhi 23, 180, 247 n.3, 248 n.4
Baoliang 寶亮 110, 252 n.43
and *Da boniepan jing jijie* 54, 94, 239 n.19
terminology of *66*, 71, 75, *76–8*, *81–9*, *91*, 234 n.79
baoshen 報身 41, 43. *See also* enjoyment-body
base consciousness 22, 107–8, 110, 137, 139, 151, 154, 160, 163, 237 n.63, 253 n.72. *See also* 8th consciousness; *Shelun Jiexing* Passage (2); storehouse consciousness; T2805 *Jiexing* Passage (1)
as *atuona shi* (*see under atuona shi*)
and enjoyment-body 34–5, *117–18*, 118–21, 127–8, *128*
and *jiexing* 26–7, 29, 32, 34–5
in Jizang 127–8, *128*
and permeation 27, 103, 233 n.66
Bashi yi 八識義 60–1, *64–8*, *70*, *98*, 109, 191, 225 n.33
basis. *See also* transformation of the basis
basis for noble people 22, 31, 152–6, *158–9*, 164, 174 (*see also Shelun Jiexing* Passage (2); T2805 *Jiexing* Passage (1))
basis for ordinary people 22, 152–5, *158* (*see also Shelun Jiexing* Passage (2); T2805 *Jiexing* Passage (1))
undefiled basis 4, 137
benefits
attainment of 115–16
benefits for oneself 114–16, 237 n.56
benefits for others 114–16
benji 本記 9
benjue 本覺 4, 248 n.7. *See also* original awakening
benyou zhongzi 本有種子 160. *See also* originally existent seeds
benyou wulou zhongzi 本有無漏種子 (*see under* originally existent seeds)
bhūmi (stage) 33, 93, *95*, 152, 156, *158*, 184, 201. *See also* bodhisattva stage
bodhi 115, 204, 239 n.19

bodhicitta 161, 201. *See also* mind of enlightenment
Bodhiruci 菩提流支 42–4, 56, 79, 94, 184, 216, 230 n.20, 235 n.30, 251 n.40, 255 n.14
 and *Awakening of Faith* (*see under Awakening of Faith*)
 terminology of *54*, *63*, *68*, 75, *82–3*, *99*, 228 n.21, 231 n.35
Bodhisattvabhūmi 162–3, 166, *207*, 243 n.104, 252 n.68, 254 n.80
bodhisattvas by designation (*jiaming pusa* 假名菩薩) 76–7, 79, 91, 152
bodhisattva stage 54, 93–5, 101–2, 115–16, 152–6, *158*–61, 164–5, 169, 174, 197, 205, 221 n.31, 236 n.37, 236 n.38, 243 n.5, 243 n.8, 243 n.9, 244 n.11, 244 n.22. *See also* first bodhisattva stage
 division of 232 n.48, 232 n.49, 245 n.28
 tenth bodhisattva stage 112–14, *158*, 236 n.32, 237 n.59
body of liberation (*jietuo shen* 解脫身) 32, 116, 118, 226 n.50
Brown, Brian E. 179
Buddha-body 43, 117–18, 120–1, 180, 192–3, 209, 226 n.56, 250 n.29. *See also* dharma-body; enjoyment-body; transformation-body
 mapping to five dharmas *207*, 252 n.61
 mapping to two *buddha-gotra* (*see under buddha-gotra*)
 three similes (icon, monarch, image) 197–200
Buddha-dharmas (*fofa* 佛法) 113, 167
buddha-gotra 15, 17, 56, 110–11, 129–34, 166–8, 173, 177, 191–5, 197–207, 211, 214, 230 n.16, 231 n.22, 235 n.26, 246 n.53, 252 n.67, 254 n.79, 254 n.82. *See also* attained *buddha-gotra*; cultivated *gotra*; drawn-forth [*buddha-*]*gotra*; *gotra*; innate [*buddha-*] *gotra*
 conditioned *vs.* unconditioned 173, 205
 Dilun masters on *buddha-gotra* 129–30, 203
 FDJL on *buddha-gotra* 163–5, 169, *207*
 identification with dharma-body and Thusness 166–7, 186–8, 191–2, 194–5, *204*, *207*, 239 n.26, 250 n.29
 Laṅkāvatāra-sūtra on *buddha-gotra* 173, 204–5, 253 n.72
 mapping to three Buddha-bodies 166, 192–3, 197–200, *207*, 209
 MSA on *buddha-gotra* 207
 of principle *vs.* of practice 203–6, 214, 253 n.72
 RGV on *buddha-gotra* 191–2, 197–8, 254 n.79
 three kinds of 56, 129–32, 166, 201–2
 two kinds (innate *vs.* cultivated) 162–6
 two kinds (innate *vs.* drawn-forth) 129–32, *133*, *134*, 166–9, 173, 192, 197–206, *207*, 252 n.67
 two similes: a treasure *vs.* a tree 188, 197–8, *199*
 uncontaminated *gotra* 164, 174
buddhahood 2, 27, 35, 112, *158*, 180, 251 n.38, 252 n.65
 attain/attainment of 12–13, 35, 120, 127, *128*, *133*, 166, 170, 172, 174, 188, 193, 197, 203, 220 n.6, 226 n.55, 246 n.46, 253 n.72
 and buddha-*gotra* 130–3, 214
 disclosed/disclosure of 183–5, 189, 203, 214, 253 n.72
 and disclosing cause 129–32
 as unconditioned 110–11, 131, 187, 239 n.26
 universal 3–4
Buddha nature (*foxing* 佛性) 15, 26–7, 47, 179, 225 n.31

cause. *See also* cause proper
 cause in terms of habituation (*xiyin* 習因) 90, *92*, 92–3, 232 n.42, 232 n.43
 cause in terms of production (*shengyin* 生因) 90, *92*
 cause of retribution (*baoyin* 報因) 90, *92*, 92–3

disclosing cause (*liaoyin* 了因) (*see under* disclosing cause)
generative cause (*shengyin* 生因) 110–11, 131, 235 n.25, 235 n.30, 239 n.24
six causes 90, *92*
three causal conditions *92*
three causes 93, 201–2

cause proper (*zhengyin* 正因) 111, 127, 157, 165, 170, 228 n.39, 235 n.25, 238 n.13, 239 n.22
for buddhahood/dharma-body 129–32, *132–4*, 201–3

CBETA 58, 157

CBReader 9, 58–60, *69*, 71, 73, 90, 104

Chang'an 長安 *73*, 79, 101
circulation of the *Awakening of Faith* in 37, 123–4
and T2805 54, 105, 124, 126, 132
and Tanqian, Daoni, Huiyuan, Jizang 59, 98, 105, 135, 139, 142–50, 212, 217, 241 n.75, 242 n.78, 242 n.90

A Chapter on the Distinction among the Three Bodies. See under Sanshen fenbie pin

Chengguan 澄觀 101, 221 n.16, 225 n.43

Cheng weishi lun 成唯識論 (CWSL) 12, 213, 228 n.44, 236 n.43, 243 n.9, 245 n.28, 245 n.33, 246 n.46, 246 n.48, 249 n.12, 254 n.81
on 7th consciousness 109
on 8th consciousness 120
on five dharmas 207, 252 n.61
on permeable (*see under* permeable)
on uncontaminated seeds and *gotra* 157–65, 169, 172, *207*, 211

Chinese Tathāgatagarbha tradition 法性宗 5, 14, 157

Chinese Yogācāra tradition 法相宗 5, 7, 10, 14, 42, 157, 220 n.6, 245 n.36

Chinkai 珍海 42, 124, 228 n.19

citta-mano-manovijñāna (*xinyiyishi* 心意意識) 44

citta-mano-vijñāna 108, 234 n.7

cognized (*ālambana*; *suoyuan* 所緣) 49, 140, 226 n.55, 226 n.56

cognizer (*ālambaka*) 49, 140

A Commentary on the Ten Stages [of the Bodhisattva Path] 6, 43

conditioned 29, 47, 111, 179, 187–8, 226 n.56, 238 n.10, 242 n.101, 245 n.34, 246 n.57, 247 n.68, 248 n.4, 248 n.5, 251 n.41, 253 n.72
conditioned undiscriminating *jñāna* (*see under* undiscriminating *jñāna*)
distinction between unconditioned *vs.* conditioned 6, 14, 17, 33, 132, *134*, 190–208, 214, 217
enjoyment-body as conditioned (*see under* enjoyment-body)
jiexing as conditioned (*see under jiexing*)

condition of object-support (*ālambana-pratyaya*; *suoyuanyuan* 所緣緣) 50

consciousness-and-representation-only 12, 26, 32, 163. *See also vijñapti-mātratā*

consciousness of matter (*shishi* 事識) 137

consciousness of retribution (*guobao shi* 果報識) 29, 136

"containing a Tathāgata" 2, 14, 31, 179–80, 188, 192, 200, 248 n.4. *See also tathāgatagarbha*

contributory cause (*yuanyin* 緣因) 33, 130, 155–7, 165–6, 169, 171, 239 n.24

contributory condition (*zengshang yuan* 增上緣) 125, 127, *128*, *133–4*, 247 n.75

cultivated *gotra* (*samudānīta-gotra*; *xisuocheng zhongxing* 習所成種姓) 162–4, 166, 198

Da boniepan jing jijie 大般涅槃經集解 54, 94, 239 n.19

Da boniepan jing yiji 大般涅槃經義記 37, 59, 94

D'Amato, Mario 253 n.75

Daoni 15, 135, 149–50, 211–12, 241 n.70
as author of T2805 (*see under* T2805)
XGSZ on 141–7, 239 n.35

Daosheng 道生 41, 71, *73*, 85

Daoshi 道世 102, 233 n.62

Daoyue 道岳 142, 144, 242 n.89

Daśabhūmika(-sūtra-śāstra) (*Shidi jing lun* 十地經論) 6, 44, 56, 94, 243 n.104. *See also Dilun* (text)
Daśabhūmika-sūtra (*Shidi jing* 十地經) 49
Dasheng qixin lun yiji 大乘起信論義記 38
Dasheng qixin lun yishu 大乘起信論義疏 (Huiyuan) 37, 101, 227 n.2
Dasheng qixin lun yishu 大乘起信論義疏 (Tanyan) 25. *See also Tanyan Shu*
Dasheng tongxing jing 大乘同性經 76, 78, 98, 104, 234 n.67
Dasheng yizhang 大乘義章 26, 37, *86*, 98, 101, 109, 115, 124, 191, 225 n.33. *See also Bashi yi*
Dasheng zhiguan famen 大乘止觀法門 27, 29, 45–6, 103, 225 n.37
  terminology of *63, 66–8, 77–8, 80–1, 87–9, 99*
Datang Dongjing Dajing'ai si yiqiejing lunmu [*lu*] 大唐東京大敬愛寺一切經論目[錄] *39*
Datang neidian lu 大唐內典錄 *8, 39*
Daxingshan Temple 大興善寺 105, 142, 144, 241 n.75, 242 n.76
Dazhidu lun shu 大智度論疏 75
Dazhou kanding zhongjing mulu 大周刊定眾經目錄 *39*
deguo foxing 得果佛性 129, 246 n.53. *See also* attained [*buddha-*]*gotra*
Delhey, Martin 247 n.79, 254 n.79
Demiéville, Paul 41
dependent origination 201, 206
  on the basis of the storehouse consciousness 11
  on the basis of the *tathāgatagarbha* 10–11, 23, 27, 221 n.16
dharma-body (*dharmakāya*; *fashen* 法身) 220 n.11, 224 n.2, 226 n.50, 236 n.43, 237 n.50, 237 n.59, 246 n.57, 249 n.12, 249 n.27, 250 n.28. *See also* Impermanence Reading; Permanence Reading; T2805 *jiexing* Passage (1)
  Asaṅga on 112–15, 180–1, 236 n.32, 248 n.5, 249 n.15, 249 n.20, 249 n.23
  attainment at 1st or 10th stage 112–16, 236 n.32, 236 n.37, 236 n.38
  as a basis 110–12, 118–20
  as both Thusness and *jñāna* about Thusness 113–14, 166–7, 169, 177, 193–6, 199–200, 206, 209, 213, 233 n.58
  disclosed through Thusness 150, 184, *185*, 200
  vs. enjoyment-body 34–5, 114–22, 174, *199*, 226 n.55, 226 n.56, 227 n.16, 237 n.56, 253 n.72
  FXL on (*see under Foxing lun*)
  identification with Thusness and innate *buddha-gotra* 14, 17, 166, 182, 184, 187–8, 191–2, 195, *207*, 211, 239 n.26, 250 n.29
  and *jiexing* 7, 25–6, 31–6, 123–4, *125*, *134*, 154, 168–70, *204*, 214
  and original awakening (*see under* original awakening)
  and permeation *128*, 238 n.12
  Shelun on 112–14, 121–2
  and *tathāgatagarbha* 14–15, 17, 24, 31, 119, 140, 173, 177, 179, *185*, 185–96, 200, 214, 253 n.72, 254 n.81
  and transformation of the basis (*see under* transformation of the basis)
  and unconditioned undiscriminating *jñāna* (*see under* unconditioned undiscriminating *jñāna*)
  as unconditioned 17, 31, 46–8, 121–2, *132*, 166, 181, 187, 198–200
  Vasubandhu on 179–86, 248 n.5
Dharma-element (*dharmadhātu*; *fajie* 法界) 33–4, 114, 128, 163, 246 n.57
  Asaṅga on 182, 236 n.46
  Awakening of Faith on 25
  as dharma-body 182
  as innate purity 178
  MAV on 194
  T2805 on 33, 155
  as unconditioned 46, 122, 187
Dharmagupta 達摩笈多 80, *117*, 241 n.64
  terminology of *61, 63–70, 78, 84, 86*
Dharmakṣema 曇無讖 57, 79, 110, 252 n.68

terminology of *66, 69, 82–3, 87*
Dharmapāla 247 n.65
dhātu 245 n.38
meaning "element (*hetu*)" 21, 22, 24, 151, 162
meaning "realm" 6, 139, 221 n.22
diamond-like concentration 112, 164, 180–1, 246 n.46, 247 n.48
Dichi lun 地持論 204
Dichi lun yiji 地持論義記 94
Dilun (text) 6, 36, 148–9. *See also Daśabhūmika-sūtra-śāstra*
Dilun master 42, 237 n.54, 243 n.105, 252 n.67
on *buddha-gotra* (*see under buddha-gotra*)
and Shelun master 29, 36, 129–30, 148–9, 212, 227 n.59, 243 n.104, 243 n.107
Dilun Tradition 5–6, 255 n.14. *See also* Dilun Masters
and *Awakening of Faith* 5, 42–5, 212, 217
on buddha-*gotra* 203, 206
and Huiyuan 26, 191, 240 n.50
and Jingsong 135, 223 n.44, 239 n.39
in northern *vs*. southern region 42, 135, 148–9, 217, 221 n.24, 243 n.104
and Shelun (tradition) 14–15, 40, 148–9
and Tanqian 135, 223 n.44
disclosing cause (*liaoyin* 了因) 109–11, 129–32, 235 n.22, 235 n.25, 235 n.30, 239 n.22, 239 n.24
distinction of the six sense bases (*ṣaḍāyatana-viśeṣa*) 204–5, 207
Doryun 道倫/遁倫 171
double-layered soteriological structure 194, 200
drawn-forth [*buddha-*]*gotra* 129–32, 166–9, 173–4, 197, *199*, 199–203, *204*, 205–6
and enjoyment-body 132, *134*, 166, 168, 194, *199*, 199–200, 203–4
Dunhuang 敦煌 6, 25, 28, 52, 56, 59, 242 n.92
and T2805 1, 18, 21, 50–2
International Dunhuang Project (IDP) 51, 229 n.3
8th consciousness 29, 120, 136–40, 148, 165, 241 n.60. *See also* base consciousness, storehouse consciousness
element. *See under dhātu*; Dharma-element
Emperor Taiwu 太武帝 79
Emperor Wu 武帝 38–9
Emptiness (*śūnyatā*) 178, 187, 194
two kinds of Emptiness 201–3
enjoyment-body 35, 41, 101, 114–22, 125, 127–8, 132–4, *158–9*, 166, 168, 170, 173–4, 197–204, 213–14, 226 n.55, 226 n.56, 227 n.57, 227 n.16, 237 n.56, 247 n.65. *See also baoshen*
Asaṅga on 116–19
as conditioned 7, 121–2, 170, 193–4, 198, 201–3, 247 n.68
vs. dharma-body (*see under* dharma-body)
and drawn-forth [*buddha-*]*gotra* (*see under* drawn-forth [*buddha-*]*gotra*)
and *jiexing* (*see under jiexing*)
and permeation of hearing (*see under* permeation of hearing)
Shelun (Vasubandhu) on 116–22
and storehouse consciousness 12, 127, *134*, 173, 253 n.72
and transformation of the basis 116, *117–18*, 118–21, 168–9, 197, 201
equality *jñāna*. *See under* four *jñāna*
essence-body (*svābhāvika-kāya*; *zixing shen* 自性身) 116–21, 170, 197–8, *207*, 236 n.43, 249 n.12, 255 n.82
Etō, Sokuō 衛藤即応 23
evolving consciousnesses (*shengqi shi* 生起識) 116–21, 138
exegetical tools 80, *84*

Fachang 法常 28, 145
faculty 根 114, *159*
faculty of having learned (*ājñātendriya*; *zhigen* 知根) 33, 155–6, 199, 244 n.20
faculty of resolving to know something unknown (*ājñāsyāmīndriya*; *zhiweizhi gen* 知未知根) 33, 155–6, 199, 244 n.20, 244 n.21, 244 n.22

faculty of the perfect knowledge (*ājñātāvīndriya*; *zhiyi gen* 知已根) 156, 199, 244 n.21
having a faculty (*see under* having a faculty)
(three) uncontaminated faculties 155–6, 200, 244 n.21
fa'er 法爾 (*dharmatā*) 160, 162–4, 173, 204
Fahu 法護 241 n.64
Fahua jing yiji 法華經義記 94
Fajing 法經 38–41, 71, 124, 144, 230 n.17, 234 n.67, 242 n.92
false mind (*wangxin* 妄心) 47
Fashang 法上 *76–80, 82–3, 85–7, 89, 93–4, 98–100,* 104, 240 n.50
fashen 法身 22, 32, 41, 43, 114, 154, 182, 194, 201, 228n21, 246 n.57. *See also* dharma-body
Fatai 法泰 135, 239 n.32, 241 n.64
Faxiang zong 法相宗 5, 221 n.16. *See also* Chinese Yogācāra tradition
Faxing zong 法性宗 5, 221 n.16. *See also* Chinese Tathāgatagarbha tradition
Fayun 法雲 71, 75, *76–8, 81–9,* 93–4, 234 n.73
Fazang 法藏 29–30, 38, *97–9,* 101, 221 n.16, 225 n.43, 251 n.42
Fei Changfang 費長房 38
final mind of resolute practice (*jiexing zhongxin* 解行終心) 93–4, *95*
final mind of the *gotra* of the path (*daozhong zhongxin* 道種終心) 93–4
first bodhisattva stage 93–4, 101–2, 112–16, 243 n.8, 243 n.9, 245 n.28
and attainment of benefits 115–16
and dharma-body 112–15, 236 n.37, 236 n.38
and *jiexing* 156, 164, 169
and nobility/noble people 54, 114, 152–3, 155–6, *158*, 164–5, 174, 243 n.5
and pure land 101–2, *102*
the stage(s) before 93–4, 160–1, 221 n.31, 232 n.48, 232 n.49, 244 n.11, 244 n.22
and undiscriminating *jñāna* 115–16, 154–6, 165, 169, 197, 237 n.59
Fodijing lun (FDJL) 佛地經論 12, 120, 151, 163–5, 169–70, *207*, 213, 245 n.42, 254 n.81
on *buddha-gotra* (*see under buddha-gotra*)
on four *jñāna* (*see under* four *jñāna*)
Foshuo wushangyi jing 佛說無上依經 115–16, 195, 226 n.50
four dharmas of purity 182–4
Asaṅga on 178
Vasubandhu on 179, 183
four *jñāna*
Asaṅga/Vasubandhu on 165
equality *jñāna* 165, 170, 245 n.42
FDJL on 120, 163–5, 169–70, 245 n.42
mirror *jñāna* (*see under* mirror *jñāna*)
MSA on 165, 170, 245 n.42
observing *jñāna* 165, 170, 245 n.42
performing *jñāna* 165, 170, 245 n.42
foxing 佛性 15, 26, 56, 110-11, 129, 131, 166, 197, 204, 225 n.31, 231 n.22, 246 n.52, 252 n.56. *See also buddha-gotra*; *gotra*
Foxing lun (FXL) 佛性論 15–16, 23, 43, 193–211, 234 n.70, 252 n.56, 254 n.82
on *buddha-gotra* 130–3, 165–9, 174, 198–207, *207*, 209, 211, 230 n.16, 239 n.26, 254 n.79
on dharma-body 166–7, 198–201, 206, 246 n.57
on disclosing cause 110–11
and RGV 193–202, 206–7, 209, 254 n.29
on *tathāgatagarbha* 195–6, 200, 211
terminology of 58, 104–5
on Thusness 49, 193–4
Frauwallner, Eric 220 n.11
Fujaku 普寂 24, 30
Funan 扶南 45, 212
Funayama, Tōru 船山徹 15–16, 152, 215–16, 221 n.31, 231 n.33, 232 n.47, 251 n.43, 255 n.10

Giles, Lionel 51–2
Gimello, Robert M. 17, 223 n.54, 239 n.39

gotra *93–5*, 129–32, *133*, *134*, 161–9, 172–4, 187–8, 192–208, 246 n.46, 247 n.65, 253 n.72, 253 n.75, 254 n.77, 254 n.79, 254 n.82. *See also* attained *buddha-gotra*; *buddha-gotra*; cultivated *gotra*; drawn-forth [*buddha-*]*gotra*; innate [*buddha-*]*gotra*; tathāgata-*gotra*
Asaṅga on *207*, 254 n.80
basic meaning of 22, 129, 245 n.38, 245 n.39
five *gotras* 172, 220 n.6, 245 n.34, 247 n.79
part of Buddhist path 232 n.46, 232 n.47, 232 n.48, 232 n.50, 233 n.53
Griffiths et al. 112, *117*, 180–4
Gujin yijing tuji 古今譯經圖記 *8, 39*
Guṇabhadra 求那跋陀羅 42, 44, *54*, *99*, 228 n.22
guo 果 129, *158*, 201
guoguo 果果 129

having a faculty (*yougen* 有根) 33, 155–6, 244 n.21. *See also* T2805 *Jiexing* Passage (2)
and undiscriminating *jñāna* (*see under* undiscriminating *jñāna*)
Hearers (*śrāvaka*) 31, 101–2, 104, 167, 247 n.79
hehe 和合 6, 22–3, 152, 171
hehe shi 和合識 26
Higata, Ryūshō 干潟龍祥 224 n.6
Hirakawa, Akira 平川彰 38–40, 228 n.19
houde (*wufenbie*) *zhi* 後得(無分別)智 33, 155. *See also* subsequently acquired *jñāna*
Huayan tradition 7, 29, 37, 157, 190, 221 n.16, 223 n.56
Huida 慧達/惠達 75, *77*, *84–8*, 93–4, 236 n.37
Huijun 慧均 42, 59, 75, 228 n.19, 232 n.47, 239 n.19, 246 n.53
report about two Shelun masters 124, 128–30, 132, 205
terminology of *66*, *77*, *84–8*, *93*, 93–4
Huikai 慧愷 52, 135, 142, 146
Huisi 慧思 27
Huiying 慧影 75, 232 n.43
terminology of *63–4*, *77*, *81*, *84–9*, *93*, 101, 234 n.73
Huiyuan 慧遠 54, 56, 109–10, 115, 141–2, 225 n.31, 225 n.33, 230 n.16, 231 n.24, 233 n.58, 241 n.75
and *Awakening of Faith* 26–7, 37, 136–9, 141, 227 n.2
on bodhisattva stages 232 n.48, 232 n.49, 233 n.52, 233 n.53
and Dilun tradition 26, 191, 240 n.50
distance from strong *tathāgatagarbha* 191, 251 n.40, 251 n.45
on *jiexing* 26–7, 124
on 9th consciousness 136–9, 240 n.50
and T2805 98–105, 142
and Tanqian 139, 144, 149, 242 n.88
terminology of 59–60, *61*, *63–8*, *70*, *76–8*, 79–80, *81–9*, 90, *93*, 94, 95, *98–9*, 100–2, *102*, 104–5
Huizhao 惠沼/慧沼 96, *97*, *117*
Huyue 護月/Yuezang 月藏 171, 245 n.36

Ibuki, Atsushi 伊吹敦 230 n.19
icchantika [*yi*] *chanti* [一]闡提 167, 203, 205–6, 253 n.76
idealism 2
vs. Phenomenology 6, 220 n.5
ignorance 1–2, 111, 167, 170
as falsity/untruth/non-awakening 6, 27, 138
mind agitated/obscured by 4, 11, 14, 30, *134*, 197, 200–1, 203, 226 n.47
and permeation 6, 26–7, *34*, 47, 50, 125, 233 n.66
Ikeda, Masanori 池田將則 25, 28
illuminating cause (*zhaoliao yin*) 照了因 111
Impermanence reading [of *jiexing*] 6, 18, 30, *34*, 34–6, 50–1, 123–6, 211
impermanent 30, 32, *34*, 36, *125*, 154, 240 n.43
innate [*buddha-*]*gotra* (*prakṛtistha-gotra*; *zhu zixing foxing* 住自性佛性) 19, 174, 204–5, 208, 214, 254 n.82
CWSL on 162–3, 172, 246 n.46

vs. drawn-forth [*buddha-*]*gotra* 197–203
FDJL on 163–5
FXL on 111, 131–2, *132–3*, 165–9, 194, 196, 198–203, 206, 239 n.26
RGV on 191, 194, 197–8
and Shelun masters 129–30, 132, *132–3*
as Thusness 130–4, *207*, 253 n.72
as unconditioned 166–9, 173, 187–8, 194

innate knowledge 170
Ishii, Kōsei 石井公成 6, 16, 56–7
Iwata, Taijō 岩田諦静 11, 22–3, 222 n.35, 222 n.36, 224 n.6, 224 n.13, 247 n.3

jiandao wei 見道位/*jianwei* 見位 112–13. *See also* Path of Insight
Jiankang 建康/Jianye 建業 135. *See also* Nanjing
Jiexian 戒賢 171
jiexin 解心 28
jiexing 解行 93–5, 232 n.48, 232 n.49, 233 n.52
jiexing 解性 12, 21–36, 48, 93–4, 149–50, 191, 218, 221 n.15, 225 n.37, 225 n.43, 226 n.54, 243 n.1, 245 n.35, 253 n.72, 256 n.16. *See also* Impermanence Reading; Permanence reading; *Shelun Jiexing* Passage (1); *Shelun Jiexing* Passage (2); T2805 *Jiexing* Passage (1); T2805 *Jiexing* Passage (2)
and *Awakening of Faith* 4–7, 18–19, 24–36, 50–1, 123–8, 132–50, 157, 174, 177, 211–14
as conditioned 6, 33, *34*, 34–6, *125*, *132–3*, 154, 165–73, 197, 201, 214, 226 n.56
and dharma-body (*see under* dharma-body)
and enjoyment-body 35, 127–8, *133–4*, *158*, 168, 197, 201, *204*, 213–14, 227 n.57
and first bodhisattva stage (*see under* first bodhisattva stage)
meaning of 151–75
as original awakening 4–6, 24–31, *34*, 36, 123–5, *134*, 136, 143–5, 151, 211, 226 n.56, 241 n.60, 256 n.15
Permanence *vs.* Impermanence Reading of 21–36, 123–4, 142–3, 145
and permeation of hearing 124–8
and storehouse consciousness (*see under* storehouse consciousness)
Ui's interpretation of (*see under* Ui)
as unconditioned 31, *34*, *125*, *133* (*see also Permanence Reading*)
and undiscriminating *jñāna* 163–5, 169–71, 173–4
Wŏnch'ŭk's citation of 139–41

Jīnagupta 闍那崛多 *77–8*, 80, *85*, *88*, 104
Jin'gangxian lun 金剛仙論 *76–8*, 80, *81–7*, 216, 231 n.35
jingjie 境界 44, 47, 50, 94
jingshi 淨識 35
jingshi 精識 *76–7*, 79, 91
Jingsong 靖嵩 135, 223 n.44, 239 n.36, 239 n.39, 241 n.62, 241 n.64
Jinguangming jing 金光明經 (*Suvarṇaprabhāsottama-sūtra*) 42–3, 48, 113, 227 n.15
Jiushi pin 九識品 139, 240 n.59
Jiushi xuanyi 九識玄義 241 n.62
Jiushi zhang 九識章 16, 138, 140–1, 230 n.9, 240 n.59, 241 n.62
jiwufu 既無復 71–3, 75
Jizang 吉藏 232 n.47, 234 n.10, 240 n.50
and *Awakening of Faith* 37
on enjoyment-body 197, 226 n.56, 247 n.68
on *jiexing* 28–9, 34–5
reports about Dilun and Shelun masters 115, 124–8, 132, 136, 139, 141, 148–9, 168, 197, 231 n.29, 237 n.54, 238 n.10, 238 n.11, 242 n.90, 243 n.104, 243 n.107, 247 n.68, 252 n.67
terminology of 56, 59–60, *61–8*, *70*, 71, *72–3*, 73, 75, *77–8*, *81*, *83–9*, 93–4, 101, 104

jñāna. *See also* four *jñāna*; subsequently acquired *jñāna*; undiscriminating *jñāna*
applied *jñāna* (*jiaxing zhi* 加行智) 33, 156

jñāna about Thusness (*ruru zhi* 如如智) 48, 100, 113, 169, 177, 196, 213, 233 n.58
jñāna arising from contemplation (*guanzhi* 觀智) 32
of things as they really are (*yathābhūta-parijñāna*; *rushi zhi* 如實智) 33, 155
Johnston, E.H. 219 n.2
Jones, Christopher 192
Juedingzang lun 決定藏論 44, 49, 56, *64*, 139–40, 240 n.43

Kaiyuan shijiao lu 開元釋教錄 16, *39*
Kano, Kazuo 加納和雄 179, 192
karma 90, 96, 118, 127, 199, 206, 234
good, bad or nonpropelling 121
Kashiwagi, Hiroo 柏木弘雄
on the connection between *Shelun* and *Awakening of Faith* 55, 144, 147
on *Dasheng zhiguan famen* 27
on the origin of the *Awakening of Faith* 11, 41, 45–6, 50, 147, 150, 221 n.19, 227 n.5, 254 n.2
on *Tanyan shu* 25, 37
Katsumata, Shunkyō 勝又俊教 52
Katsura, Shōryu 桂紹隆 90
Keenan, John 21, 219 n.1
Keng, Ching 耿晴
on Dilun and the *Awakening of Faith* 6, 191, 251 n.45
on Tathāgatagarbha thought 17, 188, 192
on theory of three natures 13
on Vasubandhu 184, 248 n.5, 252 n.59
Kimura, Kunikazu 木村邦和 33, 226 n.54
King, Sallie B. 15, 179
Kitano, Shintarō 北野新太郎 13
kliṣṭa-manas (defiled mentation, *ranwu yi* 染污意) 103–4, 107–9
Kumārajīva 鳩摩羅什 41
terminology of 57, *61*, *63*, *66*, *69*, 79, *82*, *87*, *89*

Lamotte, Étienne 178, 228 n.44
Laṅkāvatāra-sūtra 15, 42, 137, 173, 190–1, 226 n.47, 228 n.21, 251 n.40, 251 n.45, 254 n.76
and *Awakening of Faith* (*see under Awakening of Faith*)
on *buddha-gotra* (*see under buddha-gotra*)
and Dilun 44, 191, 255 n.14
and *tathāgatagarbha* 204–5, 253 n.72
de La Vallée Poussin, Louis *69*, 245 n.43
Li, Tongxuan 李通玄 101, 225 n.43
Li, Zijie 李子捷 17
Lidai sanbao ji 歷代三寶紀 141, 227 n.7, 234 n.67, 234 n.75, 242 n.84
on *Awakening of Faith* 8, 16, 38–9, 41, 144
Liebenthal, Walter 41
Lingrun 靈潤 28
Lishi apitan lun 立世阿毘曇論 72, 231 n.31
liu dade 六大德 144
liushi xin 六識心 104–5
Luoyang 洛陽 79
Lusthaus, Dan 219 n.1, 220 n.5

Madhyāntavibhāga (MAV) 13, 49, 165, 178, 194–5, 223 n.46, 254 n.82
and Paramārtha (*see under* Paramārtha)
and Sthiramati (*see under* Sthiramati)
on Thusness (*see under* Thusness)
Wŏnch'ŭk's citation from 139, 141
Madhyāntavibhāga-bhāṣya (MAVBh) 194–5, 220 n.11
Madhyāntavibhāga-ṭīkā (MAV-*ṭīkā*) 207
Mahāparinirvāṇa-mahāsūtra 大般涅槃經 79, 110, 130, 231 n.33, 239 n.24
and *tathāgatagarbha* 173, 179, 192
**Mahāyāna-abhidharma-sūtra* 大乘阿毘達磨經 21, 162
Mahāyānasaṃgraha (MSg) 3, 21–3, 47–8, 107–8, 112–14, *117*, 139, 151, 159, 178, 180–4, 202, 220 n.11, 228 n.44, 234 n.7, 236 n.46, 243 n.1, 248 n.5, 250 n.37. *See also* Asaṅga; *Shelun*
vs. Awakening of Faith 11
and T2805 52, 54
Ui's interpretation of (*see under* Ui)
Mahāyānasaṃgrahabhāṣya (MSgBh) 3, 11, 14, 47–8, 107–8, 116–18, 165,

178, 180–4, 186, 187, 189–90, 220 n.11, 221 n.15, 222 n.35, 226 n.49, 229 n.5, 233 n.62, 234 n.8, 243 n.1, 247 n.3, 248 n.9, 250 n.28, 252 n.59, 253 n.75, 254 n.77, 254 n.82. *See also Shelun*; Vasubandhu
other translations than Paramārtha's *Shelun* 28, 241 n.64, 245 n.24
and T2805 52
and Tathāgatagarbha 190, 194–6, 205–6, 208–9, 214
Mahāyānasaṃgrahopanibandhana 237 n.50, 248 n.9
Mahāyānasūtrālaṃkāra (MSA) 165, 170, 245 n.42, 251 n.38
on *buddha-gotra* (*see under buddha-gotra*)
on four *jñāna* (*see under* four *jñāna*)
and Tathāgatagarbha 177–9, 189–90, 194, 205, 207–8, 214, 253 n.75
and the theory of three natures 13
on Thusness (*see under* Thusness)
Mahāyānasūtrālaṃkāra-bhāṣya (MSABh) 178, 189, 220 n.11, 251 n.38
Maitreya 11, 13, 101
Makransky, John 250 n.28
manovijñāna 32, 44
Master Ji 基法師 5, 161, 219 n.3, 245 n.36
agreement with T2805 213
on *buddha-gotra* 173, 204–5, 214
criticism of Paramārtha's translation 194, 234 n.3
four senses of *tathāgatagarbha* 253 n.72
maturing consciousness (*vipāka-vijñāna*; *yishu shi* 異熟識) 164
mentation *yi* 意 44, 103–4, 107–9, 234 n.3, 234 n.7, 234 n.8. *See also kliṣṭa-manas*
mind 25–6, 30–2, 38, 44, 93–6, 130–1, 134, 137–8, 154, 160–1, 167–74, 192, 200–5, 208, 220 n.5, 226 n.47, 232 n.48, 238 n.12, 245 n.33, 251 n.41, 251 n.42, 252 n.65, 255 n.14. *See also* final mind; mind of enlightenment; One Mind in Two Aspects
deluded mind 6, 12
false mind 47
innate pure mind (*zixing qingjing xin* 自性清淨心) 35, 128–9, 136, 223 n.46, 240 n.46
mind-mentation-consciousness 104, 107–8, 234 n.7
pure element of the mind (*xin qingjing jie* 心清淨界) 195
pure mind 6, 27–8, 31, 128, 223 n.56, 244 n.22 (*see also* T2805 *Jiexing* Passage (1))
state(s) of mind (*xinpin* 心品) 163–4, 169–70, 172, 174, 197, 246 n.48
true mind (*zhenxin* 真心) 12, 26–7, 124, 138, 149
undeluded mind 12, 27
mind of enlightenment. *See also bodhicitta*
generation of 161, 164, 167–8, 200–2, 204–5, 245 n.33, 252 n.65
mirror *jñāna* (*ādarśa-jñāna*; *dayuanjing zhi* 大圓鏡智) 120, 165, 213, 236 n.43, 245 n.42, 246 n.48
unconditioned *vs.* conditioned 170
mixture 22, 26–7, 128, 152–3, 155–6, *159*, 164, 171–4, 200
between arising-and-ceasing and neither-arising-nor-ceasing 6, 29, 31, 42, 136
between permeation of hearing and *jiexing* (*see under* permeation of hearing)
between pure and impure aspects (*ranjing hehe* 染淨和合) 23–4
between truth and untruth (*zhenwang hehe* 真妄和合) 6, 23
Mochizuki, Shinkō 望月信亨 228 n.22, 255 n.14
on the author of *Awakening of Faith* 5, 40–3, 45, 212, 217
Moriya, Kōzō 守屋孝藏 28
**mūla-vijñāna* 22, 32, 152, 154

Nagao, Gajin 長尾雅人 *70*, 117–18, 178
on *jiexing* 23, *159*, 223 n.59, 224 n.13, 224 n.21
on MSg/MSgBh 222 n.35, 228 n.44, 243 n.9, 248 n.7
Nālandā 213
Nanjing 南京 *73*, 135

Narendrayaśas 那連提耶舍 80, *82–3*, 100, 105
Nattier, Jan 215, 255 n.5
nature of dharmas (*dharmatā*; *faxing* 法性) 121, 149, 188, 204, 233 n.61
neither-arising-nor-ceasing (*busheng bumie* 不生不滅) 6, 24, 28–31, 42, 136, 138. *See also* arising-and-ceasing
New Buddhism 17–18, 223 n.56
NGSM 16, 56
nian 念 (thought) 25, 44–5
Niepan ji 涅槃記 56, 230 n.17
ninth consciousness (*jiushi* 九識) 14, 29, 136–8, 140–1, 143, 149, 240 n.50
nirvana 21, 34, 46–7, 116, 128, 131, 233 n.58, 239 n.19, 253 n.75
 being unconditioned 46, 166–7
nobility 152, 154. *See also* noble people
noble path 22, 32, 152, 154, 171–2. *See also Shelun Jiexing* Passage (2); T2805 *Jiexing* Passage (1)
noble people (*shengren* 聖人) 22, 31–2, 49, 54, 152–3, 155–6, *158–9*, 164, 174, 243 n.5. *See also* basis, basis for noble people; nobility; *Shelun Jiexing* Passage (1); *Shelun Jiexing* Passage (2); T2805 *Jiexing* Passage (1)
noble truth 231 n.30, 235 n.30
 noble truth of the cessation of suffering 110–11
 noble truth of the path 110–11

observing *jñāna*. *See under* four *jñāna*
obstruction 障 (*āvaraṇa*) 114, 178, 180–1
 obstruction related to afflictions (*kleśāvaraṇa*; *fannao zhang* 煩惱障) 43, 139, 183, 185, 189, 251 n.36
 obstructions related to cognitive objects (*jñeyāvaraṇa*; *suozhi zhang* 所知障) 43, 172, 183, 185, 189, 250 n.36
 obstruction to [the attainment of] omniscience (*sarvajñāvaraṇa*; *yiqie zhi zhang* 一切智障) 116
Oda, Akihiro 織田顕祐 28
One Mind in Two Aspects (*yixin ermen* 一心二門) 30, 149, 251 n.42
ordinary people (*fanfu* 凡夫) 32, 102–3, 114, 129, 152–5, *158*, 189, 201. *See also Shelun Jiexing* Passage (2); T2805 *Jiexing* Passage (1)
original awakening (*benjue* 本覺) 4, 6, 24–31, 46, 123, 136, 143, 151, 241 n.60, 248 n.7
 and dharma-body 24–6, 31, *34*, 124–5, *134*, 137, 140, 149, 211, 226 n.56
 jiexing as (*see under jiexing*)
 and *tathāgatagarbha* 28
 as unconditioned 6, 31, *34*, 36, *125*, 145
 Wŏnch'ŭk on 139–41
originally existent seeds (*benyou zhongzi* 本有種子) 172–3, 245 n.37
 originally existent uncontaminated seeds (*benyou wulou zhongzi* 本有無漏種子; **anādi-anāsrava-bīja*) 19, 160–3, 172, 201, 211, 213
Ōtake, Susumu 大竹晉 230 n.9, 231 n.35
 on *Awakening of Faith* 5, 41, 45
 on *Jiushi zhang* 16, 140–1, 241 n.57
ŌYA, Tokujō 大屋德城 52

paramārtha 49, 166, 178, 182, 194
 paramārtha-satya 10
Paramārtha. *See also Foxing lun* (FXL); *Madhyāntavibhāga* (MAV); *Shelun*; traditional image of Paramārtha
 and *Awakening of Faith* (*see under Awakening of Faith*)
 direct *vs.* indirect lineage/disciples 7, 11, 15, 132–50, 211–12, 241 n.64
 life and work 2–3, 220 n.8
 and MAV 49, 194–5
 successor to Vasubandhu 177, 193–209
 terminology of 9, 60–75, 228 n.22
 three dubious assumptions about 10–13, 212–14
 translations as lecture notes 4, 16, 216
 XGSZ on Paramārtha 8, 16, 55, 79, 134, 146, 231 n.21
 between Yogācāra and Tathāgatagarbha 2–5, 10–13, 157, 177, 190, 206–9, 211–14, 219 n.4, 252 n.56

path 22, 26, 32–5, *102*, 118–19, *125*, 152, 161, 168, 171–2, 178, 201–3, 205, 231 n.28, 235 n.22, 235 n.30, 236 n.38, 240 n.43. *See also* noble path
different stages of 93–5, *158–9*, 232 n.48, 232 n.50
path of [cultivating] antidotes (*duizhi dao* 對治道; **pratipakṣa-bhāvanā*) 109–10, 118, 131
Path of Cultivation (*bhāvanā-mārga*; *xiudao* 修道) 12, 131, 155, *158–9*, 193, 244 n.21, 244 n.22
Path of Insight (*darśana-mārga*; *jiandao* 見道) 113, 155, *158–9*, 221 n.31, 244 n.21, 244 n.22 (*see also jiandao wei*)
Path of Liberation (*jietuo dao* 解脫道; **vimokṣa-mārga*) 246 n.48
uncontaminated path 32, 118, 154
Paul, Diana 15, 223 n.49
Pengcheng 彭城 135, 139
The Perfection of Wisdom Scripture for Humane Kings (*Renwang bore jing* 仁王般若經) 41, 59, 221 n.31
performing *jñāna*. *See under* four *jñāna*
Permanence Reading [of *jiexing*] 6, 18, 30–1, *34*, 50–1, 123–6, 211, 226 n.56
permanent 128, 143, 151, 154, 179–83, 240 n.43, 245 n.34
dharma-body as permanent 24, 31–6, 48, 114, *125*, 128, 181–2, 226 n.56, 248 n.9, 249 n.12
jiexing as permanent 4, 30–1, 33–4, *125*, *133* (*see also* Permanence Reading)
and permeation 32, 36, 48, 154
as unconditioned 31, 33–6, 48, 111, *125*, *133*, 180–1, 226 n.56
permeable/permeated
Asaṅga and Vasubandhu on 47
CWSL on 48
jiexing being permeated 26, 32–6, 48, *125*, 154–64, 173–4
and Thusness 5–6, 37, 46–8, 50, 154, 191, 214
and unconditioned (dharmas) 5–6, 33, 37, 46–8, *125*, *133*, 154
permeation of hearing (*śruta-vāsanā*; *wenxunxi* 聞熏習) 24, 26, 32, 34, 48, 160, 243 n.1, 247 n.75. *See also Shelun Jiexing* Passage (2); T2805 *Jiexing* Passage (1)
ceases *vs.* not ceases by two Shelun masters 124–8, *133*, 238 n.11
and enjoyment-body 125, 127–8, *128*, *133*
and *gotra* *133*, 162–4, 168, 172–4, 253 n.72
mixture with *jiexing* 22, 128, 152–6, *159*, 164, 171–4, 243 n.1 (*see also Shelun Jiexing* Passage (2); T2805 *Jiexing* Passage (1))
primary *vs.* secondary sense of 126–7
persecution [of Buddhism] 17, 75, 79, 135, 139, 143
pervasion (*sarvatraga*/[*pari-*]*spharaṇa*) 92, 186
Phenomenology
vs. idealism 6, 220
piboshena guan 毘鉢舍那觀
vs. shemota guan 奢摩他觀 44
pin 品 230 n.11
and *zhang* 章 55–6
Platform Scripture 六祖壇經 7
Prabhākaramitra 波羅頗蜜多羅 *61–8*, *70*, 101
prabhāvita 183–7, 189, 249 n.19, 249 n.23, 249 n.27, 250 n.28, 251 n.38, 252 n.59. *See also rab tu phye ba*; *suoxian*/*xiancheng*
prajñā. *See under* three kinds of understanding
Prasad, H.S. 219 n.2
pure element of the mind (*xin qingjing jie* 心清淨界). *See under* mind
purity 30, 102, 113, 121, 130, 182–5, 189, 223 n.56, 237 n.59
four dharmas of purity (*see under* four dharmas of purity)
innate purity (*prakṛti-vyavadāna*; *zixing qingjing* 自性清淨) 127, 178–9, 184–5, 202
natural purity 191, 251 n.45
purity devoid of defilement (*vaimalya-vyavadāna*; *ligou qingjing* 離垢清淨) 183, 185, 202

Pusa dichi jing 菩薩地持經 83, 93–5, 232 n.48, 232 n.49, 252 n.68
Pusa yingluo benye jing 菩薩瓔珞本業經 41, *82*, 93–5, 232 n.47, 232 n.50, 233 n.53

qifuyou 豈復有 72–3

rab tu phye ba 183–6, 249 n.19. *See also prabhāvita; suoxian/xiancheng*
Radich, Michael 16, 216, 227 n.15, 230 n.19, 235 n.19, 235 n.25, 239 n.22, 255 n.12
ranjing hehe 染淨和合 23. *See under* mixture
Ratnagotravibhāga (RGV) 14, 16–17, 23, 219 n.2, 220 n.11, 251 n.39, 252 n.59
  and *Awakening of Faith* 43–6
  on *buddha-gotra* (*see under buddha-gotra*)
  and FXL (*see under* FXL)
  on *tathāgatagarbha* 186–8, 191–3, 248 n.4, 250 n.29
  and Tathāgatagarbha thought 177–80, 189–90, 208–9, 214
Ratnagotravibhāgavyākhyā (RGVV) 186–8, 192, 198
Ratnamati (Lenamoti 勒那摩提) 17, 44, 56, 75, 79, 230 n.20
Renwang bore jing 仁王般若經 41, 93, 141, 232 n.46
Renwang jing shu 仁王經疏 221 n.31
response-body (*yingshen* 應身) 41–2, 227 n.16
reverse permeation (*huanxun* 還熏) *98*, 103
Ruegg, D.S. 192, 197–8, 247 n.3, 247 n.4
Rulaizang yuanqi zong 如來藏緣起宗 221 n.16
ruru 如如. *See also* Thusness
  rurujing 如如境 196
  ruru ruruzhi 如如如如智 113
  ruru zhi 如如智 48, 113, 196, 240 n.47 (*see under jñāna*)

śaikṣa 202
Saitō, A 齋藤明 192, 248 n.4
Sakurabe, Hajime 櫻部建 45
śamatha. See under shemota guan
Saṃdhinirmocana-sūtra 23, 44, 109, 230 n.9, 250 n.28
saṃyukta (*xiangying* 相應) 22, *32*, *62*, *64*, *74*, *92*, 163, 169
Saṃyuktābhidharma-hṛdaya-śāstra 雜阿毘曇心論 55, 92–3, 230 n.15, 232 n.42, 232 n.43
Sanlun tradition 三論宗 28, 37
Sanshen fenbie pin 三身分別品 43, 113
San wuxing lun 三無性論 49, 240 n.44, 243 n.92
sanzhong foxing 三種佛性 56
sanzhong jingtu 三種淨土 *98*, 101–2, *102*
Sarvāstivāda Abhidharma 90
satya 10, 110
Schmithausen, Lambert 186, 189, 219 n.4, 220 n.5, 220 n.11, 224 n.4, 248 n.4, 249 n.27
scribe 73, 75, 90, 142
seed (*bīja*; *zhongzi* 種子) 19, 26–7, 34–5, 49–50, 96, 103, 110, 118–20, *125*, 127–8, 130, 157–74, 191, 193, 198, 201, 205, 211, 213, 219 n.4, 225 n.31, 245 n.37, 247 n.76, 253 n.72. *See also* originally existent seeds; uncontaminated seed
  contaminated seed 160
  seeds [born from] having Thusness as the cognitive object 171, 229 n.59
  seeds for wisdom (*zhihui zhongzi* 智慧種子) 35
  in six contexts 32, 154, 226 n.49
self-view (*wojian* 我見) 103, 109
Sengzhao 僧肇 41, *63*, *82*, *87*
Sengzong 僧宗 55
seventh (7th) consciousness 29, 165
  as *atuona shi* 103–4, 107–9, 137, 139, 234 n.10
  as [*kliṣṭa-*]*manas* 103–4, 107–9
shame (*lajjā*; *cankui* 慚愧) 160
shangen 善根 (*kuśala-mūla*) *64*, 161
Shanzhou 善冑 59, 231 n.23
Shedasheng lun chao 攝大乘論抄. *See under* T2806
Shedasheng shi 攝大乘師 29, 34, 127, 136
Shelun (text) 3–4, 9–11, 21–4, 26–9, 31, 35–7, 42–50, 51–6, 59–60,

71, 100, 102–3, 107–77, 195, 208, 211–13, 224 n.9, 231 n.28, 233 n.62, 235 n.30, 236 n.32, 237 n.56, 237 n.59, 239 n.36. *See also Shelun Jiexing* Passage (1); *Shelun Jiexing* Passage (2), Shelun/*Awakening of Faith* lineage, Shelun/T2805 lineage
on attainment of benefits 115–16
on *atuona shi* (*see under atuona shi*)
and *Awakening of Faith* 43–50, 136, 147
on *buddha-gotra* 166
on dharma-body (*see under* dharma-body)
on disclosing cause 109–12
on enjoyment-body (*see under* enjoyment-body)
on *jiexing* *158*, 168, 171–3
spread of 135, 139, 142–7, 148–50, 241 n.64
and T2805 *52–6,* 141–2
on *tathāgatagarbha* 252 n.56
terminology of *86–9*
two views about nobility 152, 221 n.31
on undiscriminating *jñāna* 156

Shelun (tradition) 12, 135, 145, 193, 223 n.47, 243 n.107
and Dilun (tradition) 14–15, 40, 42, 148–9, 223 n.44, 227 n.59, 240 n.50, 243 n.107

Shelun/*Awakening of Faith* Lineage 132–50, 177
on ninth consciousness 136–8
and Tanqian 138–47, 150

Shelun jiexing passage (1) 21, 151, 162
Shelun jiexing passage (2) 22–4, 26, 31, 151–2, 224 n.7

Shelun masters 34–6, 71, 115, 168–9, 212, 227 n.59, 231 n.29, 238 n.10, 247 n.68
and *Awakening of Faith* 11, 29, 46, 223 n.44
and Dilun master (*see under* Dilun master)
and T2806 28
two lineages of 14–15, 124–50, 238 n.11, 240 n.50, 241 n.64, 242 n.90, 243 n.104

Shelun/T2805 lineage 132, 134, 141–3, 147, 150, 177

shemota guan 奢摩他觀
vs. piboshena guan 毘鉢舍那觀 44

shengjie 勝解. *See under adhimukti*

Shengjun 勝軍 171, 245 n.36

Shengkai 聖凱 11–13, 52, 222 n.36, 223 n.44, 231 n.25

shengmie 生滅 6, 29–30, 44, 48, 136. *See also* arising-and-ceasing

shengren 聖人 22, 31–2, 152, *158*, 243 n.5. *See also* noble people

shengsi 生死 35, *64*, 110

shengwen 聲聞 61, 101. *See also* Hearers
shengwen shidi 聲聞十地 98, 104

shengyin 生因. *See under* cause

Shentai 神泰 171–2

Shiba kong lun 十八空論 16, 58, 240 n.46

shi bianyi 識變異 *64, 70*

Shidi lun yishu 十地論義疏 *76–8, 82,* 94

shiji 實際 (*bhūtakoṭi*). *See* Apex of Reality

shijue 始覺 248 n.7

Shi moheyan lun 釋摩訶衍論 *77–8,* 80, *84, 87–9, 98–9*

Shindai sanzō kenkyū ronshū 真諦三藏研究論集 16

Sidi lun 四諦論 *69*

Śikṣānanda 42, 254 n.2

Siku quanshu 四庫全書 71

Silun xuanyi 四論玄義 42, 228 n.19

Sinpyeon jejong gyojang chongnok 新編諸宗教藏總錄 141

sixth [mental] consciousness 103, 109–10, 165, 235 n.23

Solitary Realizers (*pratyekabuddha*) 31, *102*, 167, 247 n.79

spotless consciousness (*amoluo shi* 阿摩羅識; **amalavijñāna*) 14, 129, 136–43, 148, 240 n.43, 240 n.44, 240 n.45, 240 n.46, 240 n.59
as unconditioned 136–7

sprout 167–8

Śrīmālādevīsiṃhanāda-sūtra 23, 173, 204–5, 253 n.72

stage (*bhūmi* 地, *avasthā* 位) 13, 26, 33, 35, 54, 93–5, 101–2, 104, 112–16, 120, 122, 128–9, 152–65, 169, 174,

180, 197, 201–5, 221 n.31, 232 n.48, 232 n.49, 236 n.32, 236 n.37, 236 n.38, 237 n.59, 238 n.10, 243 n.5, 243 n.8, 243 n.9, 244 n.11, 244 n.22, 246 n.46, 246 n.48. *See also* bodhisattva stage; first bodhisattva stage; transformative stage
Stage of Applied Practices (*prayogāvasthā; jiaxing wei* 加行位) 157, 245 n.28
Stage of [the Path of] Insight (*jianwei* 見位) 112–13
Stage of Provision (*saṃbhārāvasthā; ziliang wei* 資糧位) 157, 161, 245 n.28, 245 n.33
stage of superior advancement (*shengjin wei* 勝進位; **viśeṣāvasthā*) 160–1
states of mind (*xinpin* 心品). *See under* mind
Stein, Aurel 28, 51–2, 219 n.2
Sthiramati 140–1, 222 n.40
and MAV 141, 165, 207, 249 n.27
storehouse consciousness 11–12, 14, 42, 103–4, 116–22, 127, *134*, 160–4, *204*, 233 n.66, 234 n.7, 236 n.43, 248 n.5. *See also* base consciousness; 8th consciousness
and *atuona shi* 103, 107–9
and *Awakening of Faith* 28, 30, 136–8, 143, 190–1
as the basis 148–9
and enjoyment-body (*see under* enjoyment-body)
as fundamentally defiled/negative 6, 221 n.25, 224 n.4, 229 n.57, 240 n.44
grasped by 7th consciousness 103, 109
and *jiexing* 21–32, 139, 151–4, 172, 191
and permeation 48, 103, 243 n.1
and seeds 35, 160–2, 172–4
and *tathāgatagarbha* 173, 190–3, 253 n.72
subject (*grāhaka*) and object (*grāhya*) 113–14, 121, 137, 139
distinction between 113
duality between 114
subsequently acquired *jñāna* (*pṛṣṭhalabdha-jñāna*) 33, 112, 115–16, 155, 197, 252 n.60
Suguro, Shinjō 勝呂信静 13, 247 n.1
Sui dynasty 16, 25–6, 28, *61*, 79–80, 90
suiwang 隨妄 191, 251 n.44
suiwang liuzhuan 隨妄流轉 101, 138
suiwang sheng 隨妄生 *99*, 100, 101
Suixiang lun 隨相論 16, 71, *72–4*, 75, *85*, *87–9*, 90, 105, 142, 231 n.30
suiyuan 隨緣 29
suoxian 所顯/*xiancheng* 顯成 49, 182–6, 249 n.19, 253 n.72. *See also prabhāvita*; *rab tu phye ba*
supramundane 22, 49, 151–2, 160, 171, 243 n.8, 244 n.22
supramundane transformation of the basis. (*see under* transformation of the basis)

T2805 21, 30–6, 48, 131–4, 139, 141–5, 147, 149–59, 161–2, 164–6, 168–70, 173, 177, 211–13, 217, 223 n.60, 226 n.49, 226 n.51, 229 n.3, 230 n.9, 230 n.11, 231 n.31, 233 n.58, 233 n.66, 235 n.23, 235 n.30, 244 n.20, 256 n.16. *See also* Impermanence Reading; Shelun/T2805 Lineage; T2805 *Jiexing* Passage (1); T2805 *Jiexing* Passage (2)
affinity with Xuanzang 161–73
Daoni as the author 141–3
doctrines of 107–22, 127–8, 152
and Impermanence Reading 30–4, *125*
introduction of 1, 6–7, 9, 18–19, 51–6
terminology of 9, 60–105
T2805 *Jiexing* Passage (1) 31, 151, 153–5
T2805 *Jiexing* Passage (2) 33, 151, 155–6
T2806 28, 52, 59, *61–70*, *85–6*, 230 n.15
T2807 52, 56, 59, 109, 115, 231 n.25, 242 n.92
terminology of *62–3*, *65*, *67–8*, *70*, *85*, *93*, *97*
T2808 52, 55–6, 60, *64–6*, *68*, *85*, *87*, 109
T2809 52, 56, 60, *62–3*, *65–70*, *89*, 235 n.30, 242 n.92
Takasaki, Jikidō 高崎直道 179, 187–8, 195, 235 n.19, 235 n.25, 252 n.65

on *buddha-gotra* 166, 192
on RGV 190–2, *198*, 219 n.2, 250 n.29
Takemura, Makio 竹村牧男 5, 41, 43–5, 212, 217
Takeuchi [Shōkō] 107
Tanluan 曇鸞 75, *76–8, 82–3*
Tanqian 曇遷 15, 223 n.44, 241 n.63, 241 n.64
as author of *Dasheng zhiguan famen* 27, 225 n.35
and *Jiushi zhang* 16, 42, 141, 230 n.9, 240 n.56
and Shelun/*Awakening of Faith* lineage 46, 123, 135–50, 211–12, 239 n.36
XGSZ on 16, 138–47, 242 n.76, 242 n.78, 242 n.84, 242 n.88
Tanyan shu 曇延疏 37, 45–6, 109, 115
on *jiexing* 25–6, 30, 123–4
terminology of *61, 64–6, 78, 81–6, 88–9, 98–9,* 103
Tanyan 曇延 25, 46, 79–80, 98, 115, 123, 149, 224 n.22. *See also Tanyan shu*
terminology of 100, 101, 103–4
Tanzun 曇遵 42
Tathāgata-embryo 179
tathāgatagarbha 12, 16, 138, 223 n.47. *See also* dependent origination on the basis of the *tathāgatagarbha*; Tathāgatagarbha (tradition); *Tathāgatagarbha-sūtra*
absence in FDJL and CWSL 254 n.81
"All sentient beings are *tathāgatagarbhas*" 14, 17, 177, 179, 185–9, 192–3, 196, 205–6, 254 n.81
as *Bahuvrīhi* 180, 247 n.3, 248 n.4
basic meaning of 14, 179–80, 220 n.7, 248 n.4, 252 n.56
"containing a Tathāgata" 2, 14, 31, 179–80, 188, 200, 248 n.4
and dharma-body (*see under* dharma-body)
disclosure *vs.* development model 179
empty *vs.* non-empty 173
as example of Sinicization 217
in FXL (*see under* FXL)
and *iccantikas* 205–6
and *jiexing* 23–4, 226 n.54, 253 n.72
in MSA 189
multiple meanings of 13–14, 173, 179–80, 204–5, 253 n.72
and original awakening 24, 28, 31, 140, 149
in RGV (*see under* RGV)
and spotless consciousness 140
strong *vs.* weak 7, 14, 177, 190–3, 208, 214, 217, 251 n.45
in T2805 119
and Thusness 14, 17, 23, 31, 140, 149, 177, 179, 184–96, 200, 205–6, 208, 211, 214, 250 n.36, 253 n.72
Vasubandhu on 14, 178–80, 184–6, 189–93, 206, 208, 211, 214, 217
Tathāgatagarbha (tradition) 7, 15, 17, 174–5, 177–9, 189–93, 205, 219 n.3, 220 n.7, 250 n.29, 252 n.56. *See also* Chinese Tathāgatagarbha tradition
relation with Yogācāra (tradition) 1–5, 10–14, 19, 157, 175, 177, 186–90, 206–9, 211, 214, 219 n.4, 223 n.46, 248 n.5, 254 n.81
Tathāgatagarbha-sūtra 167–8, 179, 192, 195, 220 n.7, 248 n.4
tathāgata-gotra 166–7, 203, 207
**Tattvasiddhi* 成實論 55, *61, 64,* 79, 90, 92–3, 230 n.15, 231 n.33
ten abidings (*shizhu* 十住) 94, *95, 102,* 221 n.31, 232 n.50
ten confidences (*shi xin* 十信) *95,* 101–2, 221 n.31
ten merit-transfers (*shi huixiang* 十迴向) 94, *95,* 115, 221 n.31, 232 n.50
ten practices (*shixing* 十行) 94, *95,* 221 n.31, 232 n.50
ten understandings (*shi jie* 十解) 94, *95,* 152, 221 n.31
terminological analysis
difference between Paramārtha and Xuanzang *54, 69*
differences between *Awakening of Faith* and Paramārtha 40–5
differences between South and North 75–89

features of Paramārtha's
terminology 9, 15–16, 57–8, 212, 222 n.32
methodology of 56–60
of T2805 60–105
theory of three natures 11, 13, 222 n.41, 224 n.16
dependent nature 23, 32, 178, 240 n.44, 248 n.5
imagined nature 23, 178, 240 n.44
perfected nature 23–4, 32, 49, 136, 178, 240 n.45, 248 n.5
thirty-seven factors of enlightenment 199–200
Thirty Verses (*Triṃśikā*) 120, 165, 178, 219 n.3, 220 n.11
three greats (*sanda* 三大) 42
three kinds of pure lands 101–2
three kinds of understanding 26
understanding arising from cultivating (*bhāvanāmayī-prajñā*; *xiuhui* 修慧) 32, 153–5, *158*, 225 n.26
understanding arising from hearing (*śrutamayī-prajñā*; *wenhui* 聞慧) 32, 153–4, 225 n.26
understanding arising from hearing and from pondering (**śrutacintāmayī-prajñā*; *wensi hui* 聞思慧) 33, *34*, 125, 154–5, *158–9*, 244 n.22
understanding arising from pondering (*cintāmayī-prajñā*; *sihui* 思慧) 32, 153–4, *159*, 225 n.26, 244 n.22
Thusness (*tathatā*) 34–7, 46–50, 100, 103–4, 122, 125–6, 130–4, 136–8, 148–9, 165–7, 169–71, 177–209, 213–4, 228 n.38, 229 n.57, 229 n.59, 233 n.58, 236 n.38, 240 n.43, 240 n.44, 240 n.47, 248 n.5, 249 n.15, 249 n.20, 249 n.23, 249 n.27, 250 n.28, 252 n.61, 254 n.81, 255 n.14. *See also ruru*
aspect of Thusness (of the Mind) (*see under* aspect of Thusness)
Awakening of Faith on 25–6, 31, 42, 46–7, 126, 130, 137, 149, 238 n.12
as cognitive object 48–50, 165, 193–6, 199, 200, 206, 209, 226 n.55
dharma-body as both Thusness and *jñāna* about Thusness (Paramārtha) (*see under* dharma-body)
dharma-body as Thusness (RGV) 14, 186–8
dharma-body as Thusness (Vasubandhu) 180–6, 213, 249 n.5, 252 n.59
dharma-body as Thusness disclosed *134*, 184, *185*, 200, *204*, 253 n.72
entangled with defilements 173, 186–7, 202
FXL on 49, 166–7, 195–7, 200–3, 206–7, 239 n.26, 246 n.57, 252 n.56, 254 n.82
identification with *buddha-gotra* and dharma-body 14, 17, 166, 182, 184, 187–8, 191–2, 195, *207*, 211, 239 n.26, 250 n.29
as innate [*buddha-*]*gotra* (*see under innate* [*buddha-*]*gotra*)
as innate purity 178–9, 184–5, 202
as *jiexing* 23, 25–6, 29–31, *34*, *125*, 149, 211
MAV on 49, 194
MSA on 189, 250 n.36
permeable or not 5–6, 37, 46–8, 50, 154, 214
Takasaki on 252 n.65
as *tathāgatagarbha* *184–5*, 200, 253 n.72
as unconditioned 5–6, 14, 17, 46, 132, 137, 169, 180, 185–7, 191, 235 n.30
undiscriminating *jñāna* about 12, 48–50, 113–16, 177, 194–7, 213
Wŏnch'ŭk's report about 140
Tiantai tradition 27, 35, 223 n.56
traditional image of Paramārtha 10–11, 14–15, 150, 177, 219 n.4, 255 n.14
description and problematization of 1–8
refutation of 211–13, 216
transformation-body 114–16, 121–2, 132, 166, 193–4, 197–202, 227 n.16
transformation of the basis 32, 35, 112, 116–21, 125, 165, 168–9, 172, 197, 201, 237 n.63

Asaṅga on 243 n.9
basic idea 224 n.4, 243 n.9
and dharma-body 180–1, 185, 189, 236 n.32, 236 n.43
and disclosing cause 109–11
and enjoyment-body (*see under* enjoyment-body)
supramundane 22, 151
transformative stage
transformative stage of advancing the force and harming the power 26, 152–5, 157, *158*, 160–1
transformative stage of penetration 153, *158*, 243 n.9
Treatise of Proceeding the Stages (*Dichi jing* 地持經) 204. *See also Pusa dichi jing*
Triṃśikā. *See under Thirty Verses*
Triṃśikābhāṣya 141
true mind (*zhenxin* 真心) 12, 26–7, 124, 138, 149, 255 n.14
true pure mind (*zhenjing xin* 真淨心) 32, 154
Twenty Verses (*Viṃśikā*) 6, 178, 220 n.5, 220 n.11
two vehicles 114

Ueda, Yoshifumi 上田義文 213, 222 n.35, 222 n.40, 222 n.41, 223 n.45, 224 n.6
interpretation of Asaṅga and Vasubandhu 11–12
Ui, Hakuju 宇井伯寿 13, 30, 36, 40, 46, 222 n.35, 222 n.36, 224 n.13
interpretation of Asaṅga and Vasubandhu 10–11
interpretation of *jiexing* 23–4
interpretation of MSg 23
Ultimate Reality (*paramārtha*) 49, 166–7, 178, 182, 189, 194
unconditioned 1–2, 5, 31, 33–7, 46–8, 110–11, 125, 131–7, 145, 154, 165–74, 180–1, 185, 187–208, 213–4, 224 n.2, 226 n.56, 228 n.38, 228 n.39, 231 n.29, 235 n.30, 238 n.10, 239 n.26, 244 n.16, 246 n.57, 246 n.58, 247 n.75, 248 n.4, 248 n.5, 251 n.41, 253 n.72. *See also* unconditioned undiscriminating *jñāna*
buddhahood as (*see under* buddhahood)
dharma-body as (*see* under dharma-body)
distinction between unconditioned and conditioned 6–7, 14, 17, 33, 121–2, 131–4, 169, 190–208, 214, 217, 248 n.4, 251 n.41
innate [*buddha-*]*gotra* as (*see under* innate [*buddha-*]*gotra*)
jiexing as (*see under jiexing*)
original awakening as (*see under* original awakening)
and permeable (*see under* permeable)
spotless consciousness as (*see under* spotless consciousness)
Thusness as (*see under* Thusness)
unconditioned undiscriminating *jñāna* 1, 169–74, 247 n.75
about Thusness 137, 169–71, 194–7, 200–3, 213, 226 n.55, 246 n.57
vs. conditioned undiscriminating *jñāna* 7, 170, 197, 200, 226 n.56
and dharma-body 7, 169–70, 213
uncontaminated 19, 29, 31–2, *54*, 118–19, 154–7, 160–4, 169, 171–4, 193, 200–1, 205, 211, 213, 240 n.43. *See also anāsrava*
uncontaminated faculties (*see under* faculty)
uncontaminated path (*see under* path)
uncontaminated seed (*see under* seed)
uncontaminated seed 157, 169, 171–2, 193, 205, 253 n.72
originally existent uncontaminated seeds 19, 160–3, 172, 201, 211, 213
undiscriminating *jñāna* 12, 154–6, 231 n.28, 231 n.29, 244 n.16, 244 n.22, 247 n.75. *See also* T2805 *Jiexing* Passage (2); unconditioned undiscriminating *jñāna*
about Thusness 48–50, 113–14, 137, 165, 169, 177, 194–7, 200–3, 213, 226 n.55
acquired *vs.* innate 1–2, 4, 219 n.4
conditioned *vs.* unconditioned 7, 170, 197, 200–1, 226 n.56
and dharma-body 7, 113–16, 169–70, 177, 194, 196–7, 213, 226 n.55,

226 n.56, 236 n.43, 237 n.59, 246 n.57, 248 n.5
and first bodhisattva stage (*see under* first bodhisattva stage)
and *Fodijing lun* 163–5, 169
and having a faculty 33, 155–6, 244 n.21
and *jiexing* 23, 33, 155–6, 163–5, 169–71, 173–4, 197, 201

Vajracchedikā-prajñāpāramitā-sūtra 3, 184
Vasubandhu 3, 6–7, 19, 47, 52, 107–8, 116, 118–22, 148, 165, 175, 219 n.3, 220 n.5, 221 n.15, 221 n.31, 222 n.35, 222 n.40, 224 n.2, 226 n.49, 234 n.8, 234 n.9, 239 n.26, 243 n.1, 247 n.3, 248 n.9, 250 n.28, 251 n.41, 252 n.59, 253 n.75, 254 n.77, 254 n.80, 254 n.81, 254 n.82. *See also* MSgBh; *Shelun*
on *atuona shi* (*see under atuona shi*)
on dharma-body (*see under* dharma-body)
difference from Asaṅga 181, 248 n.5
on enjoyment-body (*see under* enjoyment-body)
on four dharmas of purity (*see under* four dharmas of purity)
on four *jñāna* (*see under* four *jñāna*)
on permeable (*see under* permeable)
and Tathāgatagarbha 10–14, 177–217
on *tathāgatagarbha* (*see under tathāgatagarbha*)
two Vasubandhus 220 n.11
Ueda's interpretation of (*see under* Ueda)
Ui's interpretation of (*see under* Ui)
vijñāna 11–12, 14, 21–3, 29, *54*, *64*, *70*, 104, 107–9, 116–17, 127, 129, 136–7, 139–40, 164, 192, 234 n.7, 234 n.8, 245 n.43. *See also ādāna-vijñāna*; *ālaya-vijñāna*; **amala-vijñāna*; *citta-mano-vijñāna*
vijñāna-pariṇāma 12, 64, 70
vijñapti 23, 26, 103, 139, 163
vijñapti-mātratā 26, 32, 163. *See also* consciousness-and-representation-only
Viṃśikā. *See under Twenty Verses*
Viniścayasaṃgrahaṇī (of *Yogācārabhūmi*) 171, 184, 228 n.38
vipaśyanā. *See under piboshena guan*

Wang shifei lun 亡是非論 145, 241 n.63
weishi zhi 唯識智 65
wensi hui 聞思慧. *See under* three kinds of understanding
without *gotra* 204, 206, 247 n.79
Wŏnch'ŭk 8, *69*, *98*, 139–40, 221 n.31, 230 n.9, 240 n.59
wufenbie zhi 無分別智 1, 154–5, *158*. *See also* undiscriminating *jñāna*
wumo shi 無沒識 129
Wuxiang lun 無相論 243 n.92

XGSZ 8, 16, 46, 55, 59, *61*, 79, 134, 138–9, 141–7, 231 n.21, 231 n.34, 239 n.36, 241 n.62, 241 n.64, 242 n.76, 242 n.78, 242 n.88
on *Awakening of Faith* (*see under Awakening of Faith*)
on Daoni (*see under* Daoni)
on Paramārtha (*see under* Paramārtha)
on Tanqian (*see under* Tanqian)
xiancheng 顯成. *See suoxian*
Xianshi lun 顯識論 23, *88*, 224 n.14, 234 n.73, 242 n.92
xianxing 現行 160, 164, 172
Xianyu jing 賢愚經 75, *76–7*, *81–3*
xinle 信樂. *See under adhimukti*
xinpin 心品 (states of mind). *See under* mind
xinyishi 心意識 44, 107
xiqi 習氣 (*vāsanā*) 48–9
xiuhui 修慧. *See under* three kinds of understanding
Xuanzang 玄奘 5, 28, 50, 107–8, 112, 135, 144, 165, 178, 180–4, 186, 219 n.1, 221 n.17
contrast against Paramārtha 10–14, 19, *117*, 120–1, 148, 151, 157, 171–4, 177, 190, 194, 207–8, 213, 222 n.41, 223 n.45, 240 n.59, 241 n.64
terminology of *54*, 60, *69*, 73, *74*, 96, *97–9*, 228 n.44, 229 n.56, 231 n.25, 232 n.43, 234 n.7, 245 n.24, 245 n.39, 249 n.19

yingshen 應身 41, 43, 132, 166, 199, 227 n.16
Yinshun 印順 240 n.56, 254 n.1
Yogācāra (tradition, thought) 1–8, 10–15, 19, 23, 37, 42, 103–4, 108, 120, 124, 150, 155, 162, 165–7, 169, 171, 175, 177–80, 184, 186–7, 189–90, 195, 205–9, 213–15, 221 n.17, 223 n.46, 245 n.34, 254 n.81, 254 n.82. *See also* Chinese Yogācāra tradition
  and *Awakening of Faith* 46–50, 229 n.57
  diversity of 13, 213
  relation to Tathāgatagarbha 1–5, 10–14, 157, 177, 190, 206–9, 211, 214, 219 n.4, 248 n.5
  on storehouse consciousness 127, 224 n.4
  theory about *gotra* 172, 207, 220 n.5, 245 n.36, 247 n.79
Yokoyama, Kōitsu 横山紘一 249 n.19
Yoshimura, Makoto 吉村誠 14, 15, 136, 240 n.50
Yoshizu, Yoshihide 吉津宜英 27, 45–6, 225 n.29, 227 n.2, 232 n.36
yuanle 願樂. *See under adhimukti*
Yuedeng sanmei jing 月燈三昧經 *82*, *98*, 105
Yugaron gi 瑜伽論記 171, 247 n.65
Yūki, Reimon 結城令聞 17, 18, 222 n.35, 223 n.54
Yuwen tai 宇文泰 80, 231 n.34

Zhancha shan'e yebao jing 占察善惡業報經 41, 45, *99*
zhang 章. *See under pin*
Zhanran 湛然 96, *97*, *99*, 148–9, 232 n.43
Zhaolun shu 肇論疏 75, 227 n.57, 236 n.37
Zhengfa nianchu jing 正法念處經 *67*, 75, *76–7*, *81–3*, *98*
zhengyin 正因. *See under* cause proper
zhenru yichi 真如依持 42
zhenshi 真實 29, 49, *74*, 167, 178, 191, 240 n.45
zhenxin 真心. *See under* mind
Zhenyuan xinding shijiao mulu 貞元新定釋教目錄 *39*
Zhiyan 智儼 37, 56, 60, 102, 233 n.61, 233 n.62, 241 n.63, 246 n.53
  terminology of *61–70, 98–9*
Zhiyi 智顗 27, 35–6, 56, 59–60, 75, 92–3, 148–9, 227 n.59, 232 n.42, 232 n.43, 232 n.47, 243 n.105
  terminology of *61–8*, *70*, *72*, *77–8*, *81*, *83–9*, 94, *95*, *99*, 101, 104, 233 n.56, 242 n.101
Zhizhou 智周 96, *97–8*
Zhongguanlun shu 中觀論疏 29
Zhongjing mulu 眾經目錄 (Fajing 法經) *8*, 16, 38, *39*, 40, 71, 234 n.67
Zhongjing mulu 眾經目錄 (Yancong 彥琮) *8*, *39*, 40, 234 n.67
zhuanshi 轉識 (*pravṛtti-vijñāna*) 42, 116–17. *See also* evolving consciousness
Zhuanshi lun 轉識論 15, 240 n.45, 242 n.92
Zhu Fonian 竺佛念 *61–2*, 79, *85*
Zimmermann, Michael 179, 192, 220 n.7, 247 n.3, 248 n.4